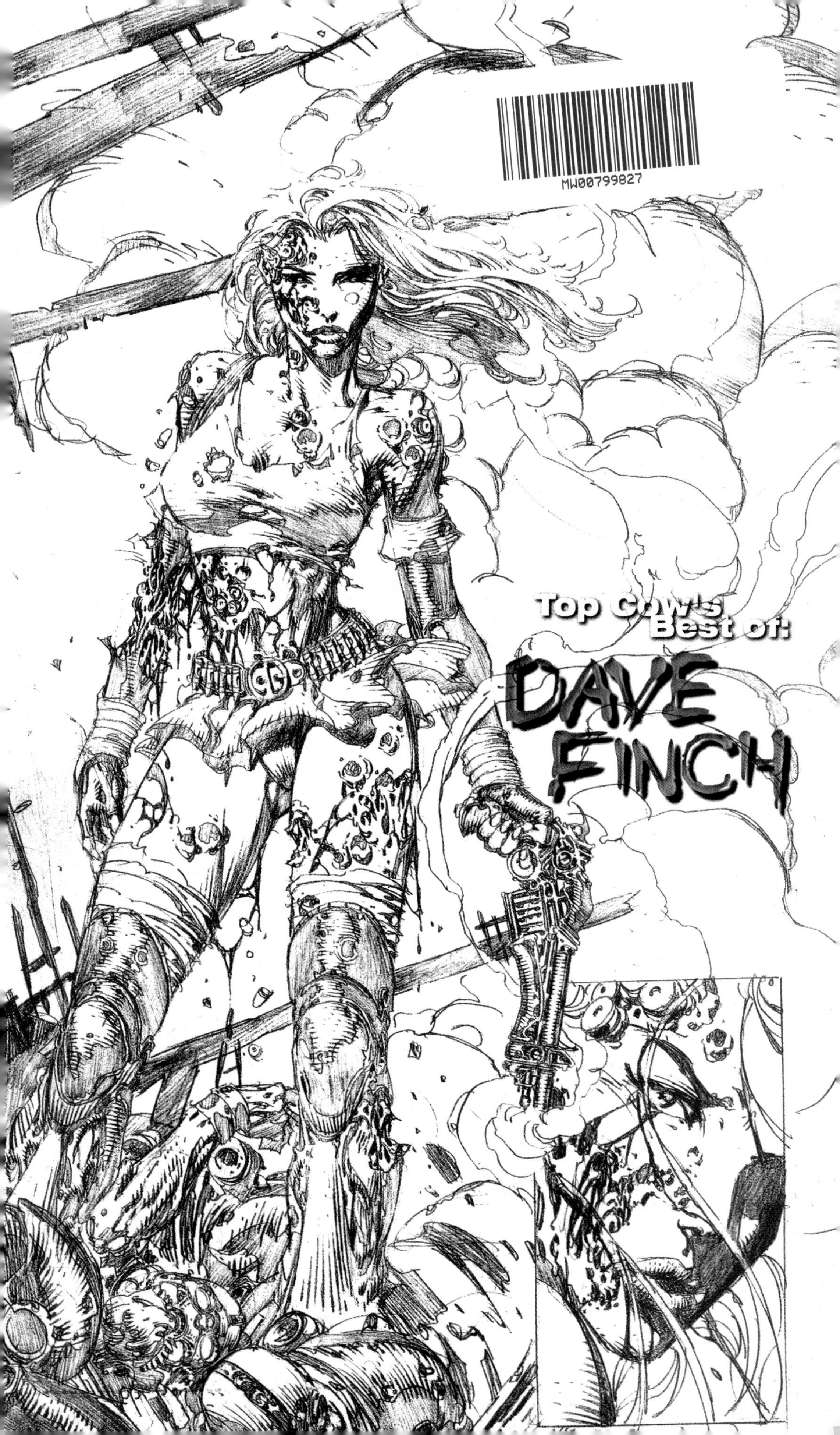
Top Cow's
Best of:
DAVE
FINCH

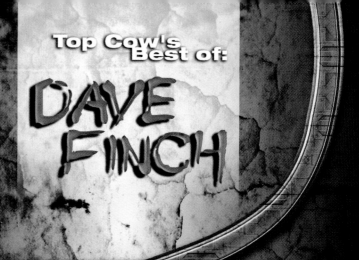

Top Cow's Best of:

DAVE FINCH

for Top Cow Productions
Marc Silvestri_chief executive officer
Matt Hawkins_president / chief operating officer
Renae Geerlings_editor in chief
Chaz Riggs_production manager
Rob Levin_editor
Annie Pham_marketing director
Peter Lam_webmaster
Phil Smith_trades and submissions
Lena Leal-Floyd
and Viet Duc Nguyen_interns

this edition edited and designed by:
Phil Smith

special thanks to:
Eric "ebas" Basaldua
for his encyclopedic knowledge and personal
library of all things "Finch"

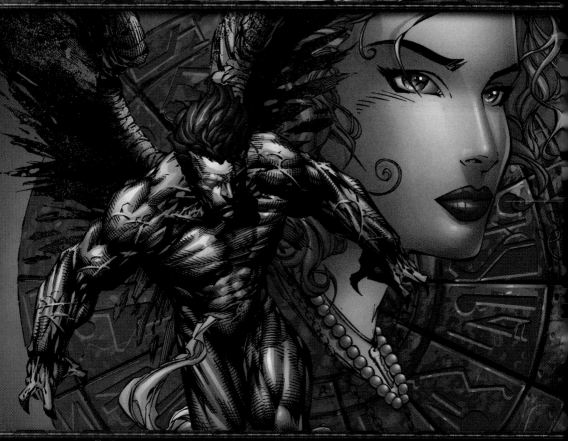

for Image Comics
publisher Erik Larsen

Top Cow's, Best of: Dave Finch trade paperback vol. 1
August 2006, FIRST PRINTING
ISBN #1-58240-638-3
Published by Image Comics Inc. Office of Publication: 1942 University Ave., Suite 305 Berkeley, CA 94704. $19.99 US. $22.27 CAN.
PRINTED IN CANADA.

Table of Contents:

Aphrodite IX
issue #0........ pg.7

Aphrodite IX
issue #1........ pg.20

Cyberforce vol. 1
issue #16.......... pg.51

Ascension
Preview...... pg.85

Ascension
issue #0..... pg.93

Ascension
issue #1..... pg.107

Tales of the Witchblade
issue #2................... pg.133

The Darkness vol. 1
issue #39............... pg.159

Finch
Gallery
pg.184

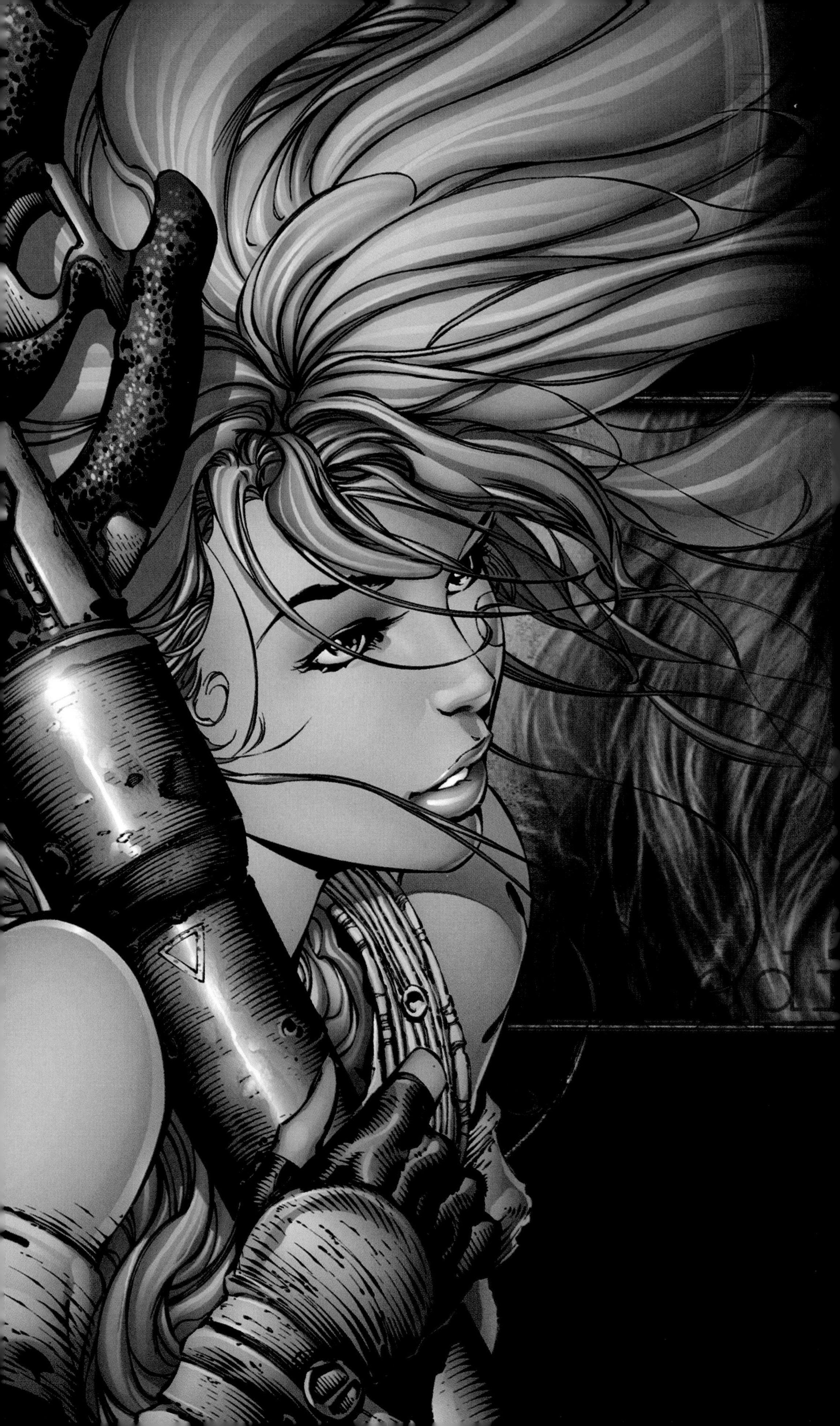

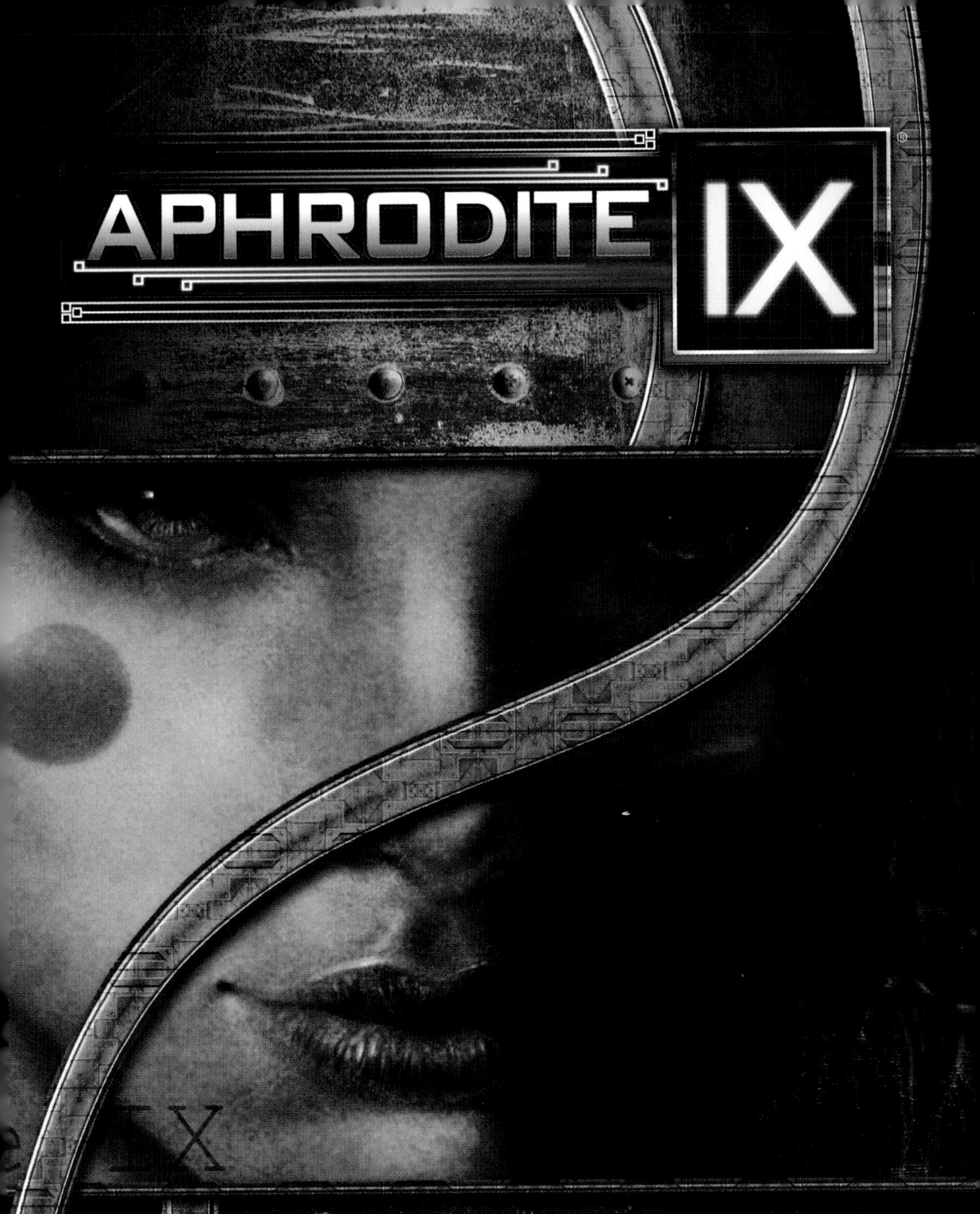
APHRODITE IX
IX

Aphrodite IX is the story of a beautiful Cyborg assassin with no memories of her past. This series showcased some of Dave Finch's best work and opened the door for readers to a unique vision of the future through the eyes of an extraordinary artist.

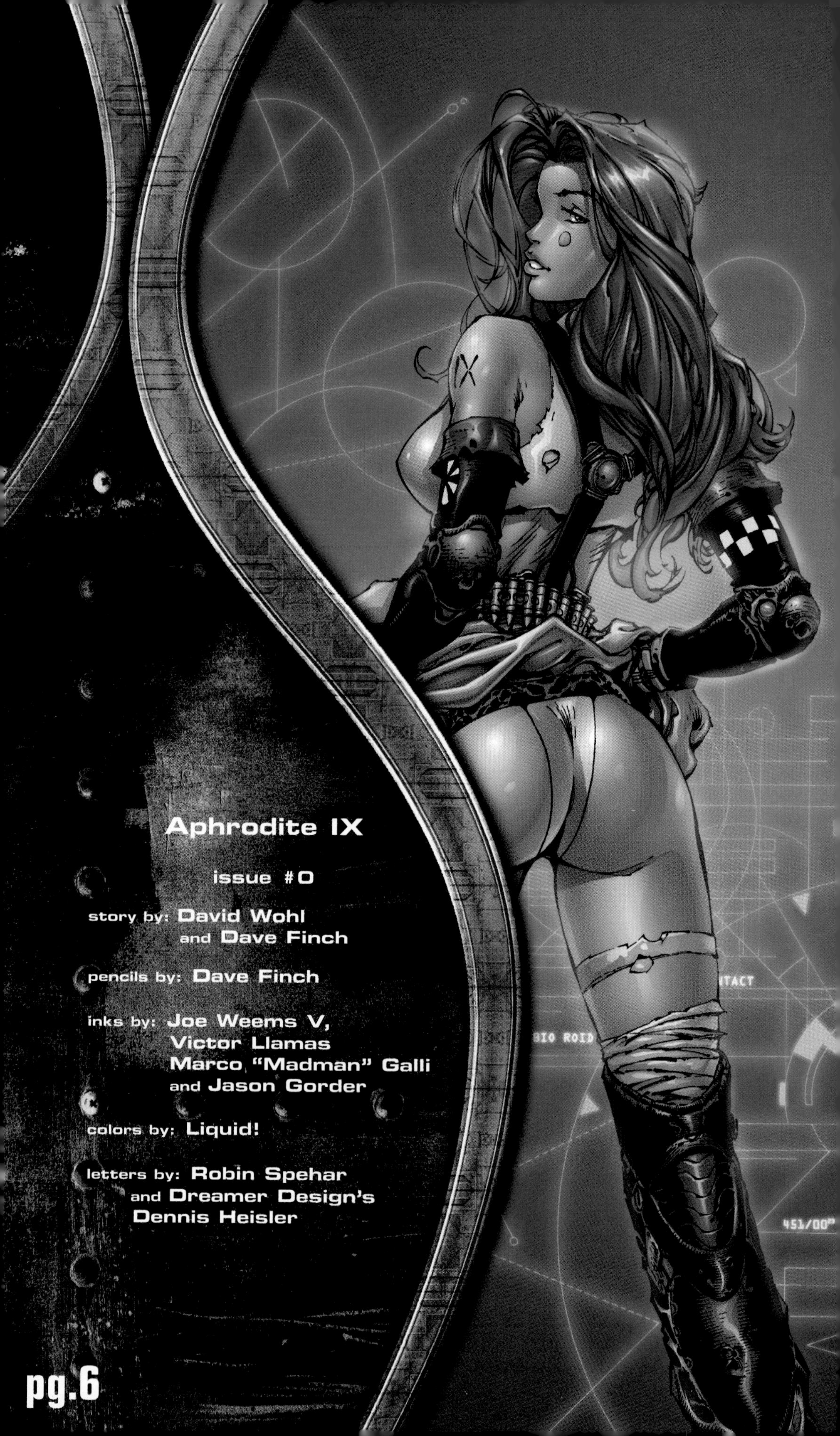
BIO ROID
451/00"

Aphrodite IX

issue #0

story by: David Wohl
and Dave Finch

pencils by: Dave Finch

inks by: Joe Weems V,
Victor Llamas
Marco "Madman" Galli
and Jason Gorder

colors by: Liquid!

letters by: Robin Spehar
and Dreamer Design's
Dennis Heisler

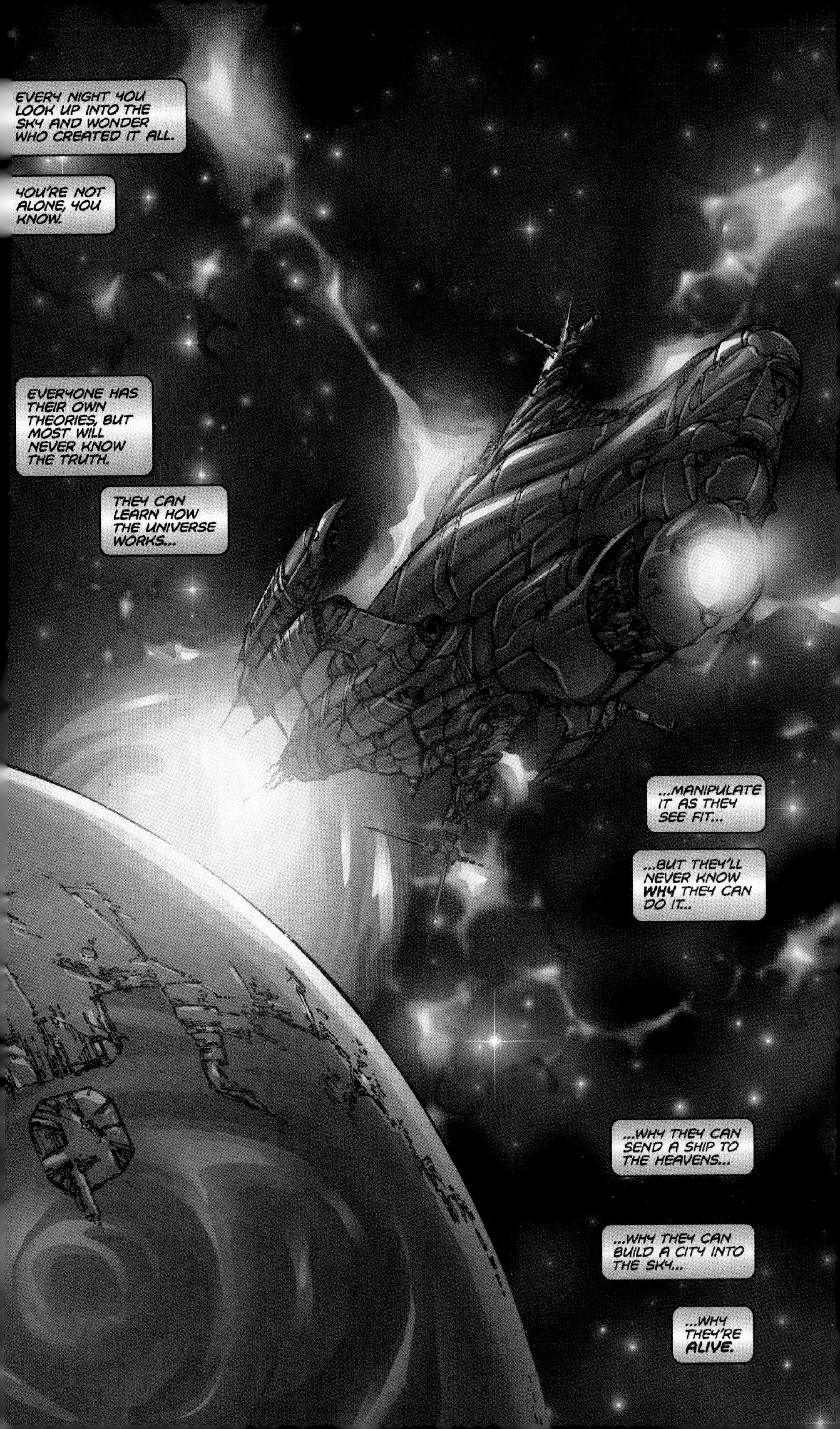
EVERY NIGHT YOU LOOK UP INTO THE SKY AND WONDER WHO CREATED IT ALL.
YOU'RE NOT ALONE, YOU KNOW.
EVERYONE HAS THEIR OWN THEORIES, BUT MOST WILL NEVER KNOW THE TRUTH.
THEY CAN LEARN HOW THE UNIVERSE WORKS...
...MANIPULATE IT AS THEY SEE FIT...
...BUT THEY'LL NEVER KNOW **WHY** THEY CAN DO IT...
...WHY THEY CAN SEND A SHIP TO THE HEAVENS...
...WHY THEY CAN BUILD A CITY INTO THE SKY...
...WHY THEY'RE **ALIVE.**

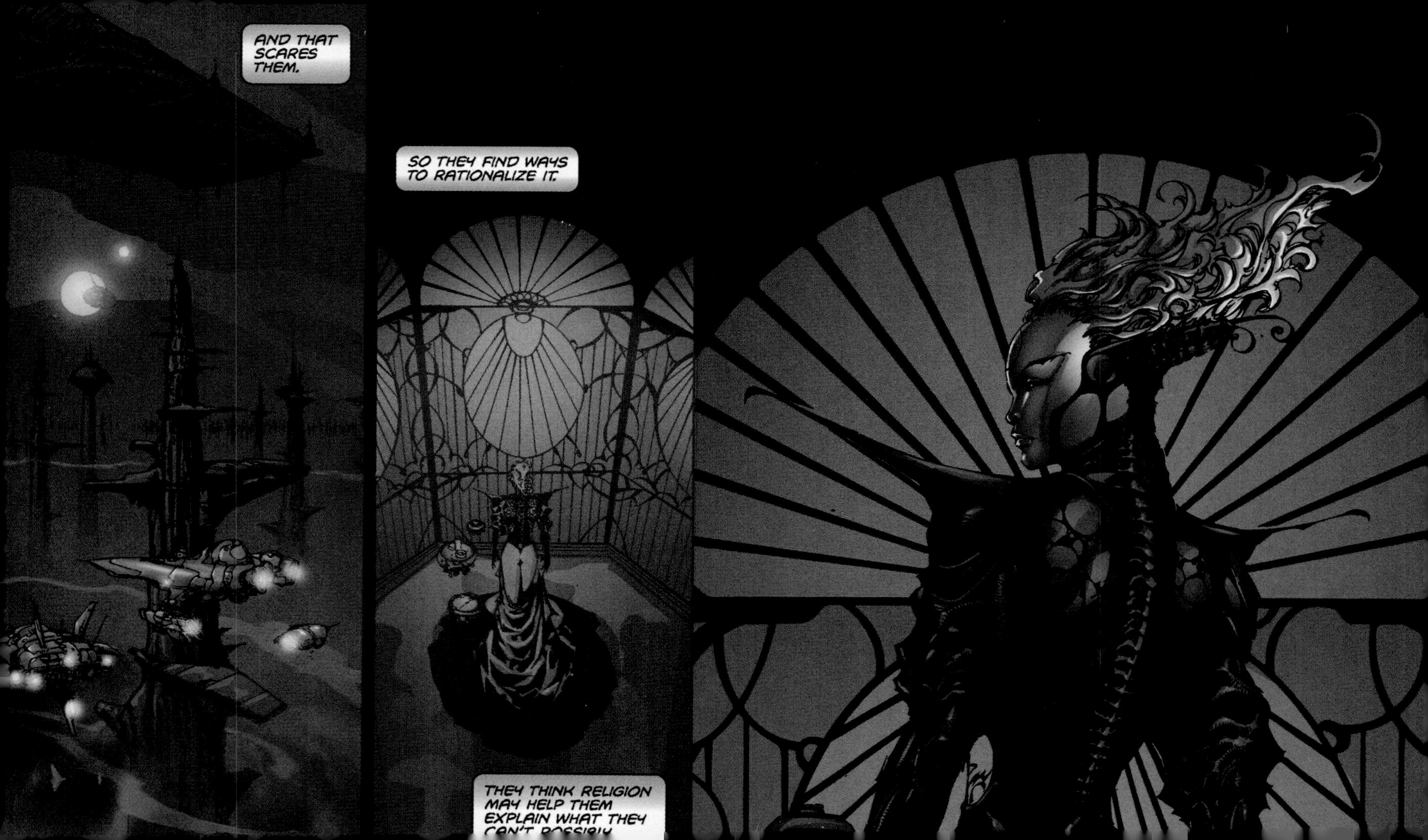
AND THAT SCARES THEM.
SO THEY FIND WAYS TO RATIONALIZE IT.
THEY THINK RELIGION MAY HELP THEM EXPLAIN WHAT THEY

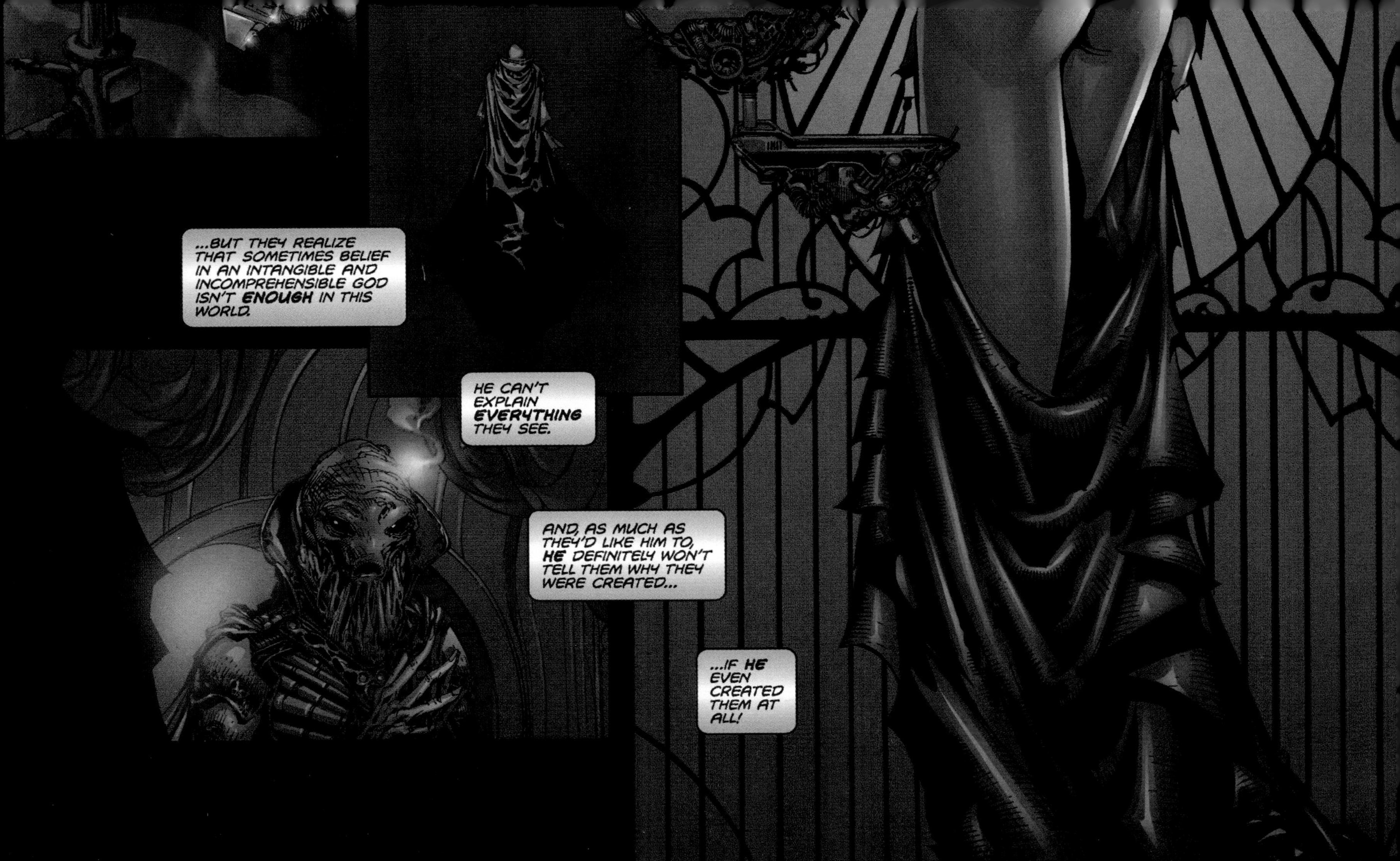
...BUT THEY REALIZE THAT SOMETIMES BELIEF IN AN INTANGIBLE AND INCOMPREHENSIBLE GOD ISN'T **ENOUGH** IN THIS WORLD.
HE CAN'T EXPLAIN **EVERYTHING** THEY SEE.
AND, AS MUCH AS THEY'D LIKE HIM TO, **HE** DEFINITELY WON'T TELL THEM WHY THEY WERE CREATED...
...IF **HE** EVEN CREATED THEM AT ALL!

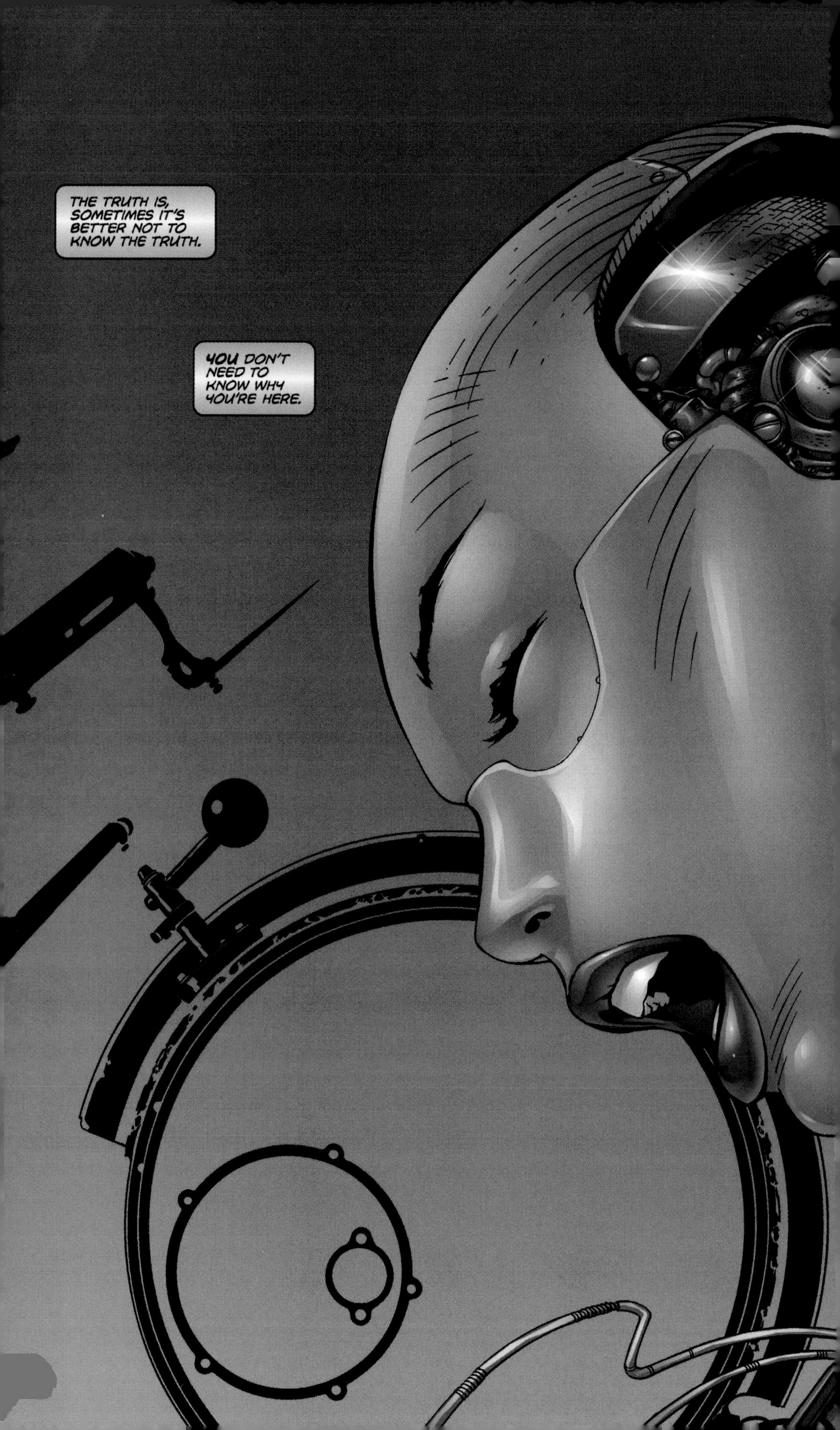
THE TRUTH IS, SOMETIMES IT'S BETTER NOT TO KNOW THE TRUTH.
YOU DON'T NEED TO KNOW WHY YOU'RE HERE.

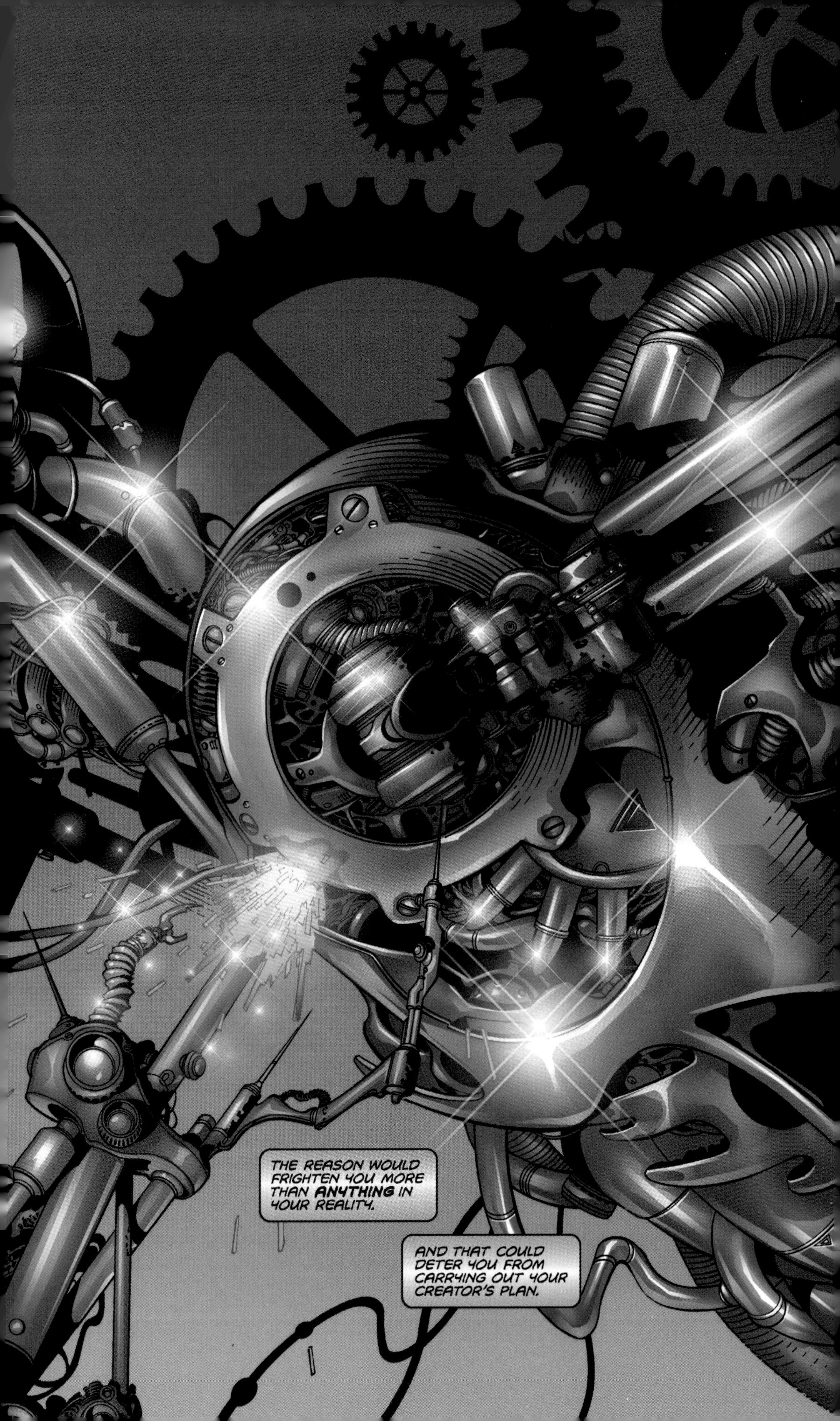
THE REASON WOULD FRIGHTEN YOU MORE THAN **ANYTHING** IN YOUR REALITY.
AND THAT COULD DETER YOU FROM CARRYING OUT YOUR CREATOR'S PLAN.

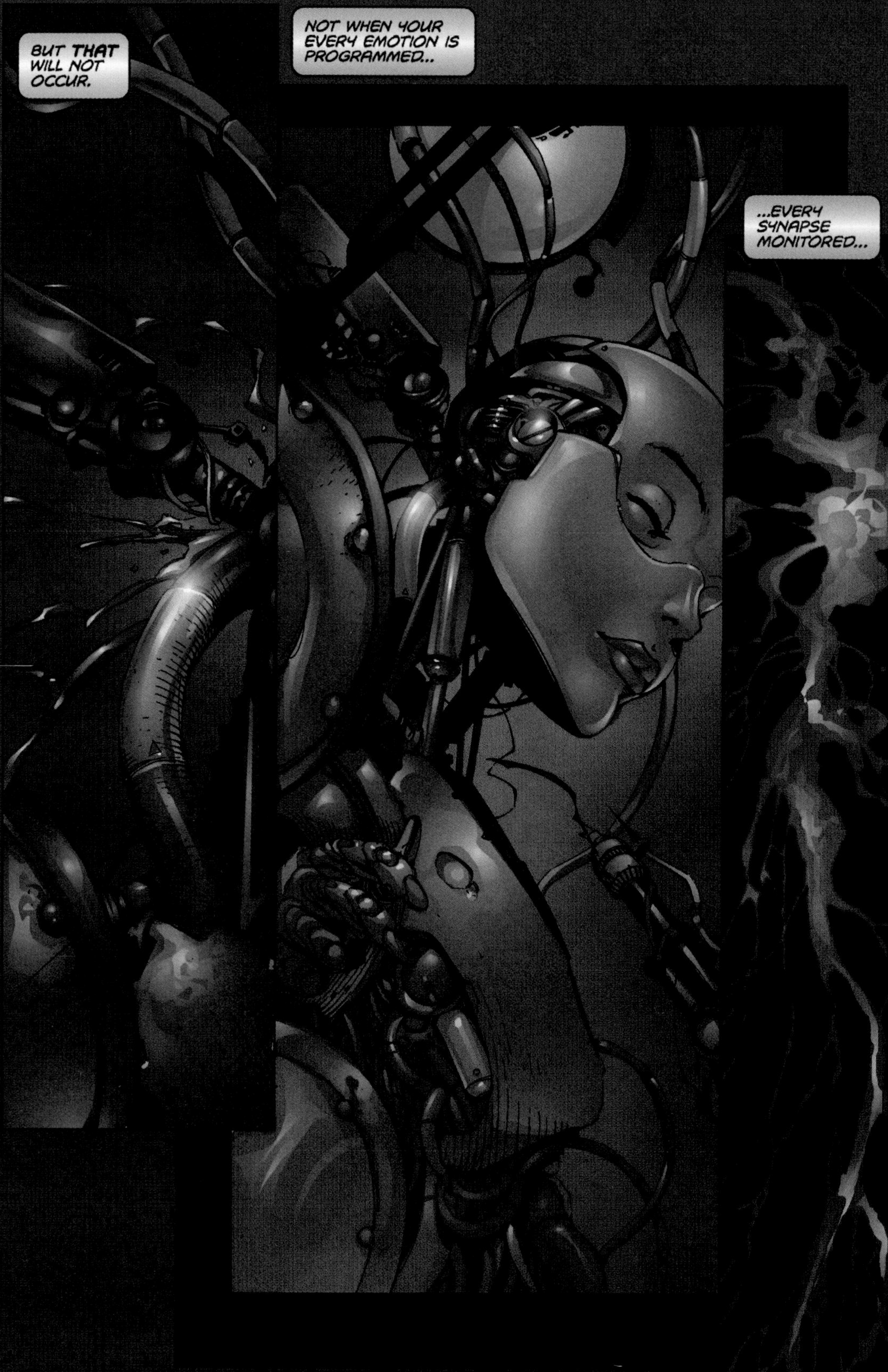
BUT THAT WILL NOT OCCUR.
NOT WHEN YOUR EVERY EMOTION IS PROGRAMMED...
...EVERY SYNAPSE MONITORED...

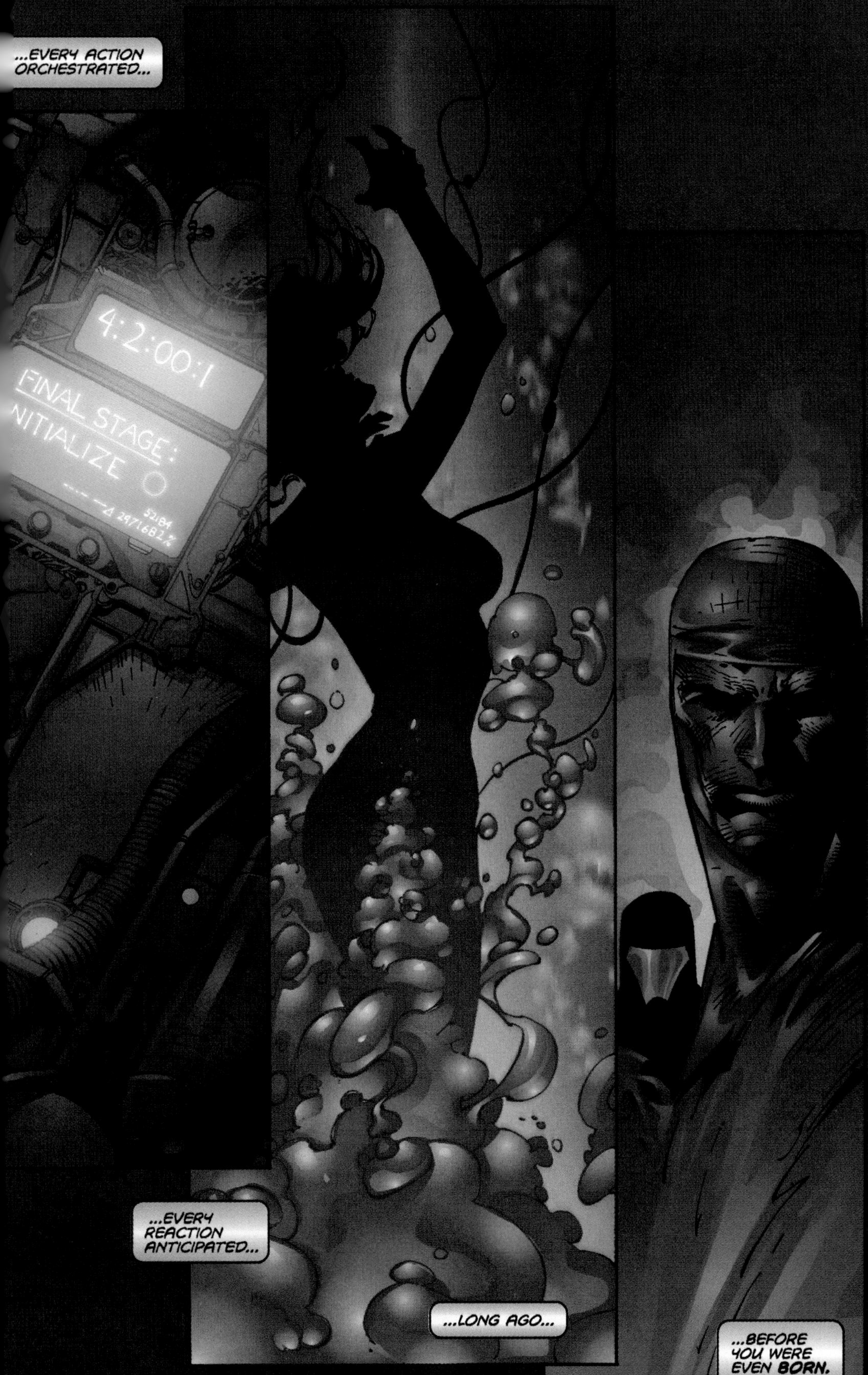
...EVERY ACTION ORCHESTRATED...
4:2:00:1
FINAL STAGE:
NITIALIZE
...EVERY REACTION ANTICIPATED...
...LONG AGO...
...BEFORE YOU WERE EVEN BORN.

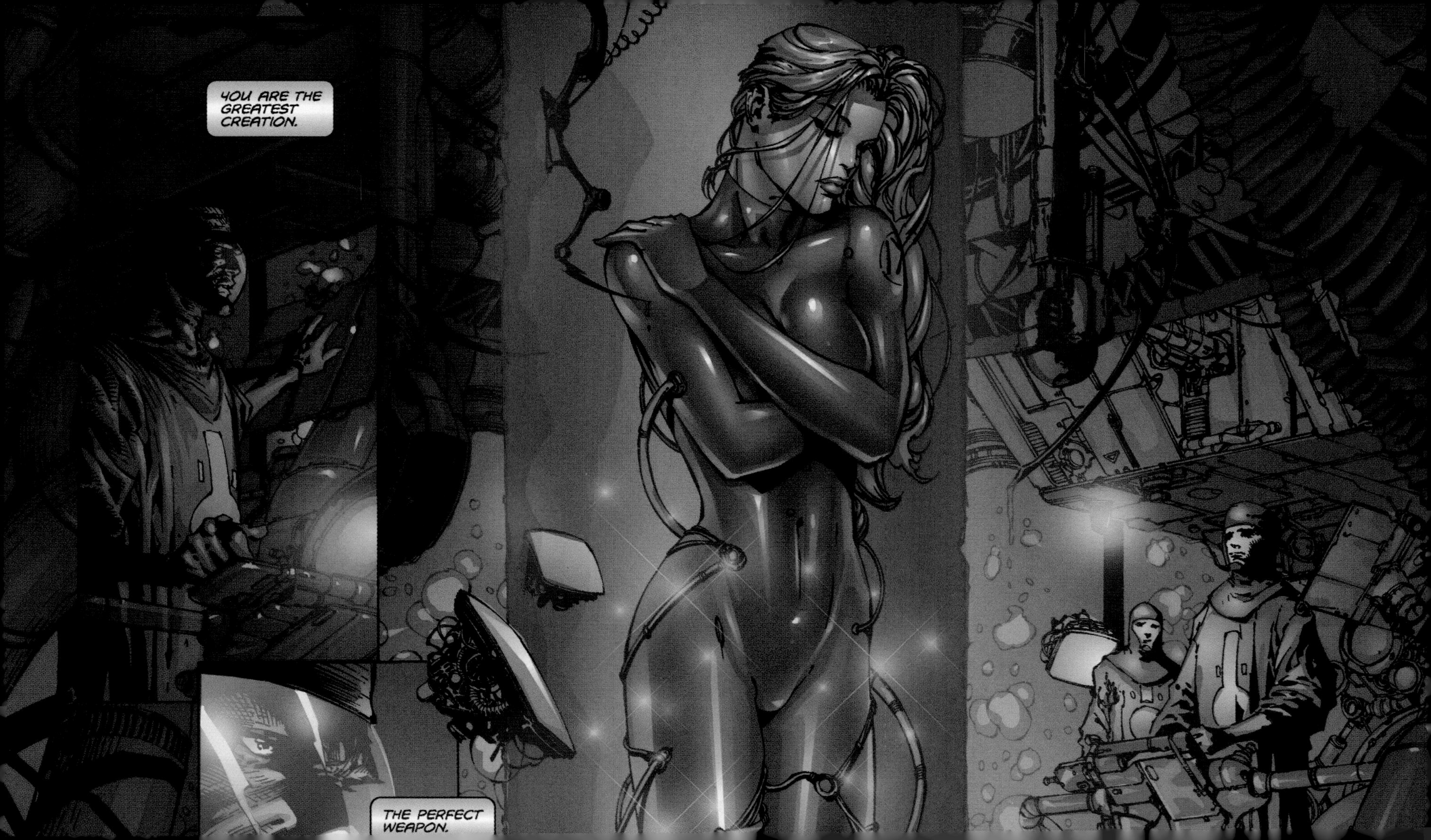
YOU ARE THE GREATEST CREATION.
THE PERFECT WEAPON.

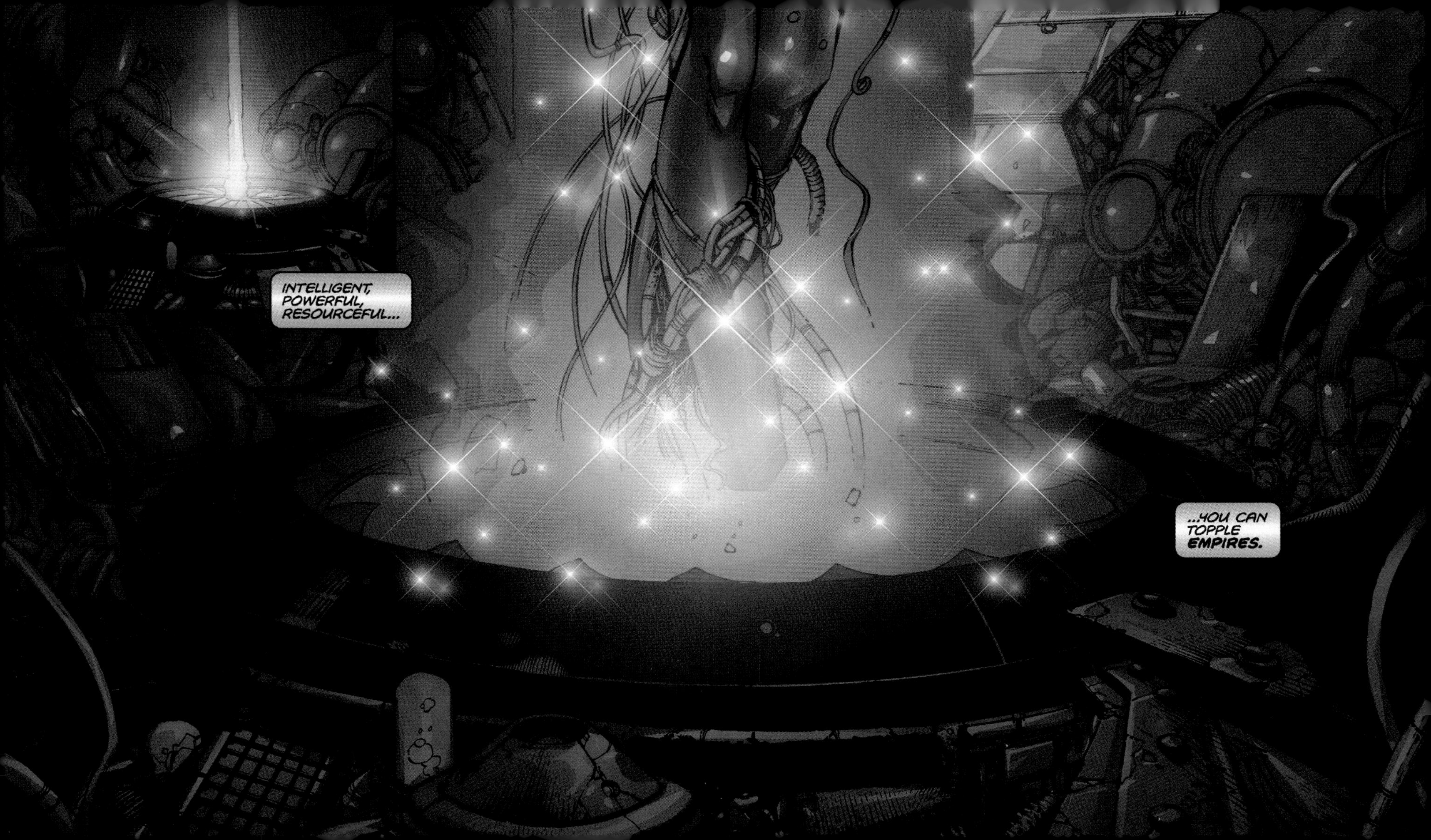
INTELLIGENT, POWERFUL, RESOURCEFUL...
...YOU CAN TOPPLE EMPIRES.

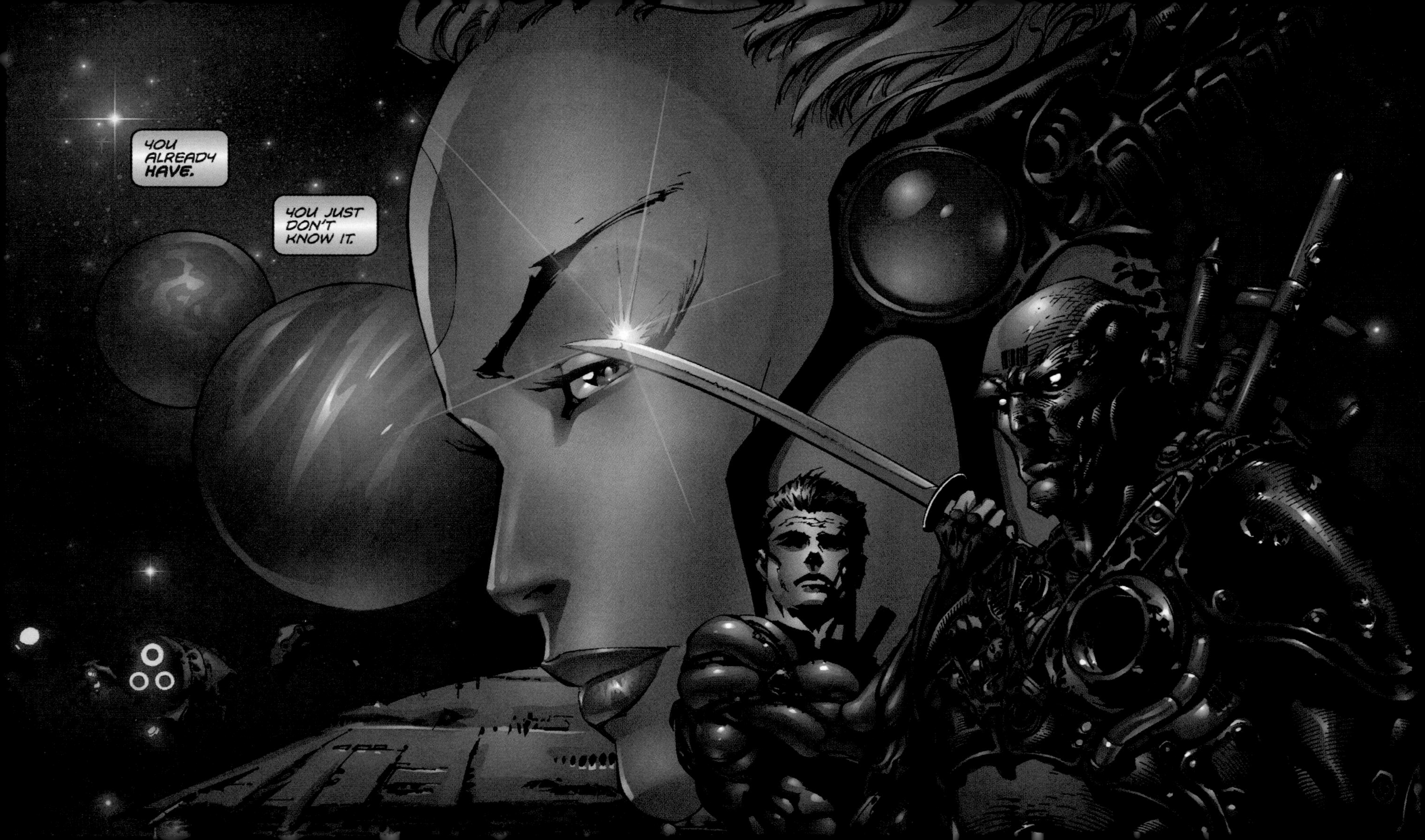
YOU ALREADY HAVE.
YOU JUST DON'T KNOW IT.

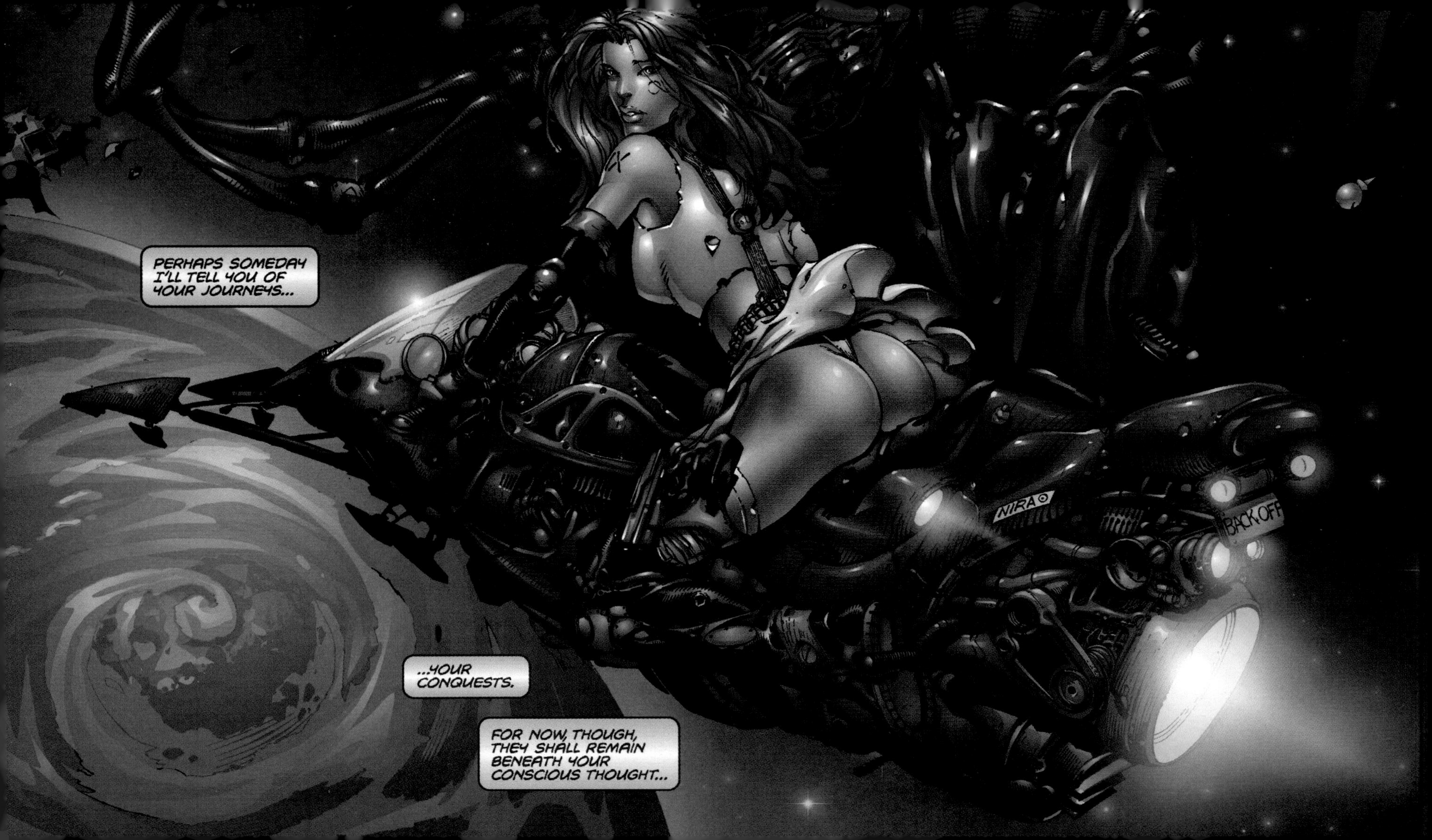
PERHAPS SOMEDAY I'LL TELL YOU OF YOUR JOURNEYS...
...YOUR CONQUESTS.
FOR NOW, THOUGH, THEY SHALL REMAIN BENEATH YOUR CONSCIOUS THOUGHT...
NIRA
BACK OFF

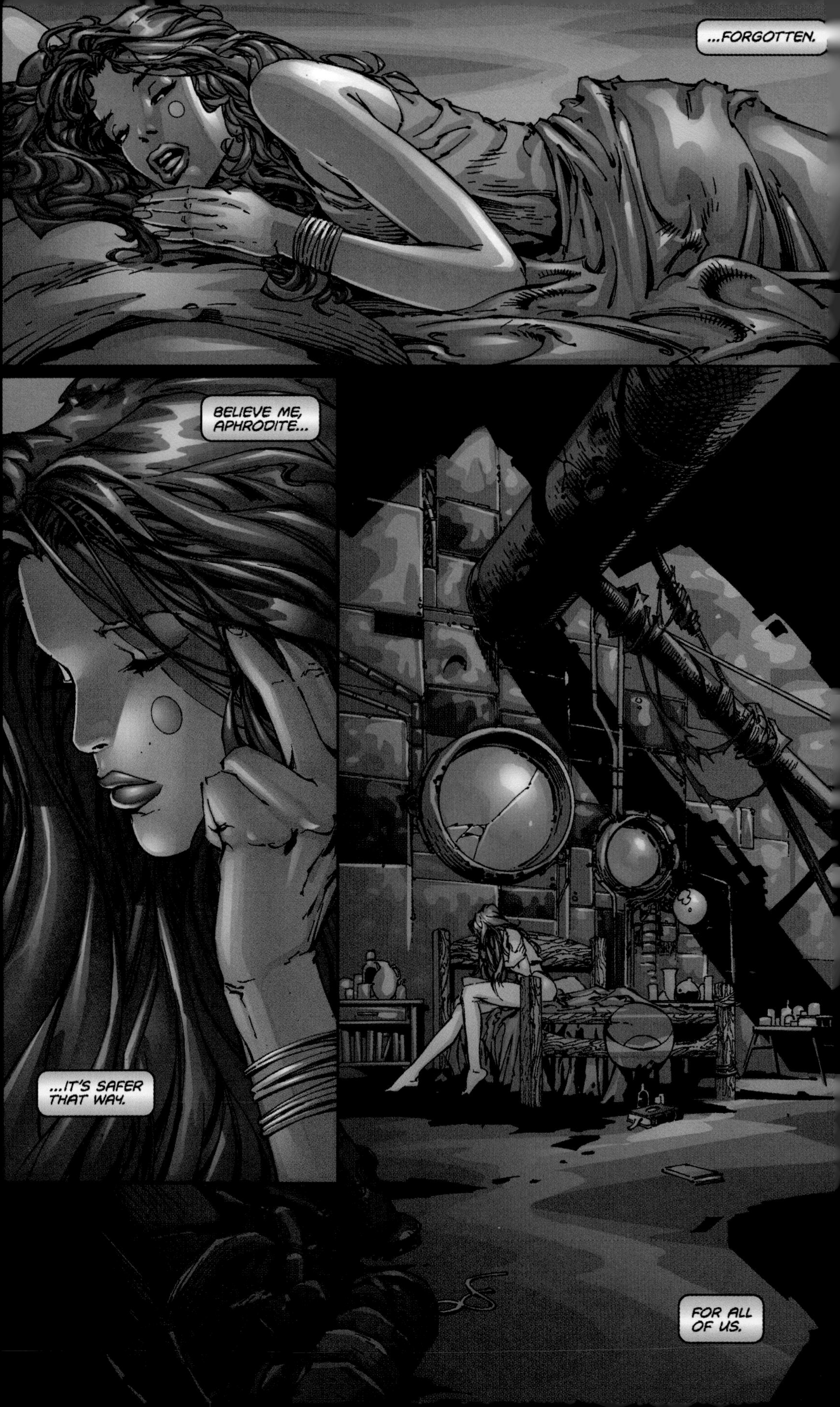
...FORGOTTEN.
BELIEVE ME, APHRODITE...
...IT'S SAFER THAT WAY.
FOR ALL OF US.

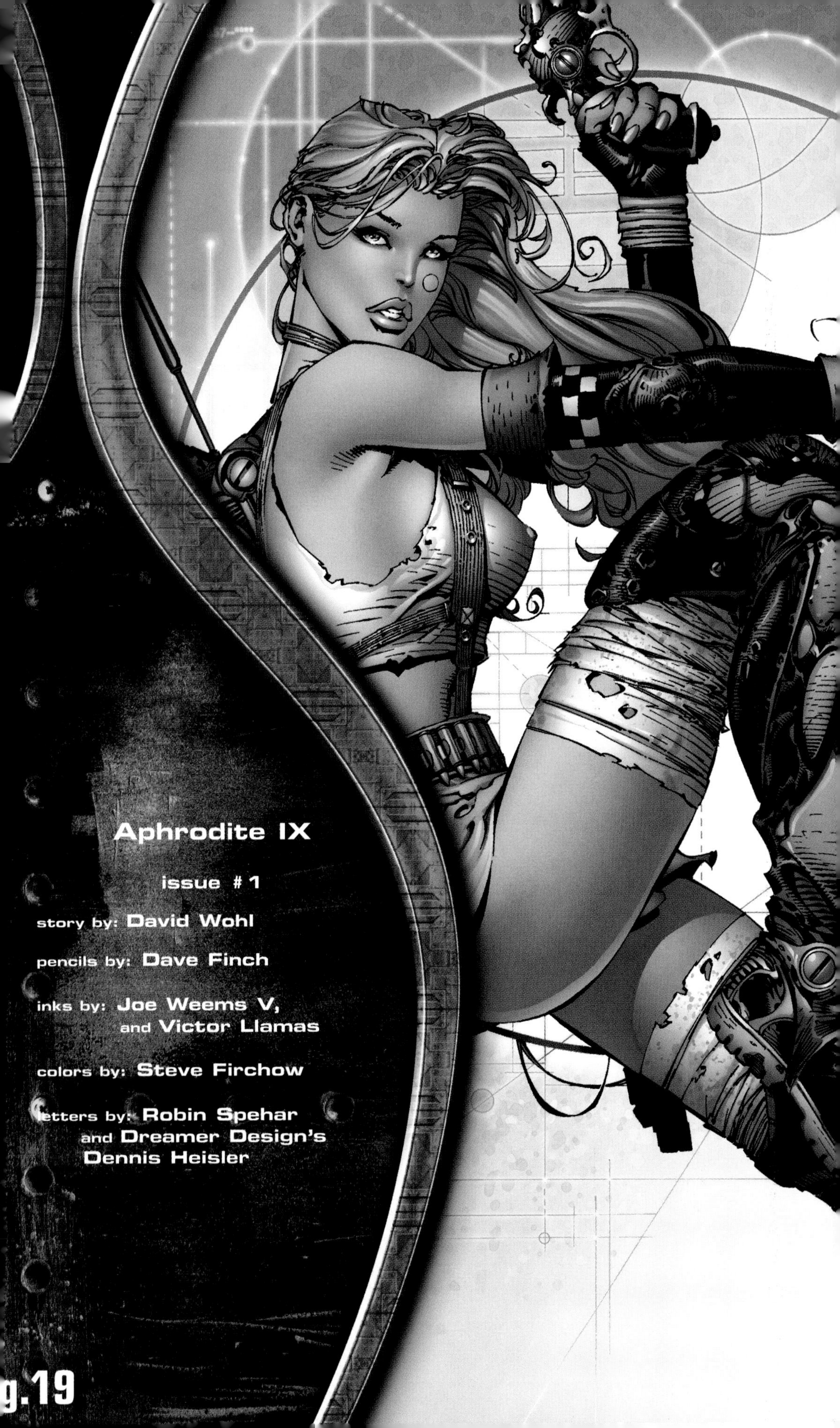
Aphrodite IX
issue # 1
story by: David Wohl
pencils by: Dave Finch
inks by: Joe Weems V, and Victor Llamas
colors by: Steve Firchow
letters by: Robin Spehar and Dreamer Design's Dennis Heisler

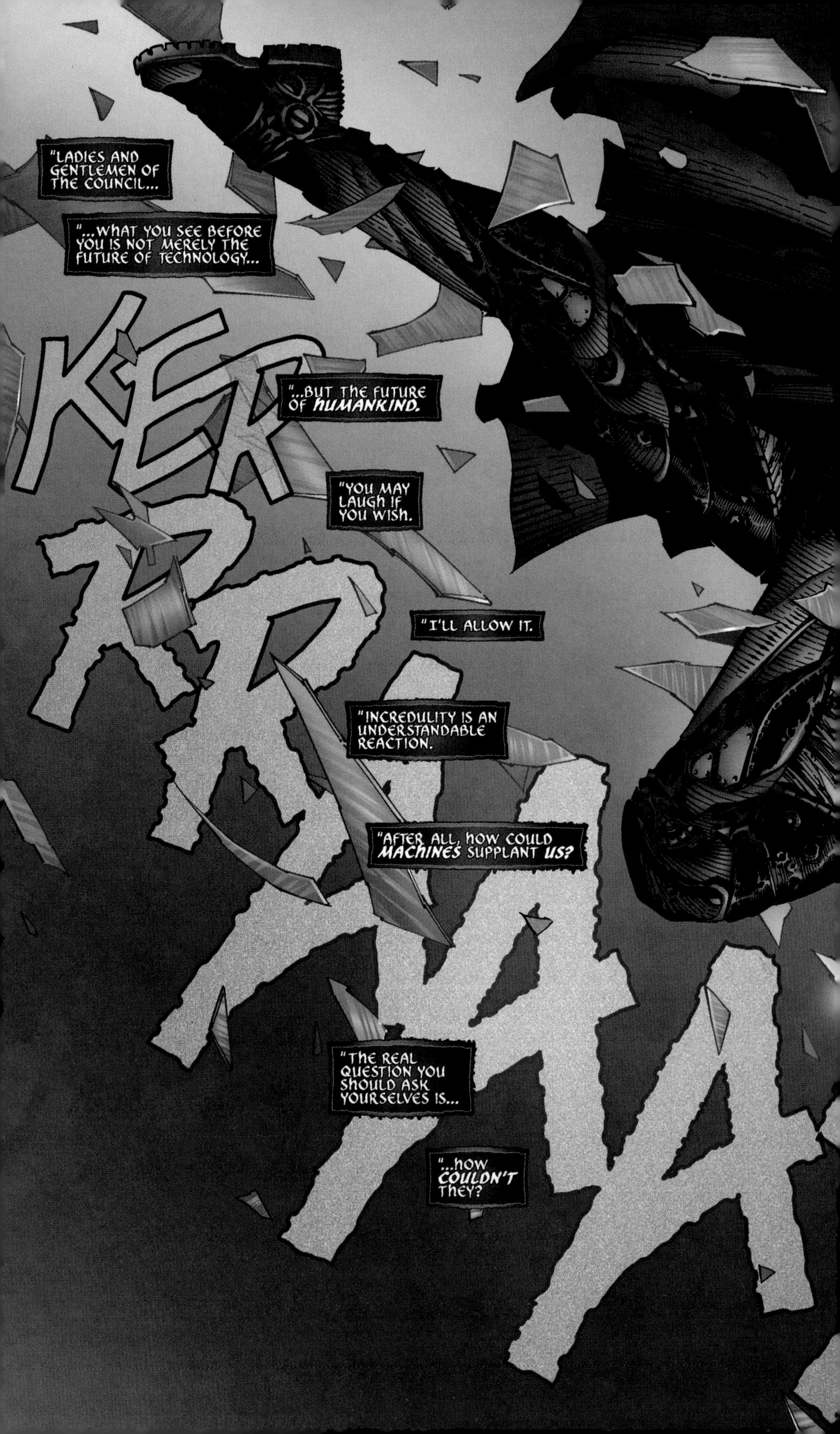
"LADIES AND GENTLEMEN OF THE COUNCIL...
"...WHAT YOU SEE BEFORE YOU IS NOT MERELY THE FUTURE OF TECHNOLOGY...
KER
"...BUT THE FUTURE OF HUMANKIND.
"YOU MAY LAUGH IF YOU WISH.
"I'LL ALLOW IT.
"INCREDULITY IS AN UNDERSTANDABLE REACTION.
"AFTER ALL, HOW COULD MACHINES SUPPLANT US?
"THE REAL QUESTION YOU SHOULD ASK YOURSELVES IS...
"...HOW COULDN'T THEY?

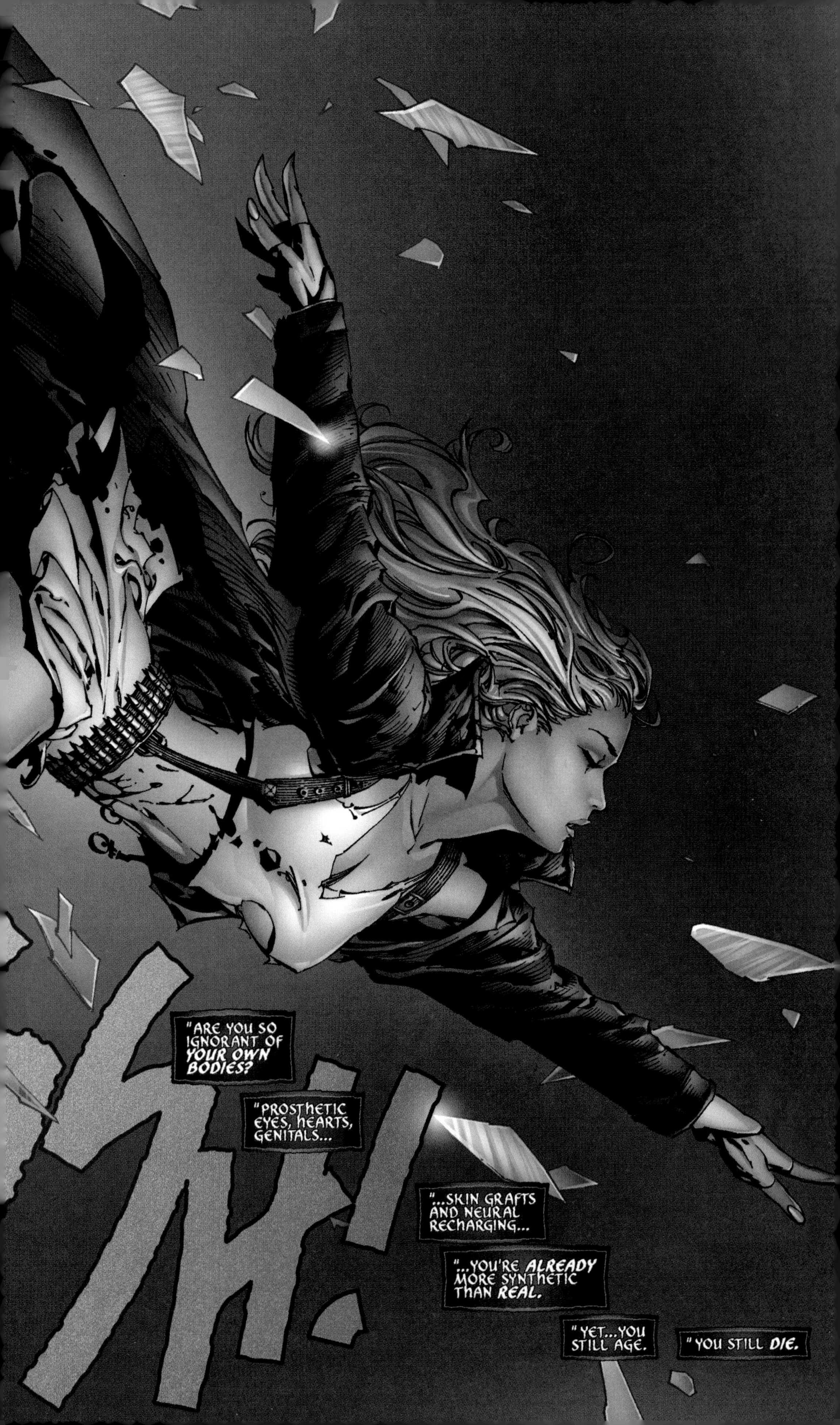
"ARE YOU SO IGNORANT OF ***YOUR OWN BODIES?***
"PROSTHETIC EYES, HEARTS, GENITALS...
"...SKIN GRAFTS AND NEURAL RECHARGING...
"...YOU'RE ***ALREADY*** MORE SYNTHETIC THAN ***REAL.***
"YET...YOU STILL AGE.
"YOU STILL ***DIE.***

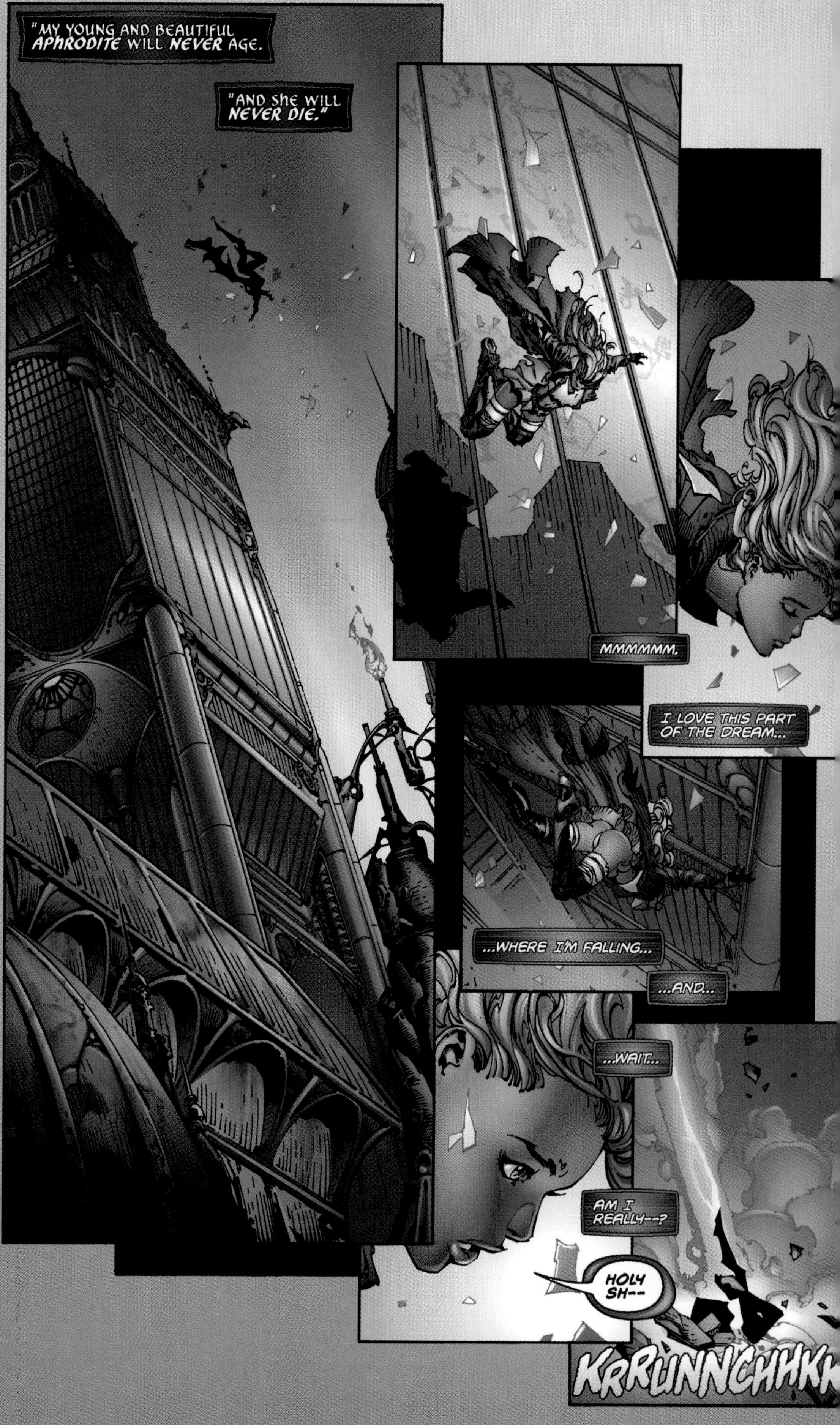

"MY YOUNG AND BEAUTIFUL APHRODITE WILL NEVER AGE.
"AND SHE WILL NEVER DIE."
MMMMMM.
I LOVE THIS PART OF THE DREAM...
...WHERE I'M FALLING...
...AND...
...WAIT...
AM I REALLY--?
HOLY SH--
KRRUNNCHHKK

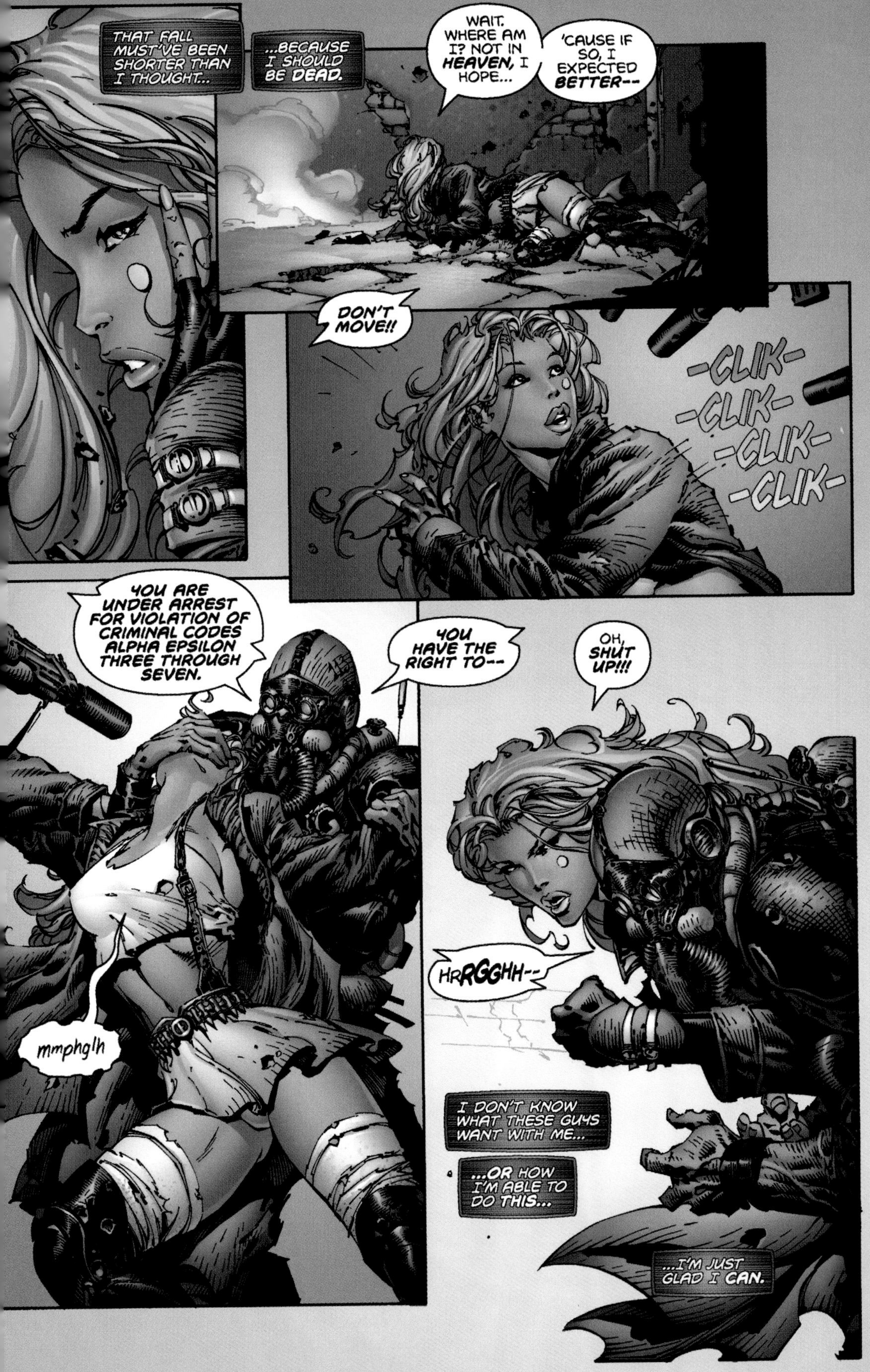
THAT FALL MUST'VE BEEN SHORTER THAN I THOUGHT...
...BECAUSE I SHOULD BE DEAD.
WAIT. WHERE AM I? NOT IN HEAVEN, I HOPE...
'CAUSE IF SO, I EXPECTED BETTER--
DON'T MOVE!!
-CLIK-
-CLIK-
-CLIK-
-CLIK-
YOU ARE UNDER ARREST FOR VIOLATION OF CRIMINAL CODES ALPHA EPSILON THREE THROUGH SEVEN.
YOU HAVE THE RIGHT TO--
mmphglh
OH, SHUT UP!!!
HRRGGHH--
I DON'T KNOW WHAT THESE GUYS WANT WITH ME...
...OR HOW I'M ABLE TO DO THIS...
...I'M JUST GLAD I CAN.

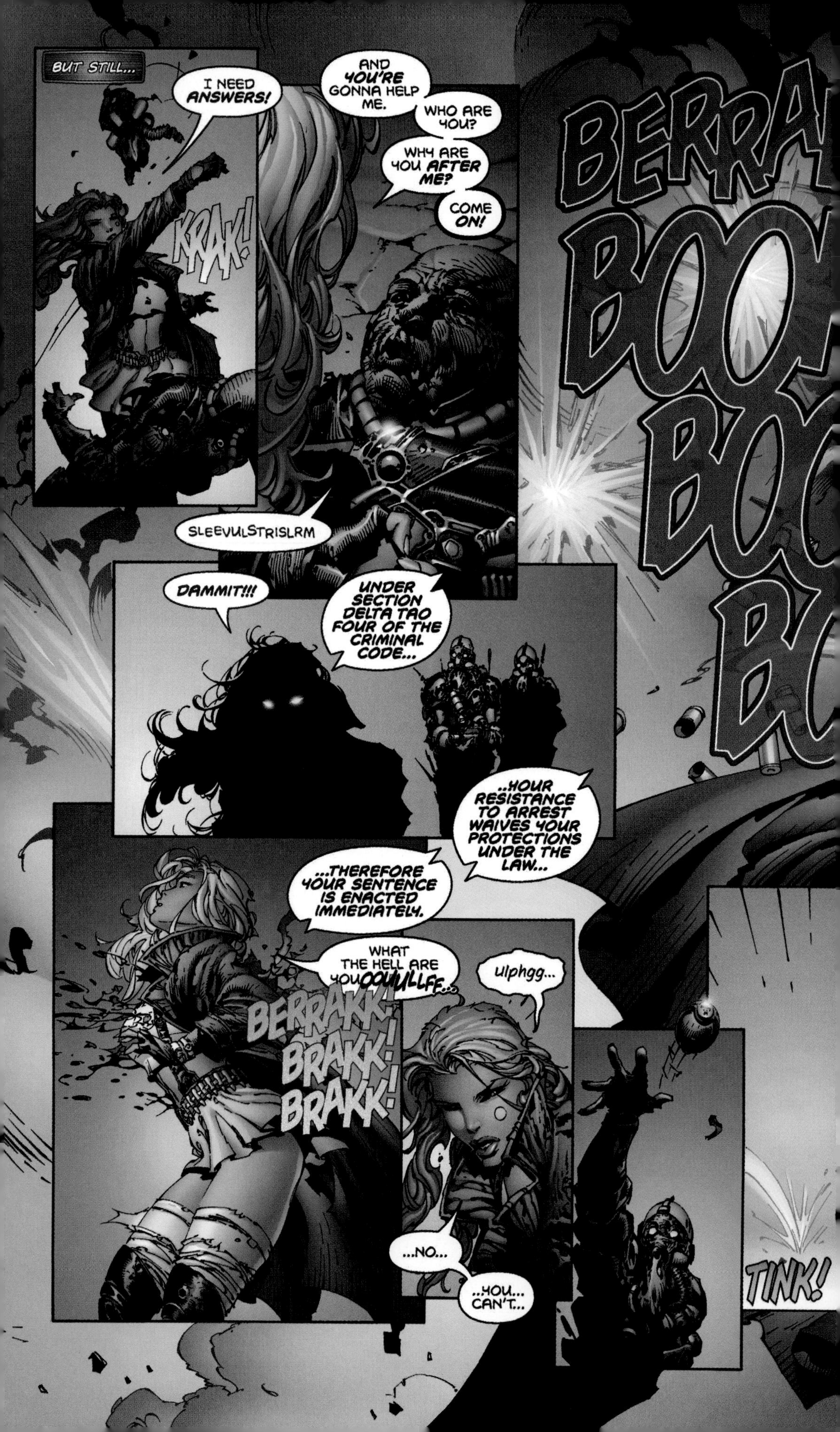

BUT STILL...
I NEED ANSWERS!
KRAK!
AND YOU'RE GONNA HELP ME.
WHO ARE YOU?
WHY ARE YOU AFTER ME?
COME ON!
SLEEVULSTRISLRM
BERRA
BOO
BOO
BO
BO
DAMMIT!!!
UNDER SECTION DELTA TAO FOUR OF THE CRIMINAL CODE...
..YOUR RESISTANCE TO ARREST WAIVES YOUR PROTECTIONS UNDER THE LAW...
...THEREFORE YOUR SENTENCE IS ENACTED IMMEDIATELY.
WHAT THE HELL ARE YOUOOUULLFF...
BERRAKK! BRAKK! BRAKK!
ulphgg...
...NO...
..YOU... CAN'T...
TINK!

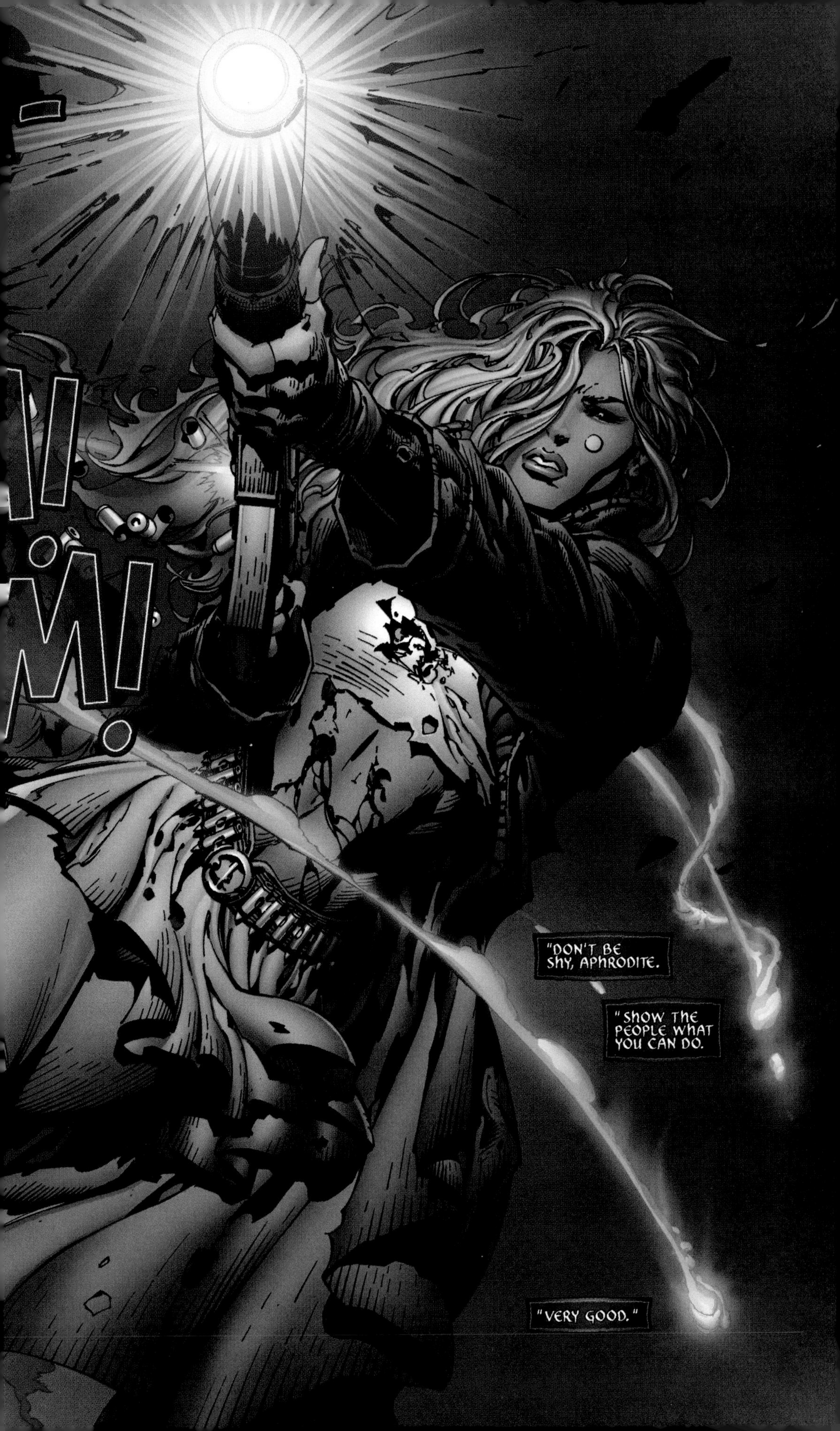
"DON'T BE SHY, APHRODITE.
"SHOW THE PEOPLE WHAT YOU CAN DO.
"VERY GOOD."

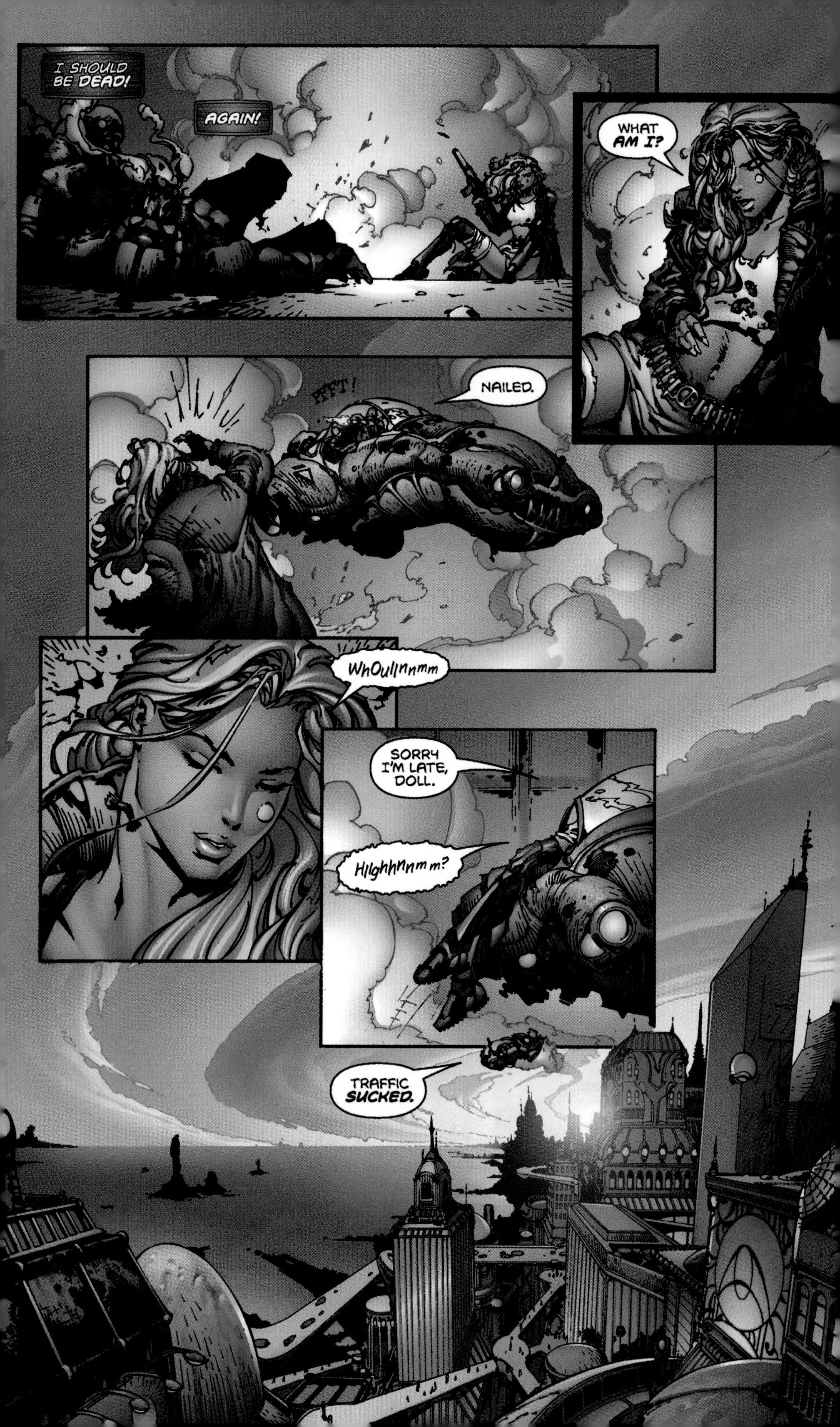
I SHOULD BE DEAD!
AGAIN!
WHAT AM I?
PFFT!
NAILED.
WhOullnnmm
SORRY I'M LATE, DOLL.
Hllghhnnmm?
TRAFFIC SUCKED.

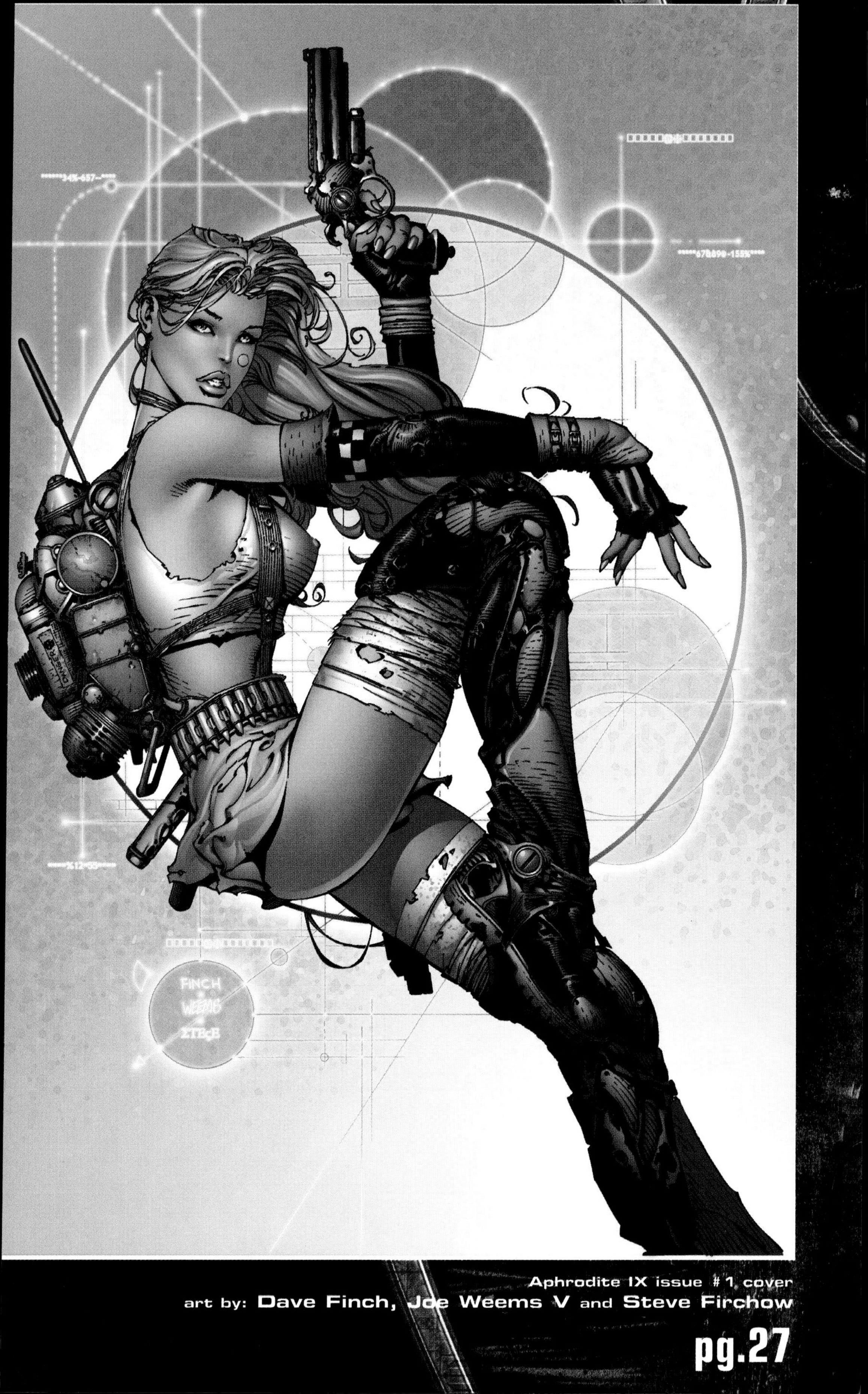
FINCH

Aphrodite IX issue # 1 cover
art by: **Dave Finch, Joe Weems V** and **Steve Firchow**

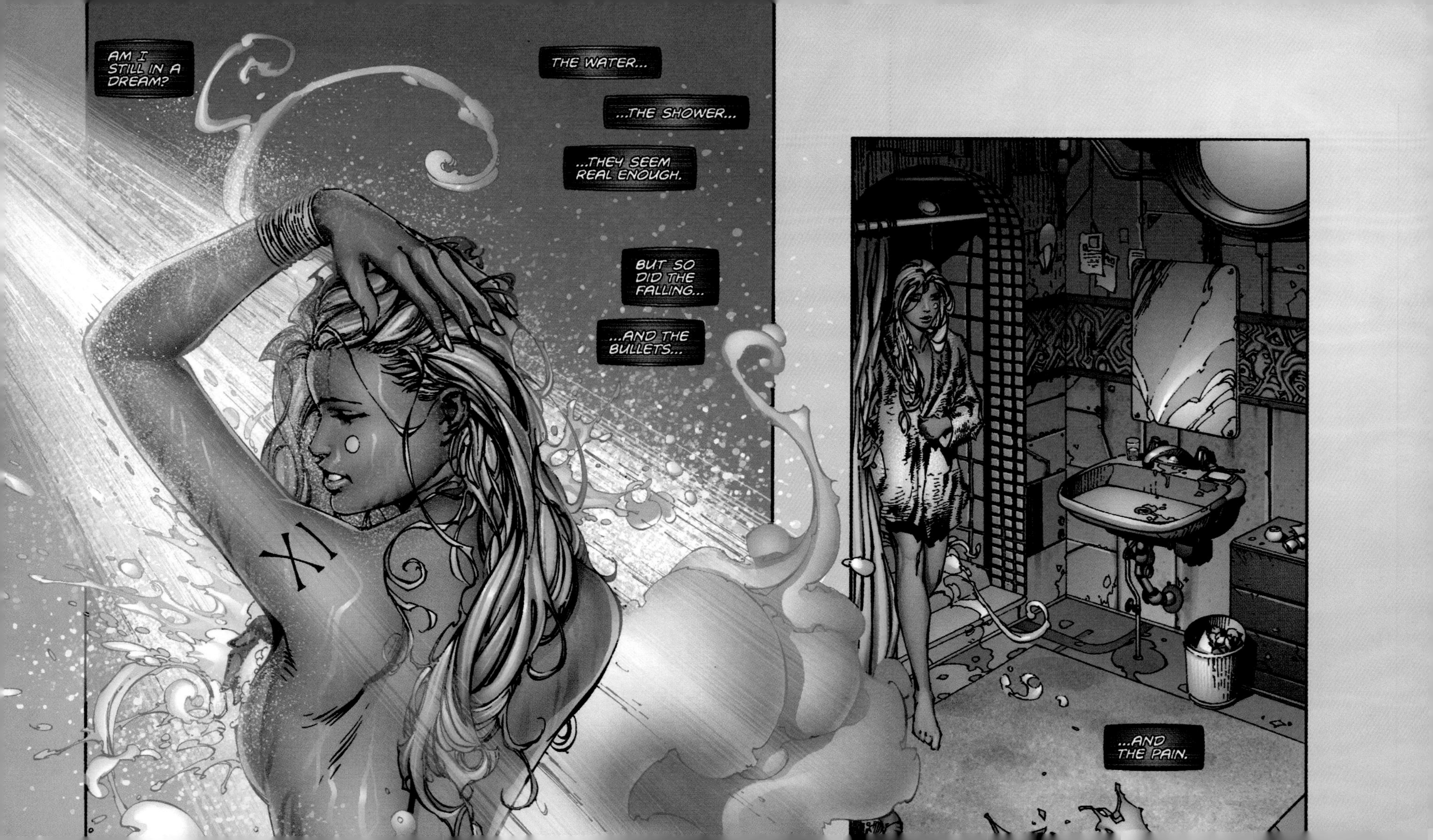
AM I STILL IN A DREAM?
THE WATER...
...THE SHOWER...
...THEY SEEM REAL ENOUGH.
BUT SO DID THE FALLING...
...AND THE BULLETS...
...AND THE PAIN.

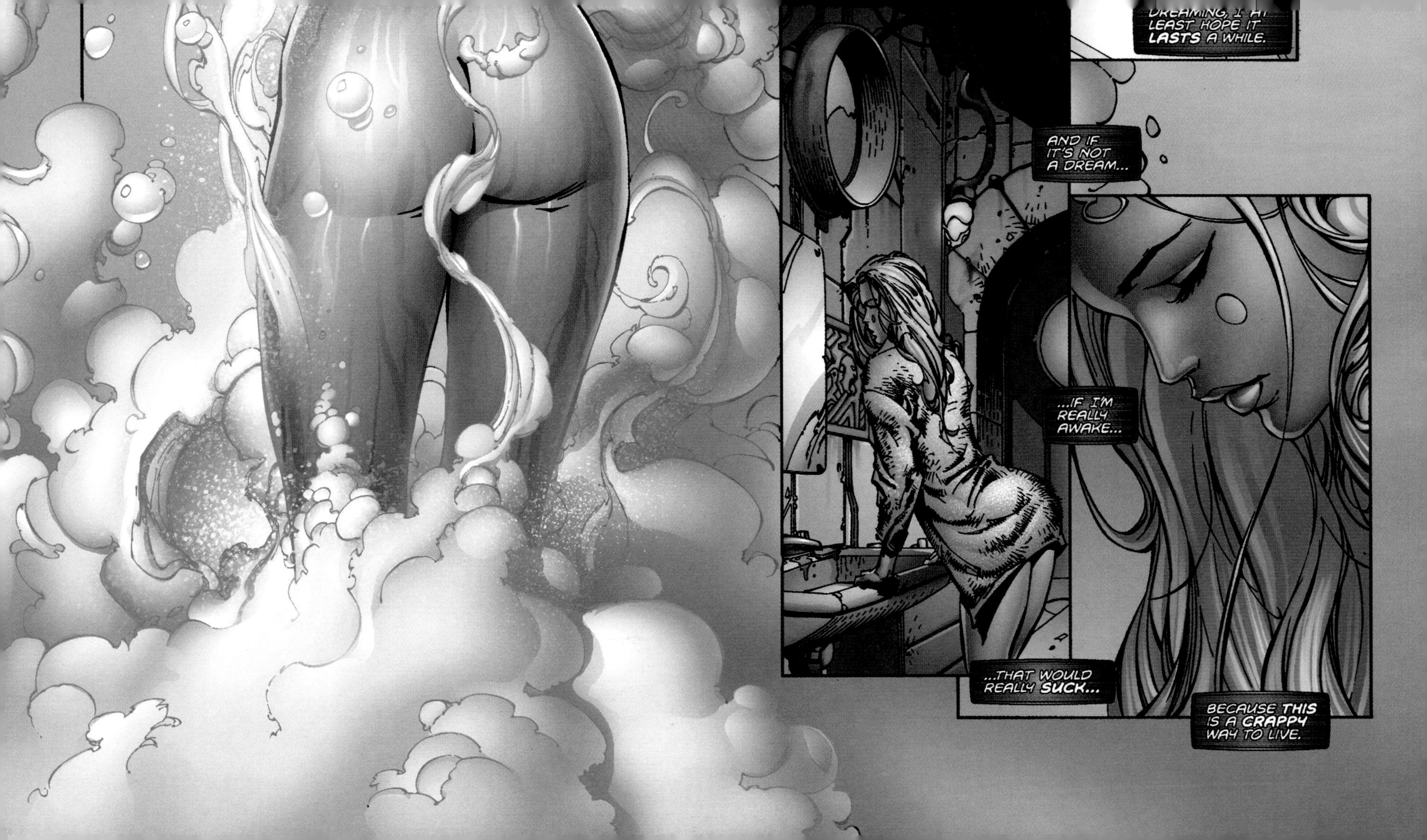
LEAST HOPE IT LASTS A WHILE.
AND IF IT'S NOT A DREAM...
...IF I'M REALLY AWAKE...
...THAT WOULD REALLY SUCK...
BECAUSE THIS IS A CRAPPY WAY TO LIVE.

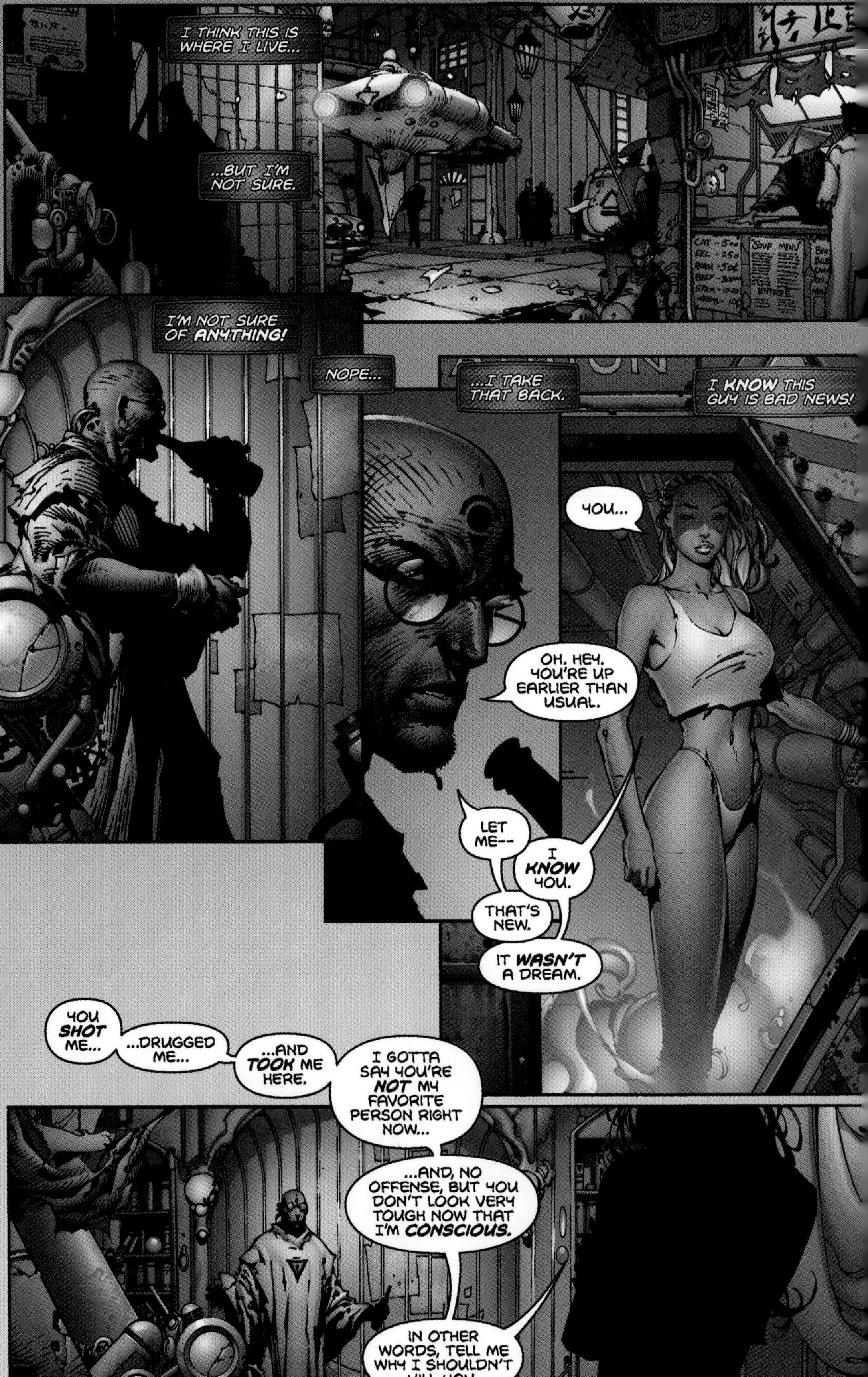
I THINK THIS IS WHERE I LIVE...
...BUT I'M NOT SURE.
CAT - 5.00
EEL - 2.50
ROACH - 5.00
BEEF - 30.00
SPAM - 10.00
WEENS - 1.00
SOUP MENU
ENTREE
I'M NOT SURE OF ANYTHING!
NOPE...
...I TAKE THAT BACK.
I KNOW THIS GUY IS BAD NEWS!
YOU...
OH. HEY. YOU'RE UP EARLIER THAN USUAL.
LET ME--
I KNOW YOU.
THAT'S NEW.
IT WASN'T A DREAM.
YOU SHOT ME...
...DRUGGED ME...
...AND TOOK ME HERE.
I GOTTA SAY YOU'RE NOT MY FAVORITE PERSON RIGHT NOW...
...AND, NO OFFENSE, BUT YOU DON'T LOOK VERY TOUGH NOW THAT I'M CONSCIOUS.
IN OTHER WORDS, TELL ME WHY I SHOULDN'T KILL YOU.

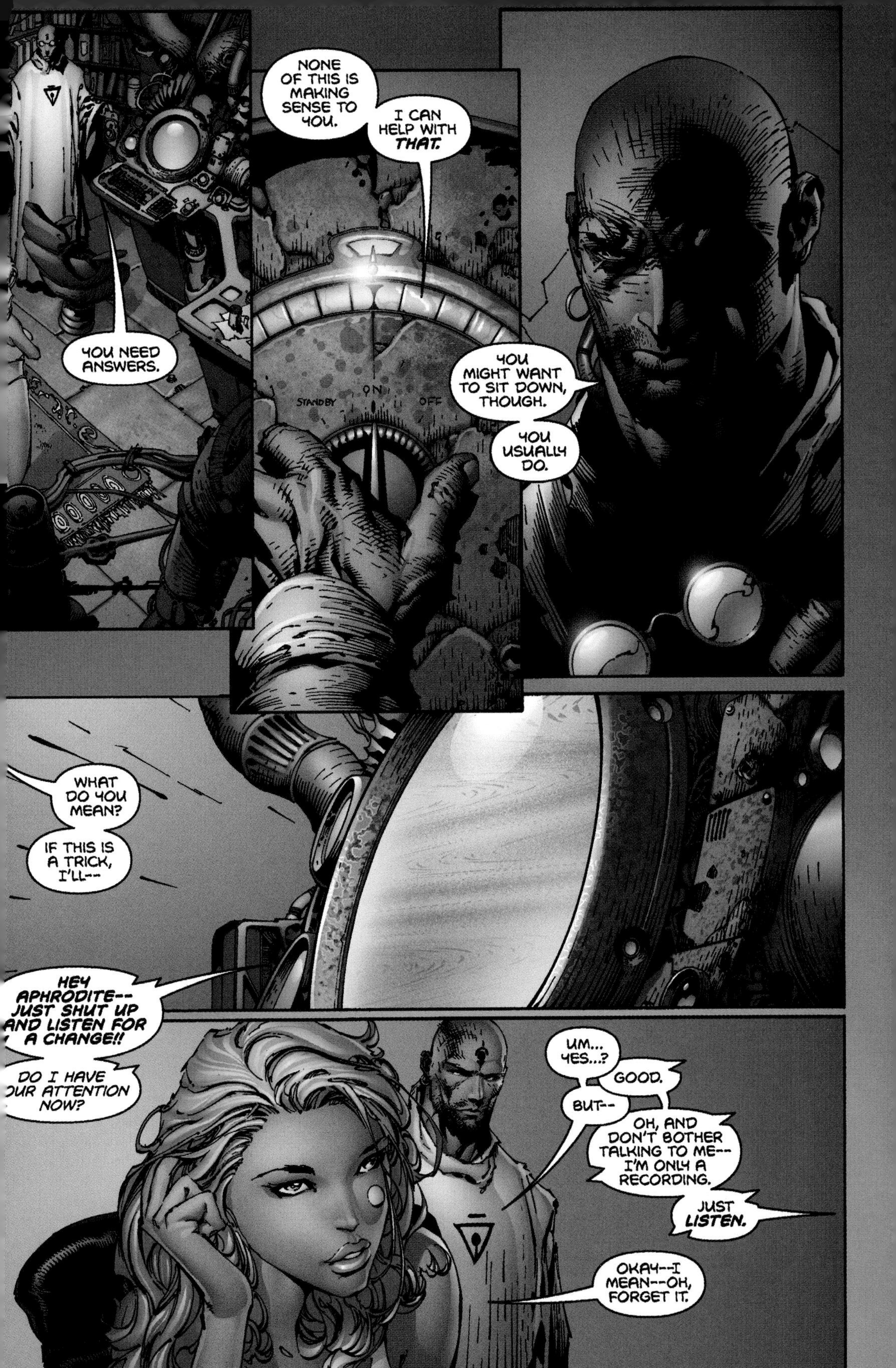
YOU NEED ANSWERS.
NONE OF THIS IS MAKING SENSE TO YOU.
I CAN HELP WITH *THAT.*
STANDBY
ON
OFF
YOU MIGHT WANT TO SIT DOWN, THOUGH.
YOU USUALLY DO.
WHAT DO YOU MEAN?
IF THIS IS A TRICK, I'LL--
HEY APHRODITE--JUST SHUT UP AND LISTEN FOR A CHANGE!!
DO I HAVE OUR ATTENTION NOW?
UM... YES...?
GOOD.
BUT--
OH, AND DON'T BOTHER TALKING TO ME--I'M ONLY A RECORDING.
JUST *LISTEN.*
OKAY--I MEAN--OH, FORGET IT.

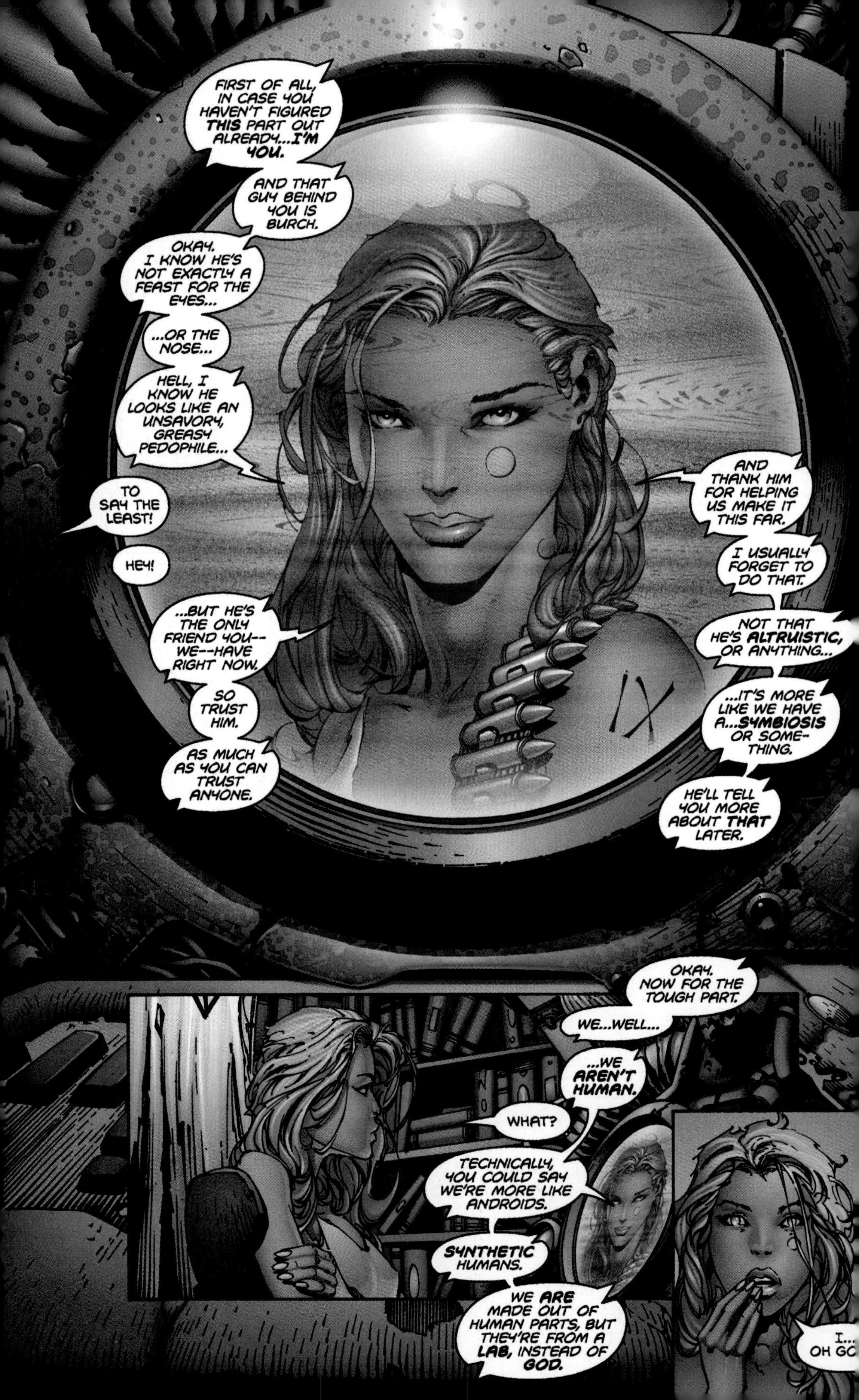
FIRST OF ALL, IN CASE YOU HAVEN'T FIGURED THIS PART OUT ALREADY...I'M YOU.
AND THAT GUY BEHIND YOU IS BURCH.
OKAY. I KNOW HE'S NOT EXACTLY A FEAST FOR THE EYES...
...OR THE NOSE...
HELL, I KNOW HE LOOKS LIKE AN UNSAVORY, GREASY PEDOPHILE...
TO SAY THE LEAST!
HEY!
...BUT HE'S THE ONLY FRIEND YOU--WE--HAVE RIGHT NOW.
SO TRUST HIM.
AS MUCH AS YOU CAN TRUST ANYONE.
AND THANK HIM FOR HELPING US MAKE IT THIS FAR.
I USUALLY FORGET TO DO THAT.
NOT THAT HE'S ALTRUISTIC, OR ANYTHING...
...IT'S MORE LIKE WE HAVE A...SYMBIOSIS OR SOME-THING.
HE'LL TELL YOU MORE ABOUT THAT LATER.
OKAY. NOW FOR THE TOUGH PART.
WE...WELL...
...WE AREN'T HUMAN.
WHAT?
TECHNICALLY, YOU COULD SAY WE'RE MORE LIKE ANDROIDS.
SYNTHETIC HUMANS.
WE ARE MADE OUT OF HUMAN PARTS, BUT THEY'RE FROM A LAB, INSTEAD OF GOD.
I... OH GO

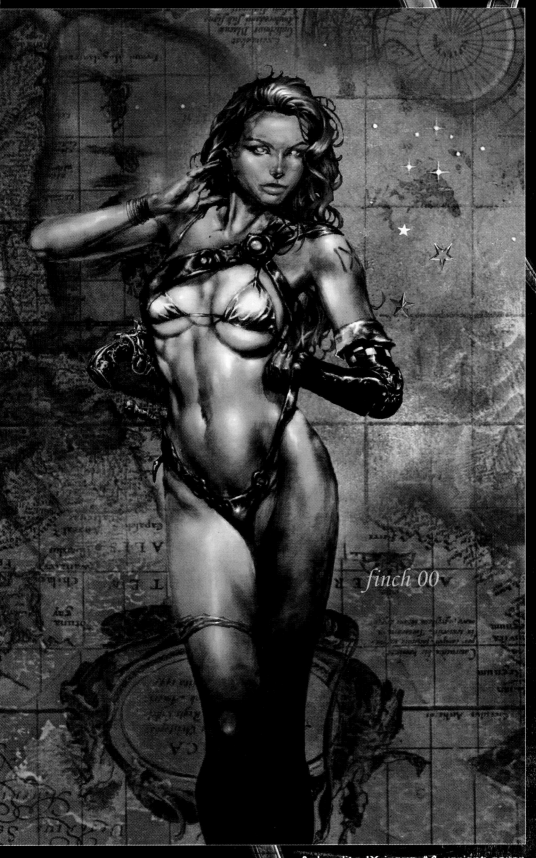

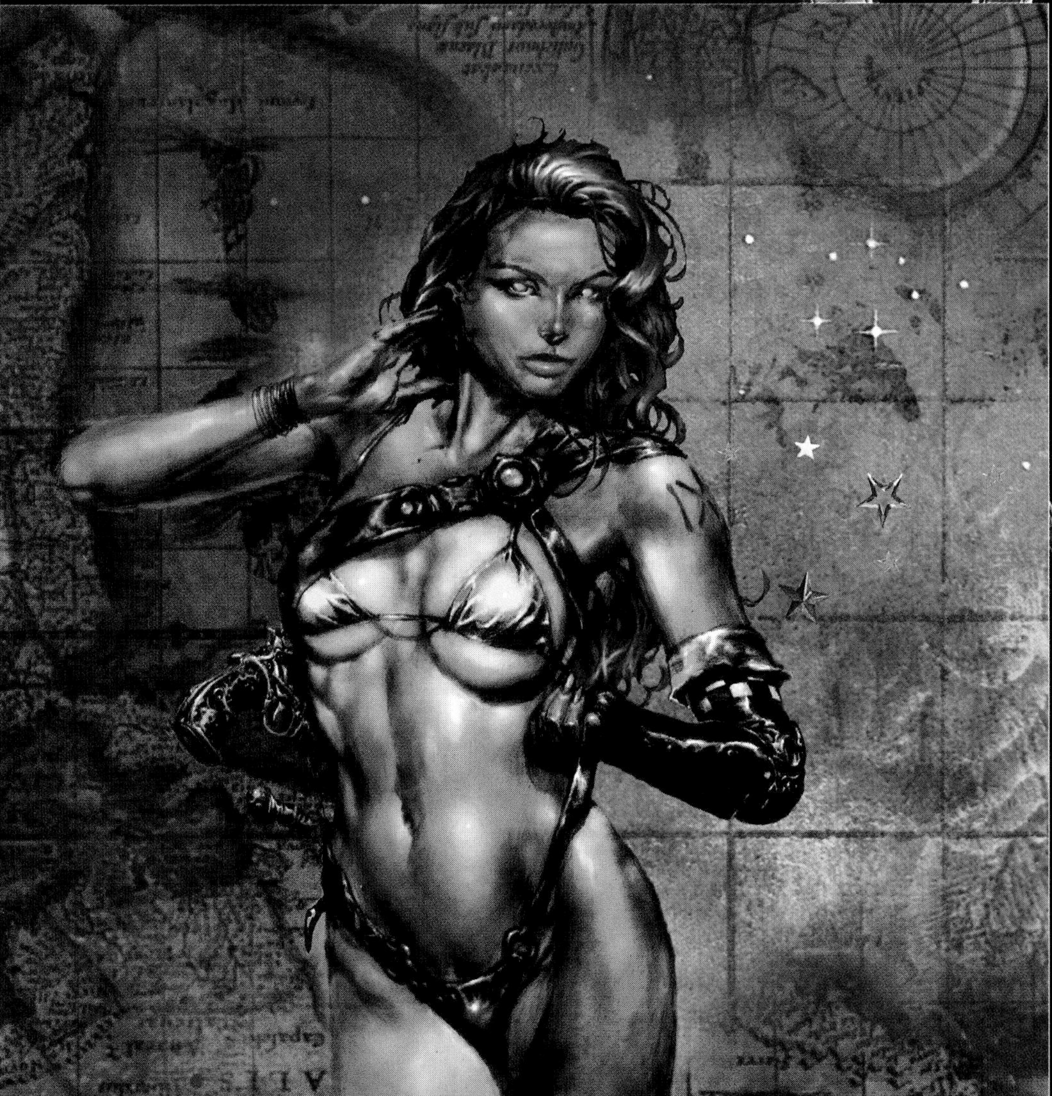
finch 00

Aphrodite IX issue #1 variant cover
art by: **Dave Finch**

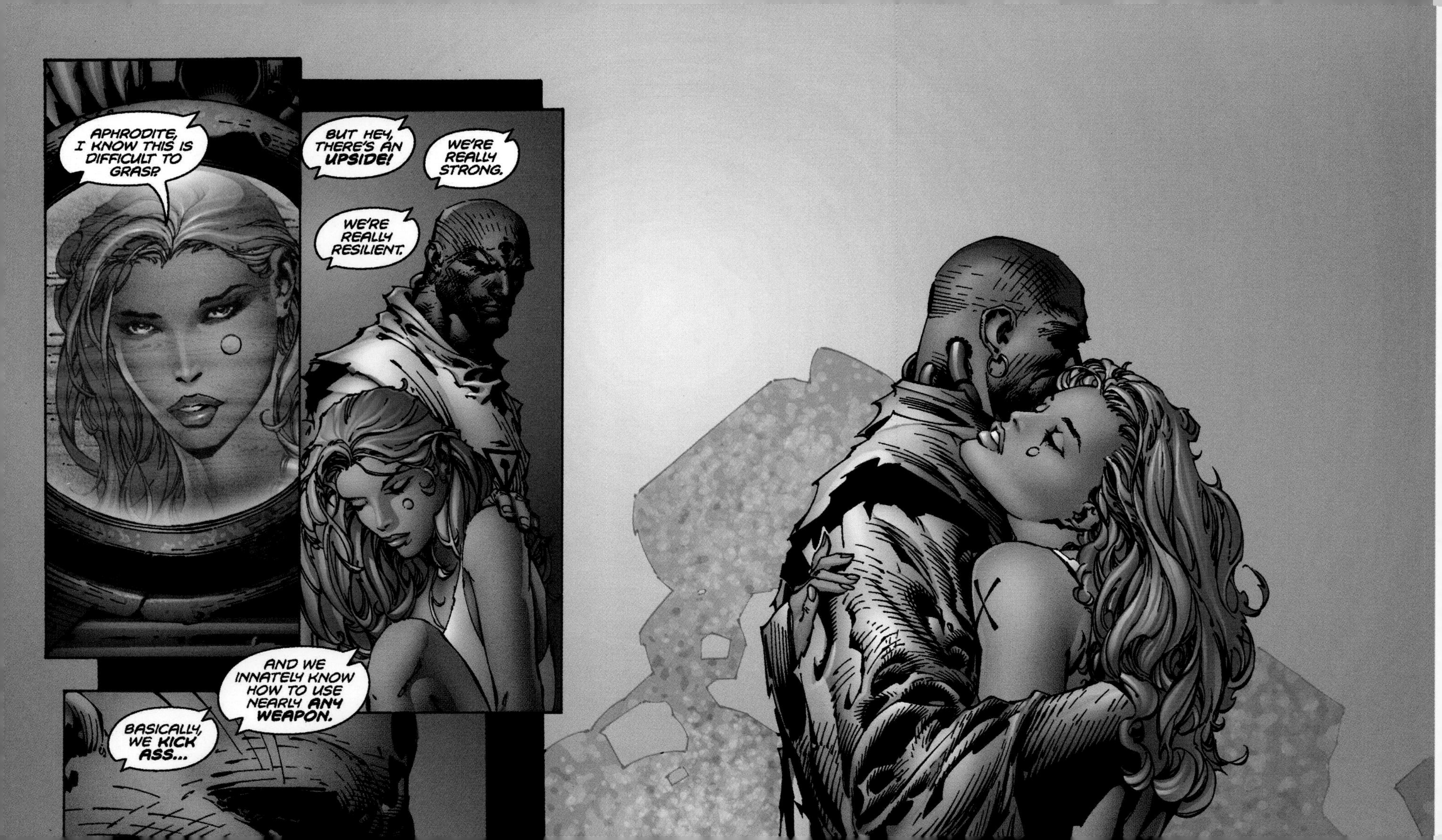
APHRODITE, I KNOW THIS IS DIFFICULT TO GRASP.
BUT HEY, THERE'S AN **UPSIDE!**
WE'RE REALLY STRONG.
WE'RE REALLY RESILIENT.
AND WE INNATELY KNOW HOW TO USE NEARLY **ANY WEAPON.**
BASICALLY, WE **KICK ASS...**

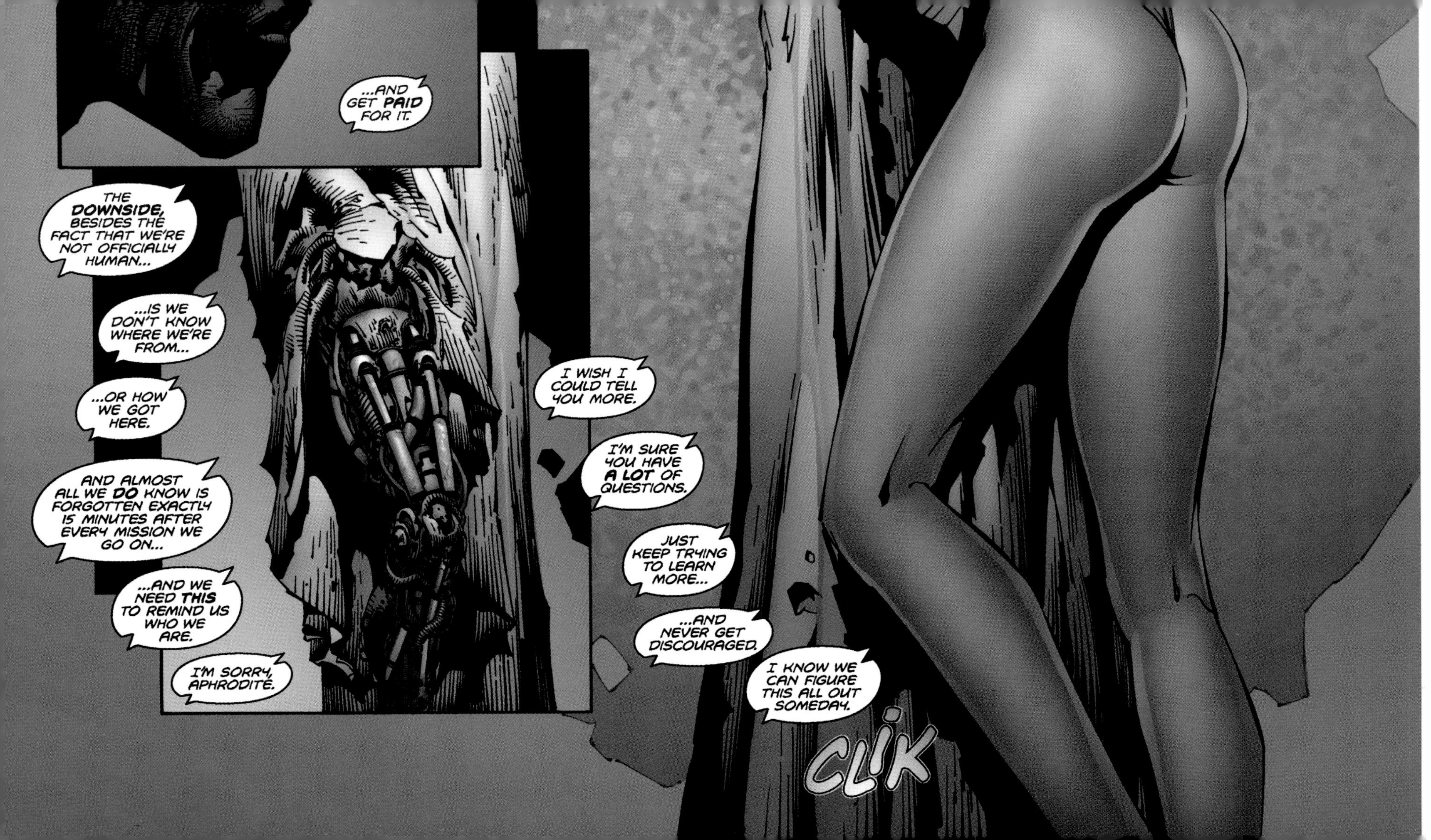
...AND GET PAID FOR IT.
THE DOWNSIDE, BESIDES THE FACT THAT WE'RE NOT OFFICIALLY HUMAN...
...IS WE DON'T KNOW WHERE WE'RE FROM...
...OR HOW WE GOT HERE.
AND ALMOST ALL WE DO KNOW IS FORGOTTEN EXACTLY 15 MINUTES AFTER EVERY MISSION WE GO ON...
...AND WE NEED THIS TO REMIND US WHO WE ARE.
I'M SORRY, APHRODITE.
I WISH I COULD TELL YOU MORE.
I'M SURE YOU HAVE A LOT OF QUESTIONS.
JUST KEEP TRYING TO LEARN MORE...
...AND NEVER GET DISCOURAGED.
I KNOW WE CAN FIGURE THIS ALL OUT SOMEDAY.
CLIK

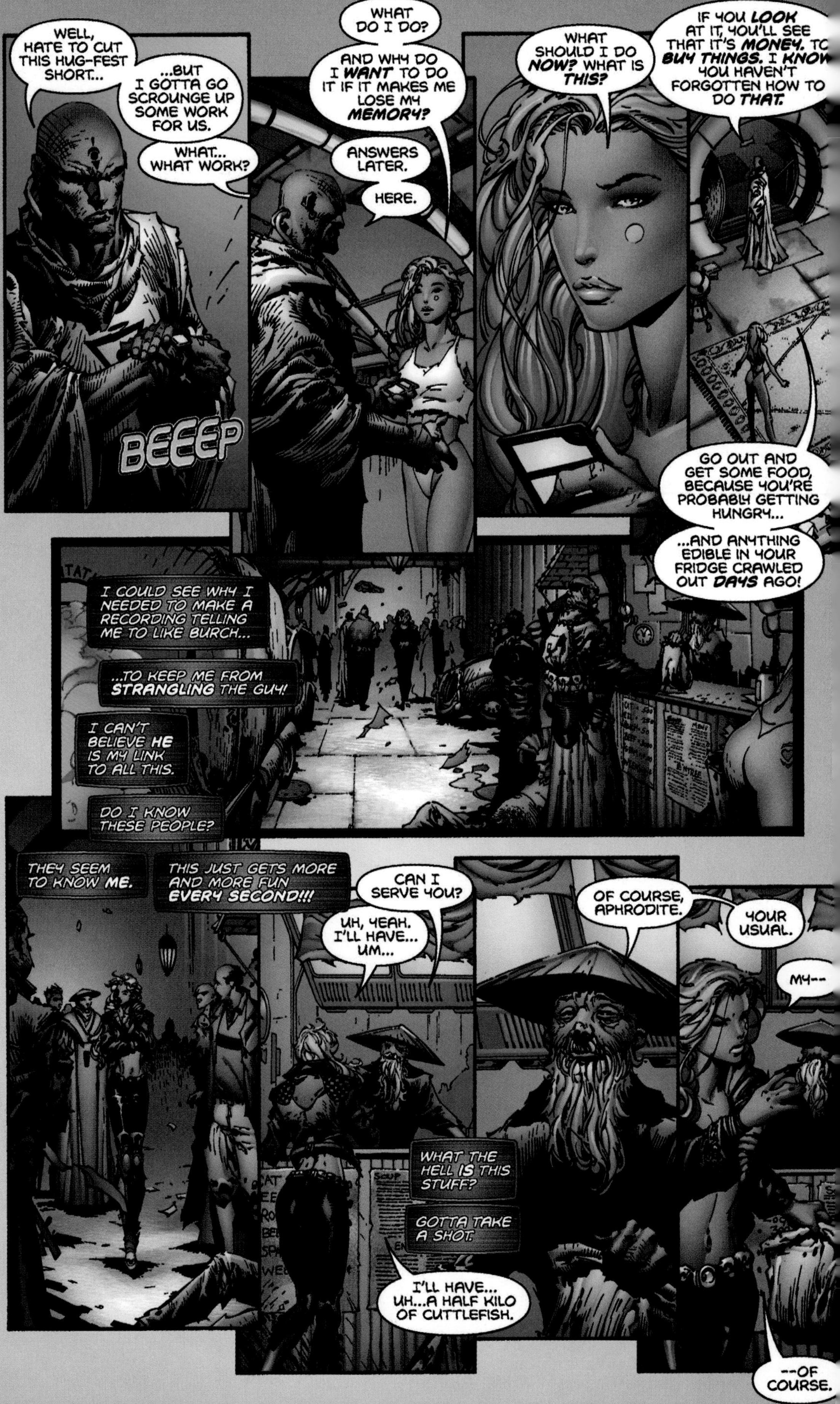
WELL, HATE TO CUT THIS HUG-FEST SHORT...
...BUT I GOTTA GO SCROUNGE UP SOME WORK FOR US.
WHAT... WHAT WORK?
BEEEP
WHAT DO I DO?
AND WHY DO I WANT TO DO IT IF IT MAKES ME LOSE MY MEMORY?
ANSWERS LATER.
HERE.
WHAT SHOULD I DO NOW? WHAT IS THIS?
IF YOU LOOK AT IT, YOU'LL SEE THAT IT'S MONEY. TO BUY THINGS. I KNOW YOU HAVEN'T FORGOTTEN HOW TO DO THAT.
GO OUT AND GET SOME FOOD, BECAUSE YOU'RE PROBABLY GETTING HUNGRY...
...AND ANYTHING EDIBLE IN YOUR FRIDGE CRAWLED OUT DAYS AGO!
I COULD SEE WHY I NEEDED TO MAKE A RECORDING TELLING ME TO LIKE BURCH...
...TO KEEP ME FROM STRANGLING THE GUY!
I CAN'T BELIEVE HE IS MY LINK TO ALL THIS.
DO I KNOW THESE PEOPLE?
THEY SEEM TO KNOW ME.
THIS JUST GETS MORE AND MORE FUN EVERY SECOND!!!
CAN I SERVE YOU?
UH, YEAH. I'LL HAVE... UM...
WHAT THE HELL IS THIS STUFF?
GOTTA TAKE A SHOT.
I'LL HAVE... UH...A HALF KILO OF CUTTLEFISH.
OF COURSE, APHRODITE.
YOUR USUAL.
MY--
--OF COURSE.

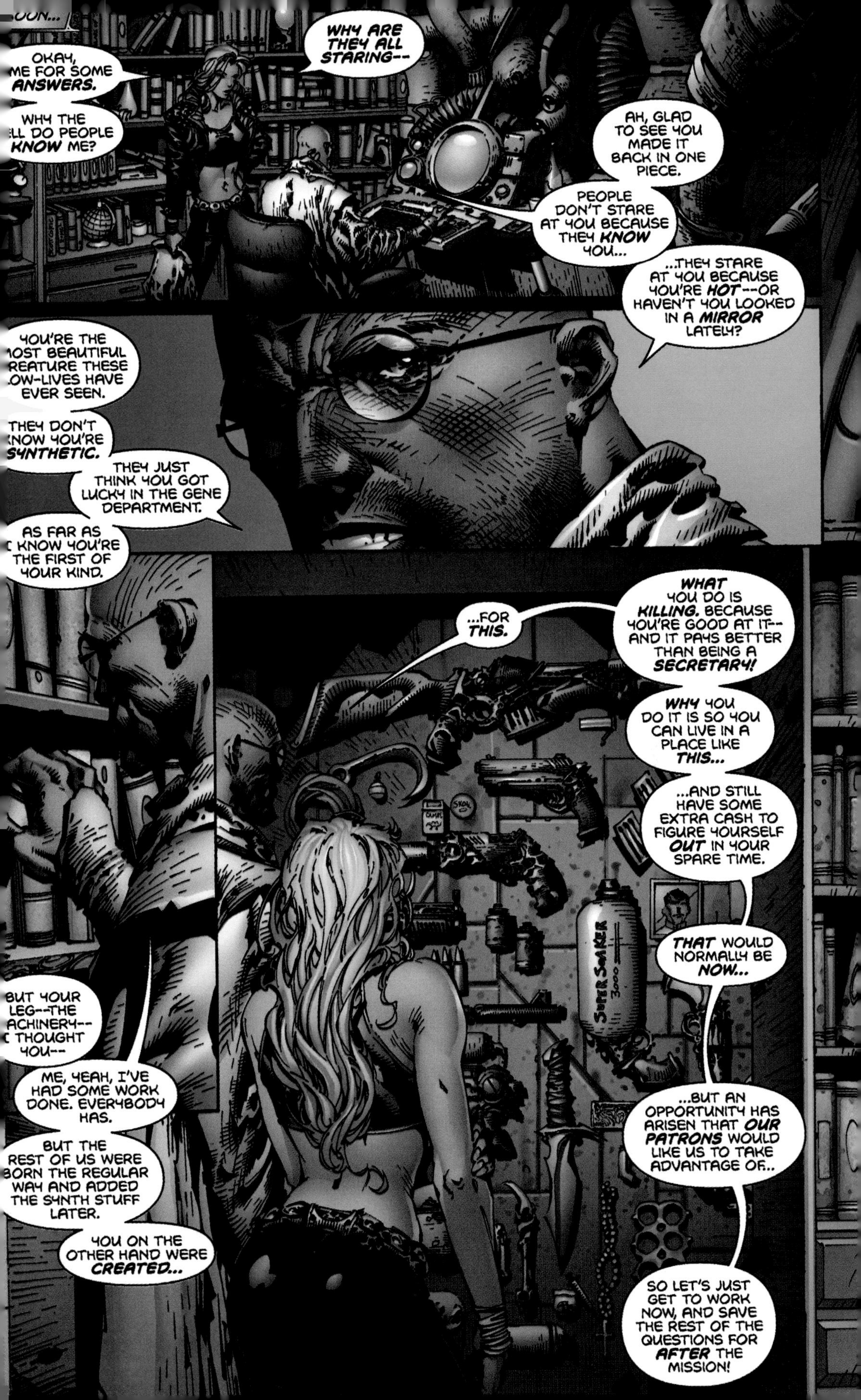

OON...
OKAY, ME FOR SOME ANSWERS.
WHY THE LL DO PEOPLE KNOW ME?
WHY ARE THEY ALL STARING--
AH, GLAD TO SEE YOU MADE IT BACK IN ONE PIECE.
PEOPLE DON'T STARE AT YOU BECAUSE THEY KNOW YOU...
...THEY STARE AT YOU BECAUSE YOU'RE HOT--OR HAVEN'T YOU LOOKED IN A MIRROR LATELY?
YOU'RE THE OST BEAUTIFUL REATURE THESE OW-LIVES HAVE EVER SEEN.
THEY DON'T NOW YOU'RE SYNTHETIC.
THEY JUST THINK YOU GOT LUCKY IN THE GENE DEPARTMENT.
AS FAR AS KNOW YOU'RE THE FIRST OF YOUR KIND.
BUT YOUR LEG--THE ACHINERY-- THOUGHT YOU--
ME, YEAH, I'VE HAD SOME WORK DONE. EVERYBODY HAS.
BUT THE REST OF US WERE BORN THE REGULAR WAY AND ADDED THE SYNTH STUFF LATER.
YOU ON THE OTHER HAND WERE CREATED...
...FOR THIS.
WHAT YOU DO IS KILLING. BECAUSE YOU'RE GOOD AT IT--AND IT PAYS BETTER THAN BEING A SECRETARY!
WHY YOU DO IT IS SO YOU CAN LIVE IN A PLACE LIKE THIS...
...AND STILL HAVE SOME EXTRA CASH TO FIGURE YOURSELF OUT IN YOUR SPARE TIME.
THAT WOULD NORMALLY BE NOW...
...BUT AN OPPORTUNITY HAS ARISEN THAT OUR PATRONS WOULD LIKE US TO TAKE ADVANTAGE OF..
SO LET'S JUST GET TO WORK NOW, AND SAVE THE REST OF THE QUESTIONS FOR AFTER THE MISSION!
SUPER SOAKER 3000

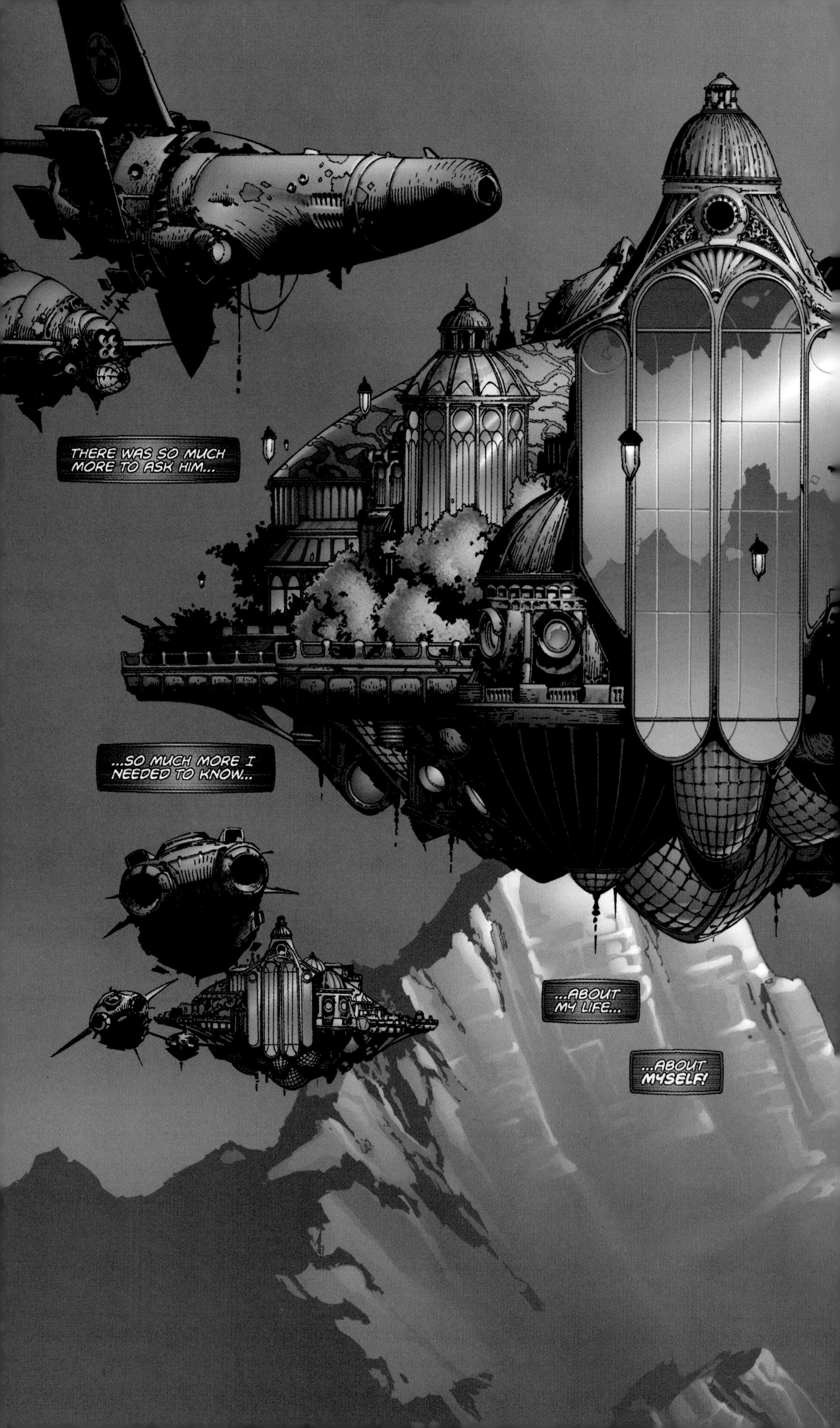
THERE WAS SO MUCH MORE TO ASK HIM...
...SO MUCH MORE I NEEDED TO KNOW...
...ABOUT MY LIFE...
...ABOUT MYSELF!

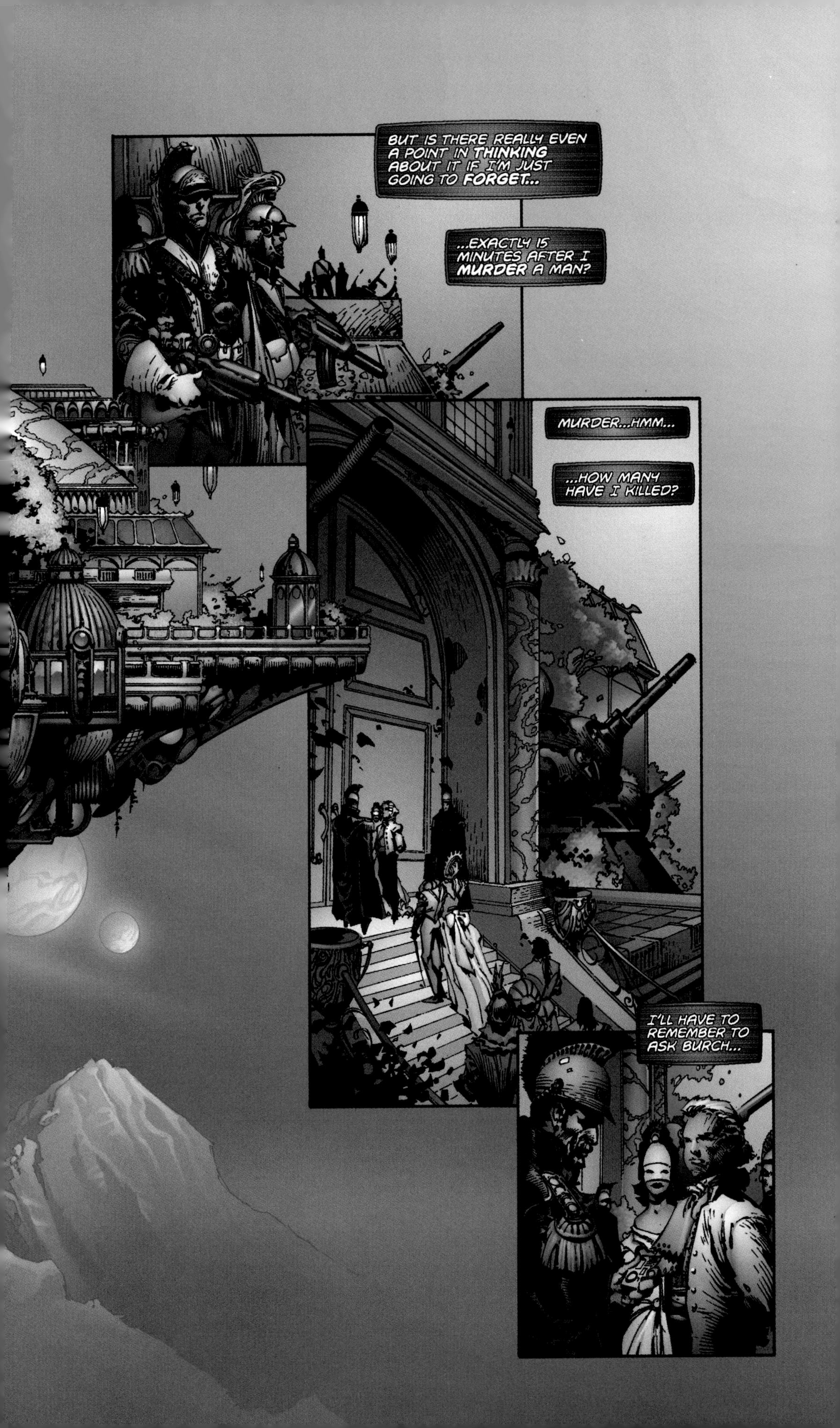
BUT IS THERE REALLY EVEN A POINT IN THINKING ABOUT IT IF I'M JUST GOING TO FORGET...
...EXACTLY 15 MINUTES AFTER I MURDER A MAN?
MURDER...HMM...
...HOW MANY HAVE I KILLED?
I'LL HAVE TO REMEMBER TO ASK BURCH...

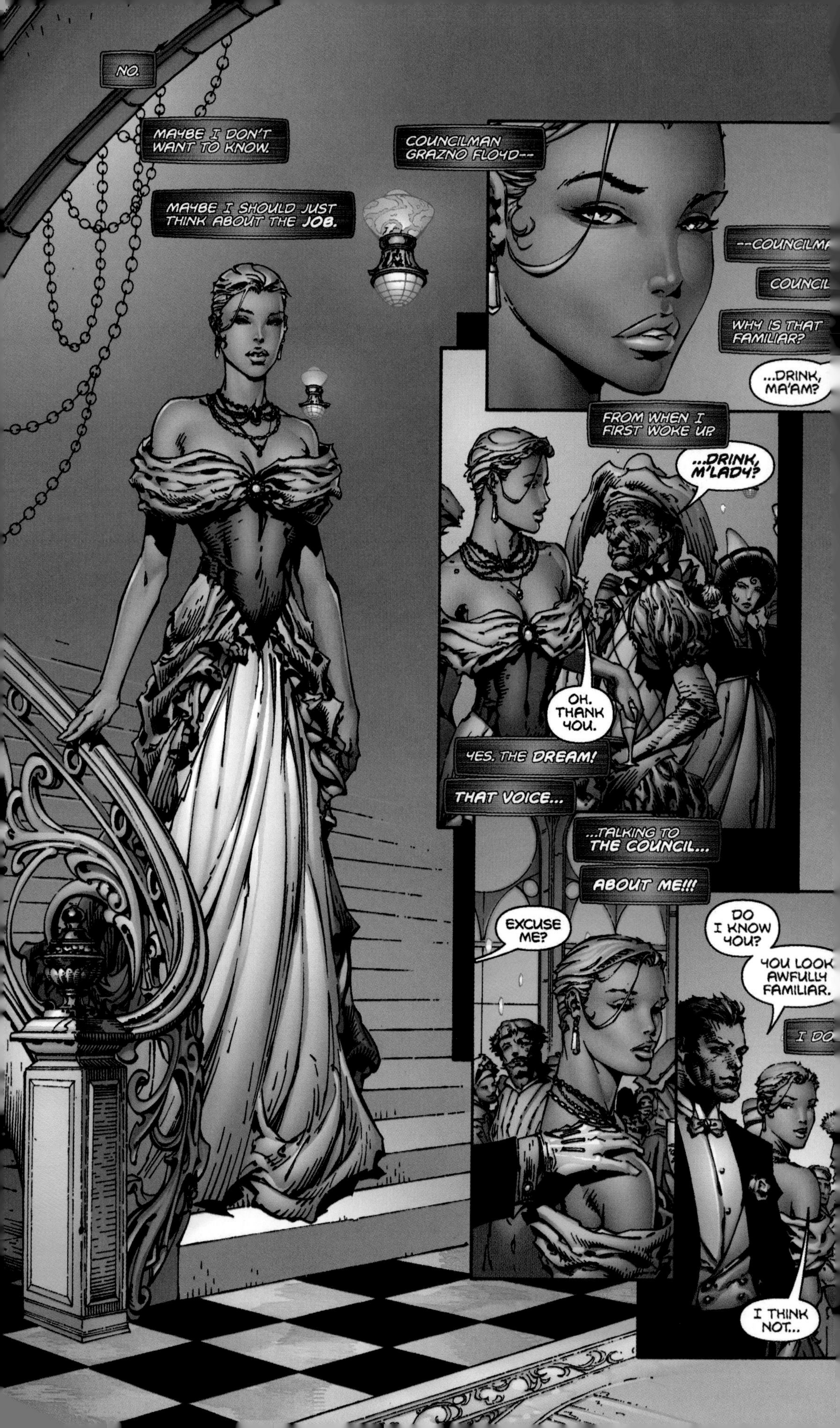
NO.
MAYBE I DON'T WANT TO KNOW.
MAYBE I SHOULD JUST THINK ABOUT THE JOB.
COUNCILMAN GRAZNO FLOYD--
--COUNCILMA
COUNCIL
WHY IS THAT FAMILIAR?
...DRINK, MA'AM?
FROM WHEN I FIRST WOKE UP.
...DRINK, M'LADY?
OH. THANK YOU.
YES. THE DREAM!
THAT VOICE...
...TALKING TO THE COUNCIL...
ABOUT ME!!!
EXCUSE ME?
DO I KNOW YOU?
YOU LOOK AWFULLY FAMILIAR.
I DO
I THINK NOT...

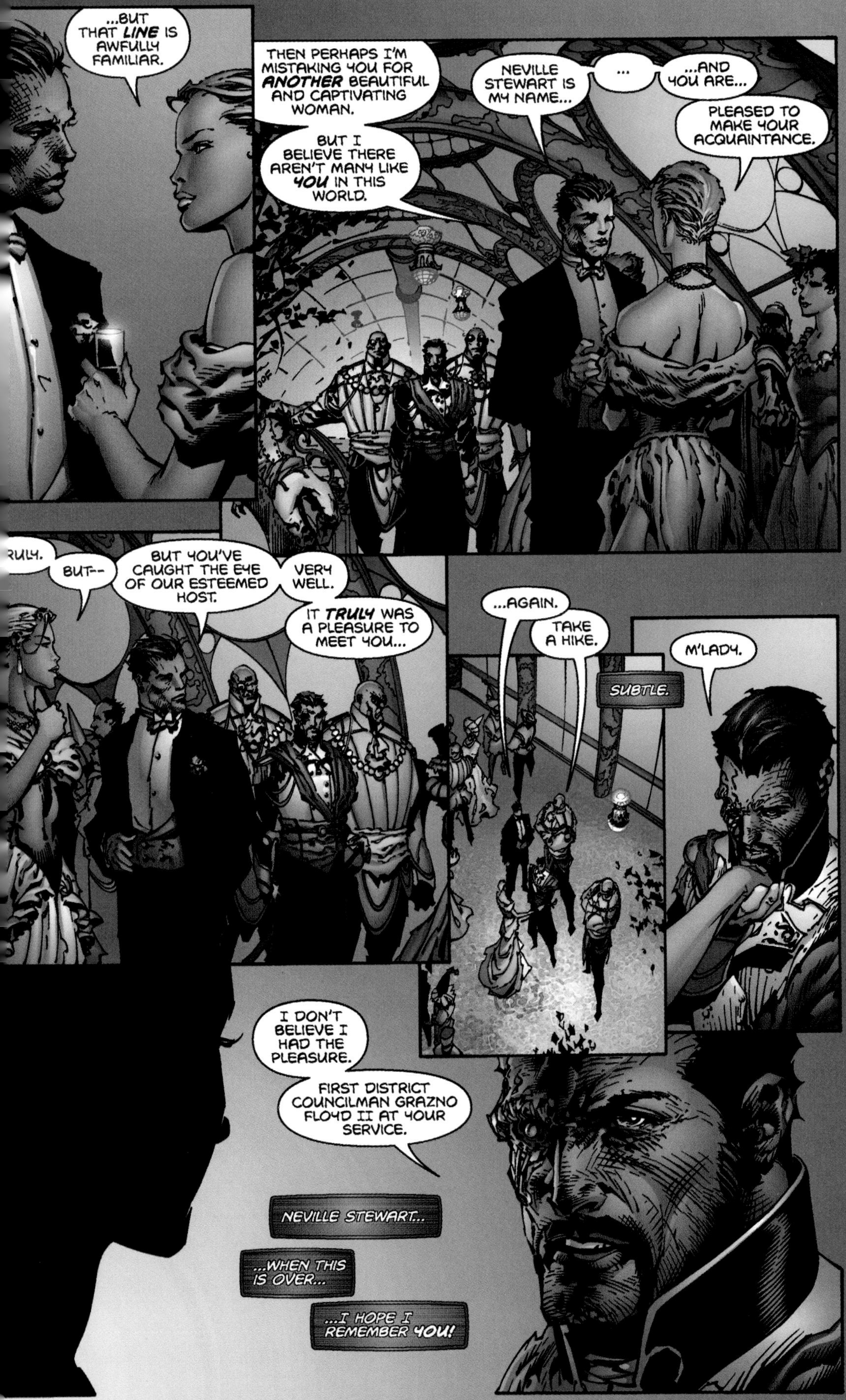
...BUT THAT **LINE** IS AWFULLY FAMILIAR.
THEN PERHAPS I'M MISTAKING YOU FOR **ANOTHER** BEAUTIFUL AND CAPTIVATING WOMAN.
BUT I BELIEVE THERE AREN'T MANY LIKE **YOU** IN THIS WORLD.
NEVILLE STEWART IS MY NAME...
...
...AND YOU ARE...
PLEASED TO MAKE YOUR ACQUAINTANCE.
RULY.
BUT--
BUT YOU'VE CAUGHT THE EYE OF OUR ESTEEMED HOST.
VERY WELL.
IT **TRULY** WAS A PLEASURE TO MEET YOU...
...AGAIN.
TAKE A HIKE.
SUBTLE.
M'LADY.
I DON'T BELIEVE I HAD THE PLEASURE.
FIRST DISTRICT COUNCILMAN GRAZNO FLOYD II AT YOUR SERVICE.
NEVILLE STEWART...
...WHEN THIS IS OVER...
...I HOPE I REMEMBER **YOU!**

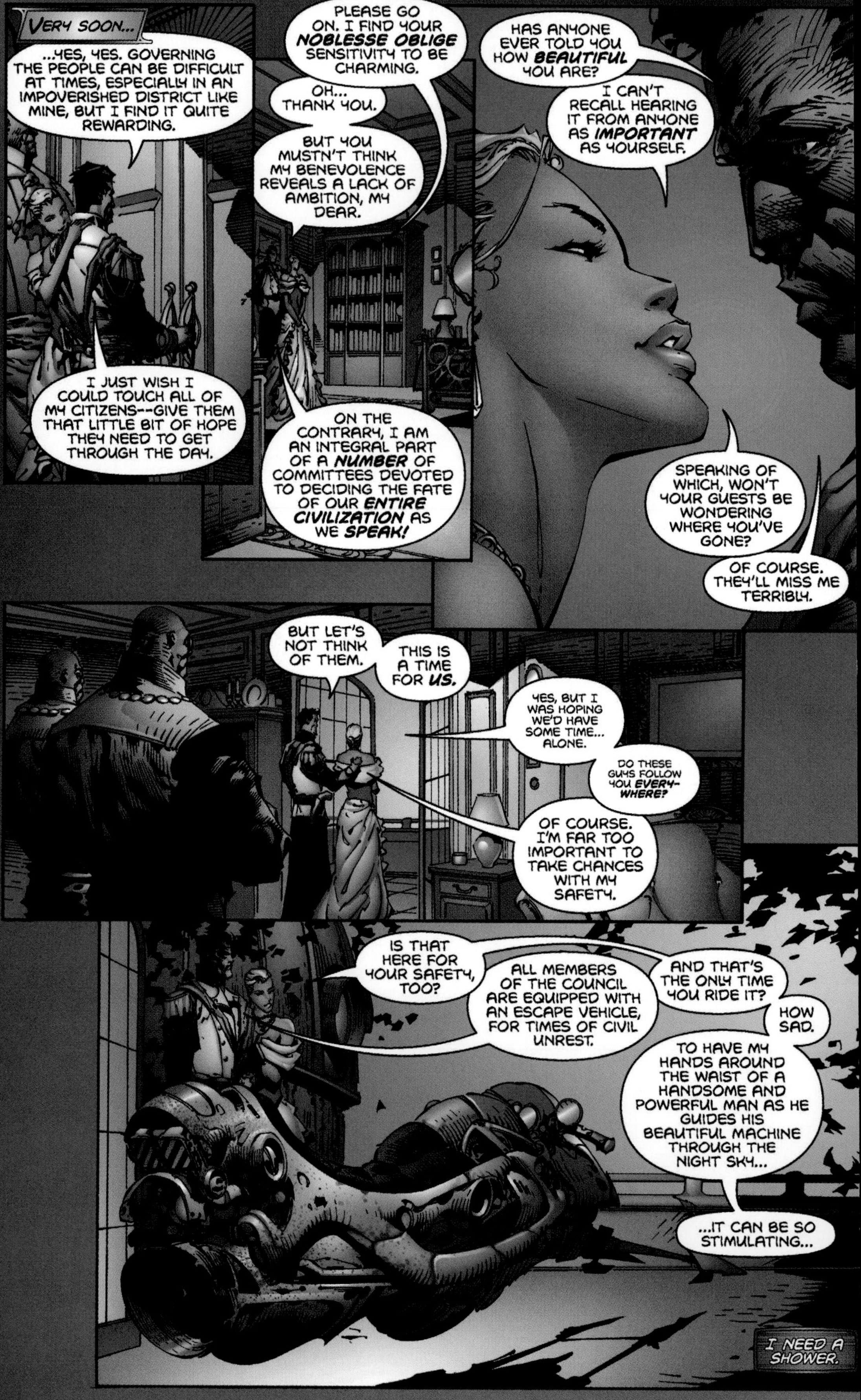

VERY SOON...
...YES, YES. GOVERNING THE PEOPLE CAN BE DIFFICULT AT TIMES, ESPECIALLY IN AN IMPOVERISHED DISTRICT LIKE MINE, BUT I FIND IT QUITE REWARDING.
I JUST WISH I COULD TOUCH ALL OF MY CITIZENS--GIVE THEM THAT LITTLE BIT OF HOPE THEY NEED TO GET THROUGH THE DAY.
PLEASE GO ON. I FIND YOUR NOBLESSE OBLIGE SENSITIVITY TO BE CHARMING.
OH... THANK YOU.
BUT YOU MUSTN'T THINK MY BENEVOLENCE REVEALS A LACK OF AMBITION, MY DEAR.
ON THE CONTRARY, I AM AN INTEGRAL PART OF A NUMBER OF COMMITTEES DEVOTED TO DECIDING THE FATE OF OUR ENTIRE CIVILIZATION AS WE SPEAK!
HAS ANYONE EVER TOLD YOU HOW BEAUTIFUL YOU ARE?
I CAN'T RECALL HEARING IT FROM ANYONE AS IMPORTANT AS YOURSELF.
SPEAKING OF WHICH, WON'T YOUR GUESTS BE WONDERING WHERE YOU'VE GONE?
OF COURSE. THEY'LL MISS ME TERRIBLY.
BUT LET'S NOT THINK OF THEM.
THIS IS A TIME FOR US.
YES, BUT I WAS HOPING WE'D HAVE SOME TIME... ALONE.
DO THESE GUYS FOLLOW YOU EVERY-WHERE?
OF COURSE. I'M FAR TOO IMPORTANT TO TAKE CHANCES WITH MY SAFETY.
IS THAT HERE FOR YOUR SAFETY, TOO?
ALL MEMBERS OF THE COUNCIL ARE EQUIPPED WITH AN ESCAPE VEHICLE, FOR TIMES OF CIVIL UNREST.
AND THAT'S THE ONLY TIME YOU RIDE IT?
HOW SAD.
TO HAVE MY HANDS AROUND THE WAIST OF A HANDSOME AND POWERFUL MAN AS HE GUIDES HIS BEAUTIFUL MACHINE THROUGH THE NIGHT SKY...
...IT CAN BE SO STIMULATING...
I NEED A SHOWER.

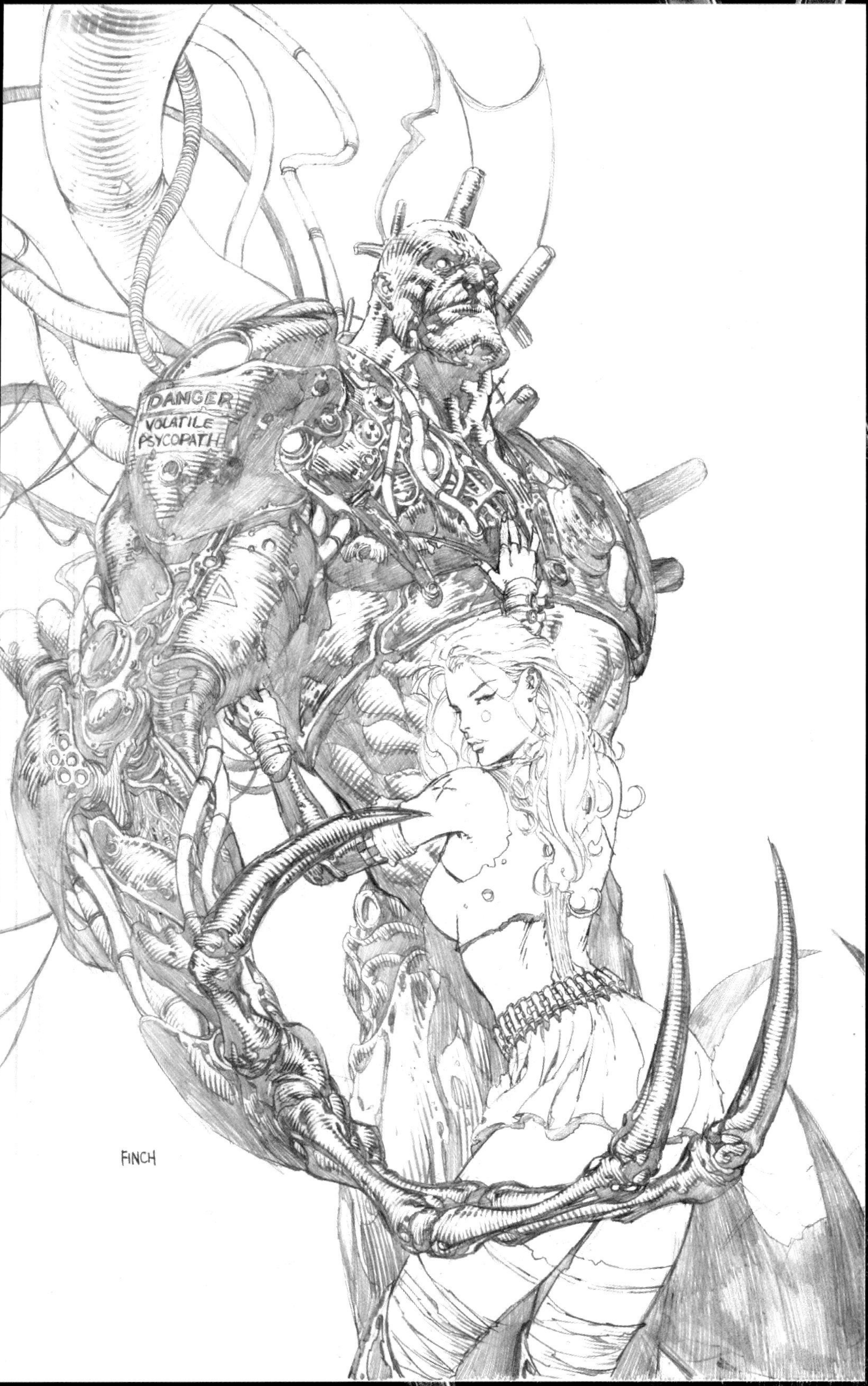
DANGER
VOLATILE
PSYCOPATH
FINCH

Aphrodite IX issue # 1 Black and White edition cover
art by: Dave Finch

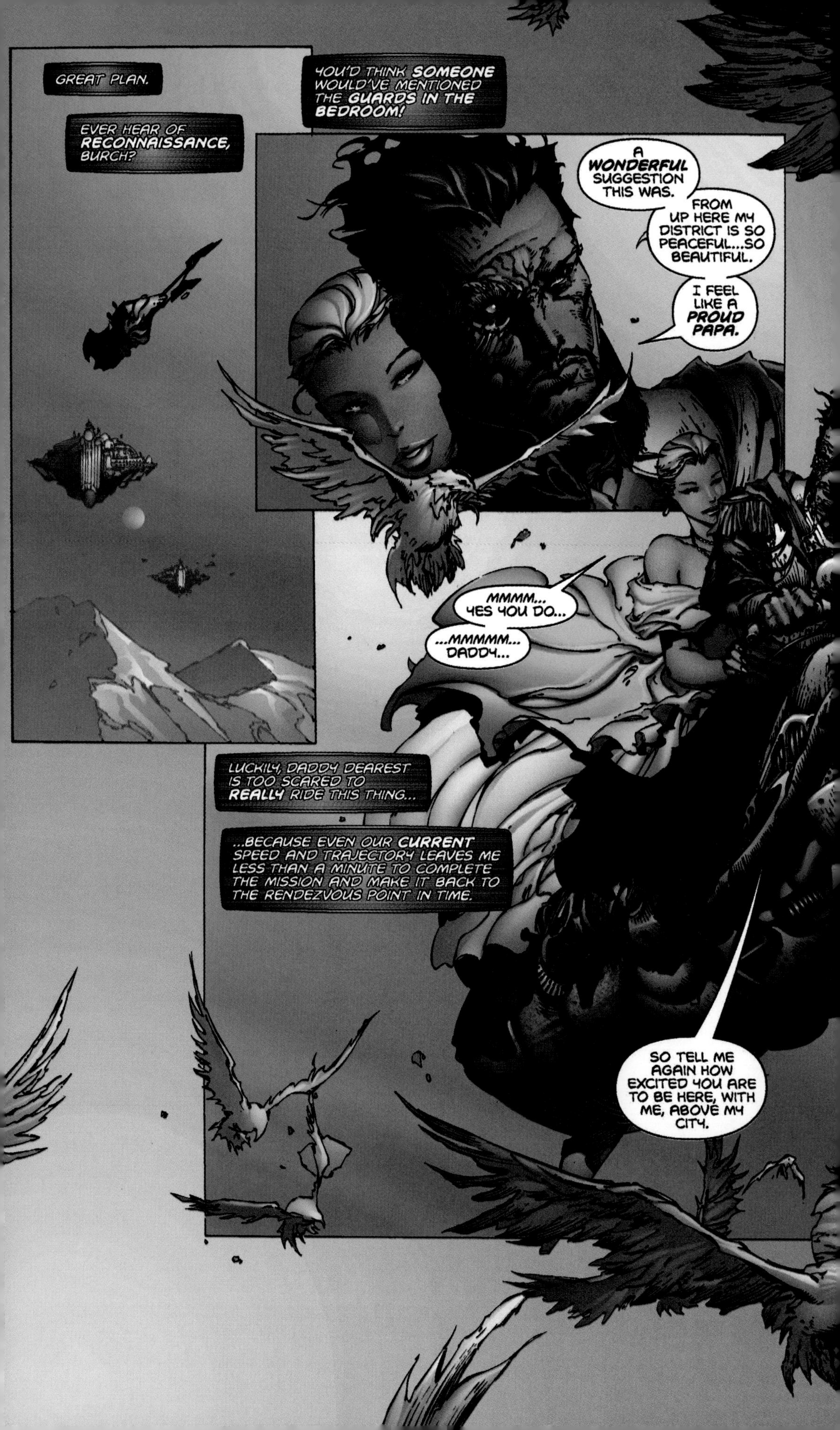
GREAT PLAN.
EVER HEAR OF RECONNAISSANCE, BURCH?
YOU'D THINK SOMEONE WOULD'VE MENTIONED THE GUARDS IN THE BEDROOM!
A WONDERFUL SUGGESTION THIS WAS.
FROM UP HERE MY DISTRICT IS SO PEACEFUL...SO BEAUTIFUL.
I FEEL LIKE A PROUD PAPA.
MMMM... YES YOU DO...
...MMMMM... DADDY...
LUCKILY, DADDY DEAREST IS TOO SCARED TO REALLY RIDE THIS THING...
...BECAUSE EVEN OUR CURRENT SPEED AND TRAJECTORY LEAVES ME LESS THAN A MINUTE TO COMPLETE THE MISSION AND MAKE IT BACK TO THE RENDEZVOUS POINT IN TIME.
SO TELL ME AGAIN HOW EXCITED YOU ARE TO BE HERE, WITH ME, ABOVE MY CITY.

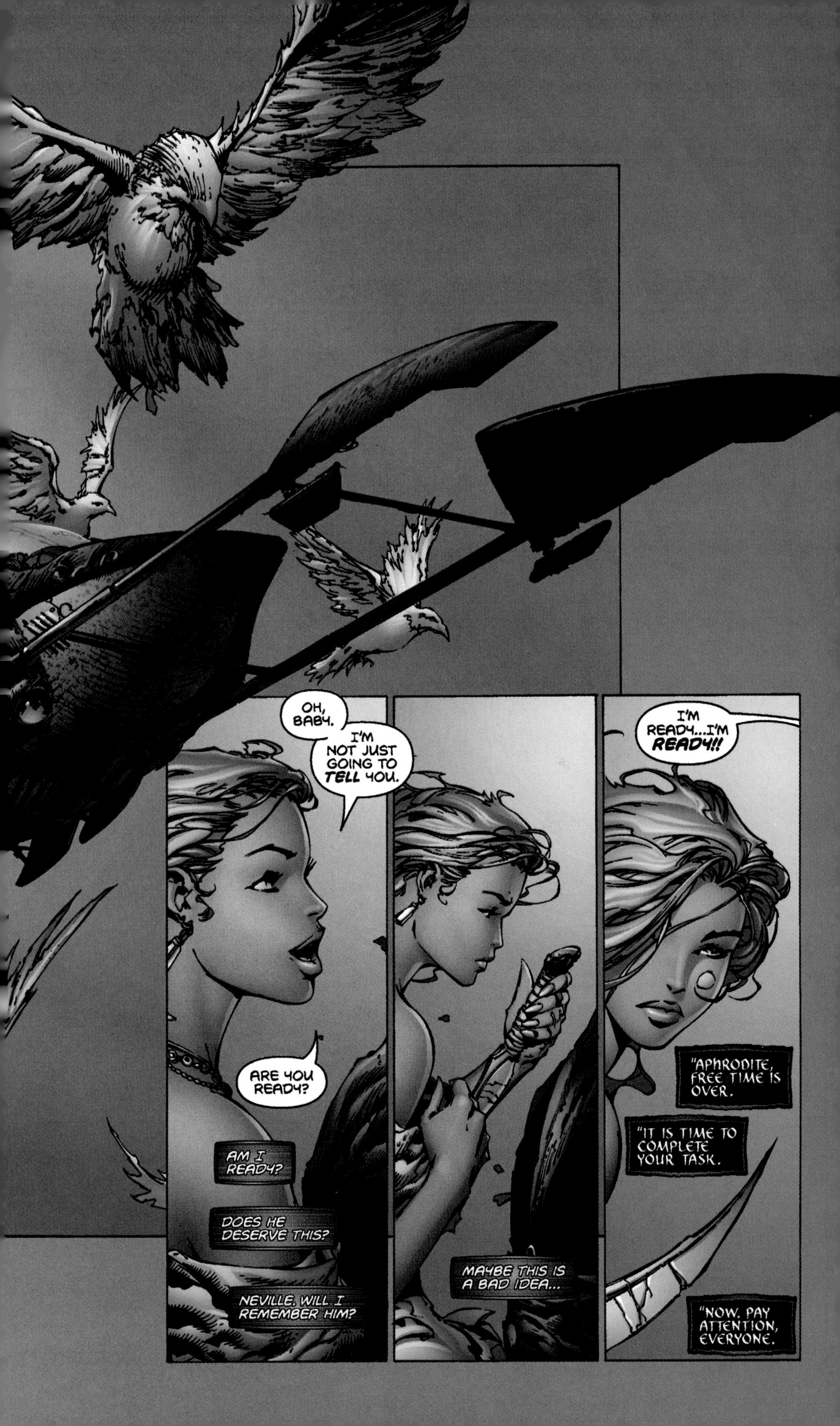
OH, BABY.
I'M NOT JUST GOING TO TELL YOU.
ARE YOU READY?
AM I READY?
DOES HE DESERVE THIS?
NEVILLE, WILL I REMEMBER HIM?
MAYBE THIS IS A BAD IDEA...
I'M READY...I'M READY!!
"APHRODITE, FREE TIME IS OVER.
"IT IS TIME TO COMPLETE YOUR TASK.
"NOW, PAY ATTENTION, EVERYONE.

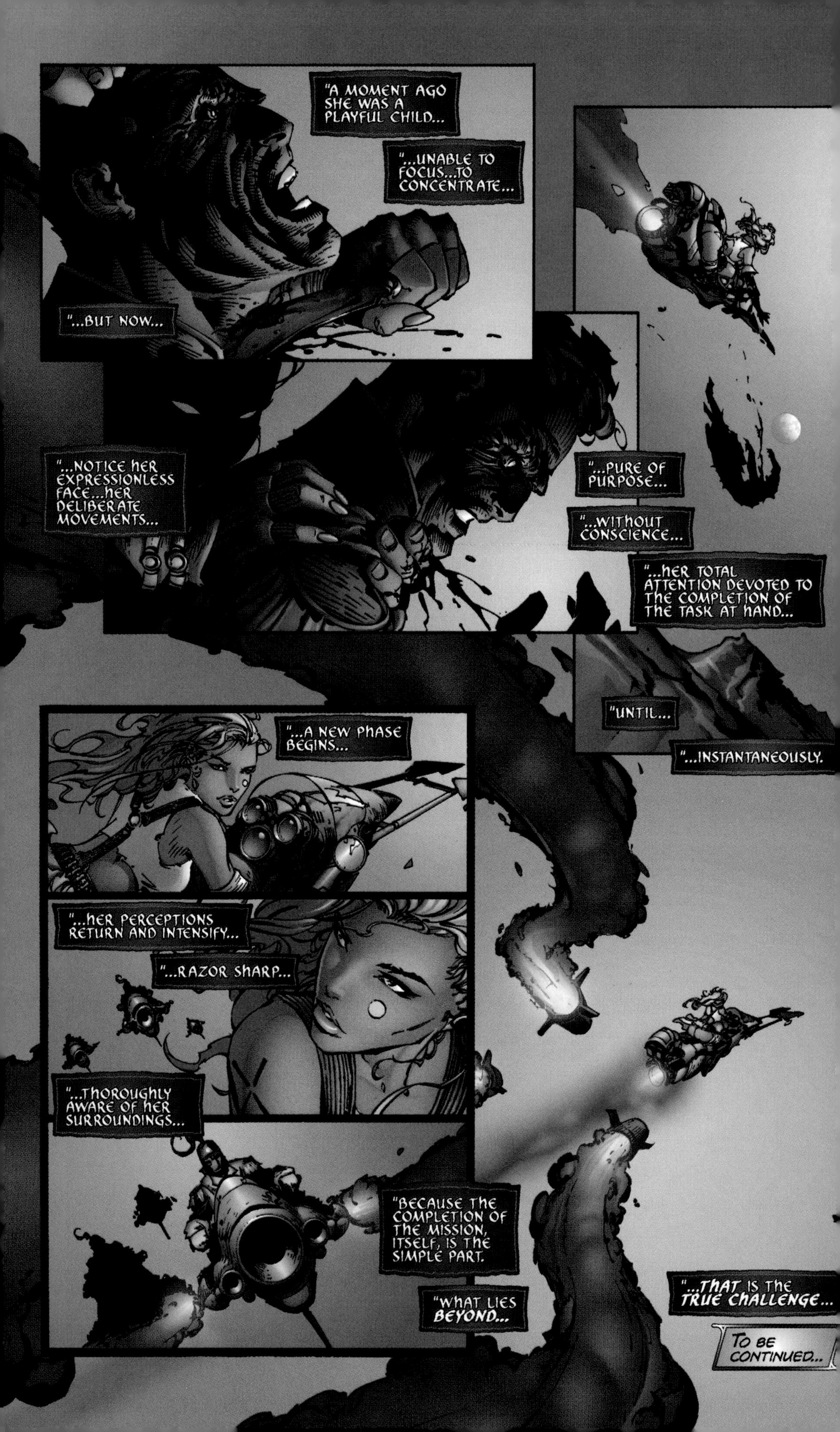
"A MOMENT AGO SHE WAS A PLAYFUL CHILD...
"...UNABLE TO FOCUS...TO CONCENTRATE...
"...BUT NOW...
"...NOTICE HER EXPRESSIONLESS FACE...HER DELIBERATE MOVEMENTS...
"...PURE OF PURPOSE...
"...WITHOUT CONSCIENCE...
"...HER TOTAL ATTENTION DEVOTED TO THE COMPLETION OF THE TASK AT HAND...
"UNTIL...
"...INSTANTANEOUSLY.
"...A NEW PHASE BEGINS...
"...HER PERCEPTIONS RETURN AND INTENSIFY...
"...RAZOR SHARP...
"...THOROUGHLY AWARE OF HER SURROUNDINGS...
"BECAUSE THE COMPLETION OF THE MISSION, ITSELF, IS THE SIMPLE PART.
"WHAT LIES *BEYOND*...
"...*THAT* IS THE *TRUE CHALLENGE*...
TO BE CONTINUED...

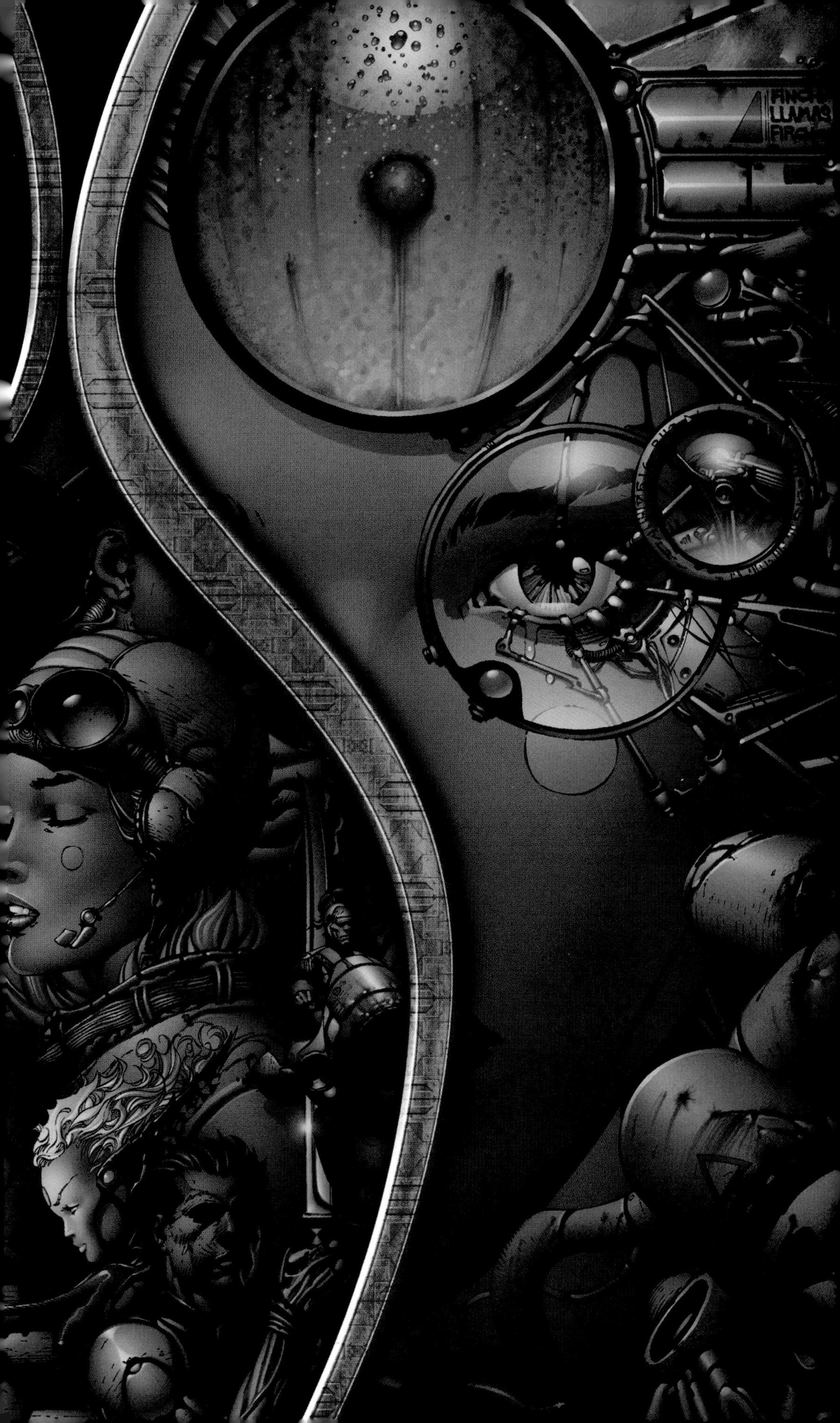

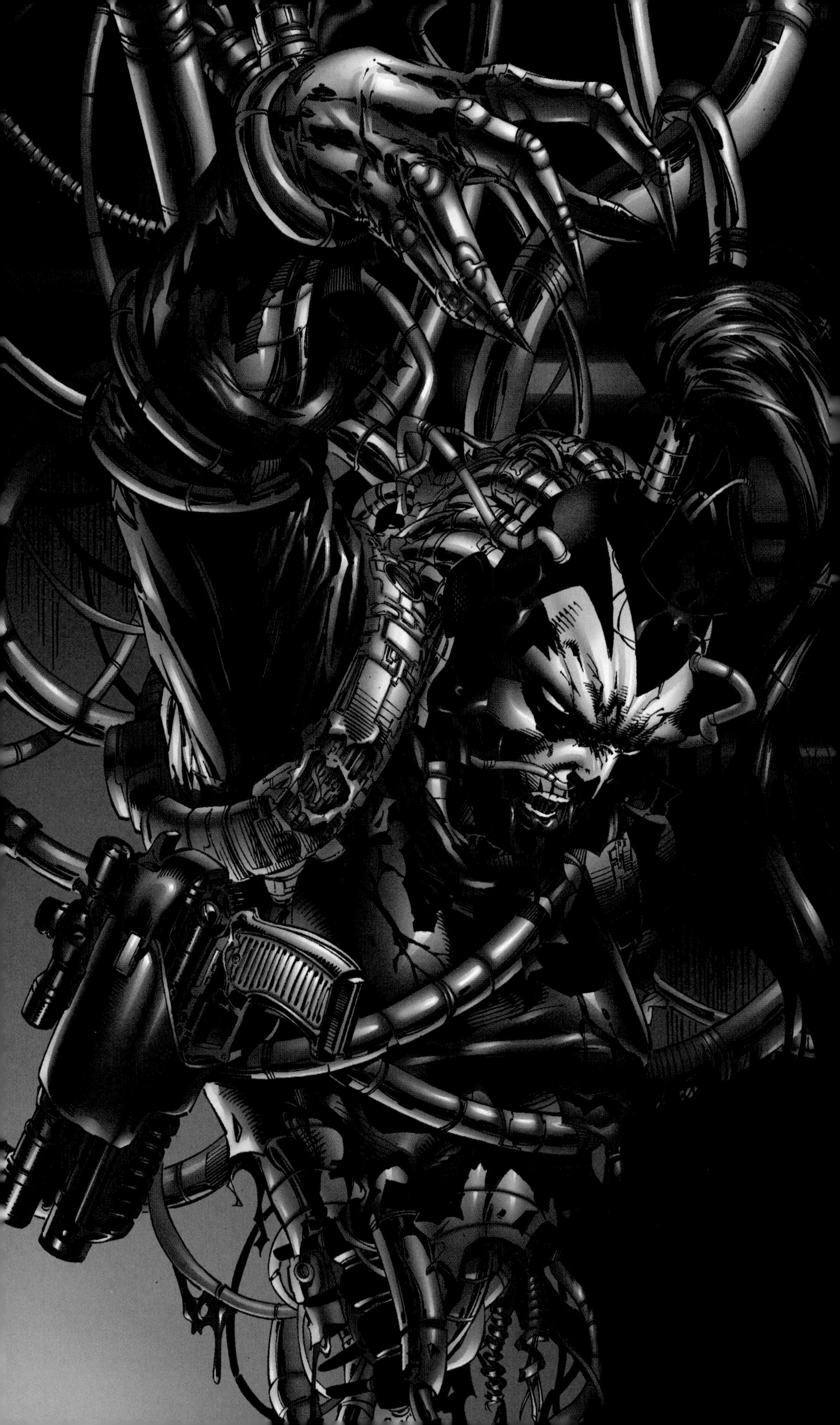

CYBER FORCE®

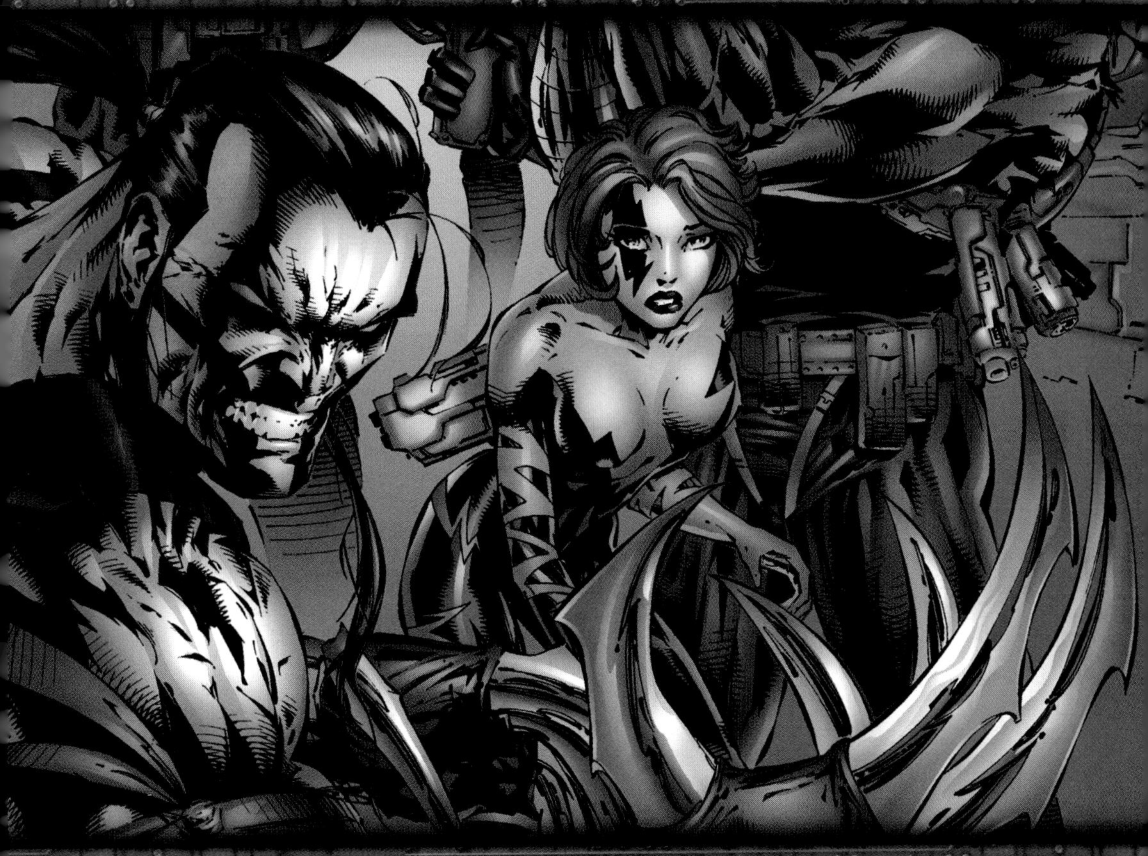

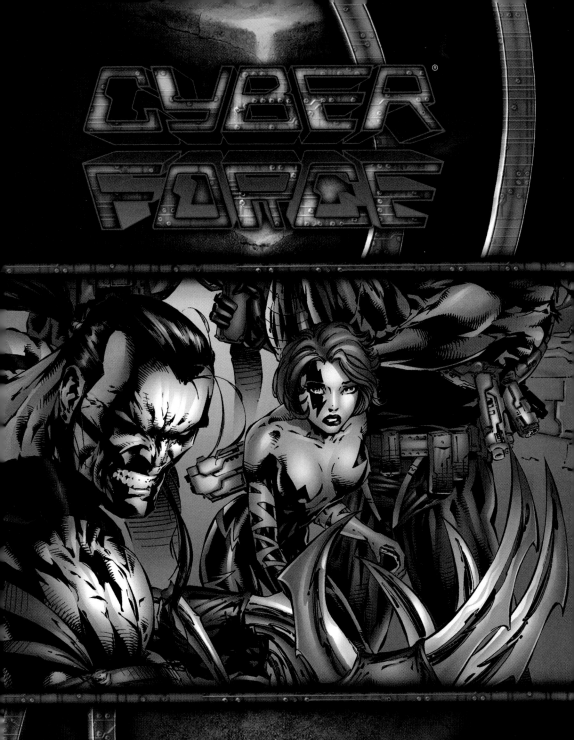

Leading into November 1995, Dave Finch had already broken into the business with his work on *Ripclaw* issue #1/2 as well as working on that year's *Cyberforce* Annual.

Cyberforce issue #16 marks Dave Finch's first full issue on the title. His work helped to establish *Cyberforce* as one of the flagship books of the Top Cow universe.

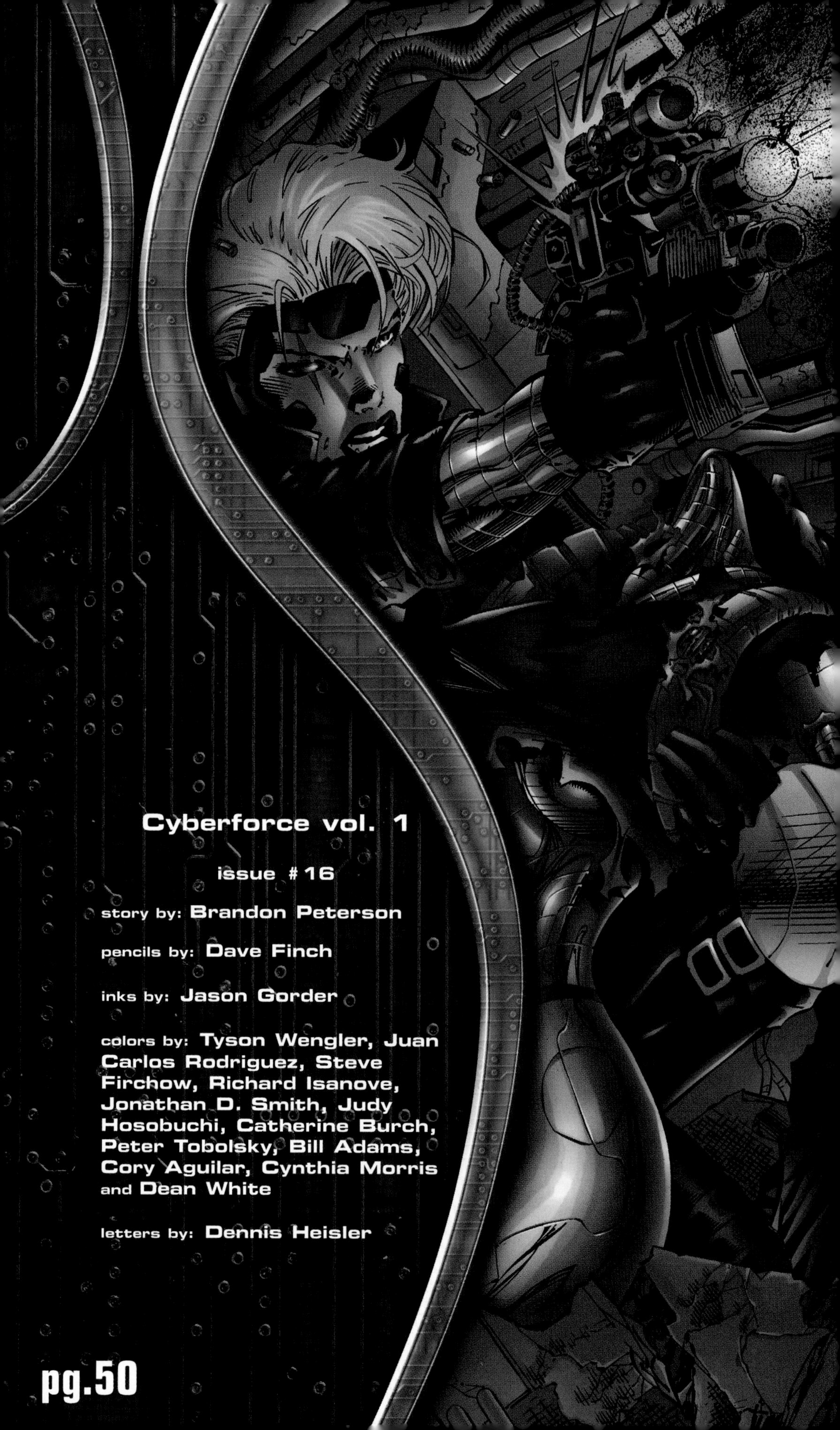

Cyberforce vol. 1

issue #16

story by: **Brandon Peterson**

pencils by: **Dave Finch**

inks by: **Jason Gorder**

colors by: **Tyson Wengler, Juan Carlos Rodriguez, Steve Firchow, Richard Isanove, Jonathan D. Smith, Judy Hosobuchi, Catherine Burch, Peter Tobolsky, Bill Adams, Cory Aguilar, Cynthia Morris** and **Dean White**

letters by: **Dennis Heisler**

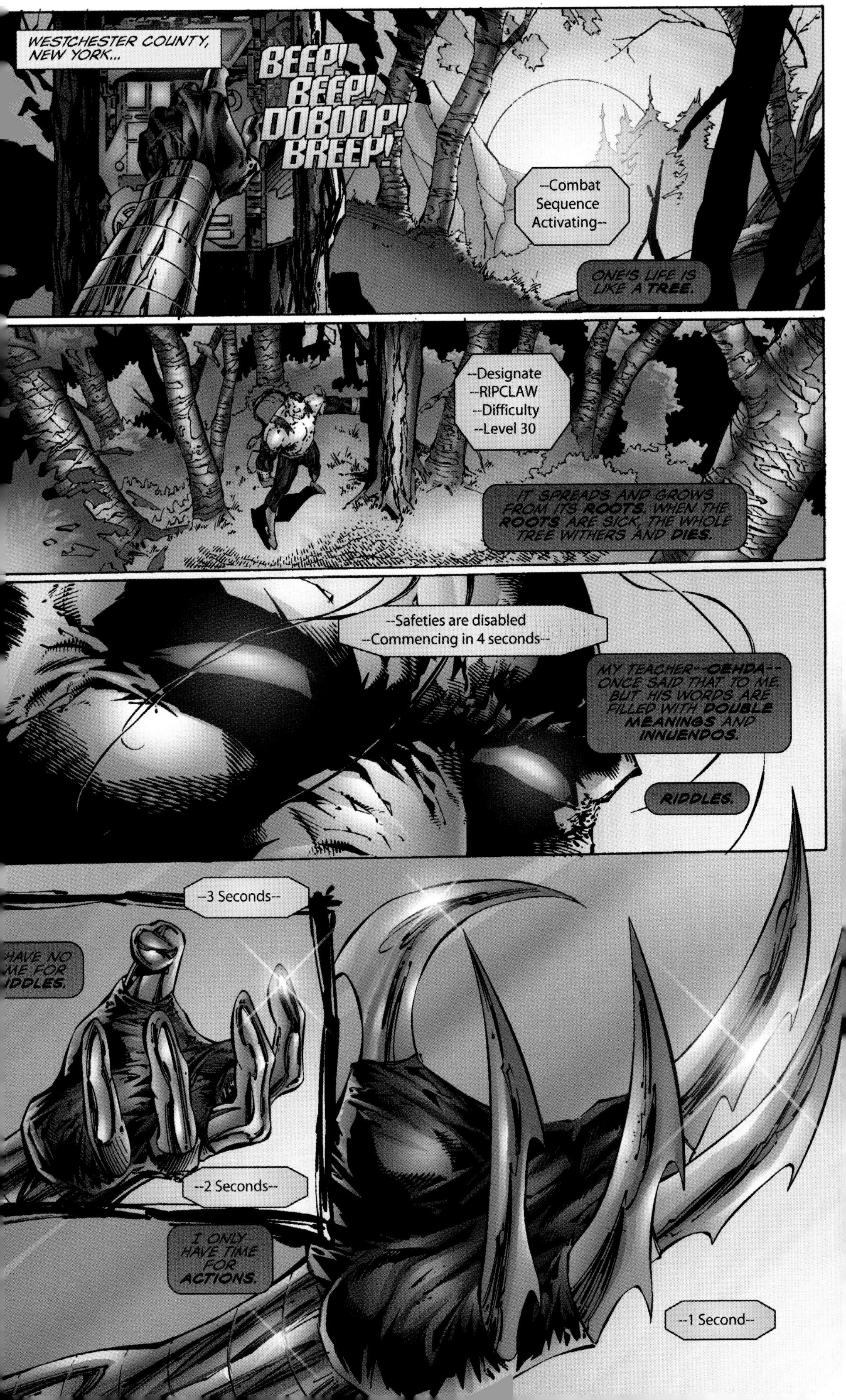
WESTCHESTER COUNTY, NEW YORK...
BEEP! BEEP! DOBOOP! BREEP!
--Combat Sequence Activating--
ONE'S LIFE IS LIKE A TREE.
--Designate --RIPCLAW --Difficulty --Level 30
IT SPREADS AND GROWS FROM ITS ROOTS. WHEN THE ROOTS ARE SICK, THE WHOLE TREE WITHERS AND DIES.
--Safeties are disabled --Commencing in 4 seconds--
MY TEACHER--OEHDA--ONCE SAID THAT TO ME. BUT HIS WORDS ARE FILLED WITH DOUBLE MEANINGS AND INNUENDOS.
RIDDLES.
--3 Seconds--
HAVE NO ME FOR IDDLES.
--2 Seconds--
I ONLY HAVE TIME FOR ACTIONS.
--1 Second--

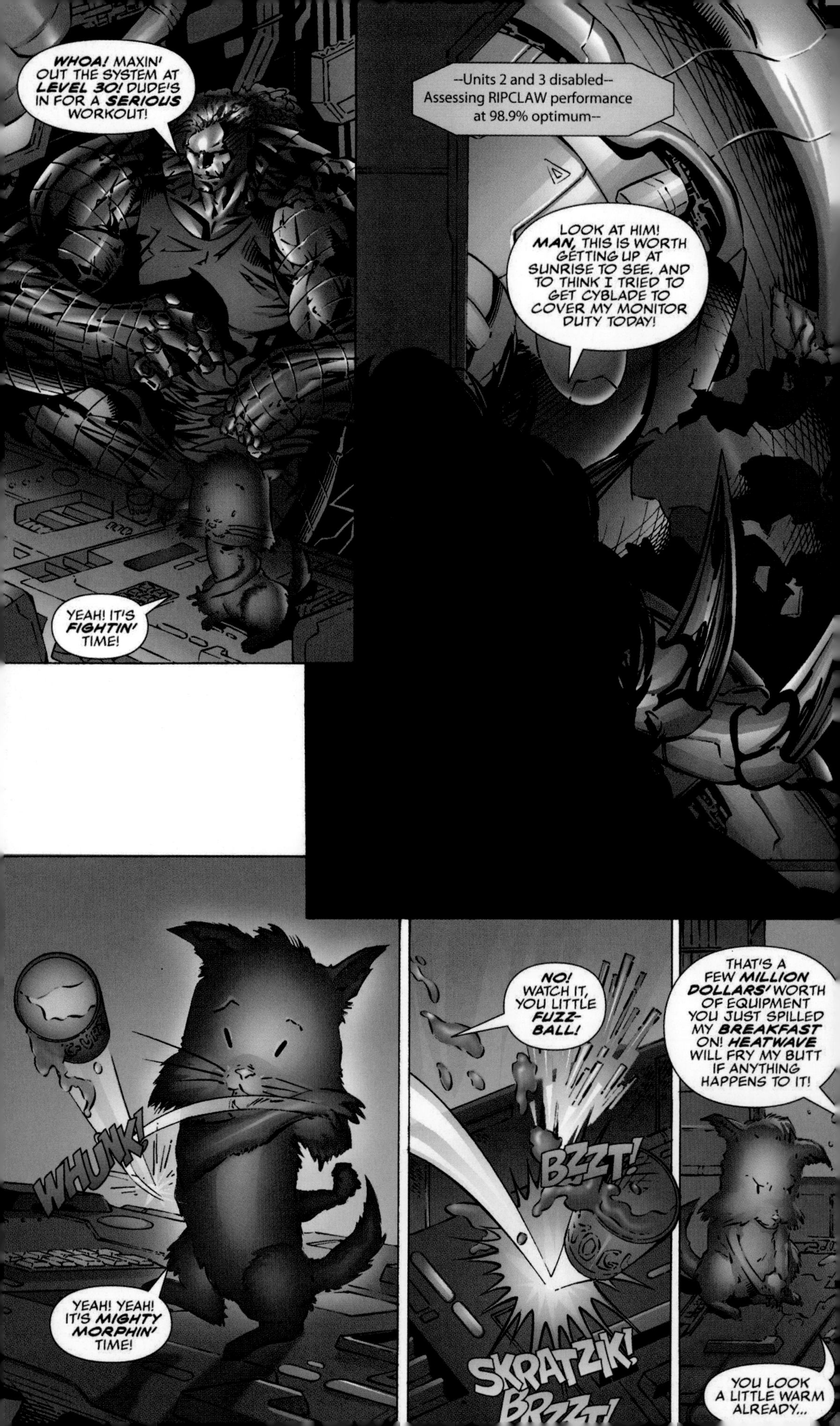
WHOA! MAXIN' OUT THE SYSTEM AT LEVEL 30! DUDE'S IN FOR A SERIOUS WORKOUT!
--Units 2 and 3 disabled-- Assessing RIPCLAW performance at 98.9% optimum--
LOOK AT HIM! MAN, THIS IS WORTH GETTING UP AT SUNRISE TO SEE. AND TO THINK I TRIED TO GET CYBLADE TO COVER MY MONITOR DUTY TODAY!
YEAH! IT'S FIGHTIN' TIME!
WHUNK!
YEAH! YEAH! IT'S MIGHTY MORPHIN' TIME!
NO! WATCH IT, YOU LITTLE FUZZ-BALL!
BZZT!
SKRATZIK!
BRZZT!
THAT'S A FEW MILLION DOLLARS' WORTH OF EQUIPMENT YOU JUST SPILLED MY BREAKFAST ON! HEATWAVE WILL FRY MY BUTT IF ANYTHING HAPPENS TO IT!
YOU LOOK A LITTLE WARM ALREADY...

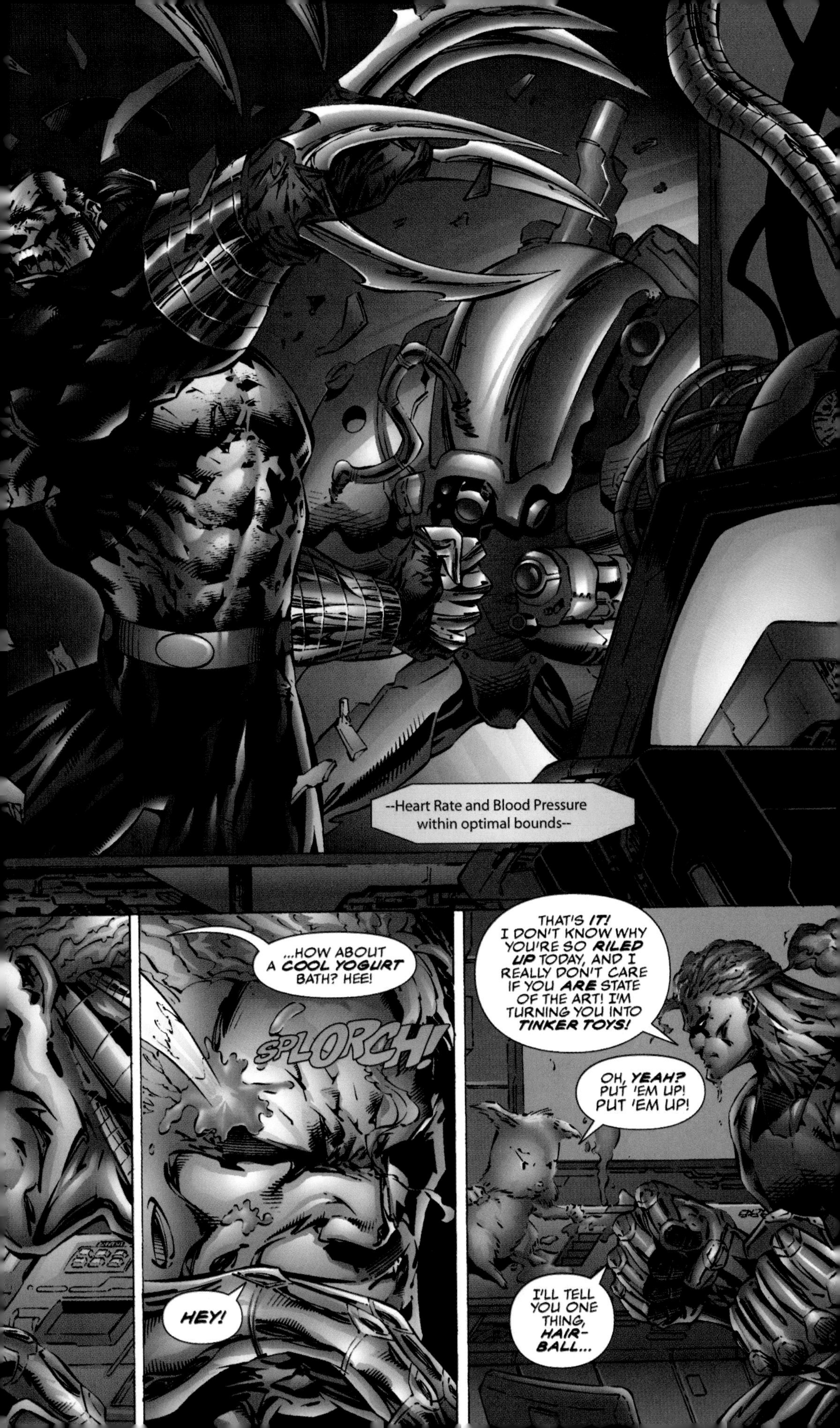
--Heart Rate and Blood Pressure within optimal bounds--
...HOW ABOUT A **COOL YOGURT** BATH? HEE!
SPLORCH!
HEY!
THAT'S **IT!** I DON'T KNOW WHY YOU'RE SO **RILED UP** TODAY, AND I REALLY DON'T CARE IF YOU **ARE** STATE OF THE ART! I'M TURNING YOU INTO **TINKER TOYS!**
OH, **YEAH?** PUT 'EM UP! PUT 'EM UP!
I'LL TELL YOU ONE THING, **HAIR-BALL...**

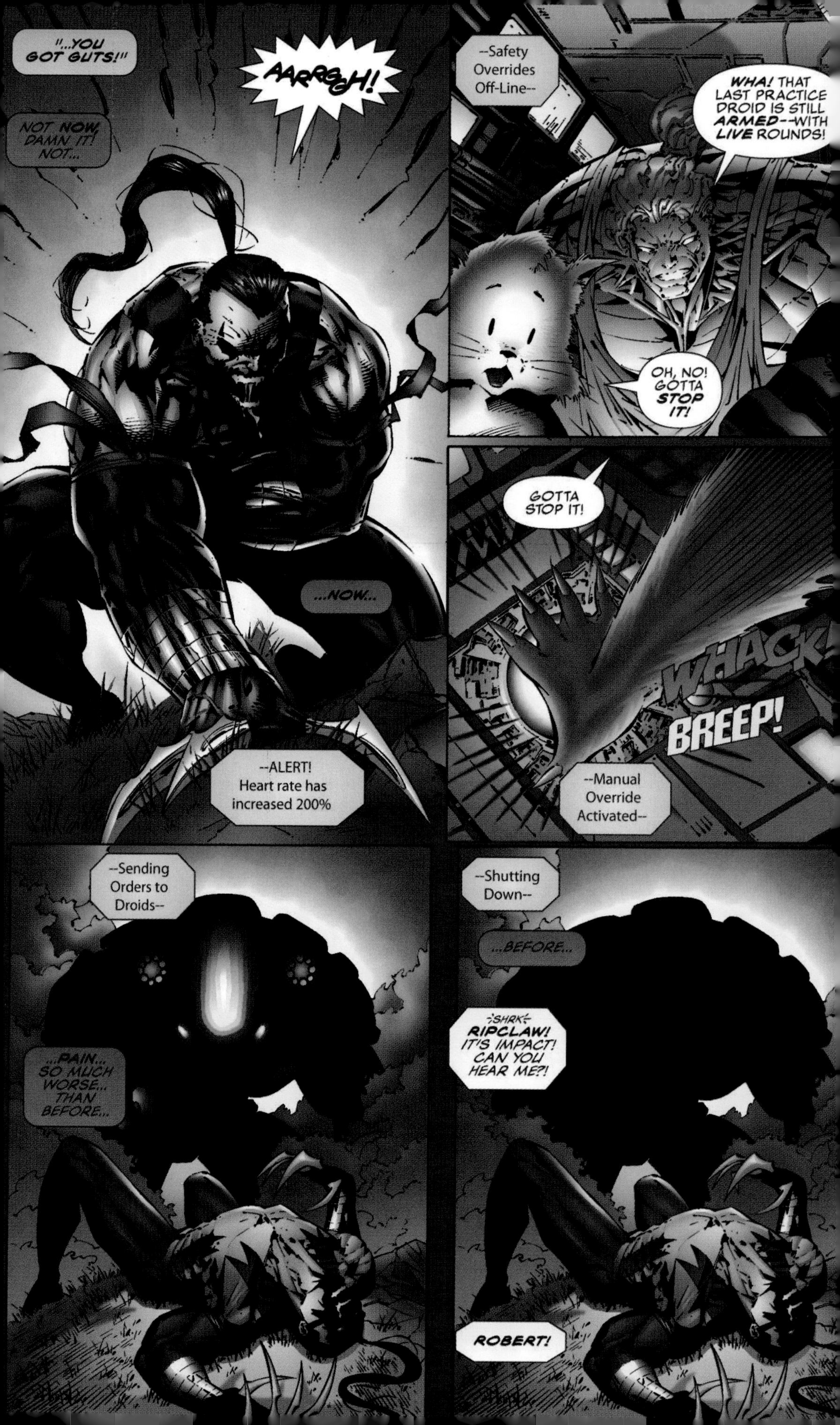
"...YOU GOT GUTS!"
AARRGGH!
NOT NOW, DAMN IT! NOT...
...NOW...
--ALERT! Heart rate has increased 200%
--Safety Overrides Off-Line--
WHA! THAT LAST PRACTICE DROID IS STILL ARMED--WITH LIVE ROUNDS!
OH, NO! GOTTA STOP IT!
GOTTA STOP IT!
WHACK!
BREEP!
--Manual Override Activated--
--Sending Orders to Droids--
...PAIN... SO MUCH WORSE... THAN BEFORE...
--Shutting Down--
...BEFORE...
SHRK
RIPCLAW! IT'S IMPACT! CAN YOU HEAR ME?!
ROBERT!

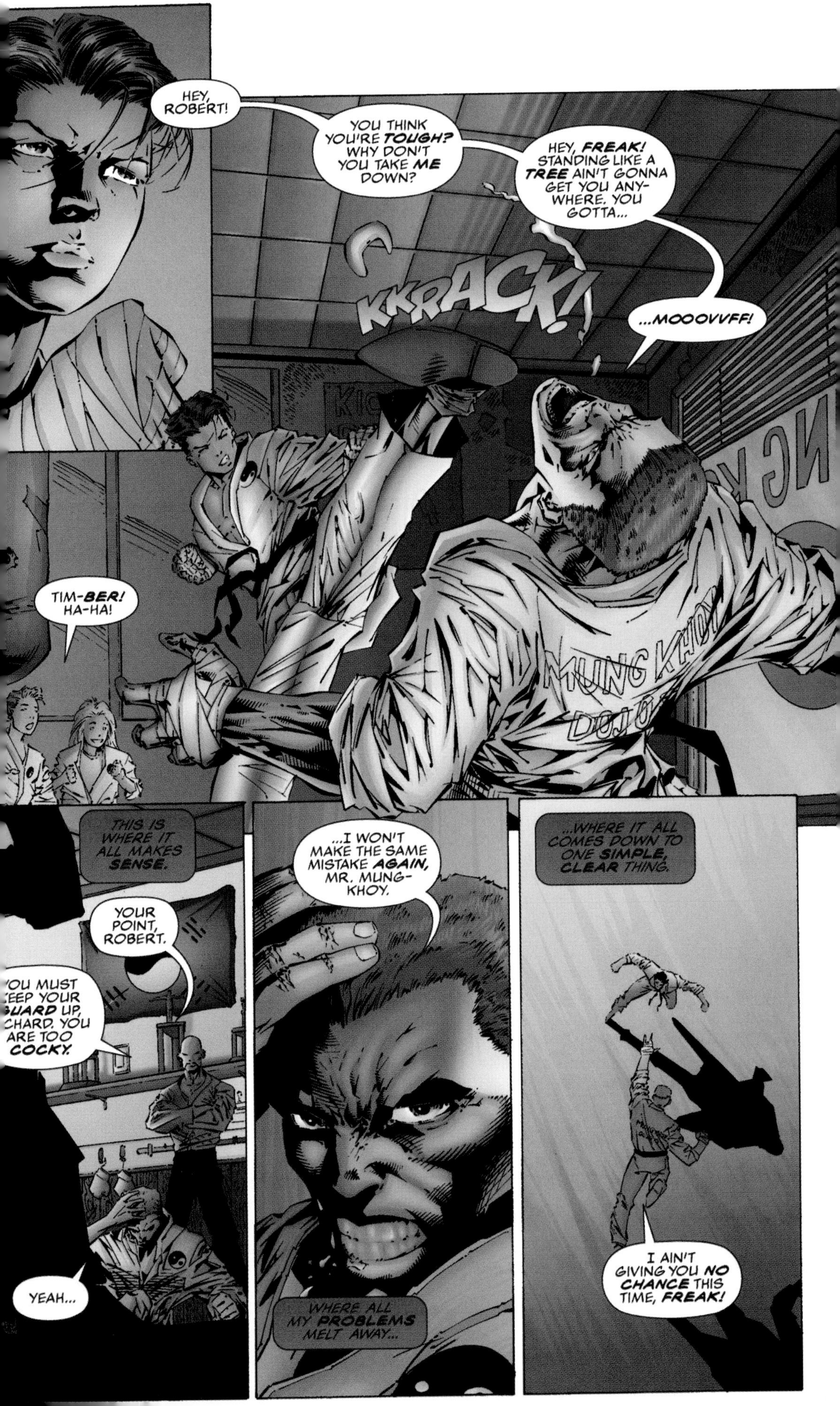
HEY, ROBERT!
YOU THINK YOU'RE TOUGH? WHY DON'T YOU TAKE ME DOWN?
HEY, FREAK! STANDING LIKE A TREE AIN'T GONNA GET YOU ANY-WHERE. YOU GOTTA...
KKRACK!
...MOOOVVFF!
TIM-BER! HA-HA!
MUNG KHOY DOJO
THIS IS WHERE IT ALL MAKES SENSE.
YOUR POINT, ROBERT.
YOU MUST KEEP YOUR GUARD UP, RICHARD. YOU ARE TOO COCKY.
YEAH...
...I WON'T MAKE THE SAME MISTAKE AGAIN, MR. MUNG-KHOY.
WHERE ALL MY PROBLEMS MELT AWAY...
...WHERE IT ALL COMES DOWN TO ONE SIMPLE, CLEAR THING.
I AIN'T GIVING YOU NO CHANCE THIS TIME, FREAK!

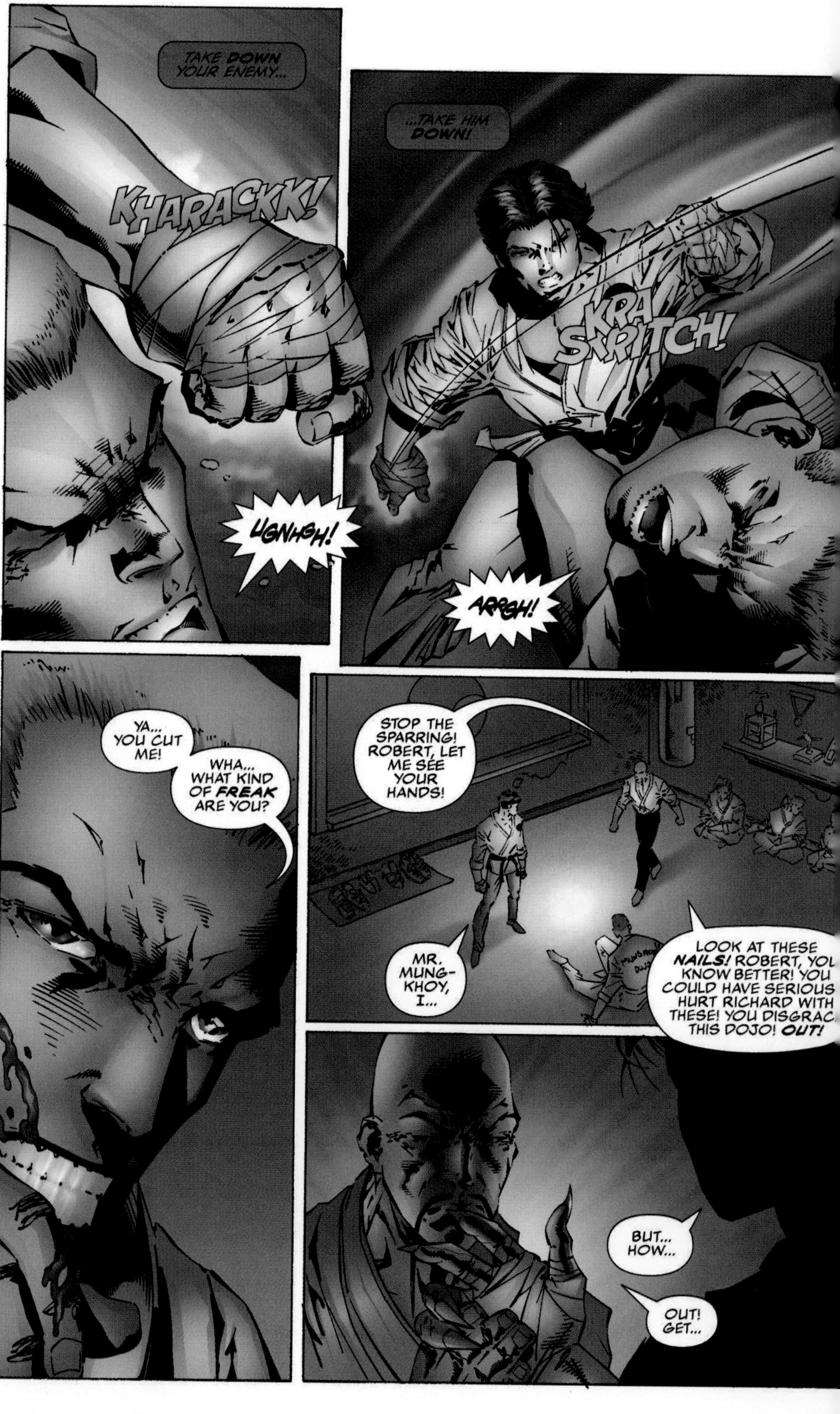
TAKE DOWN YOUR ENEMY...
KHARACKK!
UGNHGH!
...TAKE HIM DOWN!
KRA SKRITCH!
ARRGH!
YA... YOU CUT ME!
WHA... WHAT KIND OF FREAK ARE YOU?
STOP THE SPARRING! ROBERT, LET ME SEE YOUR HANDS!
MR. MUNG-KHOY, I...
LOOK AT THESE NAILS! ROBERT, YOU KNOW BETTER! YOU COULD HAVE SERIOUS HURT RICHARD WITH THESE! YOU DISGRAC THIS DOJO! OUT!
BUT... HOW...
OUT! GET...

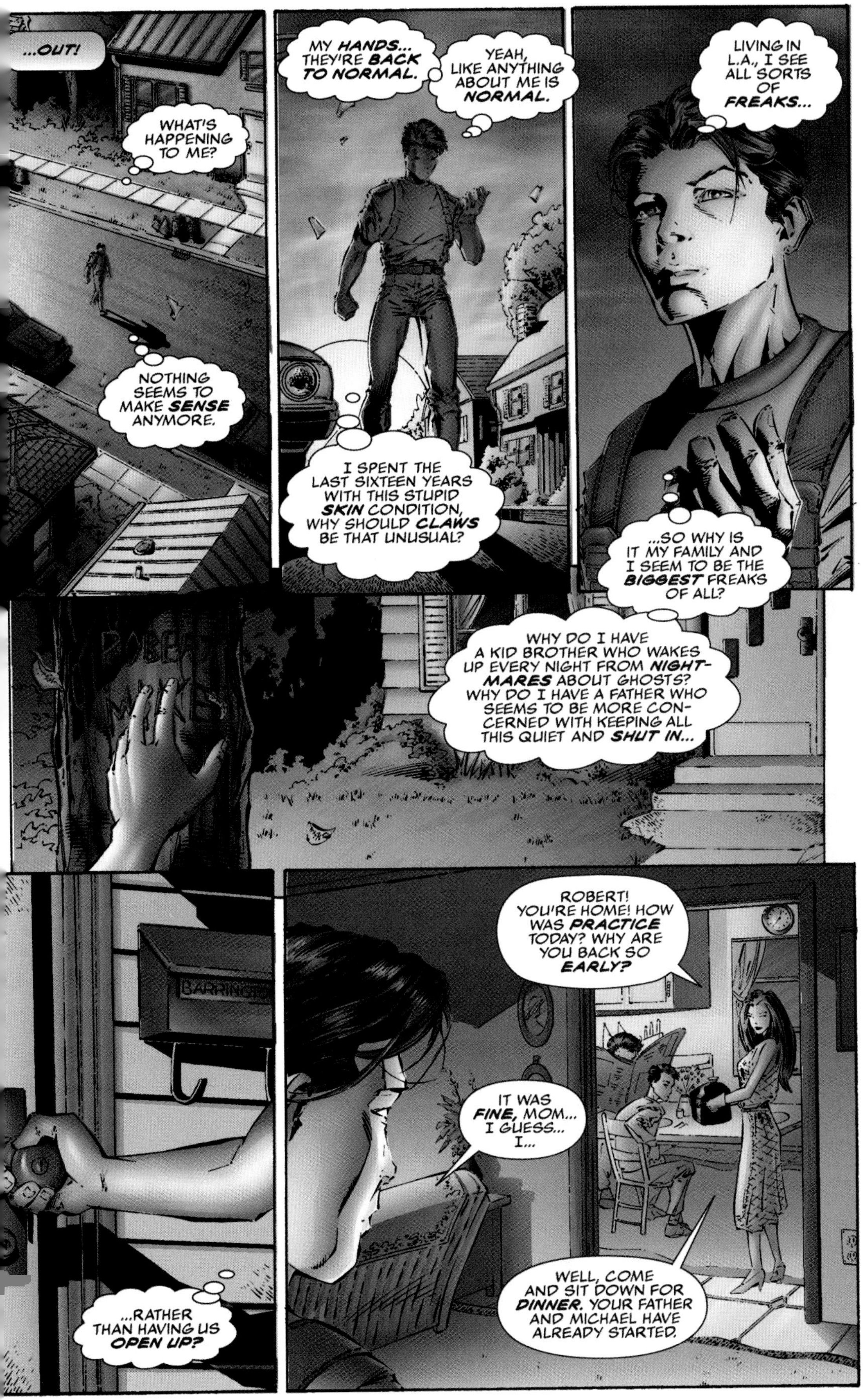
...OUT!
WHAT'S HAPPENING TO ME?
NOTHING SEEMS TO MAKE SENSE ANYMORE.
MY HANDS... THEY'RE BACK TO NORMAL.
YEAH, LIKE ANYTHING ABOUT ME IS NORMAL.
I SPENT THE LAST SIXTEEN YEARS WITH THIS STUPID SKIN CONDITION, WHY SHOULD CLAWS BE THAT UNUSUAL?
LIVING IN L.A., I SEE ALL SORTS OF FREAKS...
...SO WHY IS IT MY FAMILY AND I SEEM TO BE THE BIGGEST FREAKS OF ALL?
WHY DO I HAVE A KID BROTHER WHO WAKES UP EVERY NIGHT FROM NIGHT-MARES ABOUT GHOSTS? WHY DO I HAVE A FATHER WHO SEEMS TO BE MORE CON-CERNED WITH KEEPING ALL THIS QUIET AND SHUT IN...
BARRINGTO
...RATHER THAN HAVING US OPEN UP?
ROBERT! YOU'RE HOME! HOW WAS PRACTICE TODAY? WHY ARE YOU BACK SO EARLY?
IT WAS FINE, MOM... I GUESS... I...
WELL, COME AND SIT DOWN FOR DINNER. YOUR FATHER AND MICHAEL HAVE ALREADY STARTED.

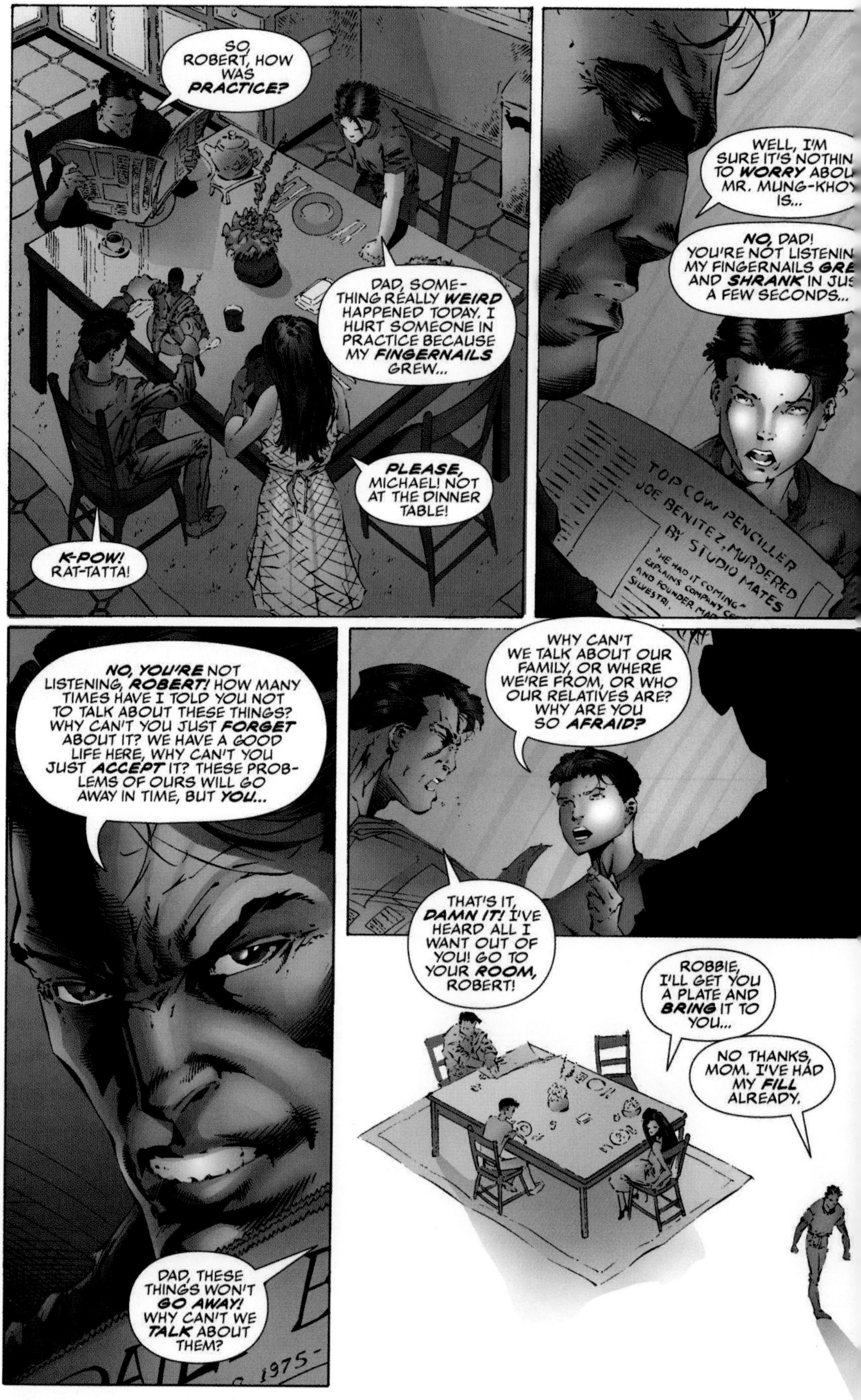
SO, ROBERT, HOW WAS PRACTICE?
DAD, SOME-THING REALLY WEIRD HAPPENED TODAY. I HURT SOMEONE IN PRACTICE BECAUSE MY FINGERNAILS GREW...
PLEASE, MICHAEL! NOT AT THE DINNER TABLE!
K-POW! RAT-TATTA!
WELL, I'M SURE IT'S NOTHIN TO WORRY ABOU MR. MUNG-KHOY IS...
NO, DAD! YOU'RE NOT LISTENIN MY FINGERNAILS GRE AND SHRANK IN JUS A FEW SECONDS...
TOP COW PENCILLER JOE BENITEZ, MURDERED BY STUDIO MATES
NO, YOU'RE NOT LISTENING, ROBERT! HOW MANY TIMES HAVE I TOLD YOU NOT TO TALK ABOUT THESE THINGS? WHY CAN'T YOU JUST FORGET ABOUT IT? WE HAVE A GOOD LIFE HERE, WHY CAN'T YOU JUST ACCEPT IT? THESE PROB-LEMS OF OURS WILL GO AWAY IN TIME, BUT YOU...
DAD, THESE THINGS WON'T GO AWAY! WHY CAN'T WE TALK ABOUT THEM?
WHY CAN'T WE TALK ABOUT OUR FAMILY, OR WHERE WE'RE FROM, OR WHO OUR RELATIVES ARE? WHY ARE YOU SO AFRAID?
THAT'S IT, DAMN IT! I'VE HEARD ALL I WANT OUT OF YOU! GO TO YOUR ROOM, ROBERT!
ROBBIE, I'LL GET YOU A PLATE AND BRING IT TO YOU...
NO THANKS, MOM. I'VE HAD MY FILL ALREADY.

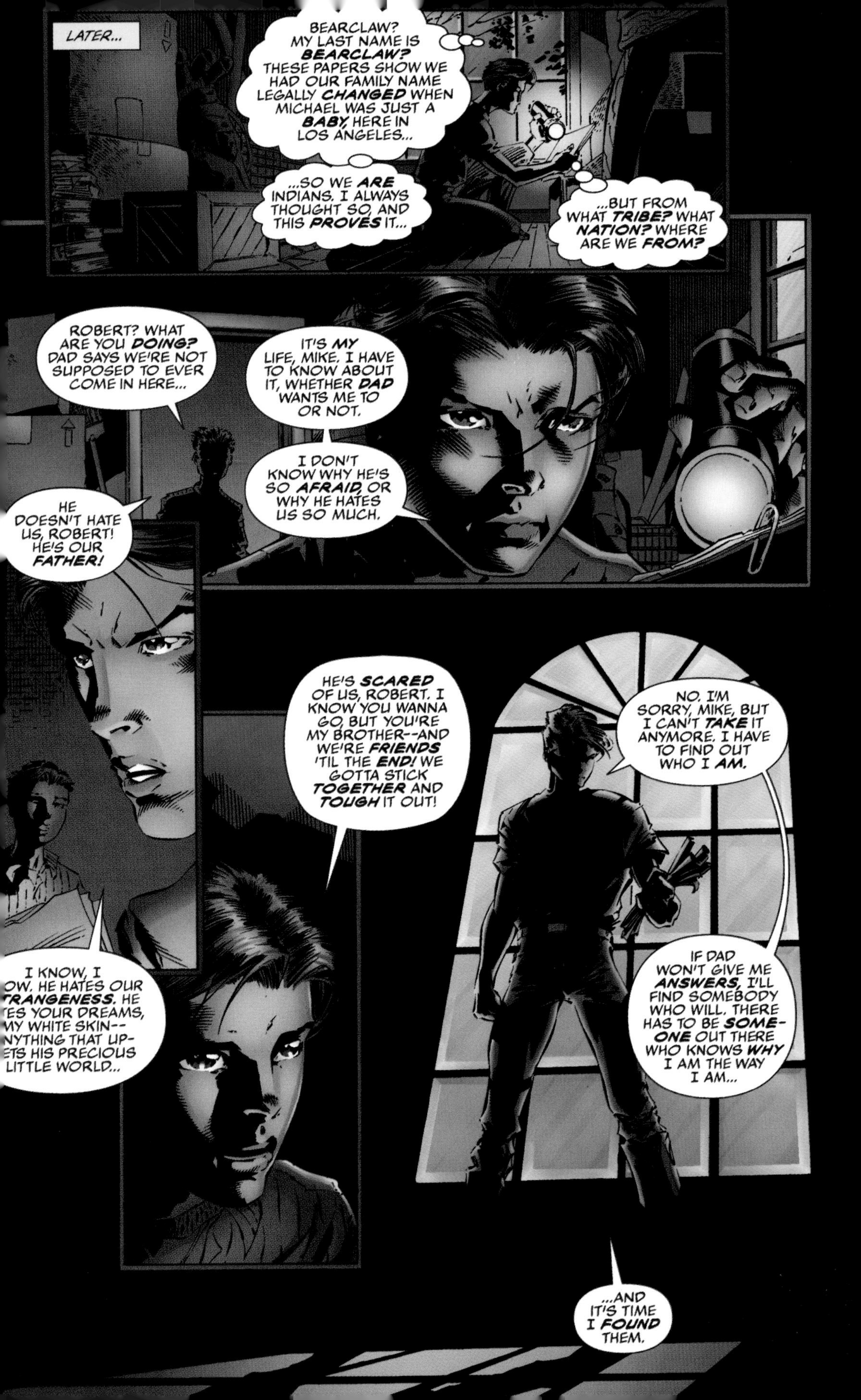

LATER...
BEARCLAW? MY LAST NAME IS BEARCLAW? THESE PAPERS SHOW WE HAD OUR FAMILY NAME LEGALLY CHANGED WHEN MICHAEL WAS JUST A BABY, HERE IN LOS ANGELES...
...SO WE ARE INDIANS. I ALWAYS THOUGHT SO, AND THIS PROVES IT...
...BUT FROM WHAT TRIBE? WHAT NATION? WHERE ARE WE FROM?
ROBERT? WHAT ARE YOU DOING? DAD SAYS WE'RE NOT SUPPOSED TO EVER COME IN HERE...
IT'S MY LIFE, MIKE. I HAVE TO KNOW ABOUT IT, WHETHER DAD WANTS ME TO OR NOT.
I DON'T KNOW WHY HE'S SO AFRAID, OR WHY HE HATES US SO MUCH.
HE DOESN'T HATE US, ROBERT! HE'S OUR FATHER!
HE'S SCARED OF US, ROBERT. I KNOW YOU WANNA GO, BUT YOU'RE MY BROTHER--AND WE'RE FRIENDS 'TIL THE END! WE GOTTA STICK TOGETHER AND TOUGH IT OUT!
I KNOW, I OW. HE HATES OUR TRANGENESS. HE ES YOUR DREAMS, MY WHITE SKIN-- NYTHING THAT UP- ETS HIS PRECIOUS LITTLE WORLD...
NO, I'M SORRY, MIKE, BUT I CAN'T TAKE IT ANYMORE. I HAVE TO FIND OUT WHO I AM.
IF DAD WON'T GIVE ME ANSWERS, I'LL FIND SOMEBODY WHO WILL. THERE HAS TO BE SOME-ONE OUT THERE WHO KNOWS WHY I AM THE WAY I AM...
...AND IT'S TIME I FOUND THEM.

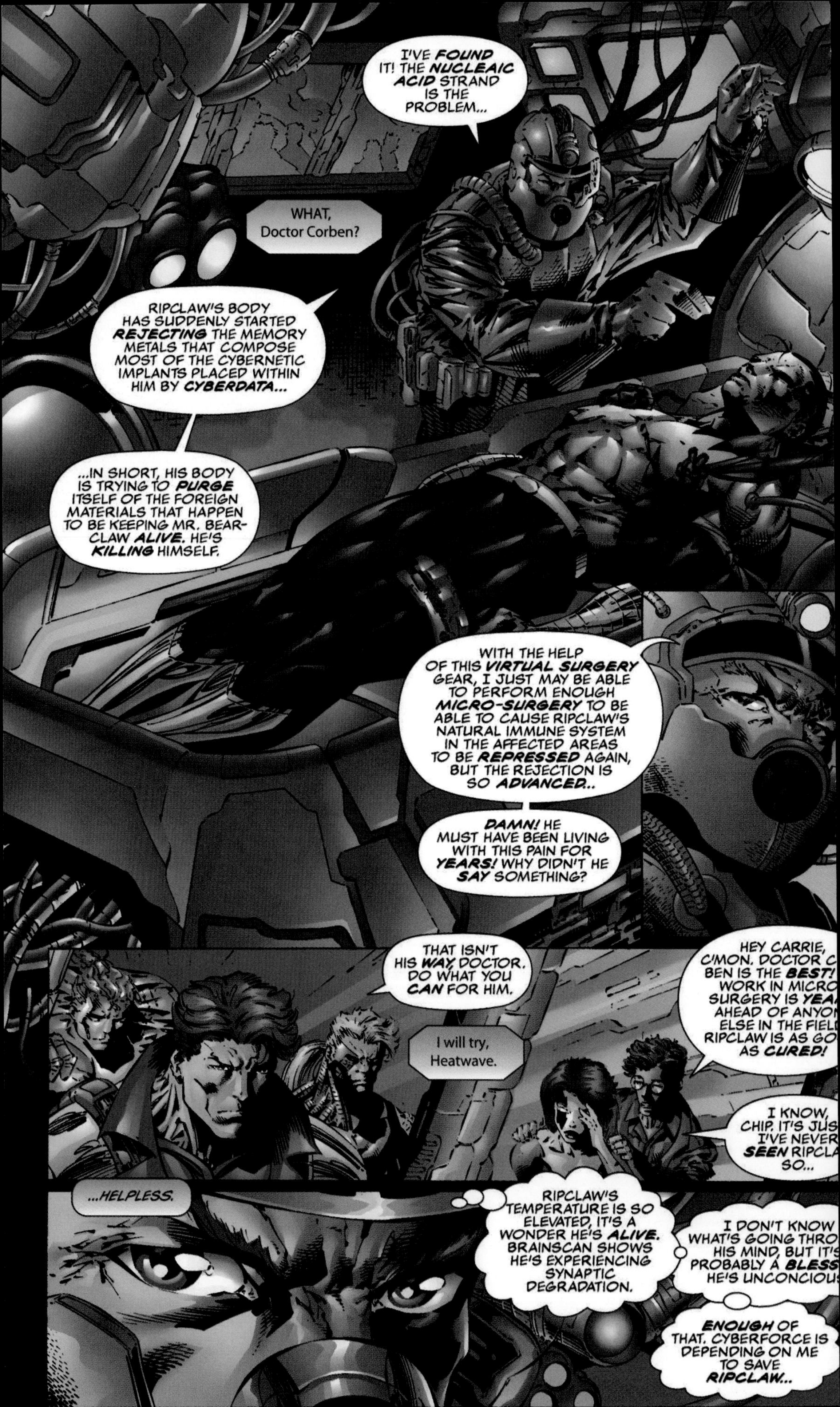
I'VE FOUND IT! THE NUCLEAIC ACID STRAND IS THE PROBLEM...
WHAT, Doctor Corben?
RIPCLAW'S BODY HAS SUDDENLY STARTED REJECTING THE MEMORY METALS THAT COMPOSE MOST OF THE CYBERNETIC IMPLANTS PLACED WITHIN HIM BY CYBERDATA...
...IN SHORT, HIS BODY IS TRYING TO PURGE ITSELF OF THE FOREIGN MATERIALS THAT HAPPEN TO BE KEEPING MR. BEAR-CLAW ALIVE. HE'S KILLING HIMSELF.
WITH THE HELP OF THIS VIRTUAL SURGERY GEAR, I JUST MAY BE ABLE TO PERFORM ENOUGH MICRO-SURGERY TO BE ABLE TO CAUSE RIPCLAW'S NATURAL IMMUNE SYSTEM IN THE AFFECTED AREAS TO BE REPRESSED AGAIN, BUT THE REJECTION IS SO ADVANCED..
DAMN! HE MUST HAVE BEEN LIVING WITH THIS PAIN FOR YEARS! WHY DIDN'T HE SAY SOMETHING?
THAT ISN'T HIS WAY, DOCTOR. DO WHAT YOU CAN FOR HIM.
I will try, Heatwave.
HEY CARRIE, C'MON. DOCTOR C BEN IS THE BEST! WORK IN MICRO SURGERY IS YEA AHEAD OF ANYON ELSE IN THE FIEL RIPCLAW IS AS GO AS CURED!
I KNOW, CHIP. IT'S JUS I'VE NEVER SEEN RIPCLA SO...
...HELPLESS.
RIPCLAW'S TEMPERATURE IS SO ELEVATED, IT'S A WONDER HE'S ALIVE. BRAINSCAN SHOWS HE'S EXPERIENCING SYNAPTIC DEGRADATION.
I DON'T KNOW WHAT'S GOING THRO HIS MIND, BUT IT'S PROBABLY A BLESS HE'S UNCONCIOU
ENOUGH OF THAT. CYBERFORCE IS DEPENDING ON ME TO SAVE RIPCLAW...

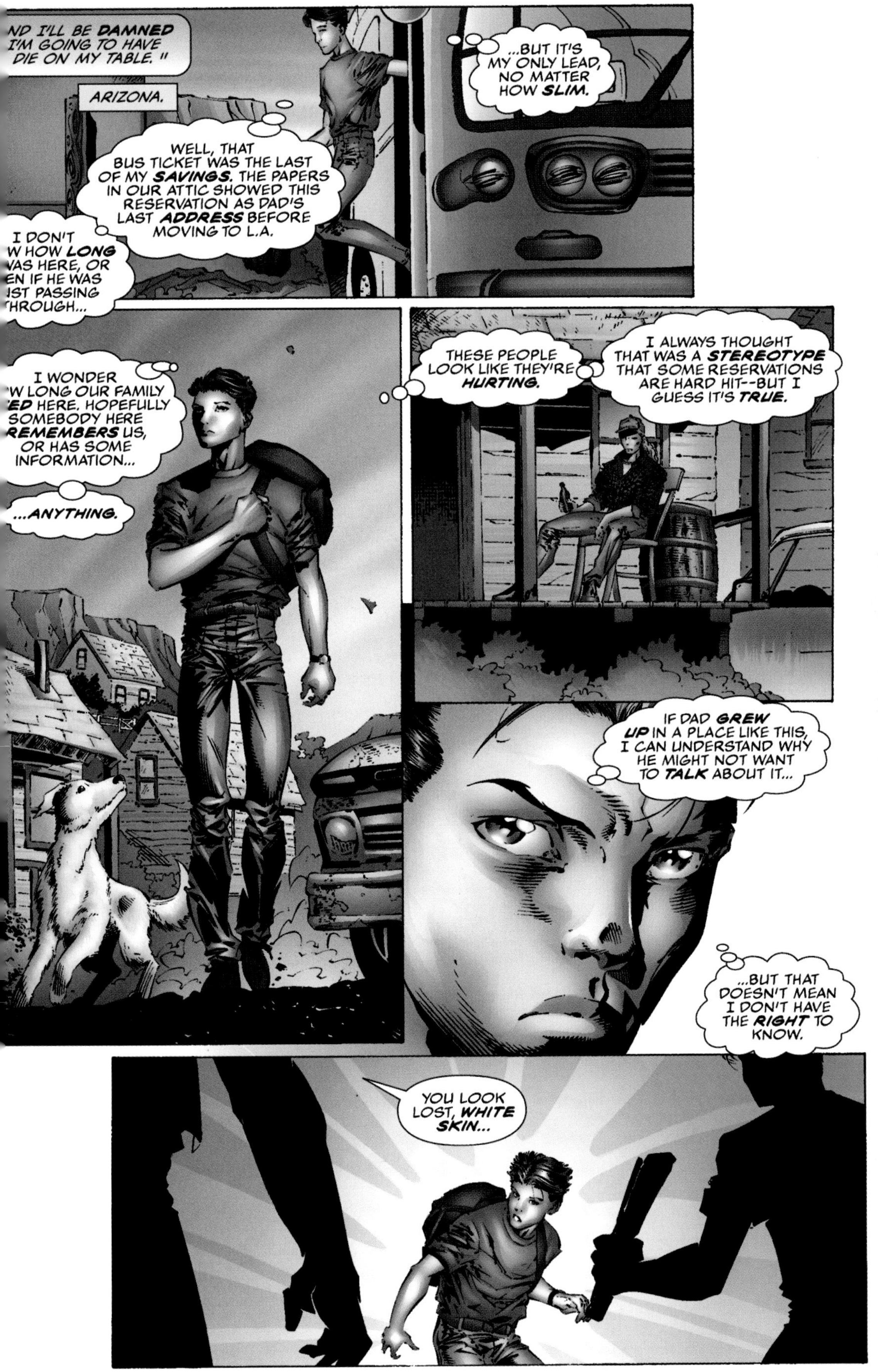
ND I'LL BE DAMNED I'M GOING TO HAVE DIE ON MY TABLE."
ARIZONA.
...BUT IT'S MY ONLY LEAD, NO MATTER HOW SLIM.
WELL, THAT BUS TICKET WAS THE LAST OF MY SAVINGS. THE PAPERS IN OUR ATTIC SHOWED THIS RESERVATION AS DAD'S LAST ADDRESS BEFORE MOVING TO L.A.
I DON'T W HOW LONG VAS HERE, OR EN IF HE WAS IST PASSING THROUGH...
I WONDER W LONG OUR FAMILY ED HERE. HOPEFULLY SOMEBODY HERE REMEMBERS US, OR HAS SOME INFORMATION...
...ANYTHING.
THESE PEOPLE LOOK LIKE THEY'RE HURTING.
I ALWAYS THOUGHT THAT WAS A STEREOTYPE THAT SOME RESERVATIONS ARE HARD HIT--BUT I GUESS IT'S TRUE.
IF DAD GREW UP IN A PLACE LIKE THIS, I CAN UNDERSTAND WHY HE MIGHT NOT WANT TO TALK ABOUT IT...
...BUT THAT DOESN'T MEAN I DON'T HAVE THE RIGHT TO KNOW.
YOU LOOK LOST, WHITE SKIN...

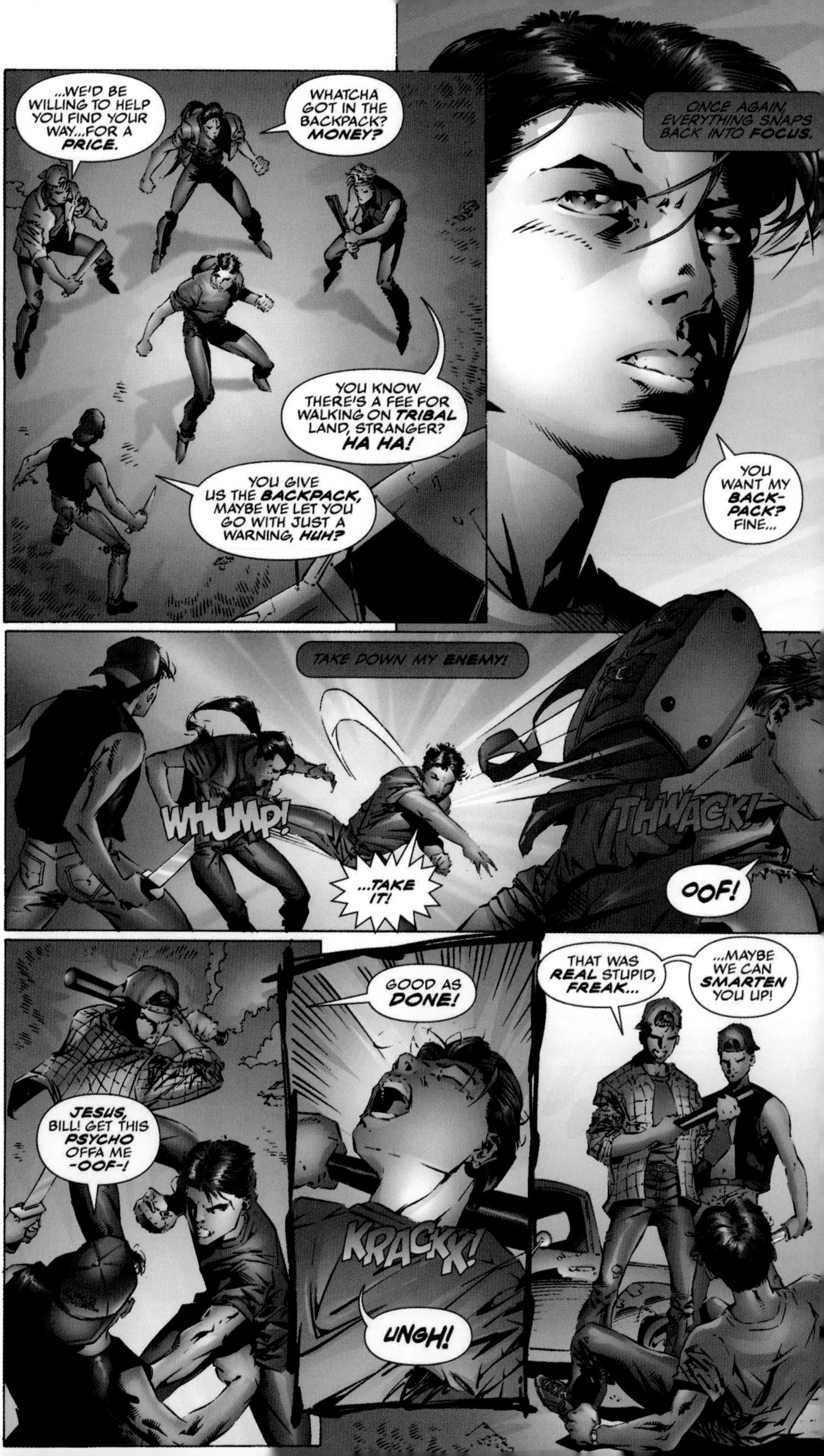
...WE'D BE WILLING TO HELP YOU FIND YOUR WAY...FOR A PRICE.
WHATCHA GOT IN THE BACKPACK? MONEY?
YOU KNOW THERE'S A FEE FOR WALKING ON TRIBAL LAND, STRANGER? HA HA!
YOU GIVE US THE BACKPACK, MAYBE WE LET YOU GO WITH JUST A WARNING, HUH?
ONCE AGAIN, EVERYTHING SNAPS BACK INTO FOCUS.
YOU WANT MY BACK-PACK? FINE...
TAKE DOWN MY ENEMY!
WHUMP!
...TAKE IT!
THWACK!
OOF!
JESUS, BILL! GET THIS PSYCHO OFFA ME -OOF-!
GOOD AS DONE!
KRACKK!
UNGH!
THAT WAS REAL STUPID, FREAK...
...MAYBE WE CAN SMARTEN YOU UP!

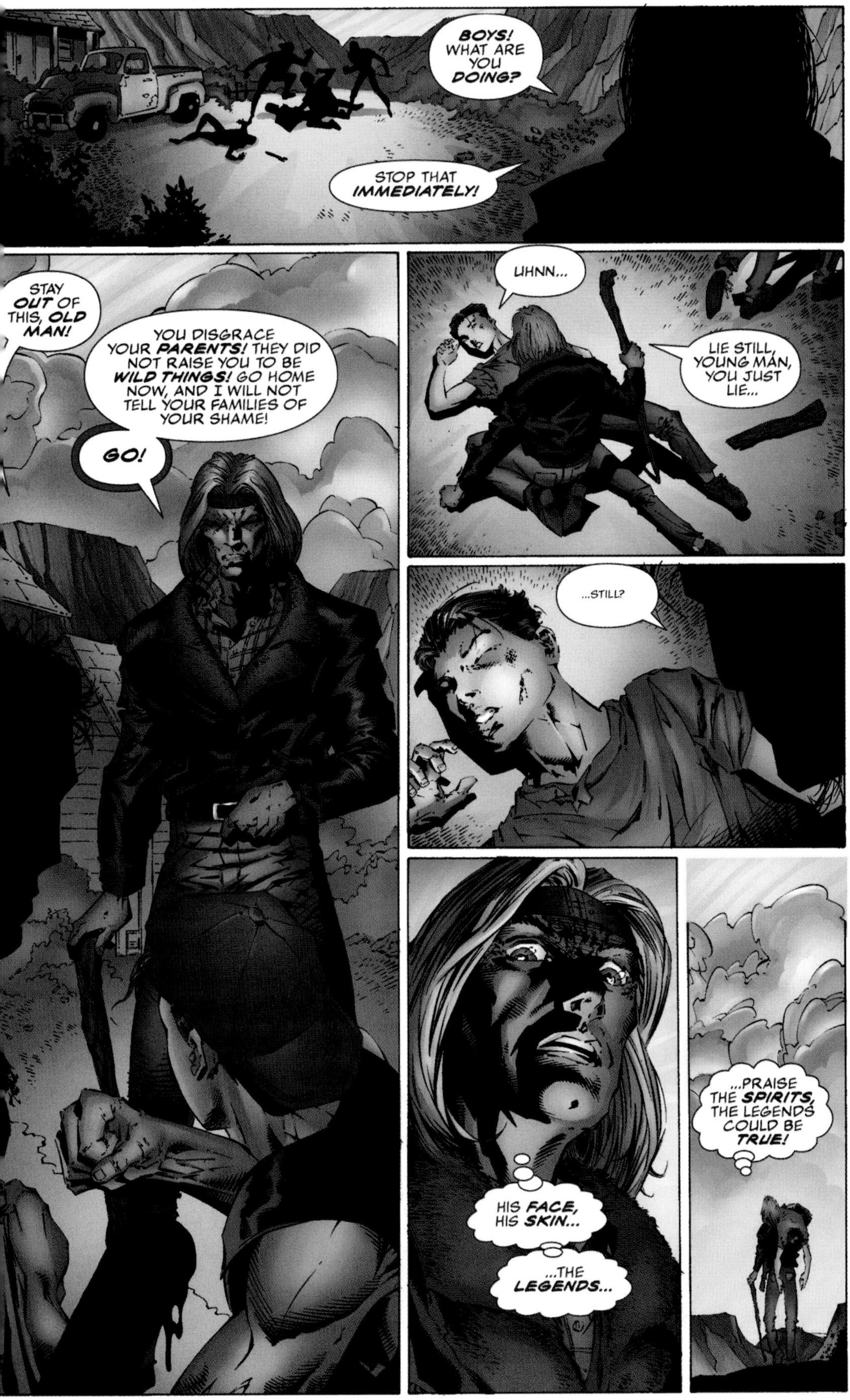
BOYS! WHAT ARE YOU DOING?
STOP THAT IMMEDIATELY!
STAY OUT OF THIS, OLD MAN!
YOU DISGRACE YOUR PARENTS! THEY DID NOT RAISE YOU TO BE WILD THINGS! GO HOME NOW, AND I WILL NOT TELL YOUR FAMILIES OF YOUR SHAME!
GO!
UHNN...
LIE STILL, YOUNG MAN, YOU JUST LIE...
...STILL?
HIS FACE, HIS SKIN...
...THE LEGENDS...
...PRAISE THE SPIRITS, THE LEGENDS COULD BE TRUE!

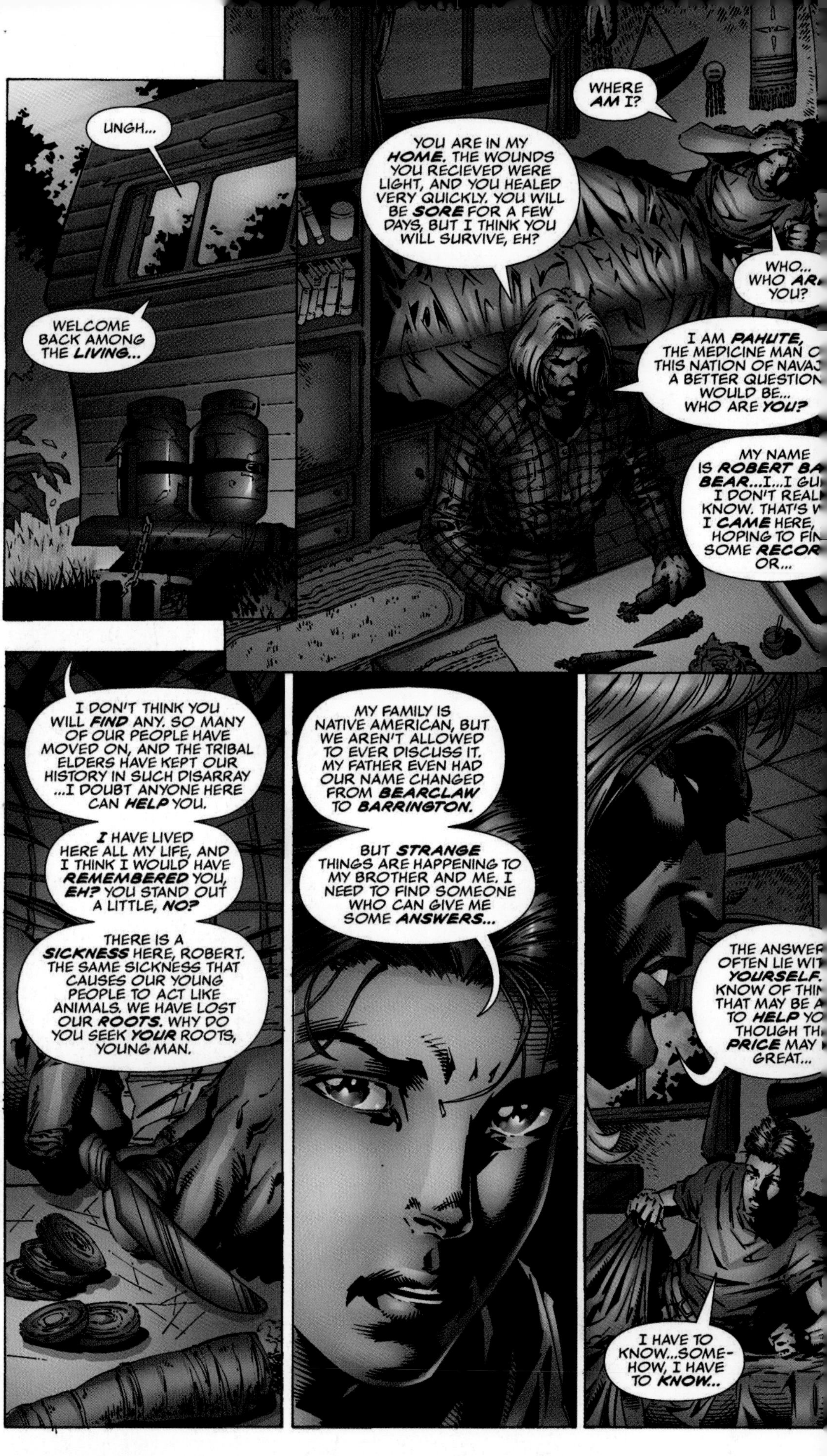
UNGH...
WELCOME BACK AMONG THE LIVING...
WHERE AM I?
YOU ARE IN MY HOME. THE WOUNDS YOU RECIEVED WERE LIGHT, AND YOU HEALED VERY QUICKLY. YOU WILL BE SORE FOR A FEW DAYS, BUT I THINK YOU WILL SURVIVE, EH?
WHO... WHO AR YOU?
I AM PAHUTE, THE MEDICINE MAN O THIS NATION OF NAVAJ A BETTER QUESTION WOULD BE... WHO ARE YOU?
MY NAME IS ROBERT BA BEAR...I...I GU I DON'T REAL KNOW. THAT'S W I CAME HERE, HOPING TO FIN SOME RECOR OR...
I DON'T THINK YOU WILL FIND ANY. SO MANY OF OUR PEOPLE HAVE MOVED ON, AND THE TRIBAL ELDERS HAVE KEPT OUR HISTORY IN SUCH DISARRAY ...I DOUBT ANYONE HERE CAN HELP YOU.
I HAVE LIVED HERE ALL MY LIFE, AND I THINK I WOULD HAVE REMEMBERED YOU, EH? YOU STAND OUT A LITTLE, NO?
THERE IS A SICKNESS HERE, ROBERT. THE SAME SICKNESS THAT CAUSES OUR YOUNG PEOPLE TO ACT LIKE ANIMALS. WE HAVE LOST OUR ROOTS. WHY DO YOU SEEK YOUR ROOTS, YOUNG MAN.
MY FAMILY IS NATIVE AMERICAN, BUT WE AREN'T ALLOWED TO EVER DISCUSS IT. MY FATHER EVEN HAD OUR NAME CHANGED FROM BEARCLAW TO BARRINGTON.
BUT STRANGE THINGS ARE HAPPENING TO MY BROTHER AND ME. I NEED TO FIND SOMEONE WHO CAN GIVE ME SOME ANSWERS...
THE ANSWER OFTEN LIE WIT YOURSELF. KNOW OF THIN THAT MAY BE A TO HELP YO THOUGH TH PRICE MAY GREAT...
I HAVE TO KNOW...SOME-HOW, I HAVE TO KNOW...

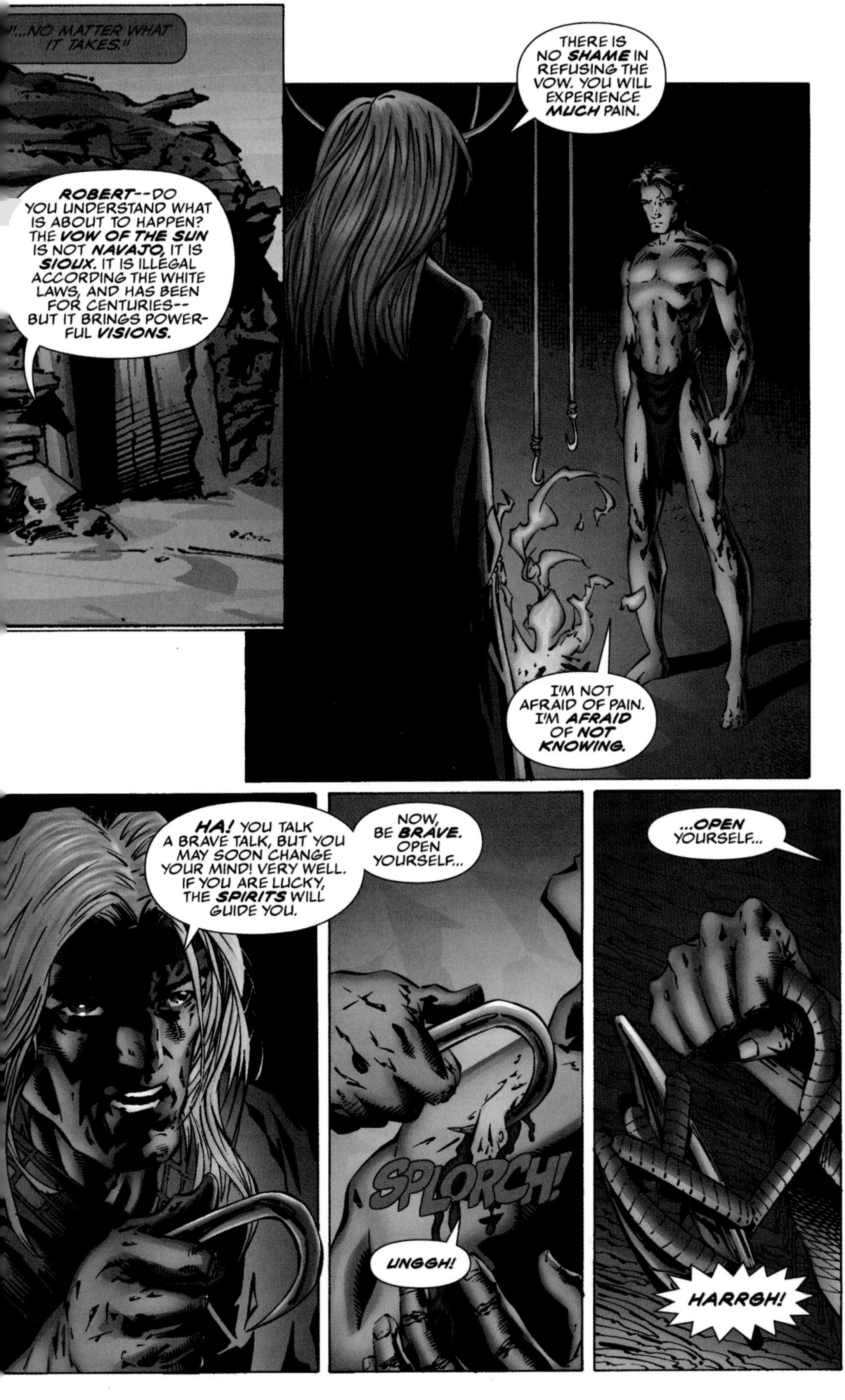
"...NO MATTER WHAT IT TAKES."
THERE IS NO SHAME IN REFUSING THE VOW. YOU WILL EXPERIENCE MUCH PAIN.
ROBERT--DO YOU UNDERSTAND WHAT IS ABOUT TO HAPPEN? THE VOW OF THE SUN IS NOT NAVAJO, IT IS SIOUX. IT IS ILLEGAL ACCORDING THE WHITE LAWS, AND HAS BEEN FOR CENTURIES--BUT IT BRINGS POWERFUL VISIONS.
I'M NOT AFRAID OF PAIN. I'M AFRAID OF NOT KNOWING.
HA! YOU TALK A BRAVE TALK, BUT YOU MAY SOON CHANGE YOUR MIND! VERY WELL. IF YOU ARE LUCKY, THE SPIRITS WILL GUIDE YOU.
NOW, BE BRAVE. OPEN YOURSELF...
SPLORCH!
UNGGH!
...OPEN YOURSELF...
HARRGH!

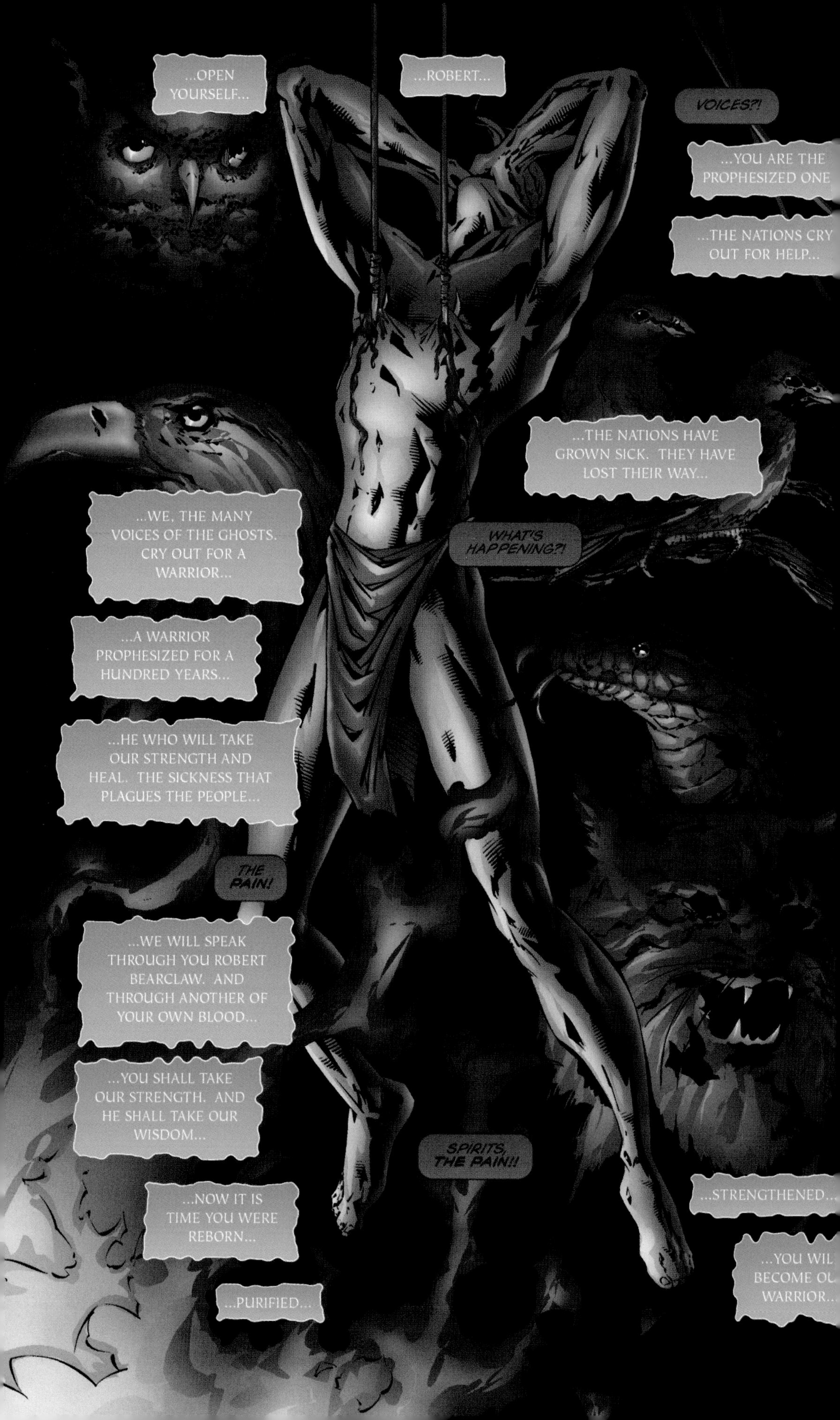
...OPEN YOURSELF...
...ROBERT...
VOICES?!
...YOU ARE THE PROPHESIZED ONE
...THE NATIONS CRY OUT FOR HELP...
...THE NATIONS HAVE GROWN SICK. THEY HAVE LOST THEIR WAY...
...WE, THE MANY VOICES OF THE GHOSTS. CRY OUT FOR A WARRIOR...
WHAT'S HAPPENING?!
...A WARRIOR PROPHESIZED FOR A HUNDRED YEARS...
...HE WHO WILL TAKE OUR STRENGTH AND HEAL. THE SICKNESS THAT PLAGUES THE PEOPLE...
THE PAIN!
...WE WILL SPEAK THROUGH YOU ROBERT BEARCLAW. AND THROUGH ANOTHER OF YOUR OWN BLOOD...
...YOU SHALL TAKE OUR STRENGTH. AND HE SHALL TAKE OUR WISDOM...
SPIRITS, THE PAIN!!
...NOW IT IS TIME YOU WERE REBORN...
...PURIFIED...
...STRENGTHENED...
...YOU WIL BECOME OU WARRIOR...

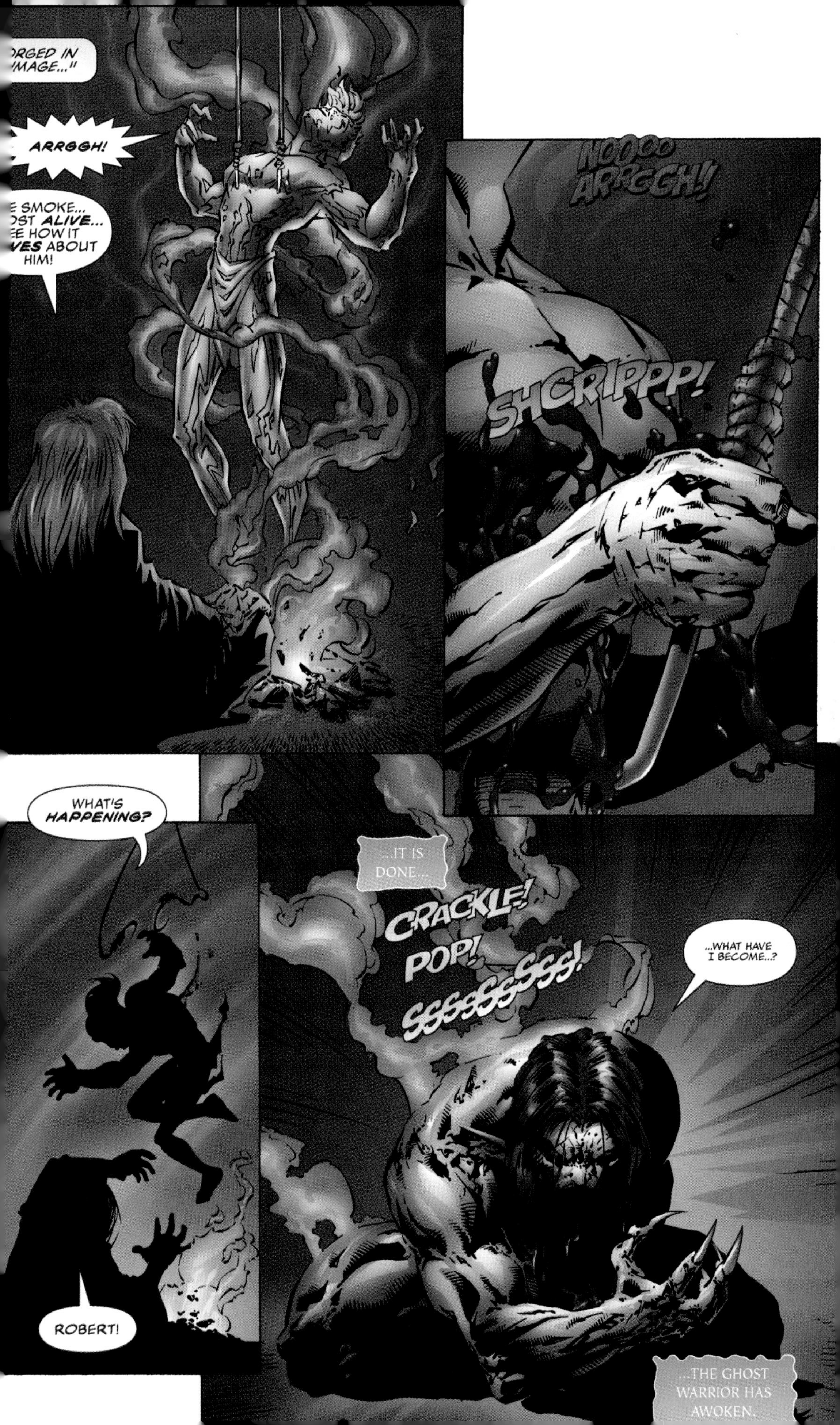
ORGED IN
IMAGE..."
ARRGGH!
E SMOKE...
OST ALIVE...
EE HOW IT
VES ABOUT
HIM!
NOOOO
ARRGGH!
SHCRIPPP!
WHAT'S
HAPPENING?
ROBERT!
...IT IS
DONE...
CRACKLE!
POP!
SSSSSSSSSS!
...WHAT HAVE
I BECOME...?
...THE GHOST
WARRIOR HAS
AWOKEN.

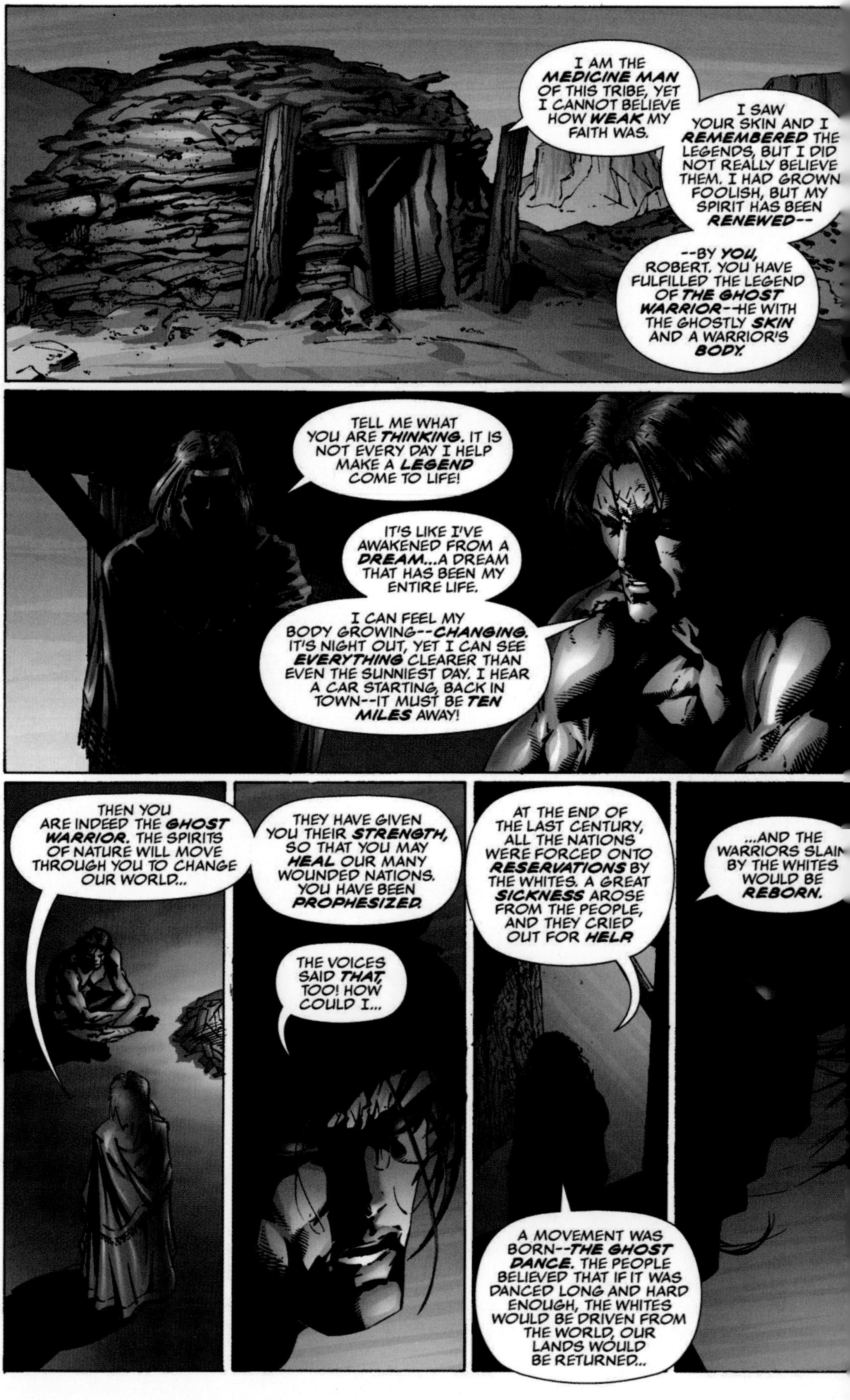
I AM THE MEDICINE MAN OF THIS TRIBE, YET I CANNOT BELIEVE HOW WEAK MY FAITH WAS.
I SAW YOUR SKIN AND I REMEMBERED THE LEGENDS, BUT I DID NOT REALLY BELIEVE THEM. I HAD GROWN FOOLISH, BUT MY SPIRIT HAS BEEN RENEWED--
--BY YOU, ROBERT. YOU HAVE FULFILLED THE LEGEND OF THE GHOST WARRIOR--HE WITH THE GHOSTLY SKIN AND A WARRIOR'S BODY.
TELL ME WHAT YOU ARE THINKING. IT IS NOT EVERY DAY I HELP MAKE A LEGEND COME TO LIFE!
IT'S LIKE I'VE AWAKENED FROM A DREAM...A DREAM THAT HAS BEEN MY ENTIRE LIFE.
I CAN FEEL MY BODY GROWING--CHANGING. IT'S NIGHT OUT, YET I CAN SEE EVERYTHING CLEARER THAN EVEN THE SUNNIEST DAY. I HEAR A CAR STARTING, BACK IN TOWN--IT MUST BE TEN MILES AWAY!
THEN YOU ARE INDEED THE GHOST WARRIOR. THE SPIRITS OF NATURE WILL MOVE THROUGH YOU TO CHANGE OUR WORLD...
THEY HAVE GIVEN YOU THEIR STRENGTH, SO THAT YOU MAY HEAL OUR MANY WOUNDED NATIONS. YOU HAVE BEEN PROPHESIZED.
THE VOICES SAID THAT, TOO! HOW COULD I...
AT THE END OF THE LAST CENTURY, ALL THE NATIONS WERE FORCED ONTO RESERVATIONS BY THE WHITES. A GREAT SICKNESS AROSE FROM THE PEOPLE, AND THEY CRIED OUT FOR HELP.
A MOVEMENT WAS BORN--THE GHOST DANCE. THE PEOPLE BELIEVED THAT IF IT WAS DANCED LONG AND HARD ENOUGH, THE WHITES WOULD BE DRIVEN FROM THE WORLD, OUR LANDS WOULD BE RETURNED...
...AND THE WARRIORS SLAIN BY THE WHITES WOULD BE REBORN.

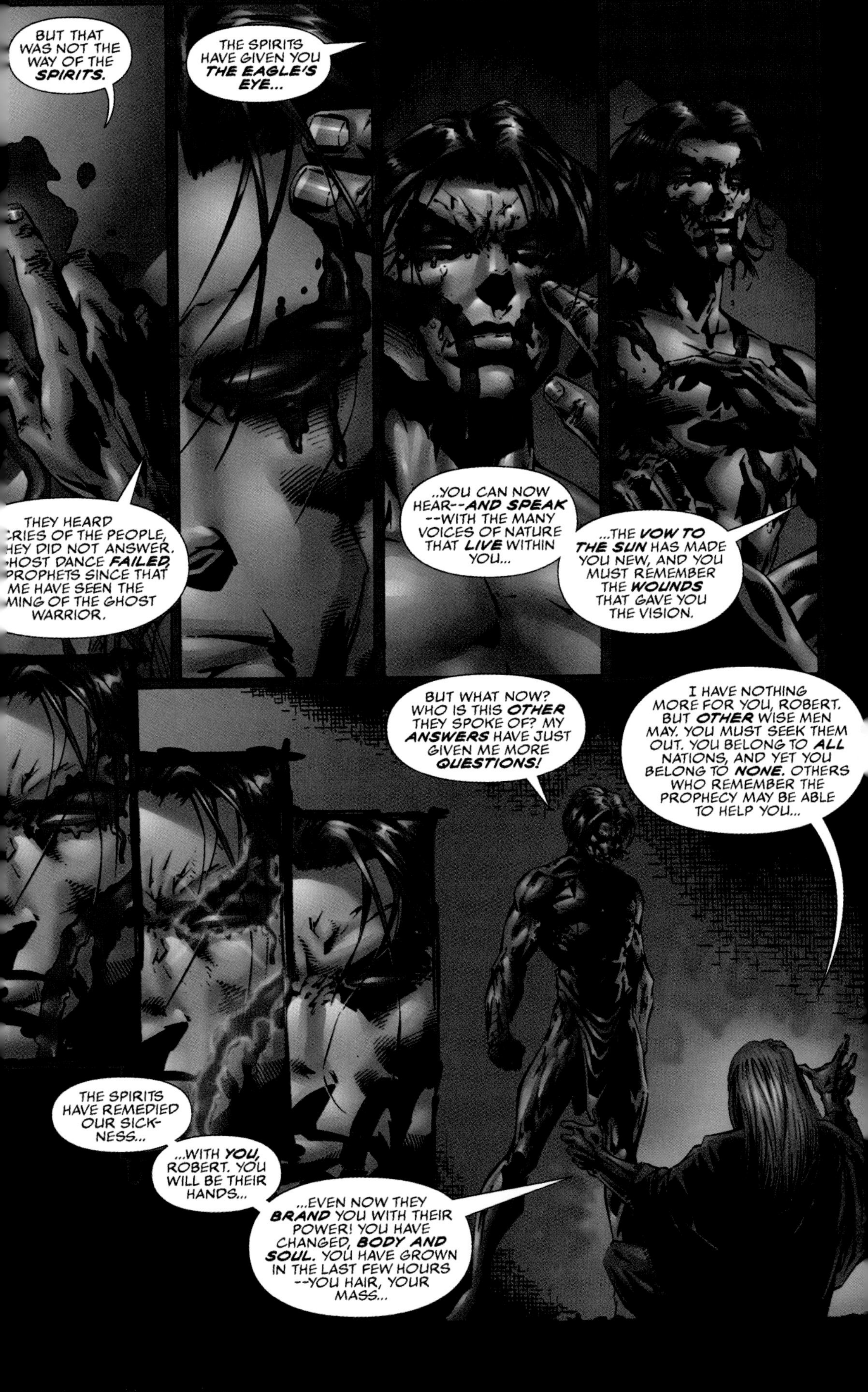

BUT THAT WAS NOT THE WAY OF THE SPIRITS.
THEY HEARD
cRIES OF THE PEOPLE, HEY DID NOT ANSWER. GHOST DANCE FAILED, PROPHETS SINCE THAT ME HAVE SEEN THE MING OF THE GHOST WARRIOR.
THE SPIRITS HAVE GIVEN YOU THE EAGLE'S EYE...
..YOU CAN NOW HEAR--AND SPEAK --WITH THE MANY VOICES OF NATURE THAT LIVE WITHIN YOU...
...THE VOW TO THE SUN HAS MADE YOU NEW, AND YOU MUST REMEMBER THE WOUNDS THAT GAVE YOU THE VISION.
THE SPIRITS HAVE REMEDIED OUR SICK-NESS...
...WITH YOU, ROBERT. YOU WILL BE THEIR HANDS...
...EVEN NOW THEY BRAND YOU WITH THEIR POWER! YOU HAVE CHANGED, BODY AND SOUL. YOU HAVE GROWN IN THE LAST FEW HOURS --YOU HAIR, YOUR MASS...
BUT WHAT NOW? WHO IS THIS OTHER THEY SPOKE OF? MY ANSWERS HAVE JUST GIVEN ME MORE QUESTIONS!
I HAVE NOTHING MORE FOR YOU, ROBERT. BUT OTHER WISE MEN MAY. YOU MUST SEEK THEM OUT. YOU BELONG TO ALL NATIONS, AND YET YOU BELONG TO NONE. OTHERS WHO REMEMBER THE PROPHECY MAY BE ABLE TO HELP YOU...

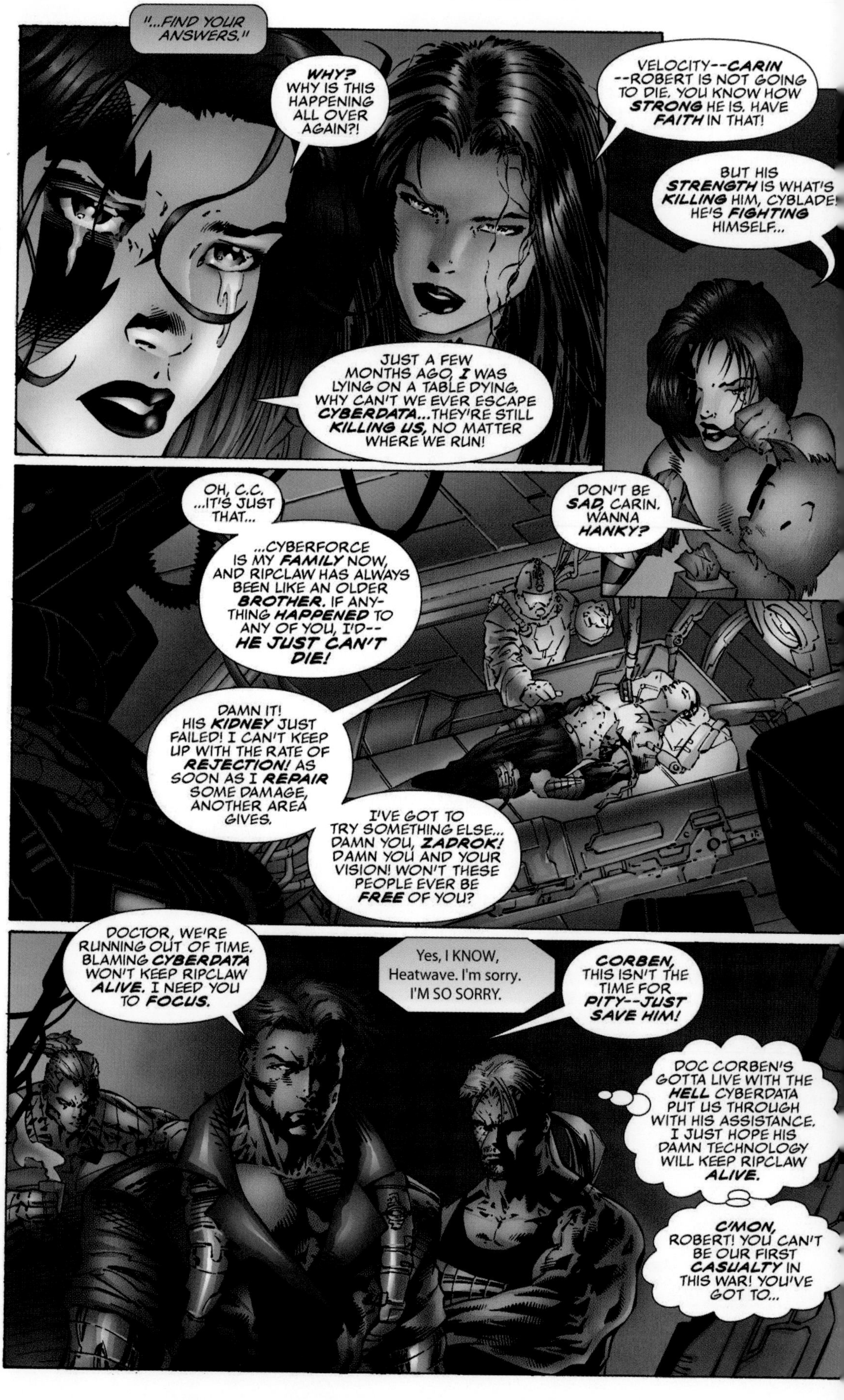
"...FIND YOUR ANSWERS."
WHY? WHY IS THIS HAPPENING ALL OVER AGAIN?!
VELOCITY--CARIN --ROBERT IS NOT GOING TO DIE. YOU KNOW HOW STRONG HE IS. HAVE FAITH IN THAT!
BUT HIS STRENGTH IS WHAT'S KILLING HIM, CYBLADE! HE'S FIGHTING HIMSELF...
JUST A FEW MONTHS AGO, I WAS LYING ON A TABLE DYING. WHY CAN'T WE EVER ESCAPE CYBERDATA...THEY'RE STILL KILLING US, NO MATTER WHERE WE RUN!
OH, C.C. ...IT'S JUST THAT...
DON'T BE SAD, CARIN. WANNA HANKY?
...CYBERFORCE IS MY FAMILY NOW, AND RIPCLAW HAS ALWAYS BEEN LIKE AN OLDER BROTHER. IF ANYTHING HAPPENED TO ANY OF YOU, I'D-- HE JUST CAN'T DIE!
DAMN IT! HIS KIDNEY JUST FAILED! I CAN'T KEEP UP WITH THE RATE OF REJECTION! AS SOON AS I REPAIR SOME DAMAGE, ANOTHER AREA GIVES.
I'VE GOT TO TRY SOMETHING ELSE... DAMN YOU, ZADROK! DAMN YOU AND YOUR VISION! WON'T THESE PEOPLE EVER BE FREE OF YOU?
DOCTOR, WE'RE RUNNING OUT OF TIME. BLAMING CYBERDATA WON'T KEEP RIPCLAW ALIVE. I NEED YOU TO FOCUS.
Yes, I KNOW, Heatwave. I'm sorry. I'M SO SORRY.
CORBEN, THIS ISN'T THE TIME FOR PITY--JUST SAVE HIM!
DOC CORBEN'S GOTTA LIVE WITH THE HELL CYBERDATA PUT US THROUGH WITH HIS ASSISTANCE. I JUST HOPE HIS DAMN TECHNOLOGY WILL KEEP RIPCLAW ALIVE.
C'MON, ROBERT! YOU CAN'T BE OUR FIRST CASUALTY IN THIS WAR! YOU'VE GOT TO...

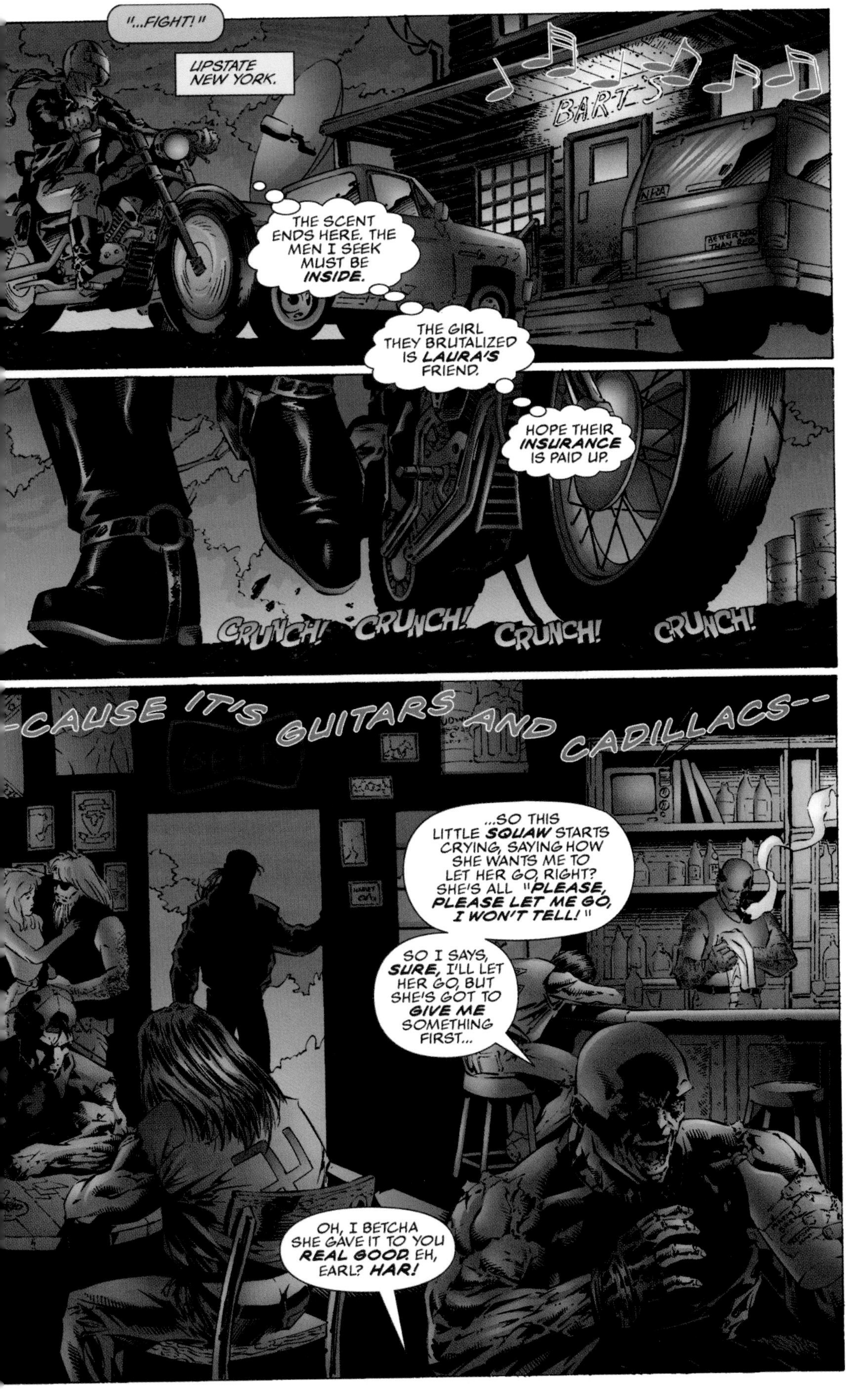
"...FIGHT!"
UPSTATE NEW YORK.
BART'S
THE SCENT ENDS HERE. THE MEN I SEEK MUST BE INSIDE.
THE GIRL THEY BRUTALIZED IS LAURA'S FRIEND.
HOPE THEIR INSURANCE IS PAID UP.
CRUNCH! CRUNCH! CRUNCH! CRUNCH!
--CAUSE IT'S GUITARS AND CADILLACS--
...SO THIS LITTLE SQUAW STARTS CRYING, SAYING HOW SHE WANTS ME TO LET HER GO, RIGHT? SHE'S ALL "PLEASE, PLEASE LET ME GO, I WON'T TELL!"
SO I SAYS, SURE, I'LL LET HER GO, BUT SHE'S GOT TO GIVE ME SOMETHING FIRST...
OH, I BETCHA SHE GAVE IT TO YOU REAL GOOD. EH, EARL? HAR!

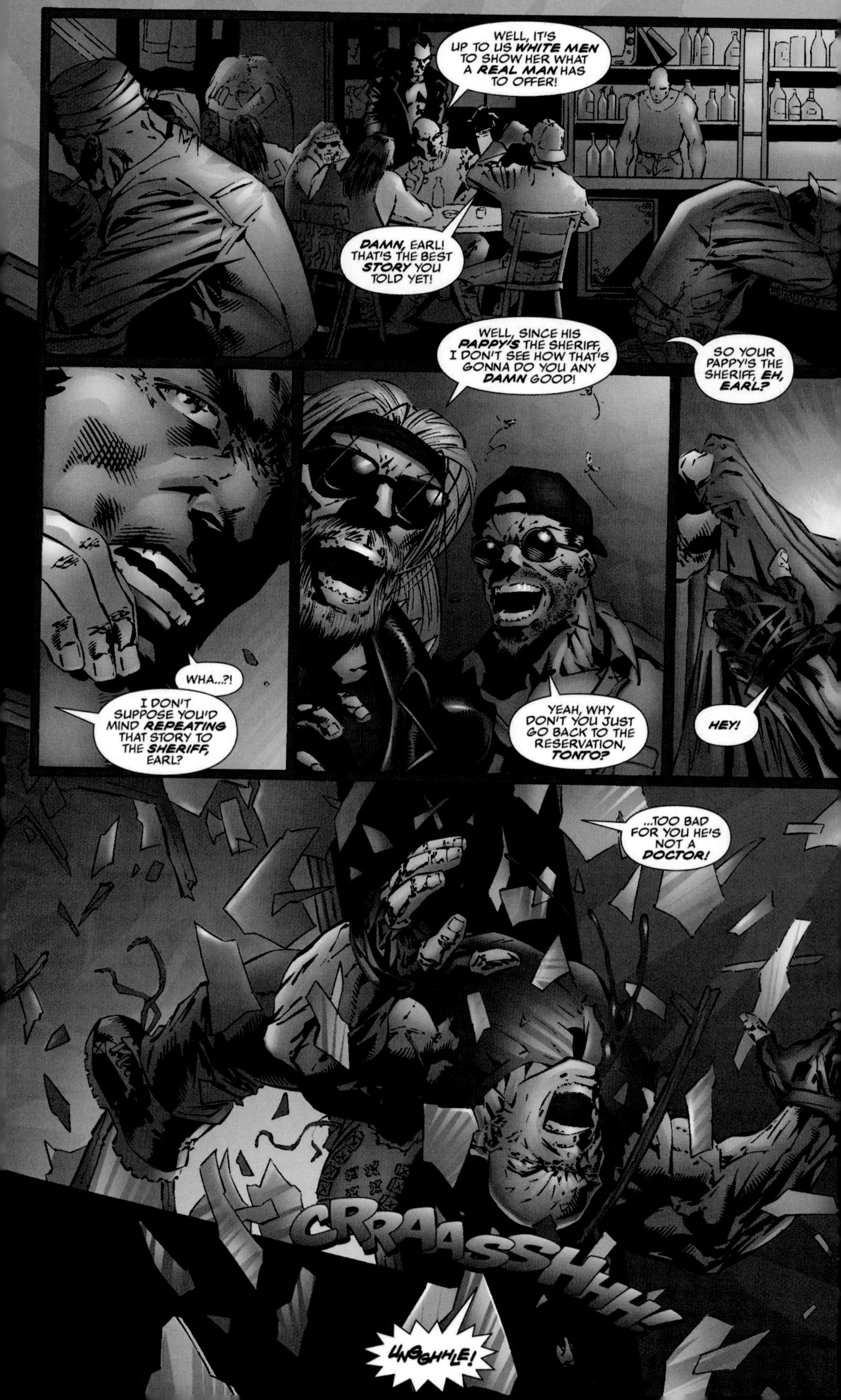
WELL, IT'S UP TO US WHITE MEN TO SHOW HER WHAT A REAL MAN HAS TO OFFER!
DAMN, EARL! THAT'S THE BEST STORY YOU TOLD YET!
SO YOUR PAPPY'S THE SHERIFF, EH, EARL?
WHA...?!
I DON'T SUPPOSE YOU'D MIND REPEATING THAT STORY TO THE SHERIFF, EARL?
WELL, SINCE HIS PAPPY'S THE SHERIFF, I DON'T SEE HOW THAT'S GONNA DO YOU ANY DAMN GOOD!
YEAH, WHY DON'T YOU JUST GO BACK TO THE RESERVATION, TONTO?
HEY!
...TOO BAD FOR YOU HE'S NOT A DOCTOR!
CRRAASSHHH!
UNGGHHLE!

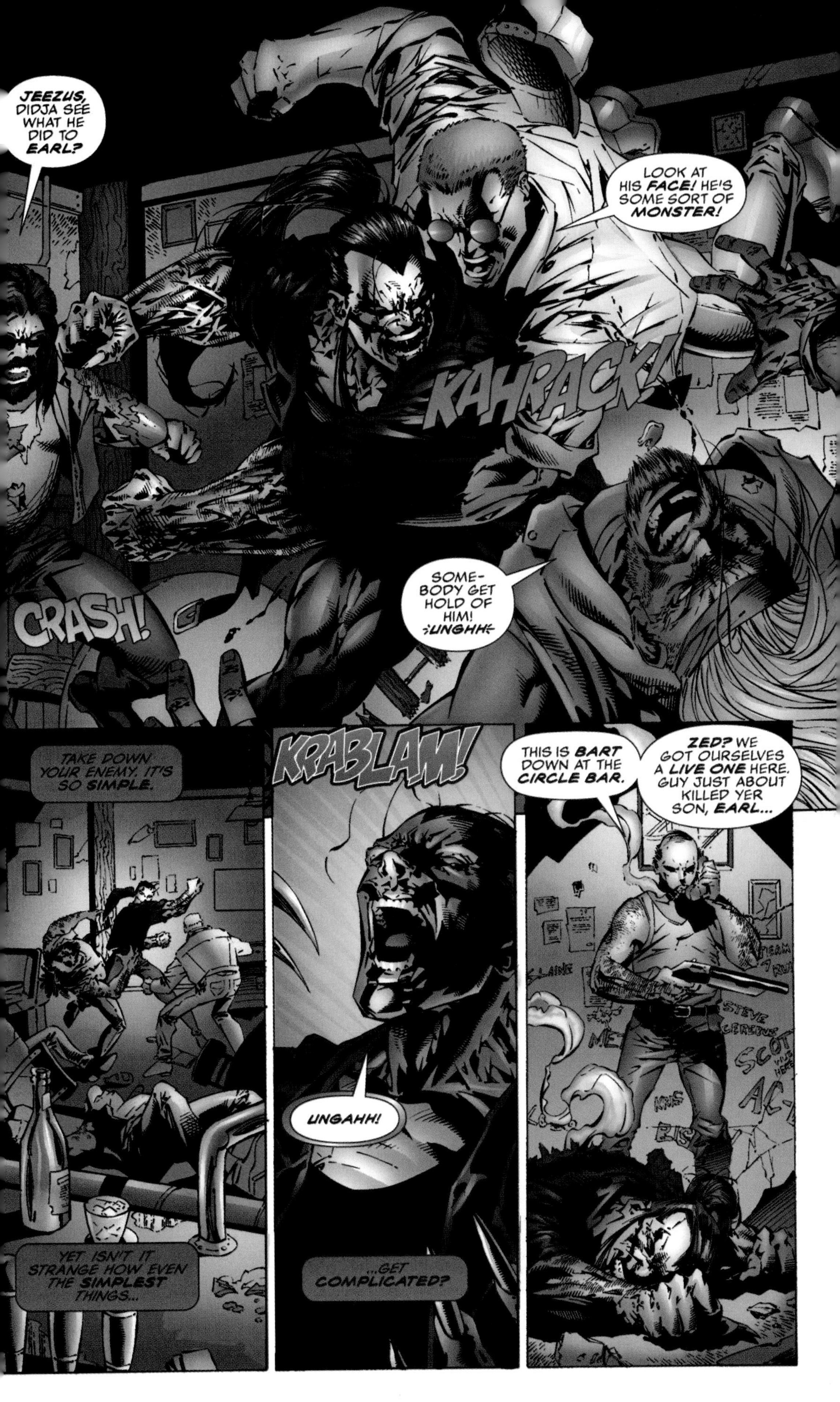
JEEZUS, DIDJA SEE WHAT HE DID TO EARL?
LOOK AT HIS FACE! HE'S SOME SORT OF MONSTER!
KAHRACK!
CRASH!
SOME-BODY GET HOLD OF HIM! UNGHH
TAKE DOWN YOUR ENEMY. IT'S SO SIMPLE.
YET ISN'T IT STRANGE HOW EVEN THE SIMPLEST THINGS...
KRABLAM!
UNGAHH!
...GET COMPLICATED?
THIS IS BART DOWN AT THE CIRCLE BAR.
ZED? WE GOT OURSELVES A LIVE ONE HERE. GUY JUST ABOUT KILLED YER SON, EARL...

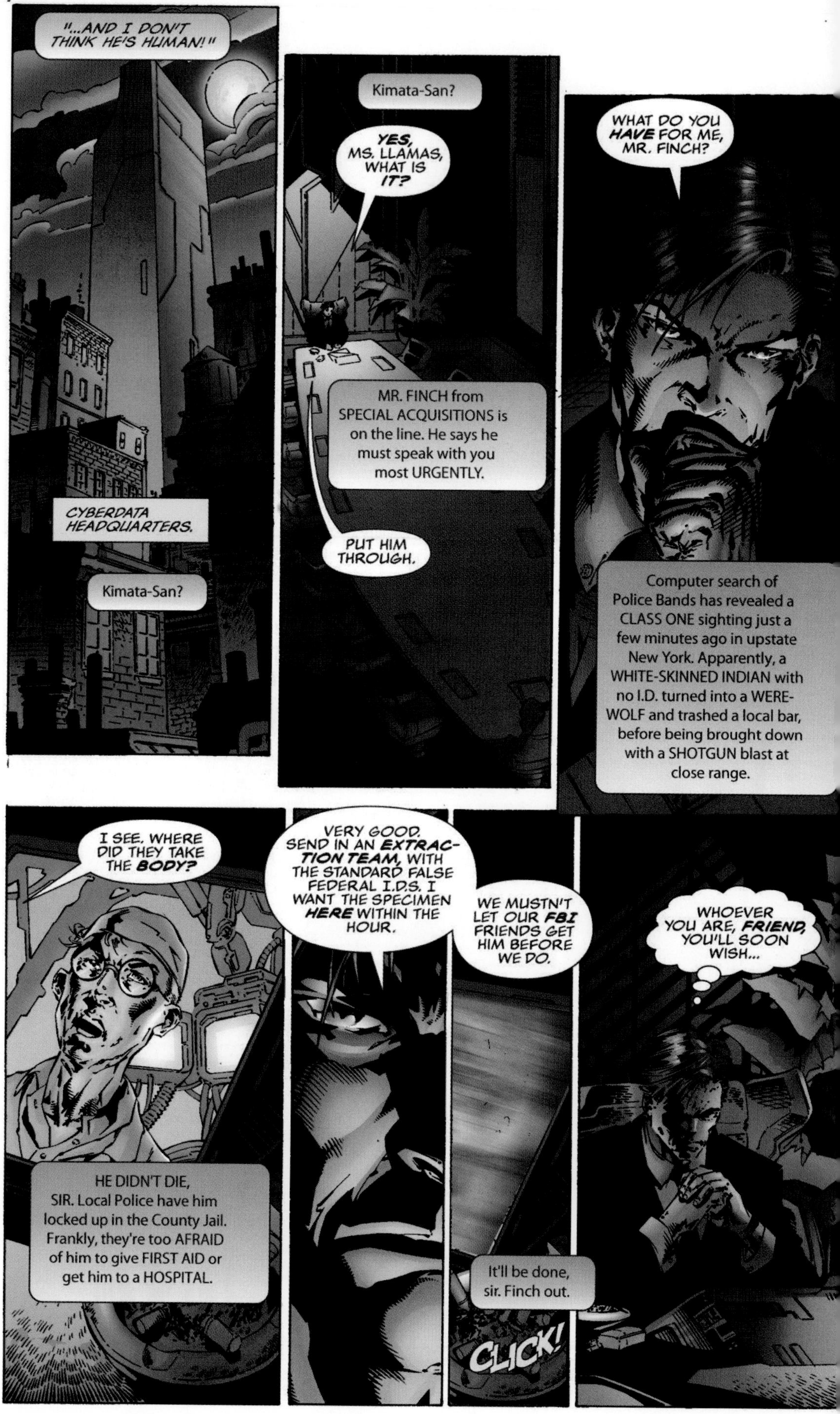
"...AND I DON'T THINK HE'S HUMAN!"
CYBERDATA HEADQUARTERS.
Kimata-San?
Kimata-San?
YES, MS. LLAMAS, WHAT IS IT?
MR. FINCH from SPECIAL ACQUISITIONS is on the line. He says he must speak with you most URGENTLY.
PUT HIM THROUGH.
WHAT DO YOU HAVE FOR ME, MR. FINCH?
Computer search of Police Bands has revealed a CLASS ONE sighting just a few minutes ago in upstate New York. Apparently, a WHITE-SKINNED INDIAN with no I.D. turned into a WERE-WOLF and trashed a local bar, before being brought down with a SHOTGUN blast at close range.
I SEE. WHERE DID THEY TAKE THE BODY?
HE DIDN'T DIE, SIR. Local Police have him locked up in the County Jail. Frankly, they're too AFRAID of him to give FIRST AID or get him to a HOSPITAL.
VERY GOOD. SEND IN AN EXTRACTION TEAM, WITH THE STANDARD FALSE FEDERAL I.D.S. I WANT THE SPECIMEN HERE WITHIN THE HOUR.
WE MUSTN'T LET OUR FBI FRIENDS GET HIM BEFORE WE DO.
It'll be done, sir. Finch out.
CLICK!
WHOEVER YOU ARE, FRIEND, YOU'LL SOON WISH...

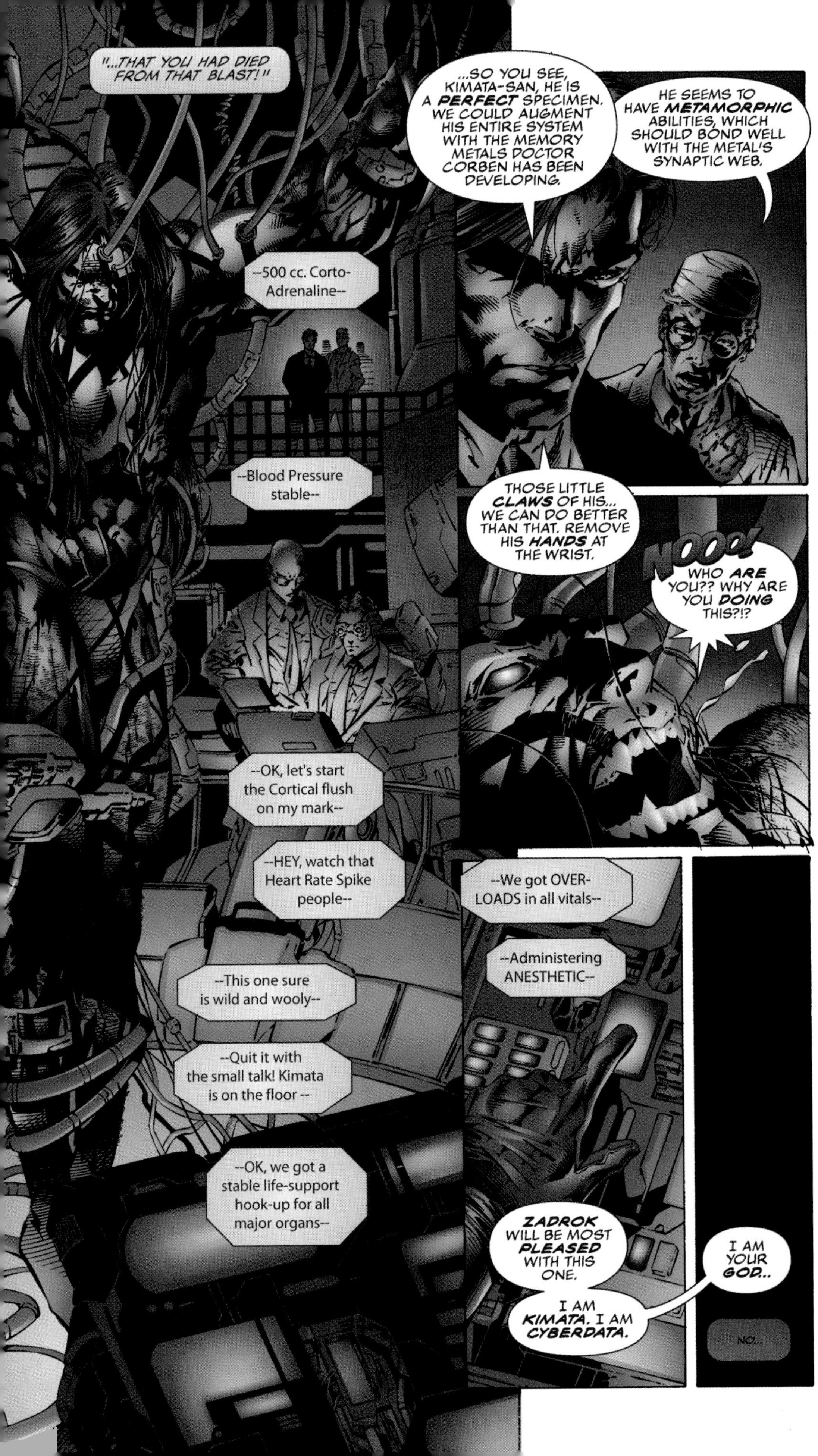
"...THAT YOU HAD DIED FROM THAT BLAST!"
--500 cc. Corto-Adrenaline--
--Blood Pressure stable--
--OK, let's start the Cortical flush on my mark--
--HEY, watch that Heart Rate Spike people--
--This one sure is wild and wooly--
--Quit it with the small talk! Kimata is on the floor --
--OK, we got a stable life-support hook-up for all major organs--
...SO YOU SEE, KIMATA-SAN, HE IS A PERFECT SPECIMEN. WE COULD AUGMENT HIS ENTIRE SYSTEM WITH THE MEMORY METALS DOCTOR CORBEN HAS BEEN DEVELOPING.
HE SEEMS TO HAVE METAMORPHIC ABILITIES, WHICH SHOULD BOND WELL WITH THE METAL'S SYNAPTIC WEB.
THOSE LITTLE CLAWS OF HIS... WE CAN DO BETTER THAN THAT. REMOVE HIS HANDS AT THE WRIST.
NOOO!
WHO ARE YOU?? WHY ARE YOU DOING THIS?!?
--We got OVER-LOADS in all vitals--
--Administering ANESTHETIC--
ZADROK WILL BE MOST PLEASED WITH THIS ONE.
I AM KIMATA. I AM CYBERDATA.
I AM YOUR GOD...
NO...

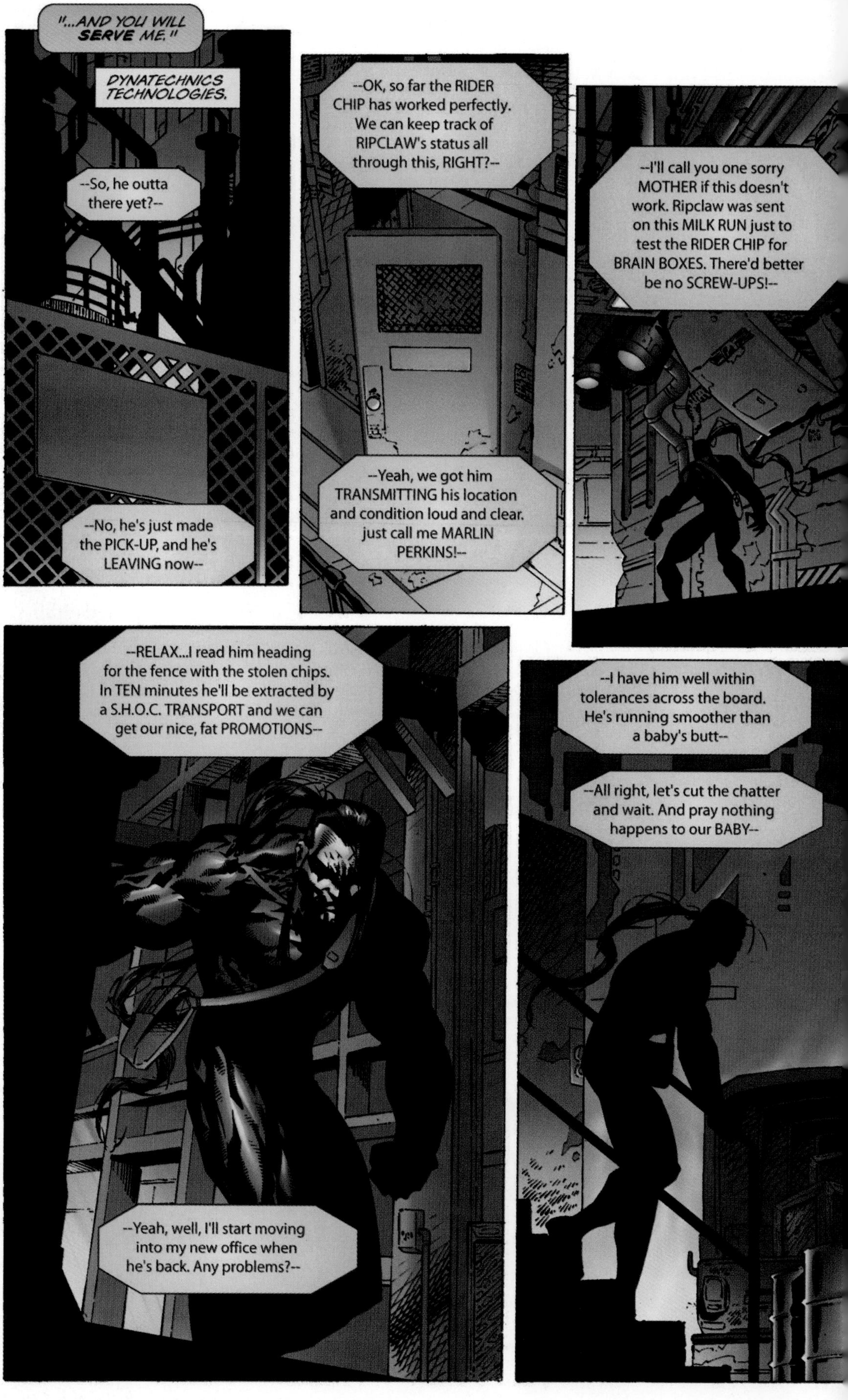
"...AND YOU WILL SERVE ME."
DYNATECHNICS TECHNOLOGIES.
--So, he outta there yet?--
--No, he's just made the PICK-UP, and he's LEAVING now--
--OK, so far the RIDER CHIP has worked perfectly. We can keep track of RIPCLAW's status all through this, RIGHT?--
--Yeah, we got him TRANSMITTING his location and condition loud and clear. just call me MARLIN PERKINS!--
--I'll call you one sorry MOTHER if this doesn't work. Ripclaw was sent on this MILK RUN just to test the RIDER CHIP for BRAIN BOXES. There'd better be no SCREW-UPS!--
--RELAX...I read him heading for the fence with the stolen chips. In TEN minutes he'll be extracted by a S.H.O.C. TRANSPORT and we can get our nice, fat PROMOTIONS--
--Yeah, well, I'll start moving into my new office when he's back. Any problems?--
--I have him well within tolerances across the board. He's running smoother than a baby's butt--
--All right, let's cut the chatter and wait. And pray nothing happens to our BABY--

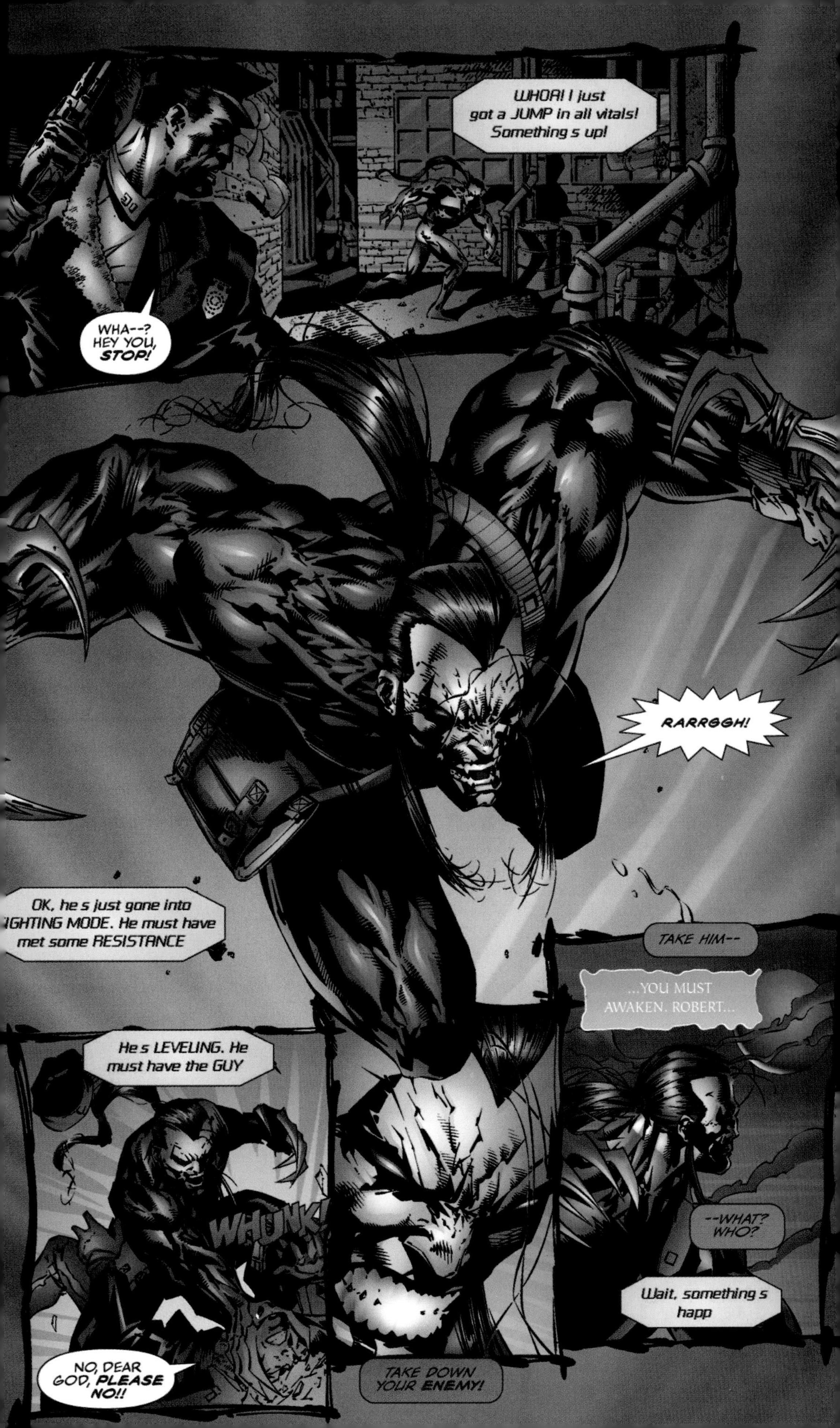
WHOA! I just got a JUMP in all vitals! Something s up!
WHA--? HEY YOU, STOP!
RARRGGH!
OK, he s just gone into IGHTING MODE. He must have met some RESISTANCE
TAKE HIM--
...YOU MUST AWAKEN, ROBERT...
He s LEVELING. He must have the GUY
WHUNK
NO, DEAR GOD, PLEASE NO!!
TAKE DOWN YOUR ENEMY!
--WHAT? WHO?
Wait, something s happ

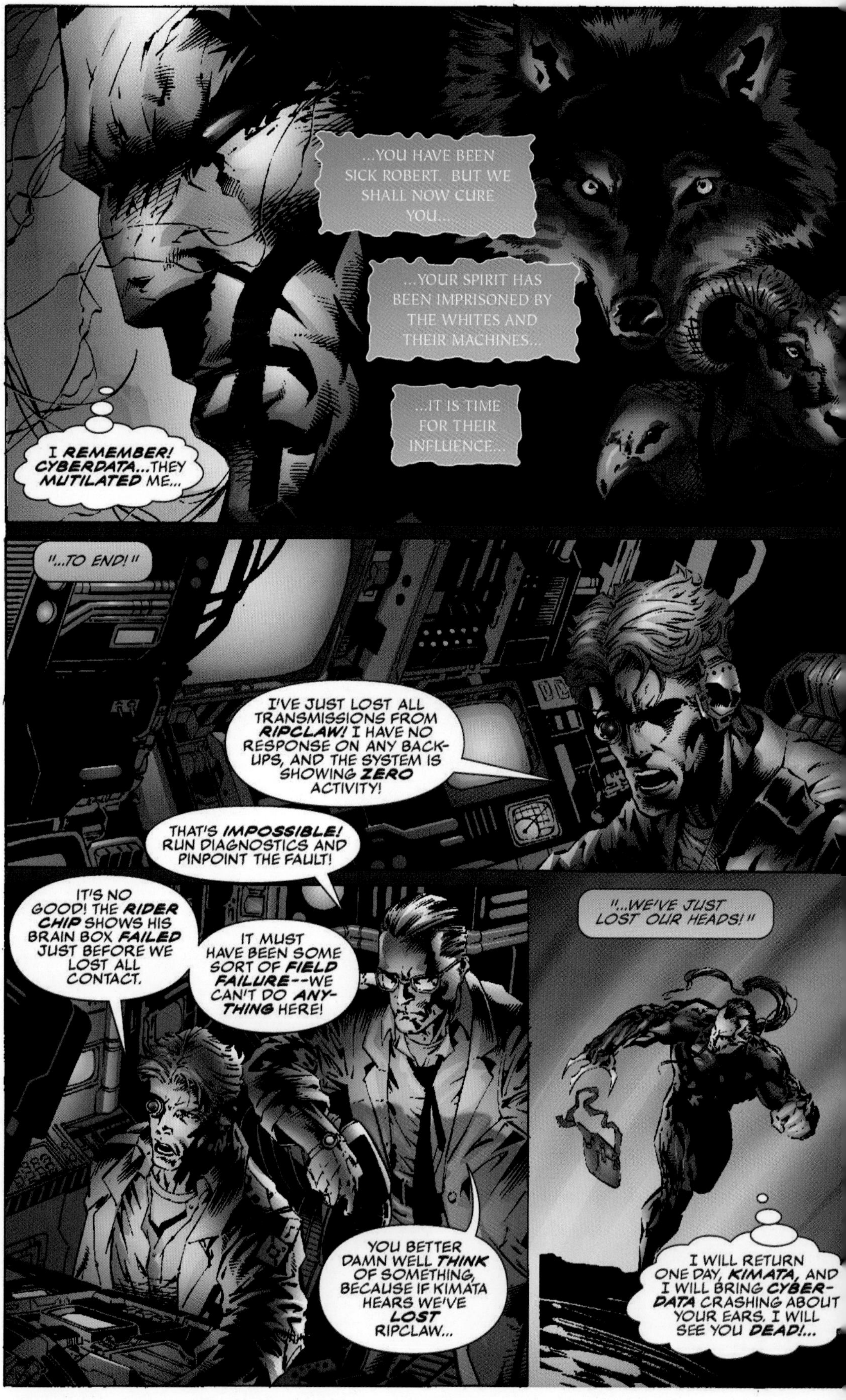
...YOU HAVE BEEN SICK ROBERT. BUT WE SHALL NOW CURE YOU...
...YOUR SPIRIT HAS BEEN IMPRISONED BY THE WHITES AND THEIR MACHINES...
...IT IS TIME FOR THEIR INFLUENCE...
I REMEMBER! CYBERDATA...THEY MUTILATED ME...
"...TO END!"
I'VE JUST LOST ALL TRANSMISSIONS FROM RIPCLAW! I HAVE NO RESPONSE ON ANY BACK-UPS, AND THE SYSTEM IS SHOWING ZERO ACTIVITY!
THAT'S IMPOSSIBLE! RUN DIAGNOSTICS AND PINPOINT THE FAULT!
IT'S NO GOOD! THE RIDER CHIP SHOWS HIS BRAIN BOX FAILED JUST BEFORE WE LOST ALL CONTACT.
IT MUST HAVE BEEN SOME SORT OF FIELD FAILURE--WE CAN'T DO ANY-THING HERE!
YOU BETTER DAMN WELL THINK OF SOMETHING, BECAUSE IF KIMATA HEARS WE'VE LOST RIPCLAW...
"...WE'VE JUST LOST OUR HEADS!"
I WILL RETURN ONE DAY, KIMATA, AND I WILL BRING CYBER-DATA CRASHING ABOUT YOUR EARS. I WILL SEE YOU DEAD!...

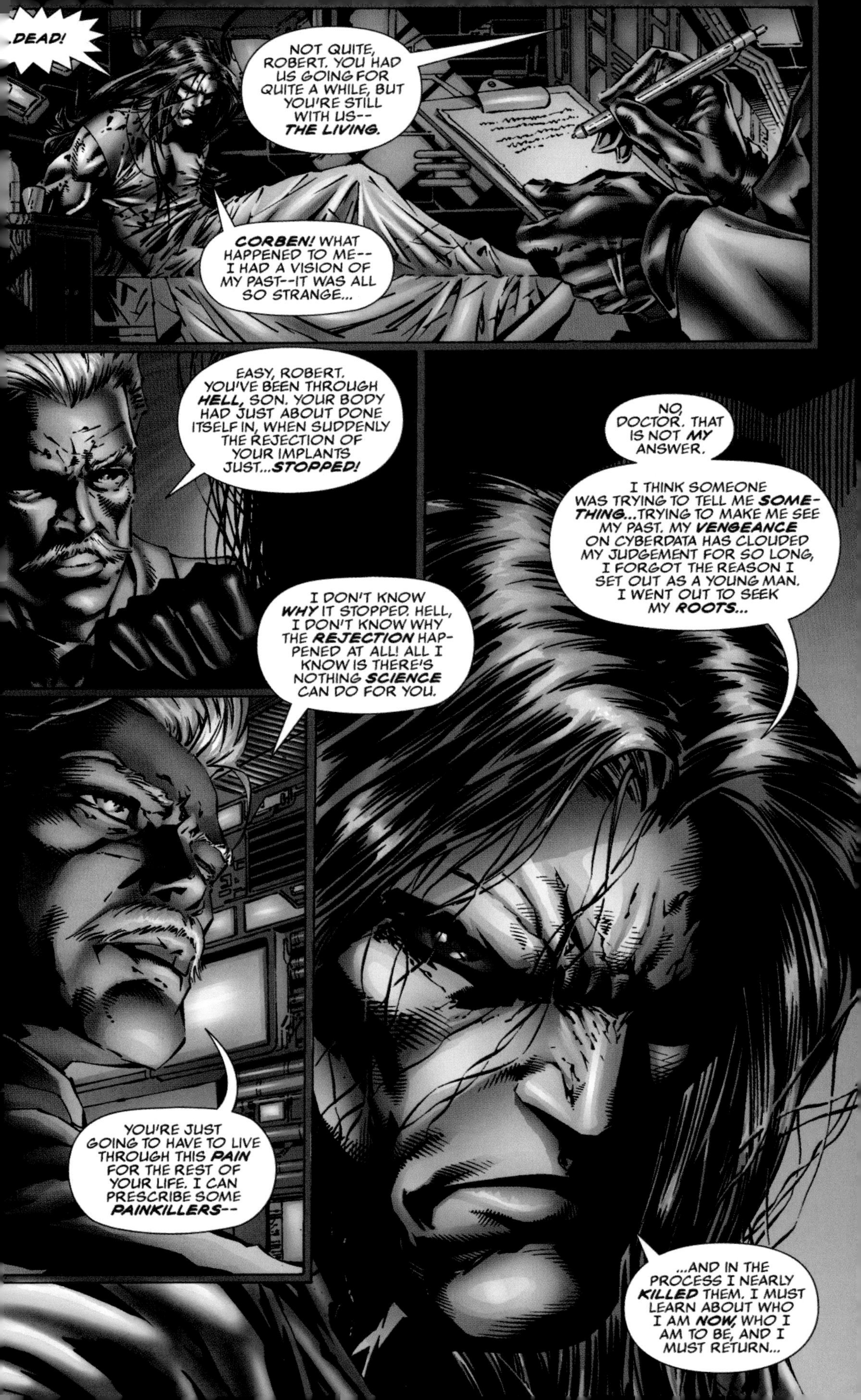
...DEAD!
NOT QUITE, ROBERT. YOU HAD US GOING FOR QUITE A WHILE, BUT YOU'RE STILL WITH US-- THE LIVING.
CORBEN! WHAT HAPPENED TO ME-- I HAD A VISION OF MY PAST--IT WAS ALL SO STRANGE...
EASY, ROBERT. YOU'VE BEEN THROUGH HELL, SON. YOUR BODY HAD JUST ABOUT DONE ITSELF IN, WHEN SUDDENLY THE REJECTION OF YOUR IMPLANTS JUST...STOPPED!
I DON'T KNOW WHY IT STOPPED. HELL, I DON'T KNOW WHY THE REJECTION HAPPENED AT ALL! ALL I KNOW IS THERE'S NOTHING SCIENCE CAN DO FOR YOU.
YOU'RE JUST GOING TO HAVE TO LIVE THROUGH THIS PAIN FOR THE REST OF YOUR LIFE. I CAN PRESCRIBE SOME PAINKILLERS--
NO, DOCTOR. THAT IS NOT MY ANSWER.
I THINK SOMEONE WAS TRYING TO TELL ME SOMETHING...TRYING TO MAKE ME SEE MY PAST. MY VENGEANCE ON CYBERDATA HAS CLOUDED MY JUDGEMENT FOR SO LONG, I FORGOT THE REASON I SET OUT AS A YOUNG MAN. I WENT OUT TO SEEK MY ROOTS...
...AND IN THE PROCESS I NEARLY KILLED THEM. I MUST LEARN ABOUT WHO I AM NOW, WHO I AM TO BE, AND I MUST RETURN...

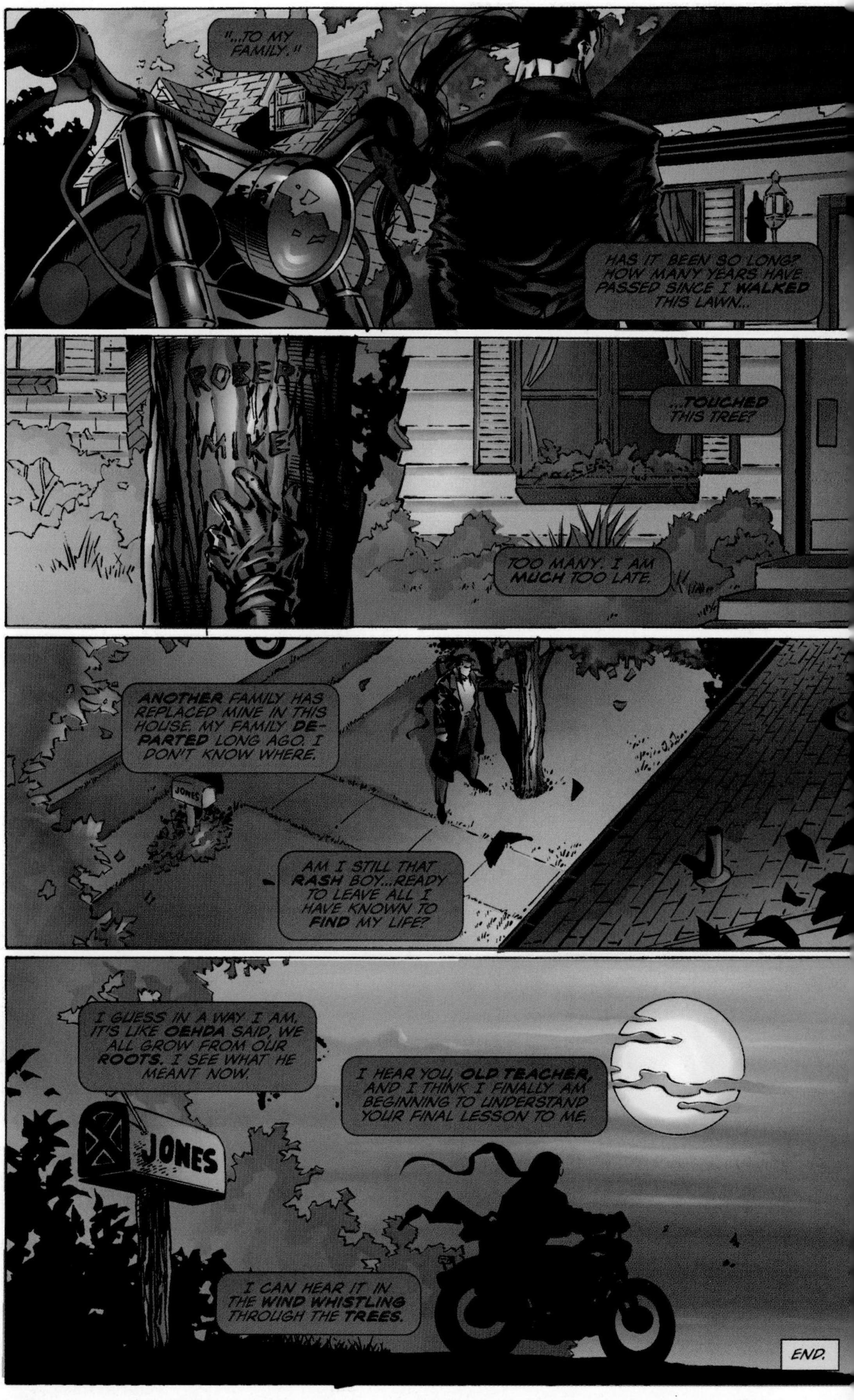
"...TO MY FAMILY."
HAS IT BEEN SO LONG? HOW MANY YEARS HAVE PASSED SINCE I WALKED THIS LAWN...
ROBERT
MIKE
...TOUCHED THIS TREE?
TOO MANY. I AM MUCH TOO LATE.
ANOTHER FAMILY HAS REPLACED MINE IN THIS HOUSE. MY FAMILY DEPARTED LONG AGO. I DON'T KNOW WHERE.
JONES
AM I STILL THAT RASH BOY...READY TO LEAVE ALL I HAVE KNOWN TO FIND MY LIFE?
I GUESS IN A WAY I AM. IT'S LIKE OEHDA SAID, WE ALL GROW FROM OUR ROOTS. I SEE WHAT HE MEANT NOW.
I HEAR YOU, OLD TEACHER, AND I THINK I FINALLY AM BEGINNING TO UNDERSTAND YOUR FINAL LESSON TO ME.
JONES
I CAN HEAR IT IN THE WIND WHISTLING THROUGH THE TREES.
END.

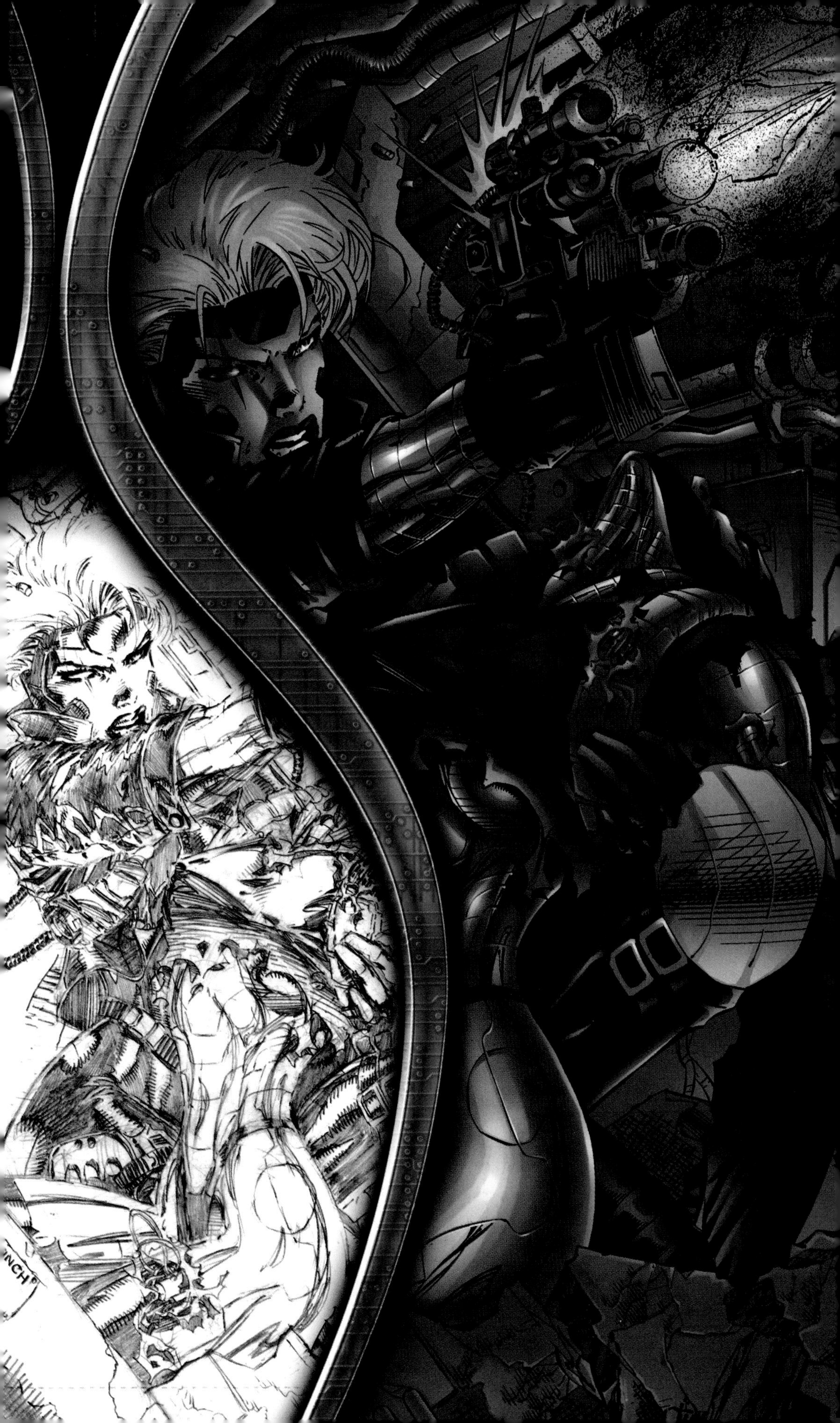

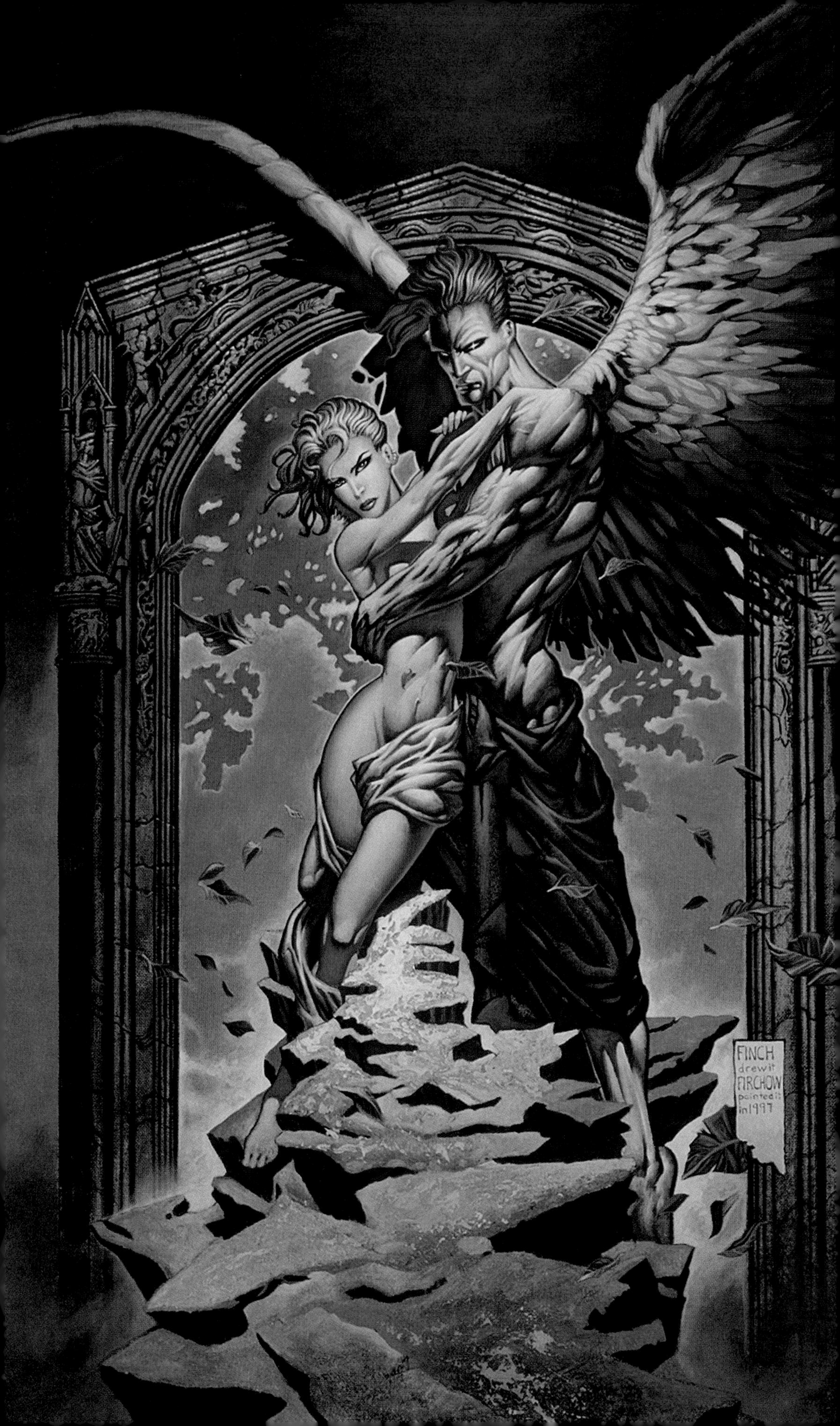
FINCH
drew it
FIRCHOW
painted it
in 1997

Ascension marks one of the major jumps in Dave Finch's career. The series, written by Dave Finch and Matt "Batt" Banning, gave him the chance to get behind the wheel creatively. Dedication to his work shows through in the following samples from the series.

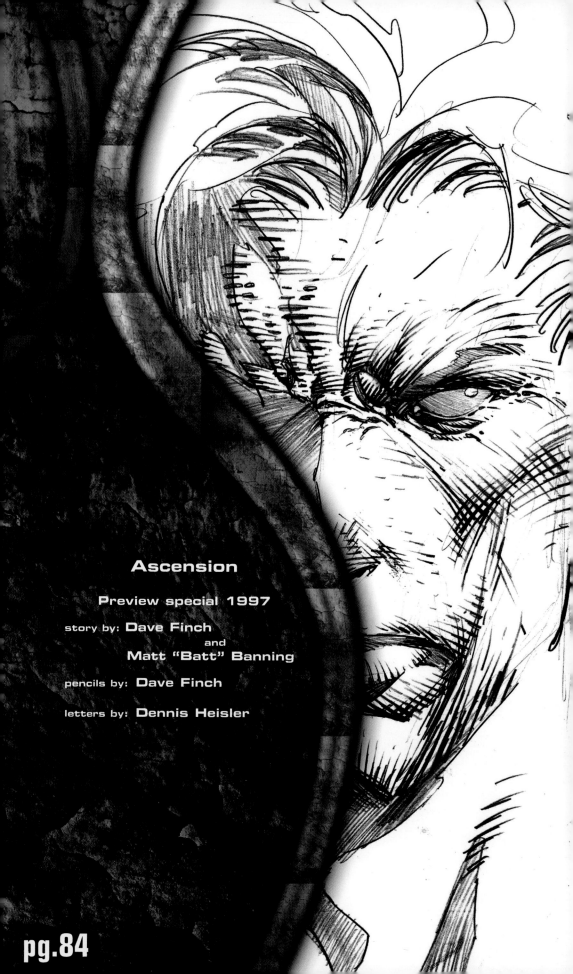

Ascension

Preview special 1997

story by: **Dave Finch**
and
Matt "Batt" Banning

pencils by: **Dave Finch**

letters by: **Dennis Heisler**

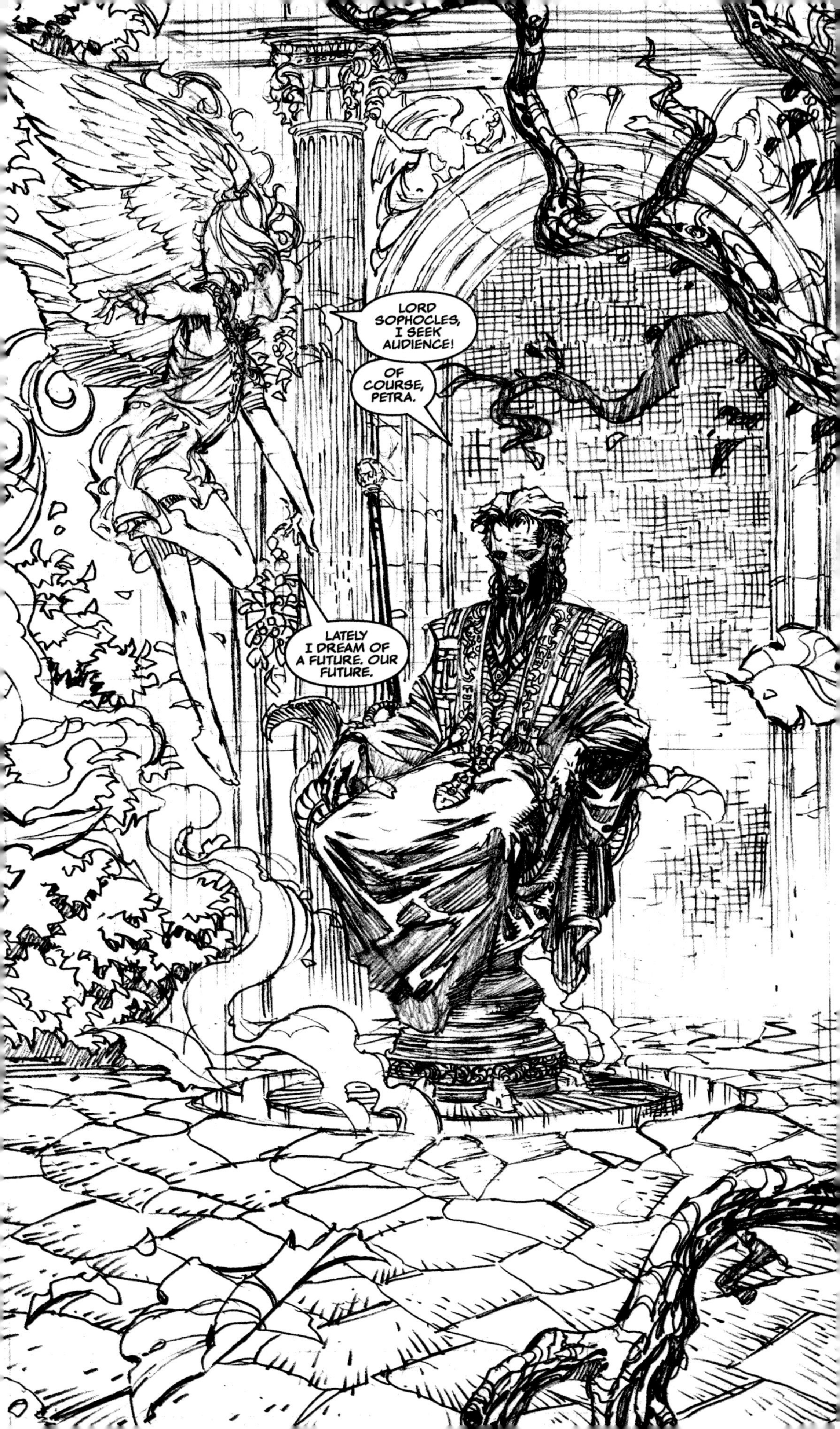
LORD SOPHOCLES, I SEEK AUDIENCE!
OF COURSE, PETRA.
LATELY I DREAM OF A FUTURE. OUR FUTURE.

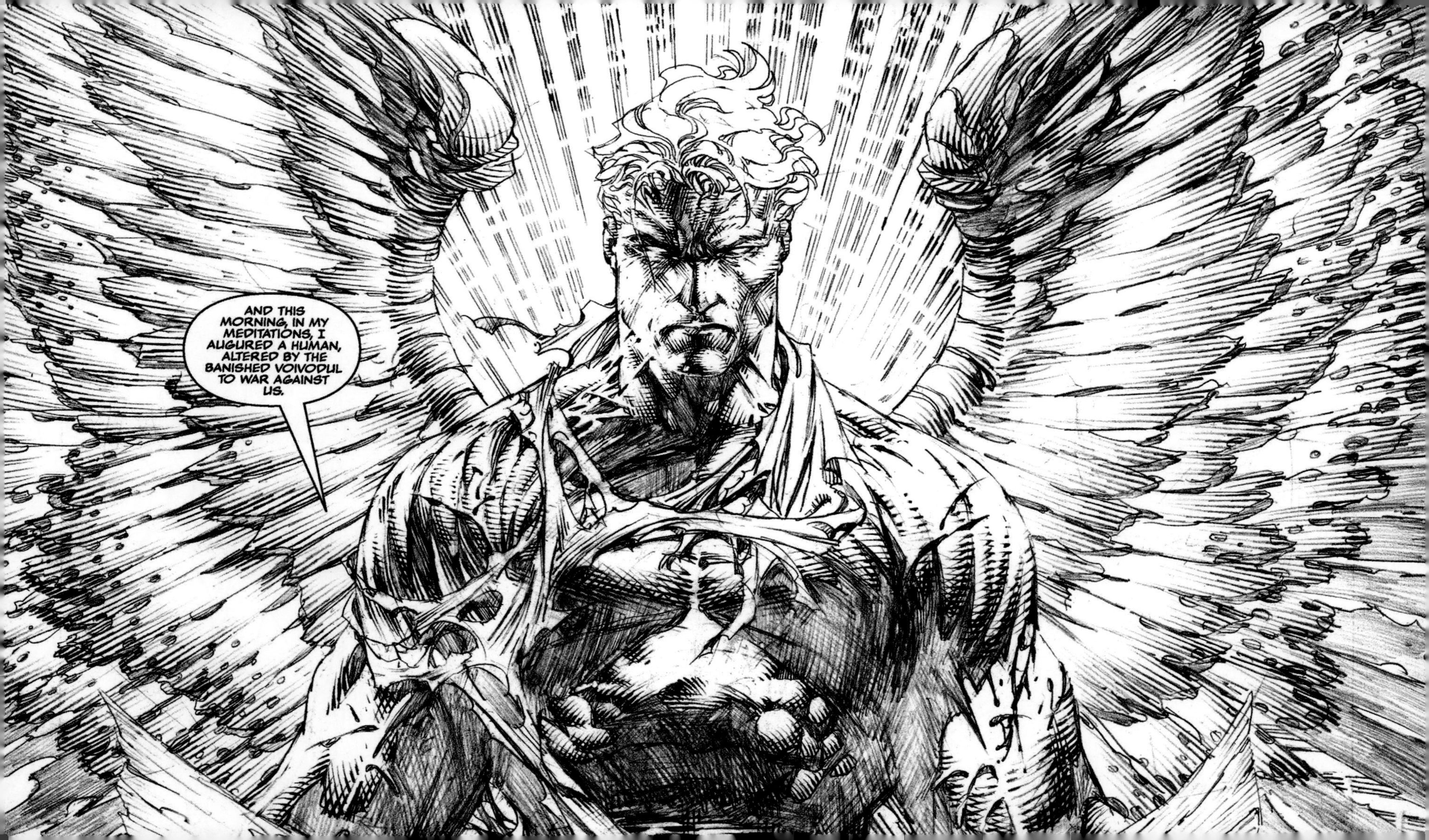
AND THIS MORNING, IN MY MEDITATIONS, I AUGURED A HUMAN, ALTERED BY THE BANISHED VOIVODUL TO WAR AGAINST US.

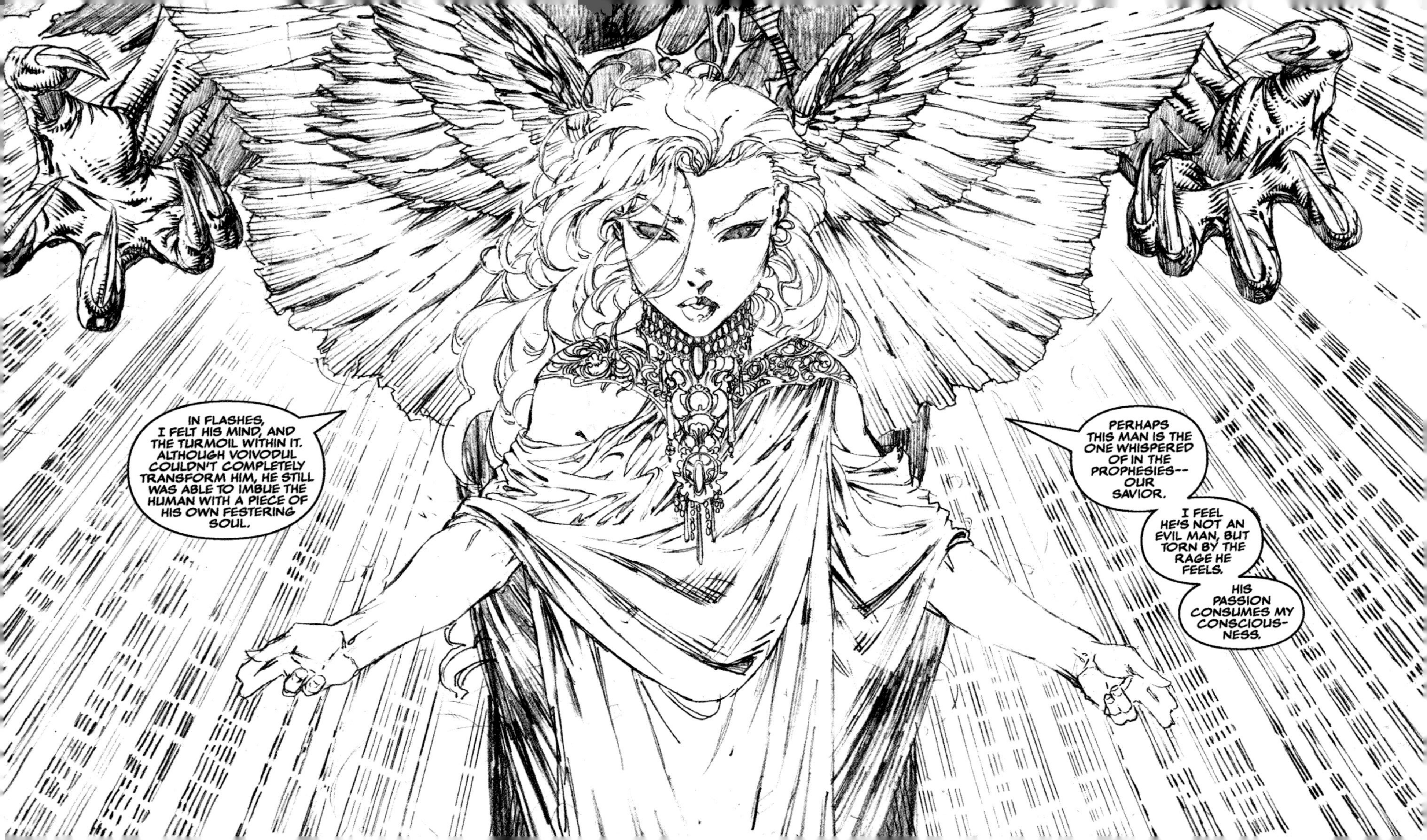
IN FLASHES, I FELT HIS MIND, AND THE TURMOIL WITHIN IT. ALTHOUGH VOIVODUL COULDN'T COMPLETELY TRANSFORM HIM, HE STILL WAS ABLE TO IMBUE THE HUMAN WITH A PIECE OF HIS OWN FESTERING SOUL.
PERHAPS THIS MAN IS THE ONE WHISPERED OF IN THE PROPHESIES-- OUR SAVIOR.
I FEEL HE'S NOT AN EVIL MAN, BUT TORN BY THE RAGE HE FEELS.
HIS PASSION CONSUMES MY CONSCIOUS-NESS.

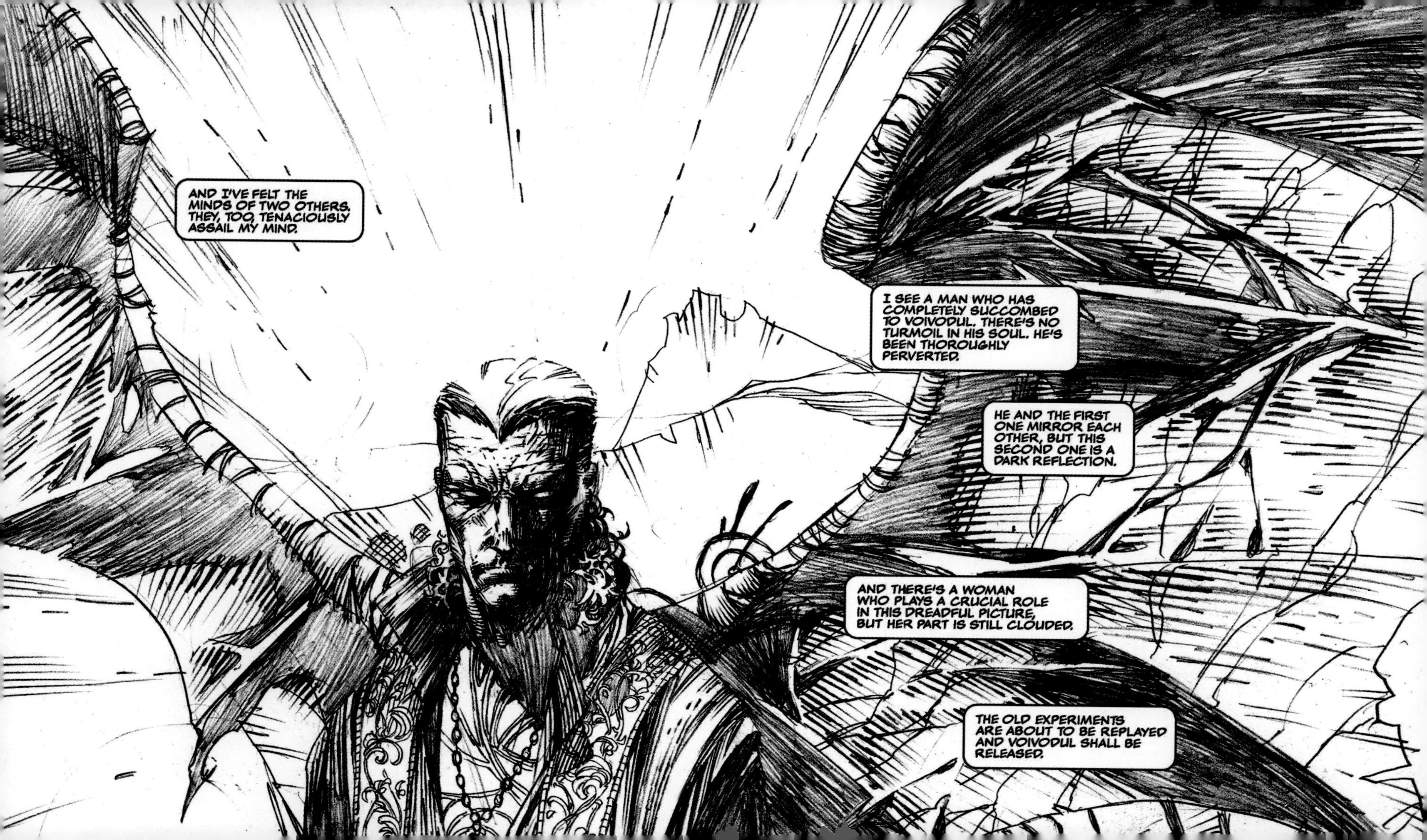
AND I'VE FELT THE MINDS OF TWO OTHERS. THEY, TOO, TENACIOUSLY ASSAIL MY MIND.
I SEE A MAN WHO HAS COMPLETELY SUCCOMBED TO VOIVODUL. THERE'S NO TURMOIL IN HIS SOUL. HE'S BEEN THOROUGHLY PERVERTED.
HE AND THE FIRST ONE MIRROR EACH OTHER, BUT THIS SECOND ONE IS A DARK REFLECTION.
AND THERE'S A WOMAN WHO PLAYS A CRUCIAL ROLE IN THIS DREADFUL PICTURE, BUT HER PART IS STILL CLOUDED.
THE OLD EXPERIMENTS ARE ABOUT TO BE REPLAYED AND VOIVODUL SHALL BE RELEASED.

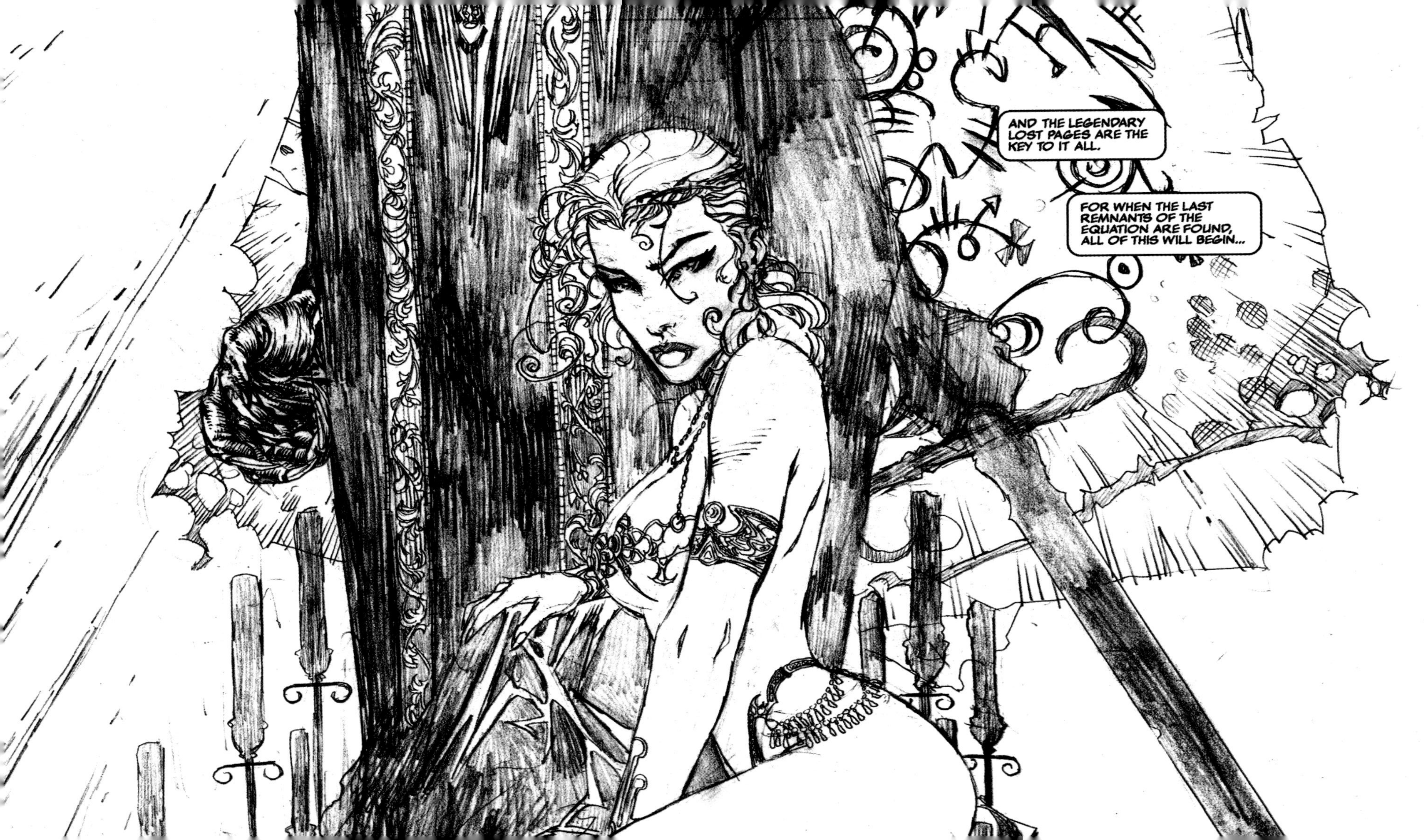
AND THE LEGENDARY LOST PAGES ARE THE KEY TO IT ALL.
FOR WHEN THE LAST REMNANTS OF THE EQUATION ARE FOUND, ALL OF THIS WILL BEGIN...

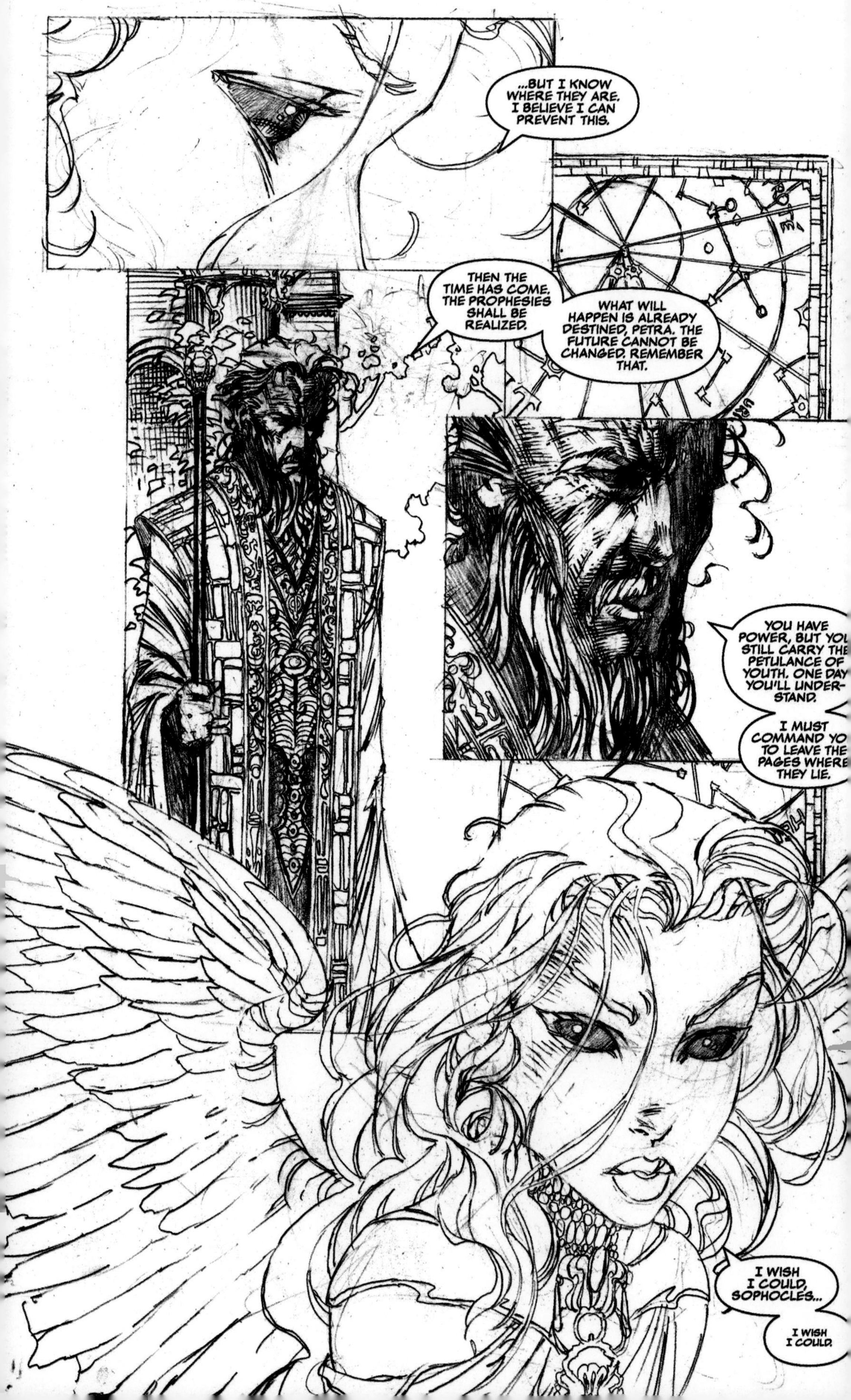
...BUT I KNOW WHERE THEY ARE. I BELIEVE I CAN PREVENT THIS.
THEN THE TIME HAS COME. THE PROPHESIES SHALL BE REALIZED.
WHAT WILL HAPPEN IS ALREADY DESTINED, PETRA. THE FUTURE CANNOT BE CHANGED. REMEMBER THAT.
YOU HAVE POWER, BUT YOU STILL CARRY THE PETULANCE OF YOUTH. ONE DAY YOU'LL UNDER-STAND.
I MUST COMMAND YOU TO LEAVE THE PAGES WHERE THEY LIE.
I WISH I COULD, SOPHOCLES...
I WISH I COULD.

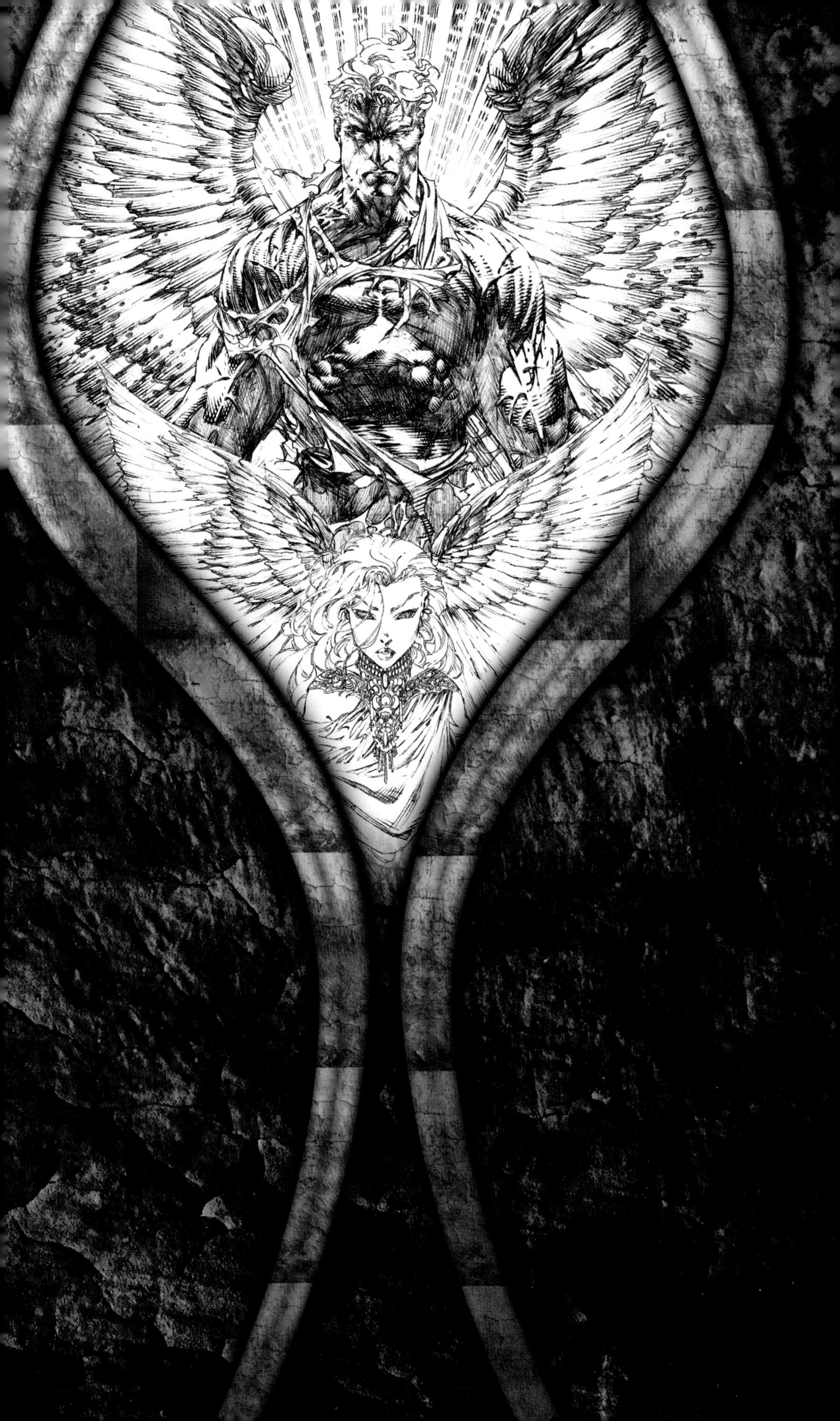

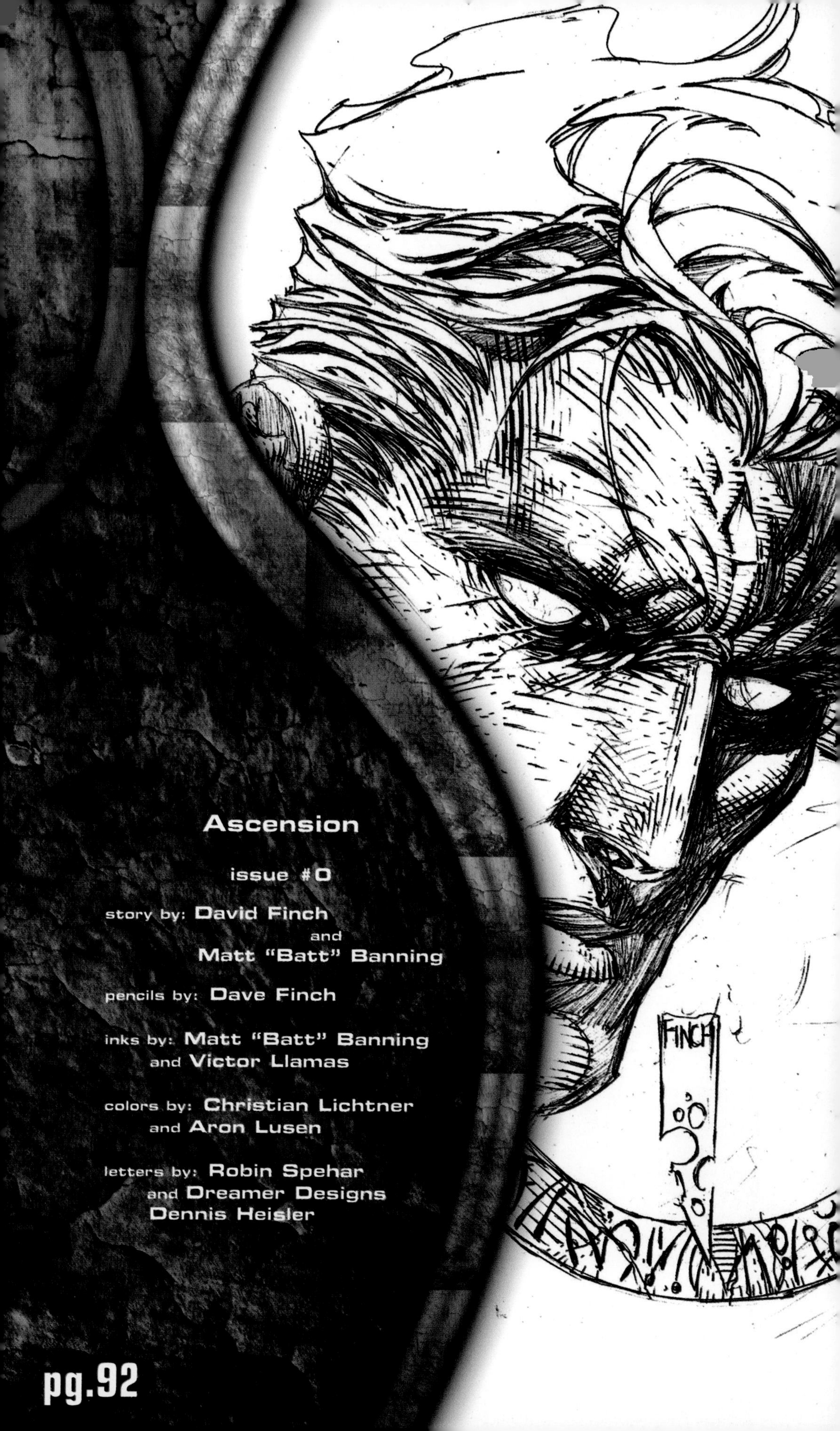
FINCH

Ascension

issue #0

story by: David Finch
and
Matt "Batt" Banning

pencils by: Dave Finch

inks by: Matt "Batt" Banning
and Victor Llamas

colors by: Christian Lichtner
and Aron Lusen

letters by: Robin Spehar
and Dreamer Designs
Dennis Heisler

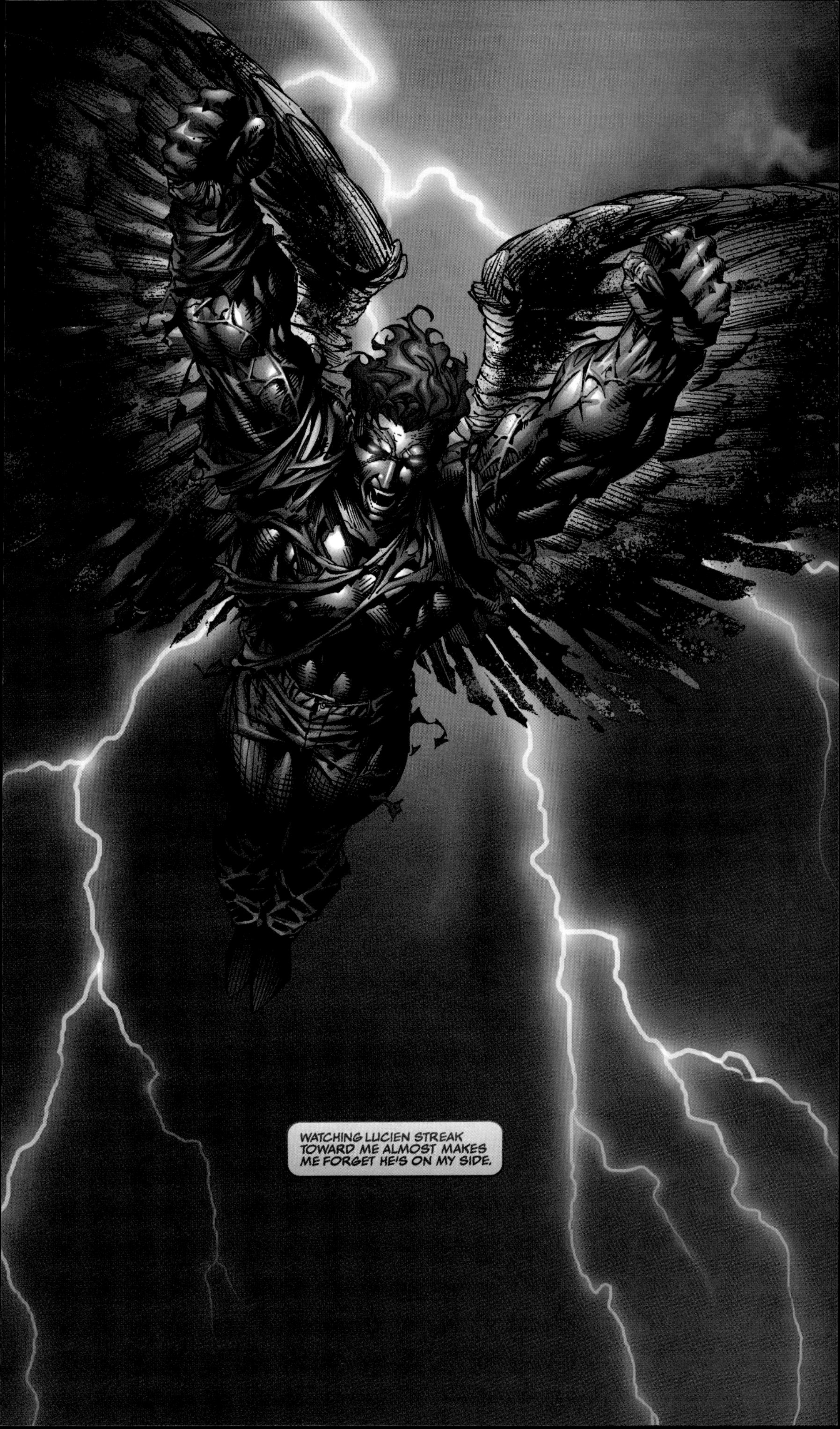
WATCHING LUCIEN STREAK TOWARD ME ALMOST MAKES ME FORGET HE'S ON MY SIDE.

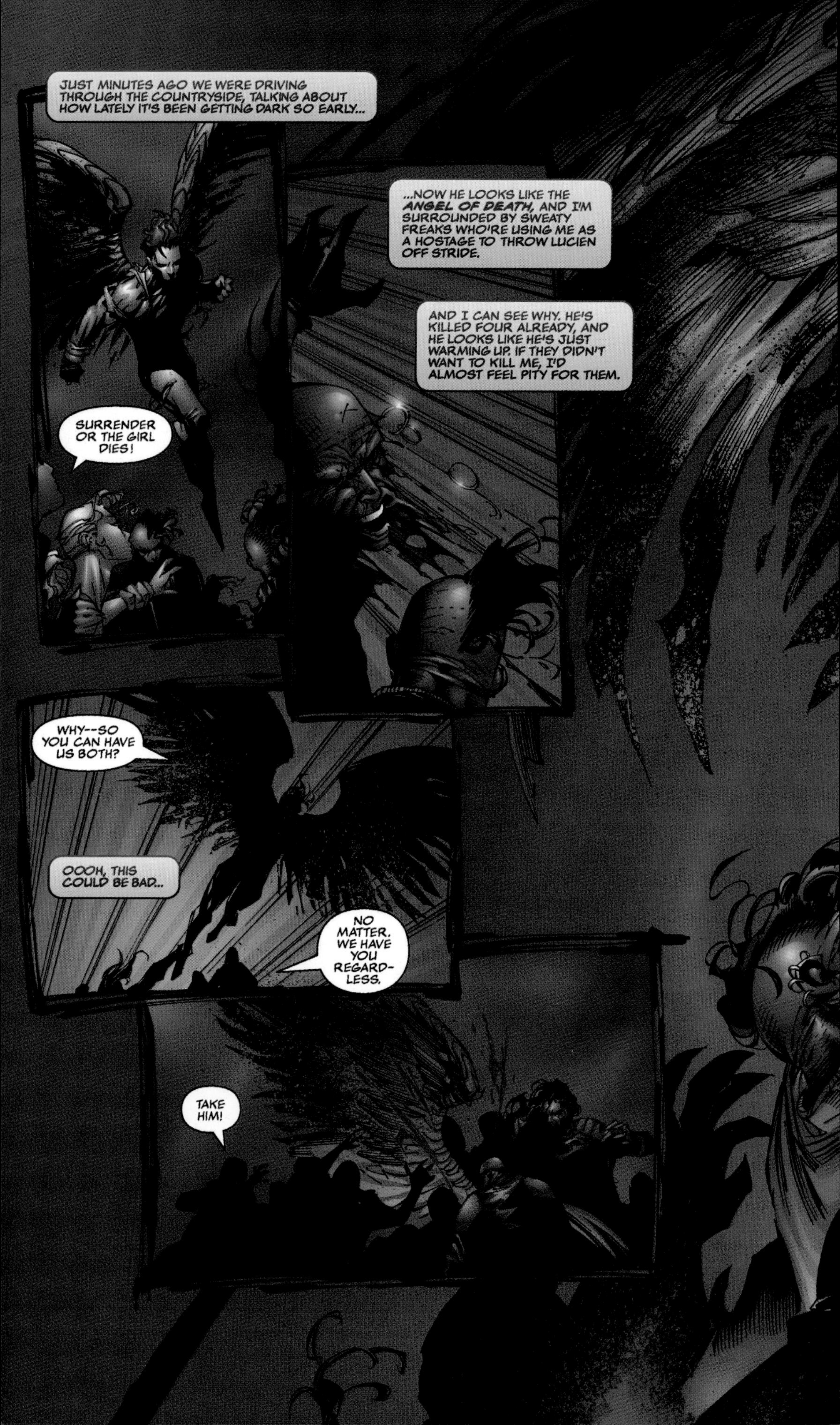
JUST MINUTES AGO WE WERE DRIVING THROUGH THE COUNTRYSIDE, TALKING ABOUT HOW LATELY IT'S BEEN GETTING DARK SO EARLY...
...NOW HE LOOKS LIKE THE ANGEL OF DEATH, AND I'M SURROUNDED BY SWEATY FREAKS WHO'RE USING ME AS A HOSTAGE TO THROW LUCIEN OFF STRIDE.
AND I CAN SEE WHY. HE'S KILLED FOUR ALREADY, AND HE LOOKS LIKE HE'S JUST WARMING UP. IF THEY DIDN'T WANT TO KILL ME, I'D ALMOST FEEL PITY FOR THEM.
SURRENDER OR THE GIRL DIES!
WHY--SO YOU CAN HAVE US BOTH?
OOOH, THIS COULD BE BAD...
NO MATTER. WE HAVE YOU REGARDLESS.
TAKE HIM!

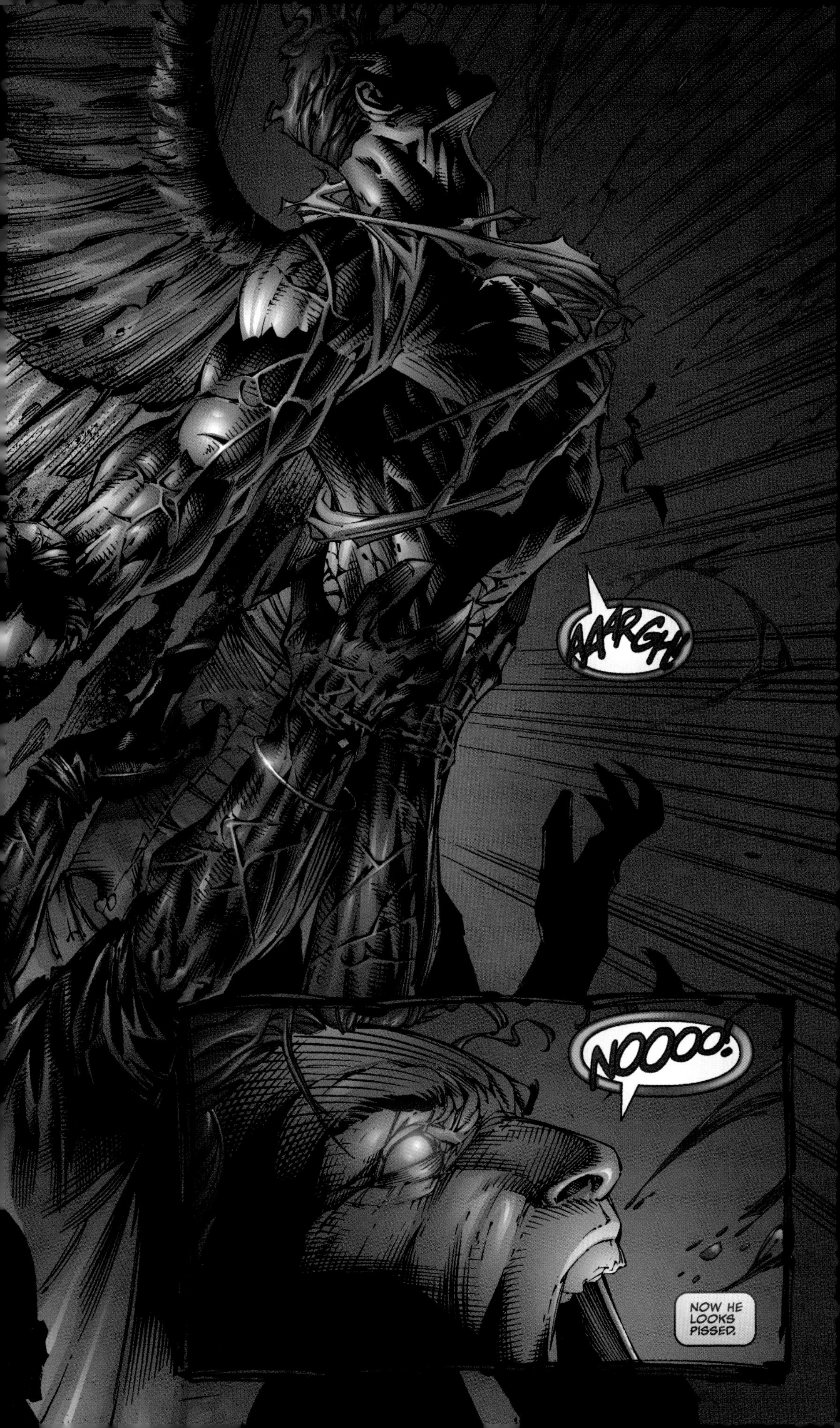
AAARGH!
NOOOO!
NOW HE LOOKS PISSED.

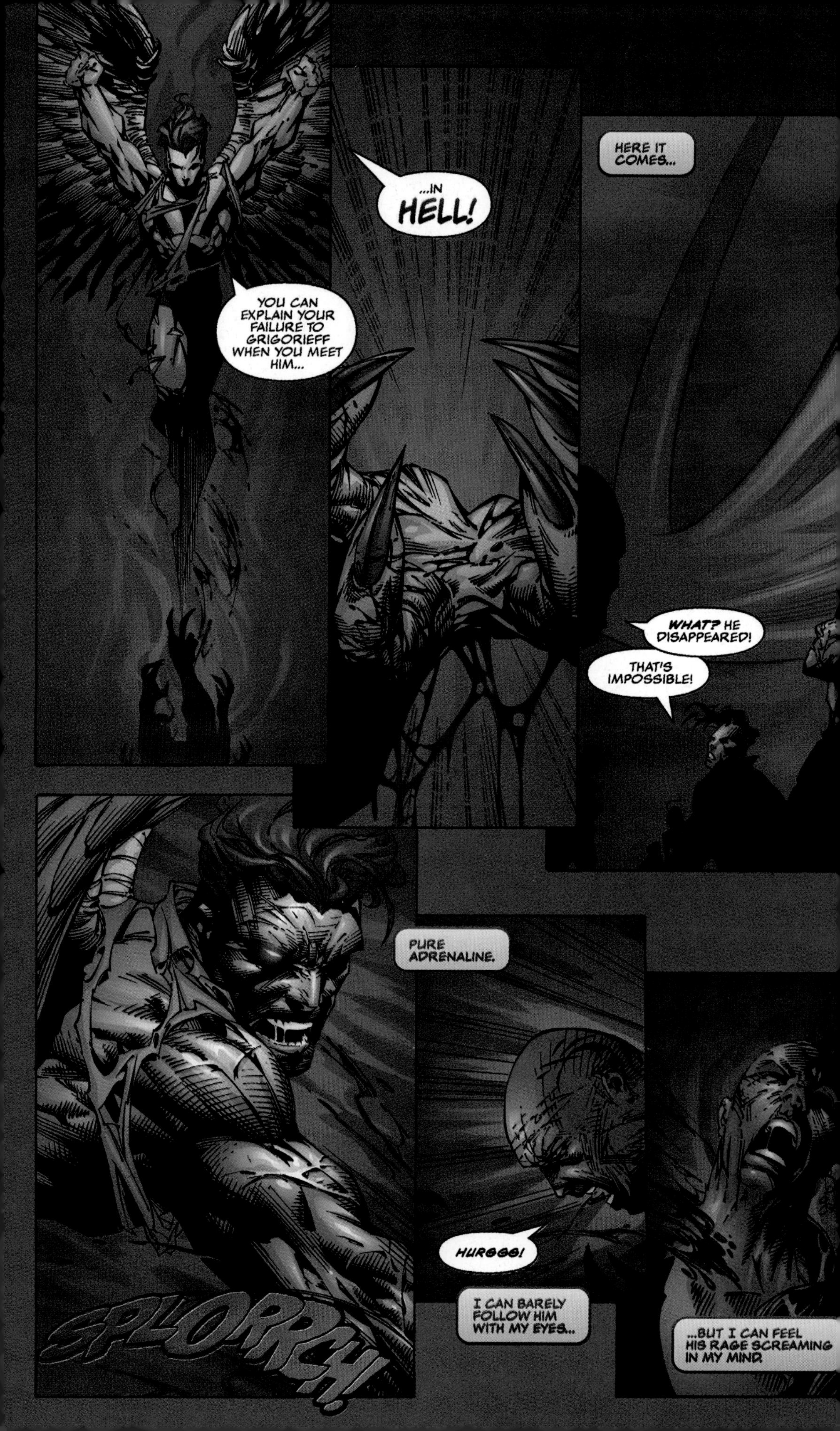
YOU CAN EXPLAIN YOUR FAILURE TO GRIGORIEFF WHEN YOU MEET HIM...
...IN HELL!
HERE IT COMES...
WHAT? HE DISAPPEARED!
THAT'S IMPOSSIBLE!
PURE ADRENALINE.
SPLORRCH!
HURGGG!
I CAN BARELY FOLLOW HIM WITH MY EYES...
...BUT I CAN FEEL HIS RAGE SCREAMING IN MY MIND.

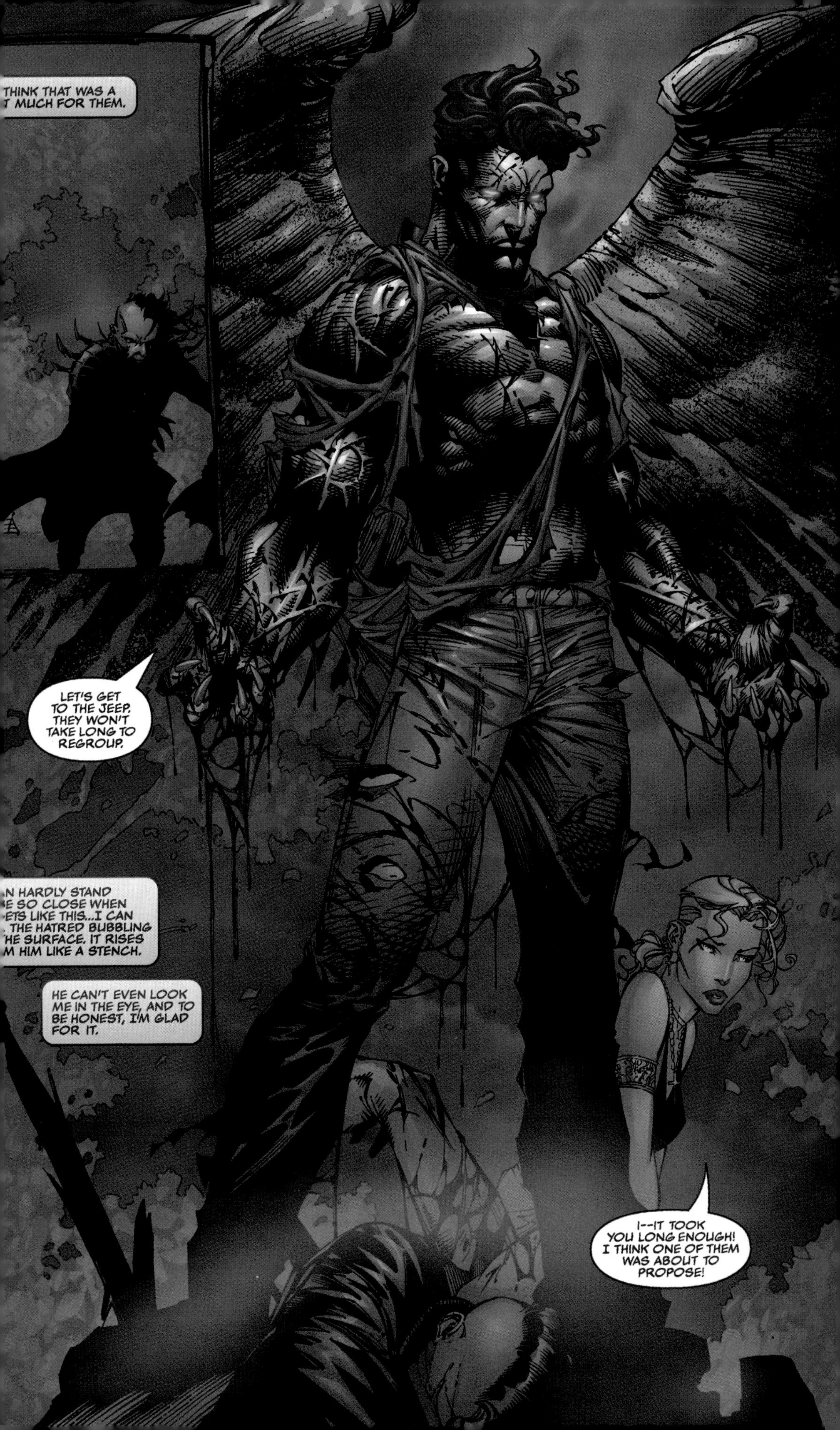
THINK THAT WAS A T MUCH FOR THEM.
LET'S GET TO THE JEEP. THEY WON'T TAKE LONG TO REGROUP.
N HARDLY STAND E SO CLOSE WHEN ETS LIKE THIS...I CAN THE HATRED BUBBLING THE SURFACE. IT RISES M HIM LIKE A STENCH.
HE CAN'T EVEN LOOK ME IN THE EYE, AND TO BE HONEST, I'M GLAD FOR IT.
I--IT TOOK YOU LONG ENOUGH! I THINK ONE OF THEM WAS ABOUT TO PROPOSE!

AS BAD AS IT LOOKS WHEN HE UNMANIFESTS HIS WINGS, THE PAIN I FEEL FROM HIM IS SO MUCH WORSE.
AARRRGGGG!
THERE'S NO TIME TO WASTE; COME ON.
THE PRICE I PAY FOR BEING AN EMPATH, I GUESS...
GRIGORIEFF IS ON US WHEREVER WE HIDE. WHY CAN'T HE LEAVE IT ALONE?

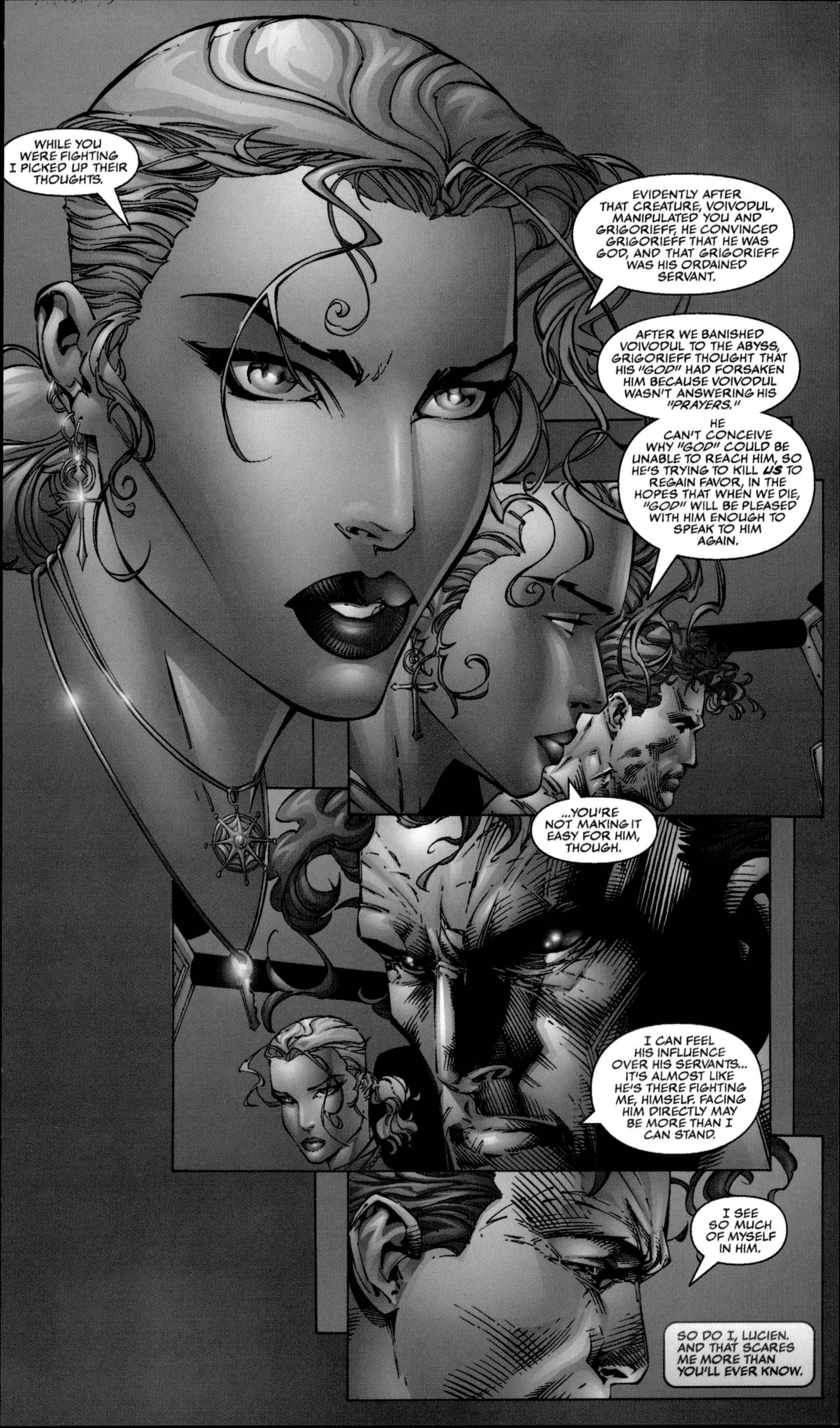
WHILE YOU WERE FIGHTING I PICKED UP THEIR THOUGHTS.
EVIDENTLY AFTER THAT CREATURE, VOIVODUL, MANIPULATED YOU AND GRIGORIEFF, HE CONVINCED GRIGORIEFF THAT HE WAS GOD, AND THAT GRIGORIEFF WAS HIS ORDAINED SERVANT.
AFTER WE BANISHED VOIVODUL TO THE ABYSS, GRIGORIEFF THOUGHT THAT HIS "GOD" HAD FORSAKEN HIM BECAUSE VOIVODUL WASN'T ANSWERING HIS "PRAYERS."
HE CAN'T CONCEIVE WHY "GOD" COULD BE UNABLE TO REACH HIM, SO HE'S TRYING TO KILL US TO REGAIN FAVOR, IN THE HOPES THAT WHEN WE DIE, "GOD" WILL BE PLEASED WITH HIM ENOUGH TO SPEAK TO HIM AGAIN.
...YOU'RE NOT MAKING IT EASY FOR HIM, THOUGH.
I CAN FEEL HIS INFLUENCE OVER HIS SERVANTS... IT'S ALMOST LIKE HE'S THERE FIGHTING ME, HIMSELF. FACING HIM DIRECTLY MAY BE MORE THAN I CAN STAND.
I SEE SO MUCH OF MYSELF IN HIM.
SO DO I, LUCIEN. AND THAT SCARES ME MORE THAN YOU'LL EVER KNOW.

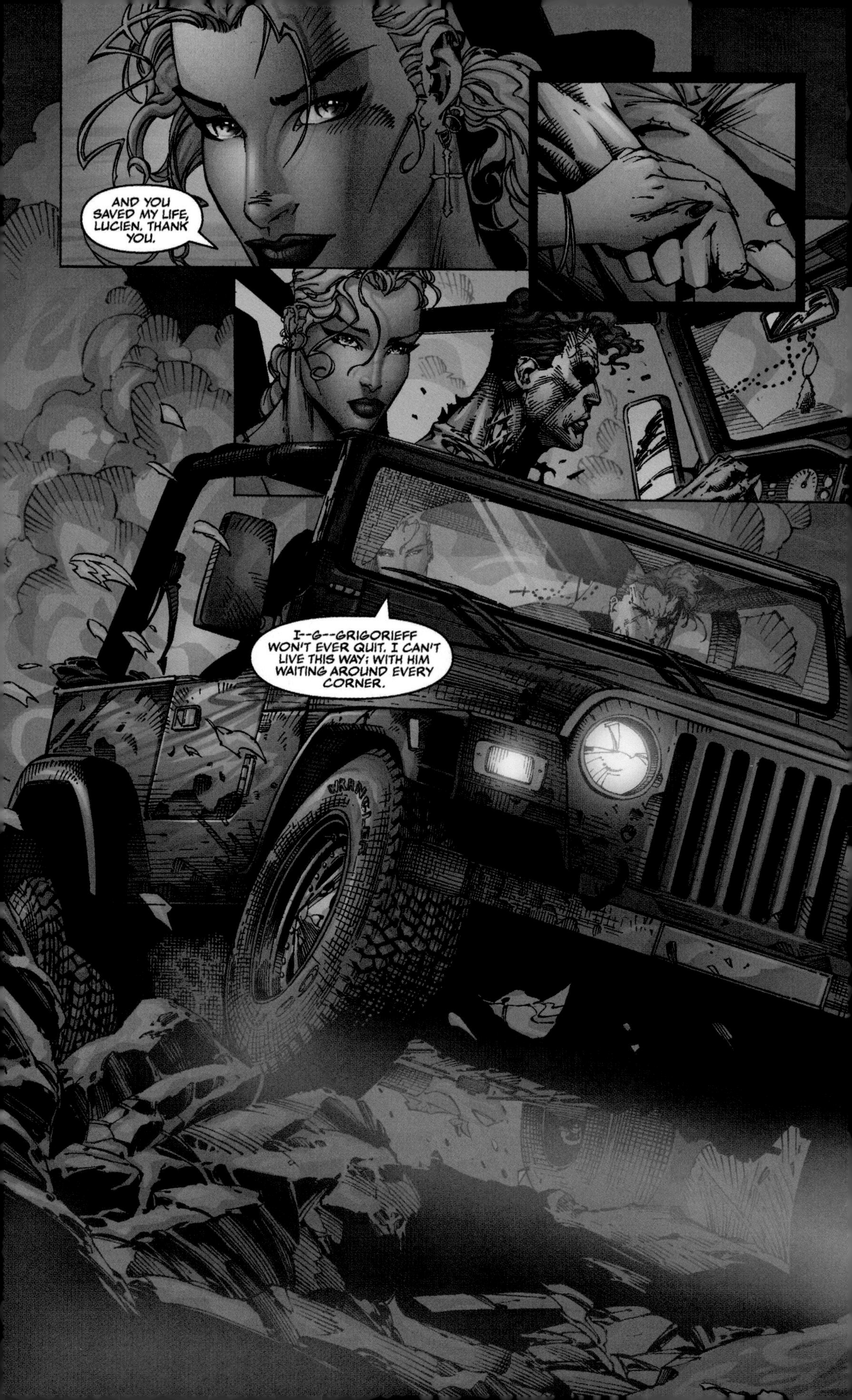
AND YOU SAVED MY LIFE, LUCIEN. THANK YOU.
I--G--GRIGORIEFF WON'T EVER QUIT. I CAN'T LIVE THIS WAY; WITH HIM WAITING AROUND EVERY CORNER.

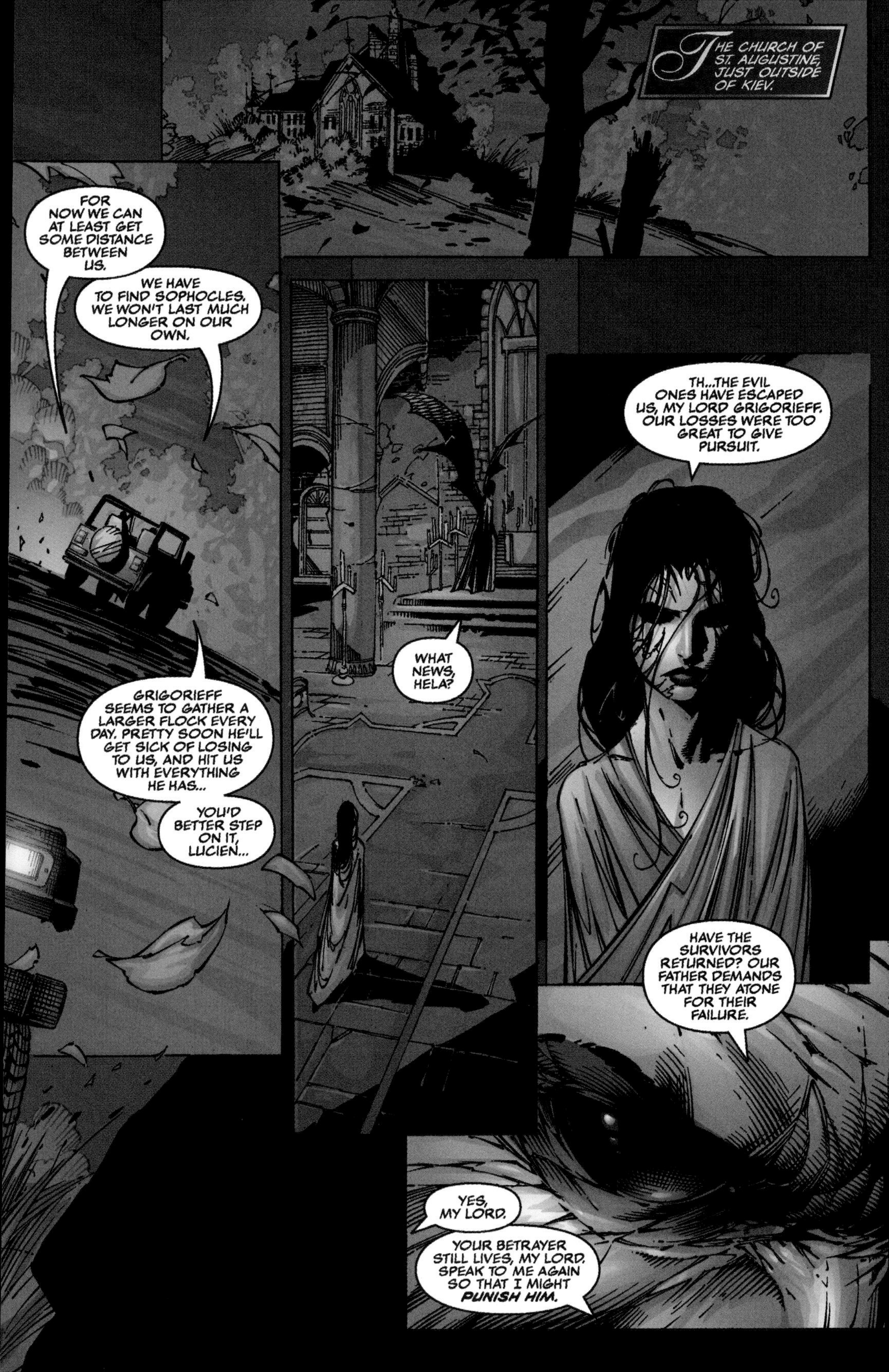
THE CHURCH OF ST. AUGUSTINE, JUST OUTSIDE OF KIEV.
FOR NOW WE CAN AT LEAST GET SOME DISTANCE BETWEEN US.
WE HAVE TO FIND SOPHOCLES. WE WON'T LAST MUCH LONGER ON OUR OWN.
GRIGORIEFF SEEMS TO GATHER A LARGER FLOCK EVERY DAY. PRETTY SOON HE'LL GET SICK OF LOSING TO US, AND HIT US WITH EVERYTHING HE HAS...
YOU'D BETTER STEP ON IT, LUCIEN...
WHAT NEWS, HELA?
TH...THE EVIL ONES HAVE ESCAPED US, MY LORD GRIGORIEFF. OUR LOSSES WERE TOO GREAT TO GIVE PURSUIT.
HAVE THE SURVIVORS RETURNED? OUR FATHER DEMANDS THAT THEY ATONE FOR THEIR FAILURE.
YES, MY LORD.
YOUR BETRAYER STILL LIVES, MY LORD. SPEAK TO ME AGAIN SO THAT I MIGHT PUNISH HIM.

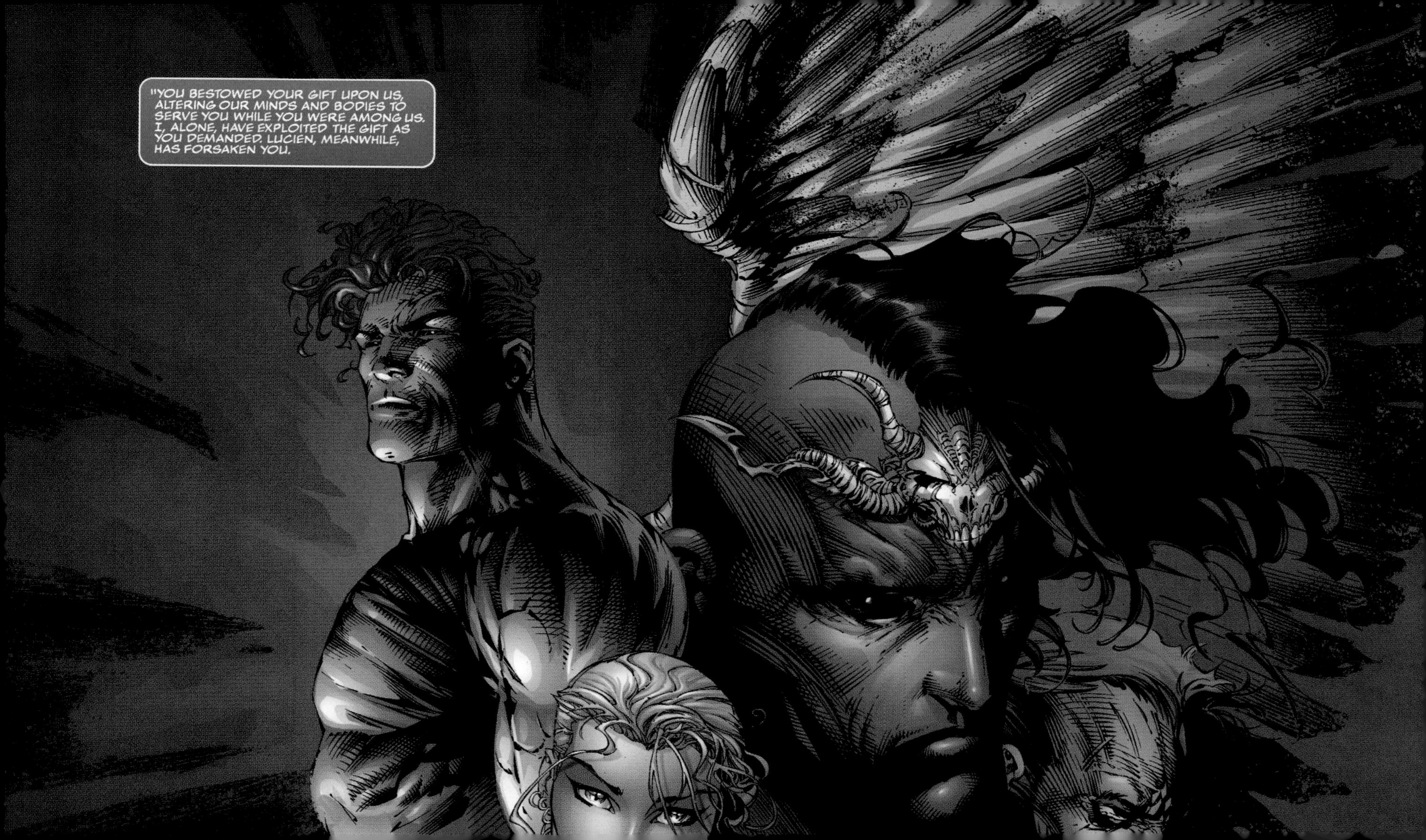
"YOU BESTOWED YOUR GIFT UPON US, ALTERING OUR MINDS AND BODIES TO SERVE YOU WHILE YOU WERE AMONG US. I, ALONE, HAVE EXPLOITED THE GIFT AS YOU DEMANDED. LUCIEN, MEANWHILE, HAS FORSAKEN YOU.

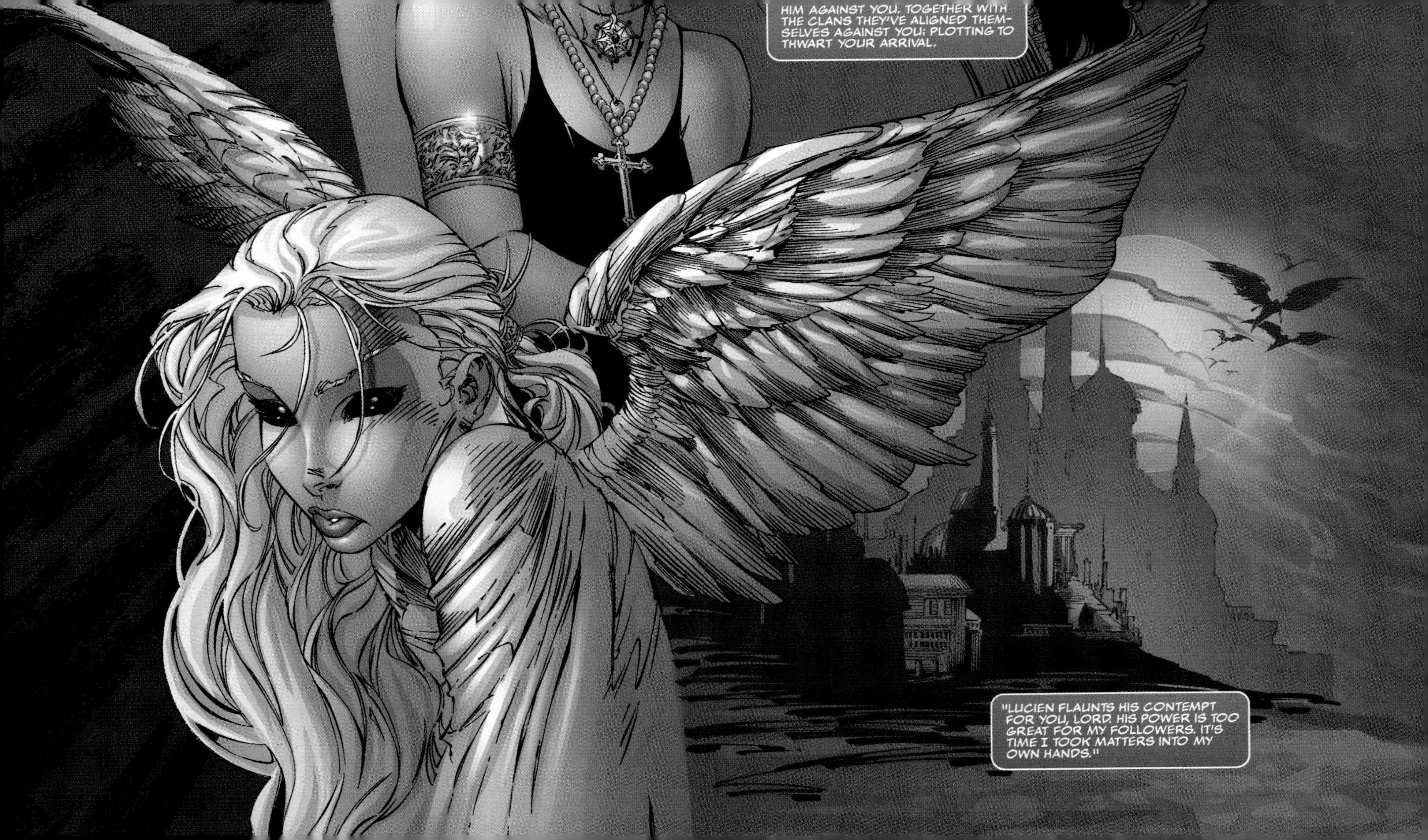
HIM AGAINST YOU. TOGETHER WITH THE CLANS THEY'VE ALIGNED THEM-SELVES AGAINST YOU; PLOTTING TO THWART YOUR ARRIVAL.
"LUCIEN FLAUNTS HIS CONTEMPT FOR YOU, LORD. HIS POWER IS TOO GREAT FOR MY FOLLOWERS. IT'S TIME I TOOK MATTERS INTO MY OWN HANDS."

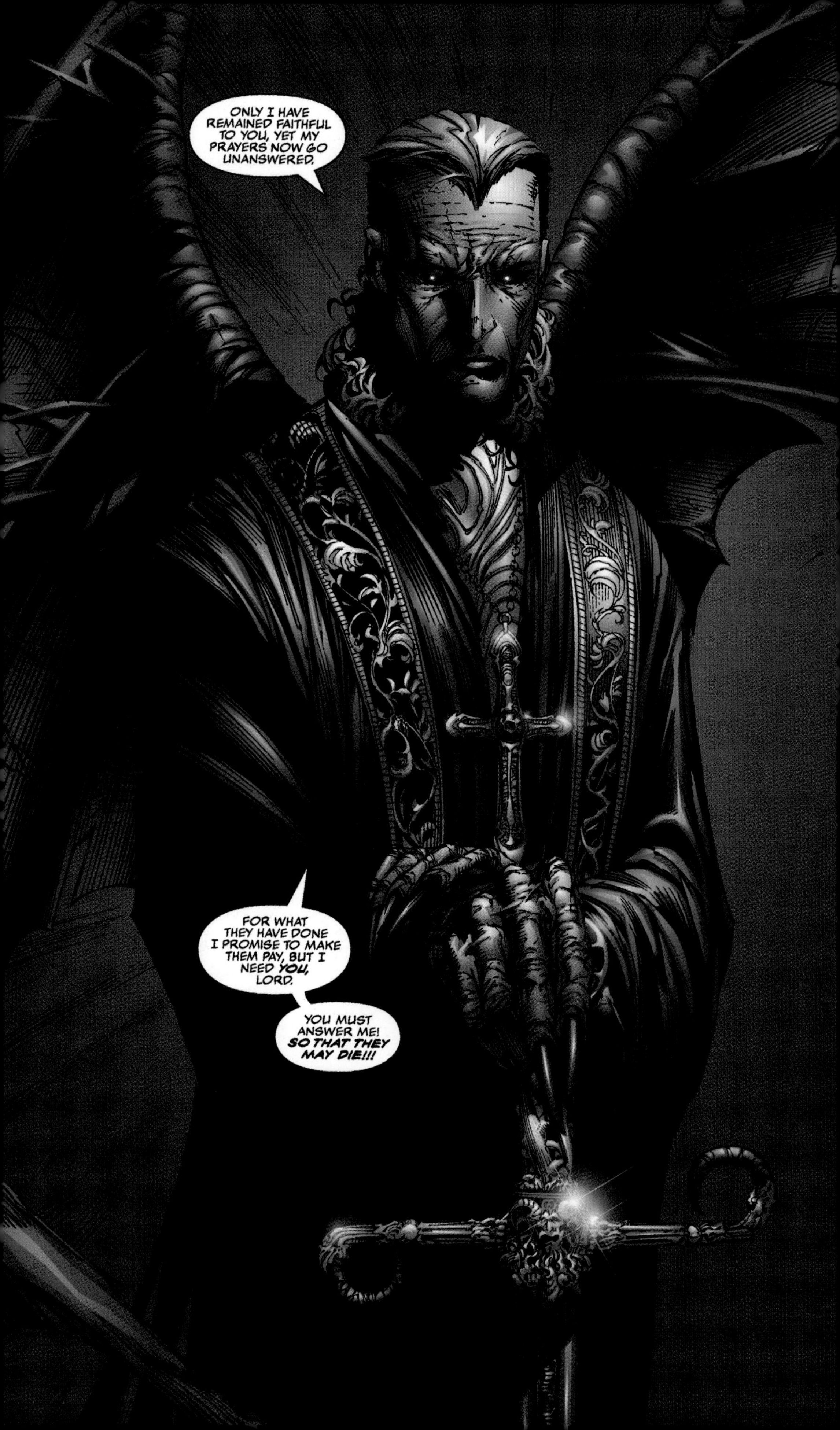
ONLY I HAVE REMAINED FAITHFUL TO YOU, YET MY PRAYERS NOW GO UNANSWERED.
FOR WHAT THEY HAVE DONE I PROMISE TO MAKE THEM PAY, BUT I NEED *YOU*, LORD.
YOU MUST ANSWER ME! ***SO THAT THEY MAY DIE!!!***

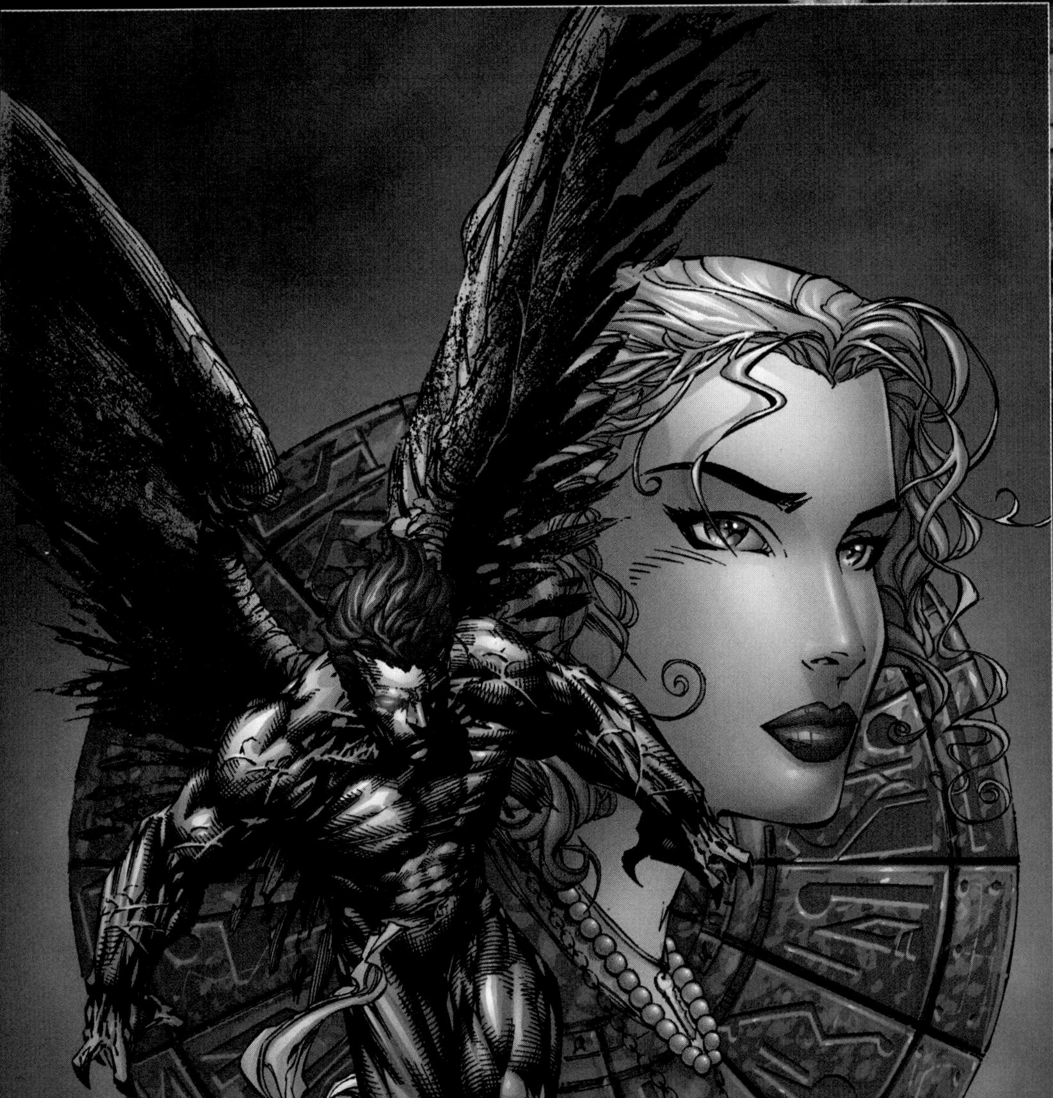
FINCH
BATT
LUSEN
LICHTNER

Ascension Preview edition cover
art by: **Dave Finch, Matt "Batt" Banning, Christian Lichtner** and **Aron Lusen**

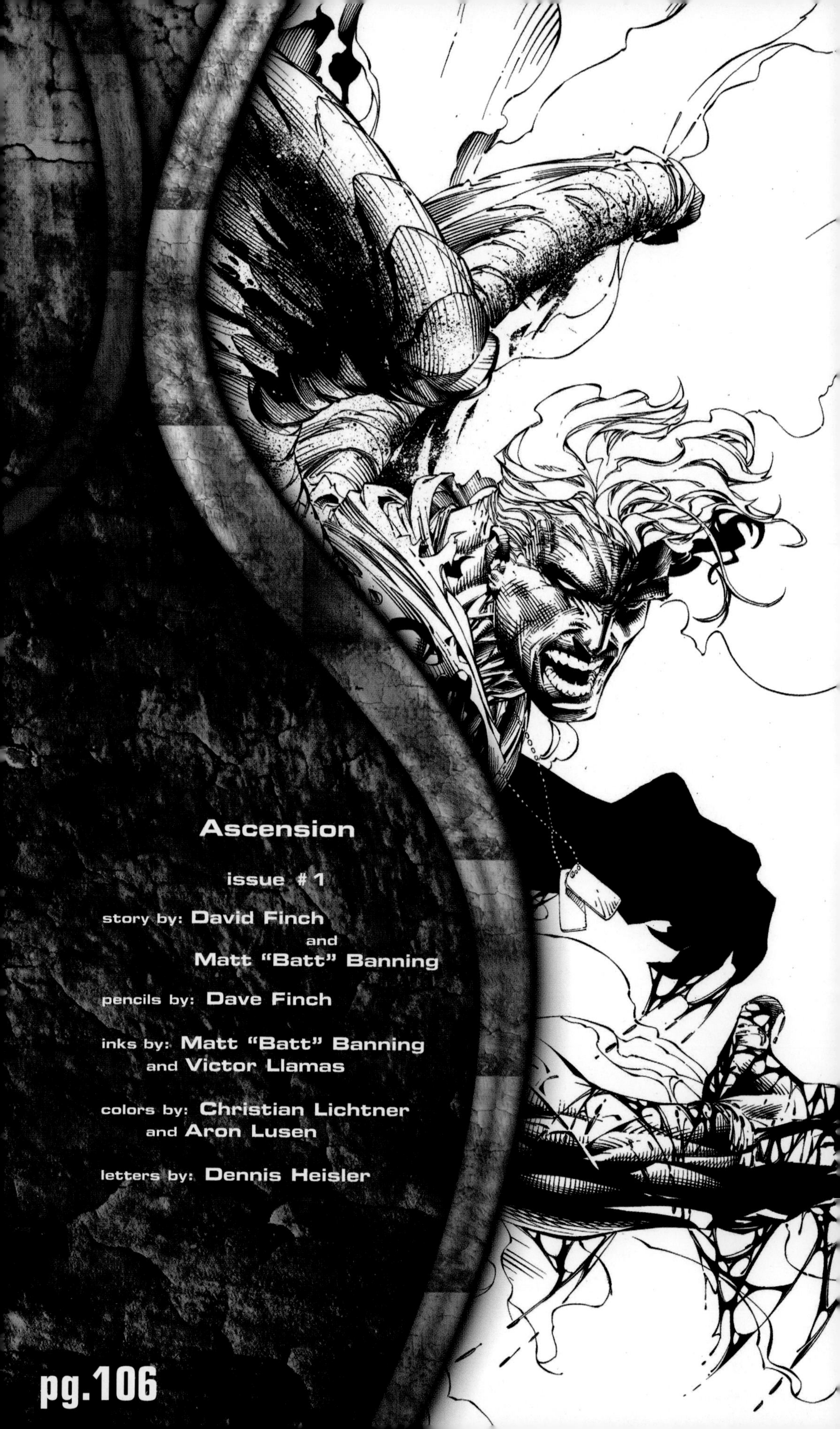

Ascension

issue #1

story by: David Finch
and
Matt "Batt" Banning

pencils by: Dave Finch

inks by: Matt "Batt" Banning
and Victor Llamas

colors by: Christian Lichtner
and Aron Lusen

letters by: Dennis Heisler

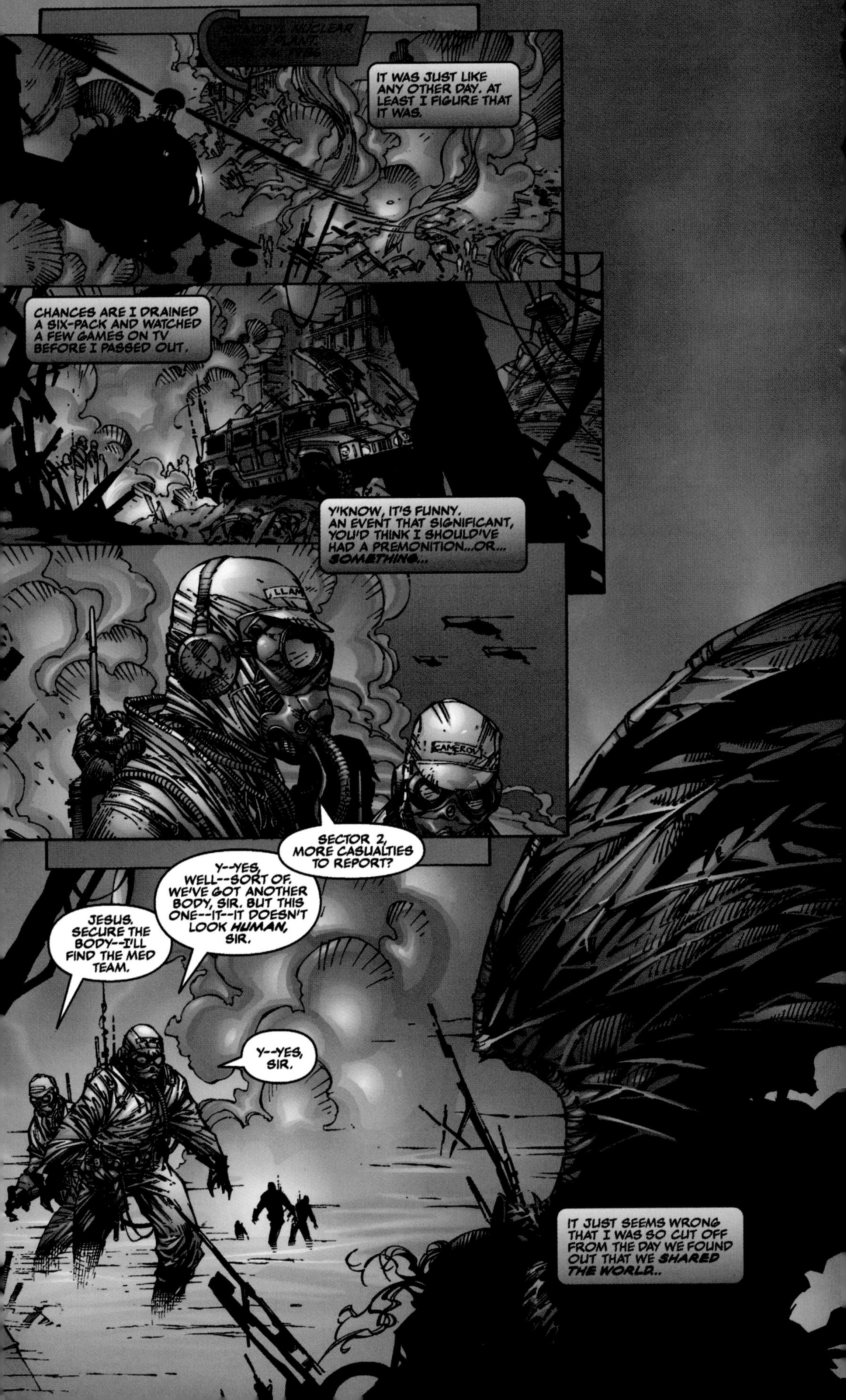
IT WAS JUST LIKE ANY OTHER DAY. AT LEAST I FIGURE THAT IT WAS.
CHANCES ARE I DRAINED A SIX-PACK AND WATCHED A FEW GAMES ON TV BEFORE I PASSED OUT.
Y'KNOW, IT'S FUNNY. AN EVENT THAT SIGNIFICANT, YOU'D THINK I SHOULD'VE HAD A PREMONITION...OR... SOMETHING...
SECTOR 2, MORE CASUALTIES TO REPORT?
Y--YES, WELL--SORT OF. WE'VE GOT ANOTHER BODY, SIR. BUT THIS ONE--IT--IT DOESN'T LOOK HUMAN, SIR.
JESUS. SECURE THE BODY--I'LL FIND THE MED TEAM.
Y--YES, SIR.
IT JUST SEEMS WRONG THAT I WAS SO CUT OFF FROM THE DAY WE FOUND OUT THAT WE SHARED THE WORLD...

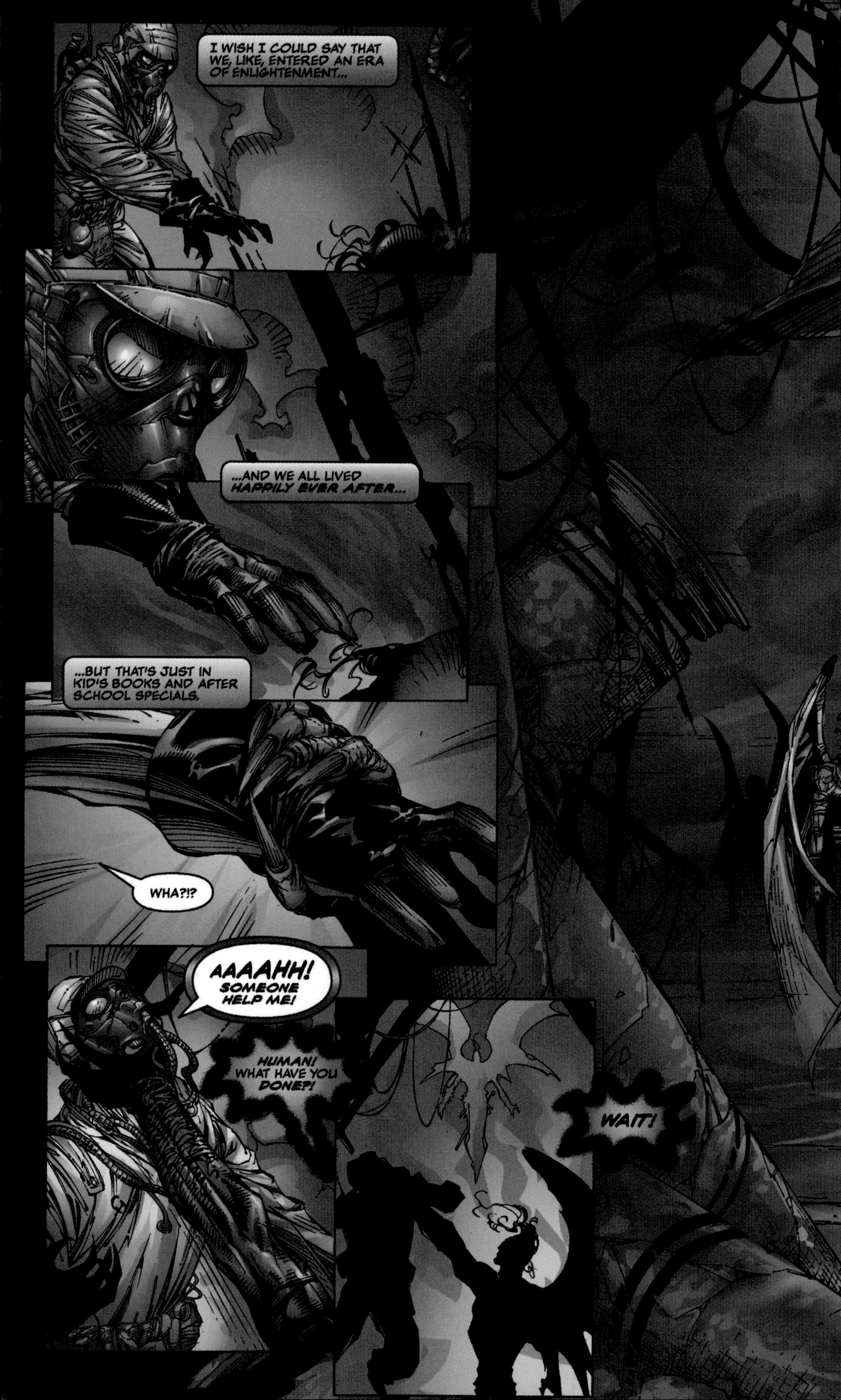
I WISH I COULD SAY THAT WE, LIKE, ENTERED AN ERA OF ENLIGHTENMENT...
...AND WE ALL LIVED HAPPILY EVER AFTER...
...BUT THAT'S JUST IN KID'S BOOKS AND AFTER SCHOOL SPECIALS.
WHA?!?
AAAAHH! SOMEONE HELP ME!
HUMAN! WHAT HAVE YOU DONE?!
WAIT!

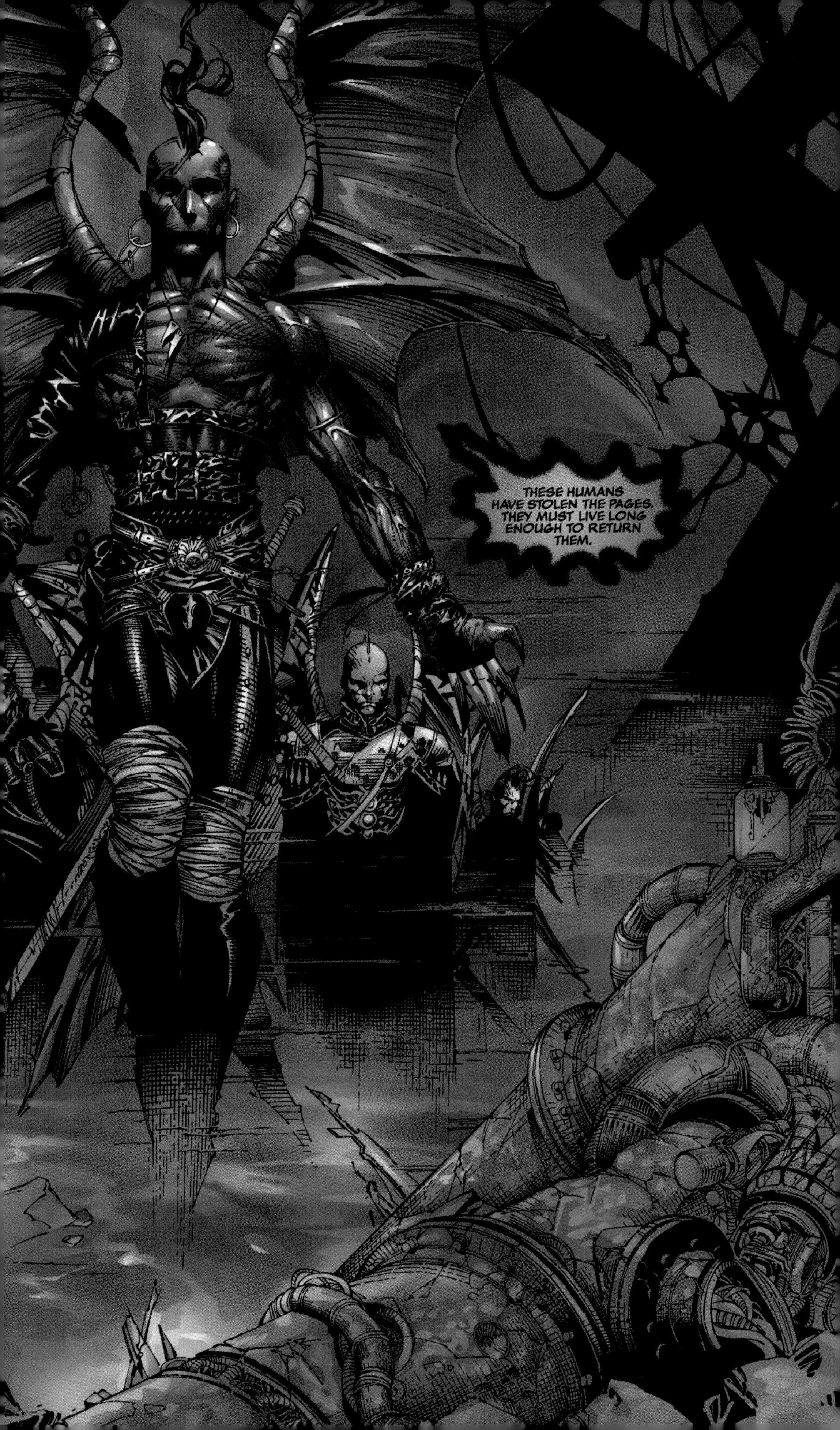
THESE HUMANS HAVE STOLEN THE PAGES. THEY MUST LIVE LONG ENOUGH TO RETURN THEM.

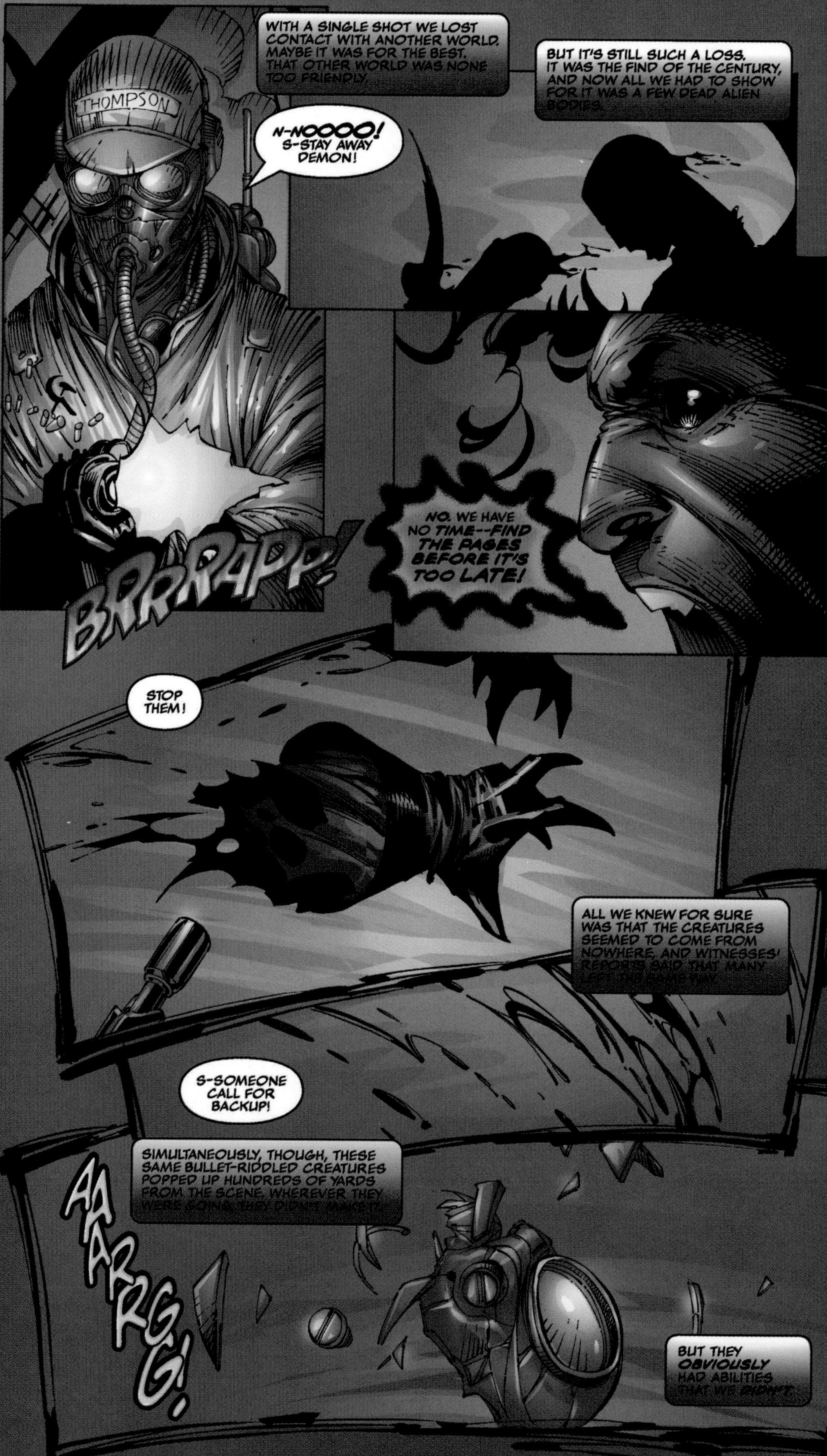
WITH A SINGLE SHOT WE LOST CONTACT WITH ANOTHER WORLD. MAYBE IT WAS FOR THE BEST. THAT OTHER WORLD WAS NONE TOO FRIENDLY.
BUT IT'S STILL SUCH A LOSS. IT WAS THE FIND OF THE CENTURY, AND NOW ALL WE HAD TO SHOW FOR IT WAS A FEW DEAD ALIEN BODIES.
THOMPSON
N-NOOOO! S-STAY AWAY DEMON!
BRRRAPP!
NO. WE HAVE NO *TIME*--FIND THE PAGES BEFORE IT'S TOO LATE!
STOP THEM!
ALL WE KNEW FOR SURE WAS THAT THE CREATURES SEEMED TO COME FROM NOWHERE, AND WITNESSES' REPORTS SAID THAT MANY
S-SOMEONE CALL FOR BACKUP!
SIMULTANEOUSLY, THOUGH, THESE SAME BULLET-RIDDLED CREATURES POPPED UP HUNDREDS OF YARDS FROM THE SCENE. WHEREVER THEY
AAARRGG!
BUT THEY *OBVIOUSLY* HAD ABILITIES THAT WE *DIDN'T*.

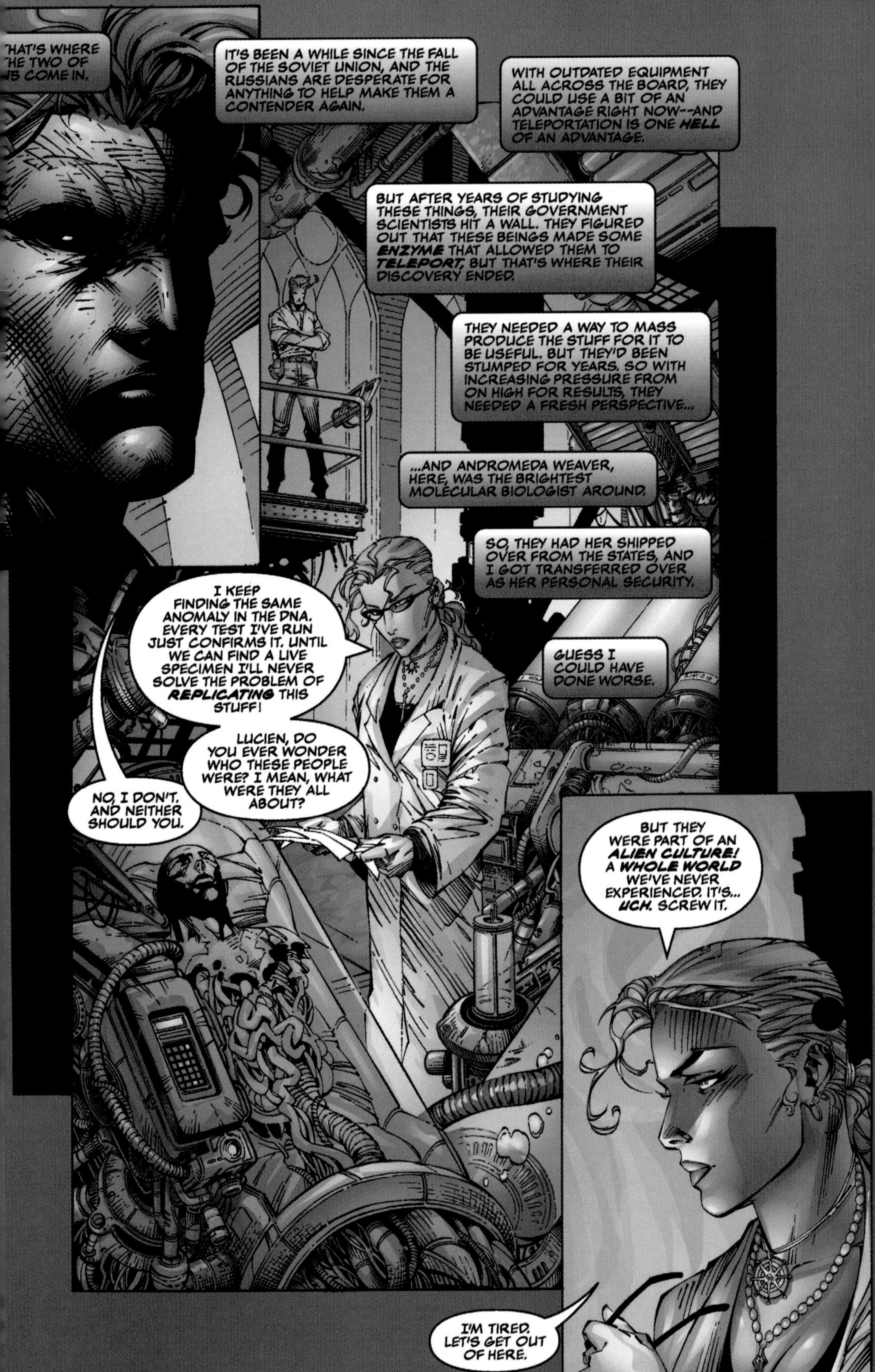

THAT'S WHERE THE TWO OF US COME IN.
IT'S BEEN A WHILE SINCE THE FALL OF THE SOVIET UNION, AND THE RUSSIANS ARE DESPERATE FOR ANYTHING TO HELP MAKE THEM A CONTENDER AGAIN.
WITH OUTDATED EQUIPMENT ALL ACROSS THE BOARD, THEY COULD USE A BIT OF AN ADVANTAGE RIGHT NOW--AND TELEPORTATION IS ONE HELL OF AN ADVANTAGE.
BUT AFTER YEARS OF STUDYING THESE THINGS, THEIR GOVERNMENT SCIENTISTS HIT A WALL. THEY FIGURED OUT THAT THESE BEINGS MADE SOME ENZYME THAT ALLOWED THEM TO TELEPORT, BUT THAT'S WHERE THEIR DISCOVERY ENDED.
THEY NEEDED A WAY TO MASS PRODUCE THE STUFF FOR IT TO BE USEFUL. BUT THEY'D BEEN STUMPED FOR YEARS. SO WITH INCREASING PRESSURE FROM ON HIGH FOR RESULTS, THEY NEEDED A FRESH PERSPECTIVE...
...AND ANDROMEDA WEAVER, HERE, WAS THE BRIGHTEST MOLECULAR BIOLOGIST AROUND.
SO, THEY HAD HER SHIPPED OVER FROM THE STATES, AND I GOT TRANSFERRED OVER AS HER PERSONAL SECURITY.
GUESS I COULD HAVE DONE WORSE.
I KEEP FINDING THE SAME ANOMALY IN THE DNA. EVERY TEST I'VE RUN JUST CONFIRMS IT. UNTIL WE CAN FIND A LIVE SPECIMEN I'LL NEVER SOLVE THE PROBLEM OF REPLICATING THIS STUFF!
LUCIEN, DO YOU EVER WONDER WHO THESE PEOPLE WERE? I MEAN, WHAT WERE THEY ALL ABOUT?
NO, I DON'T. AND NEITHER SHOULD YOU.
BUT THEY WERE PART OF AN ALIEN CULTURE! A WHOLE WORLD WE'VE NEVER EXPERIENCED. IT'S... UGH. SCREW IT.
I'M TIRED. LET'S GET OUT OF HERE.

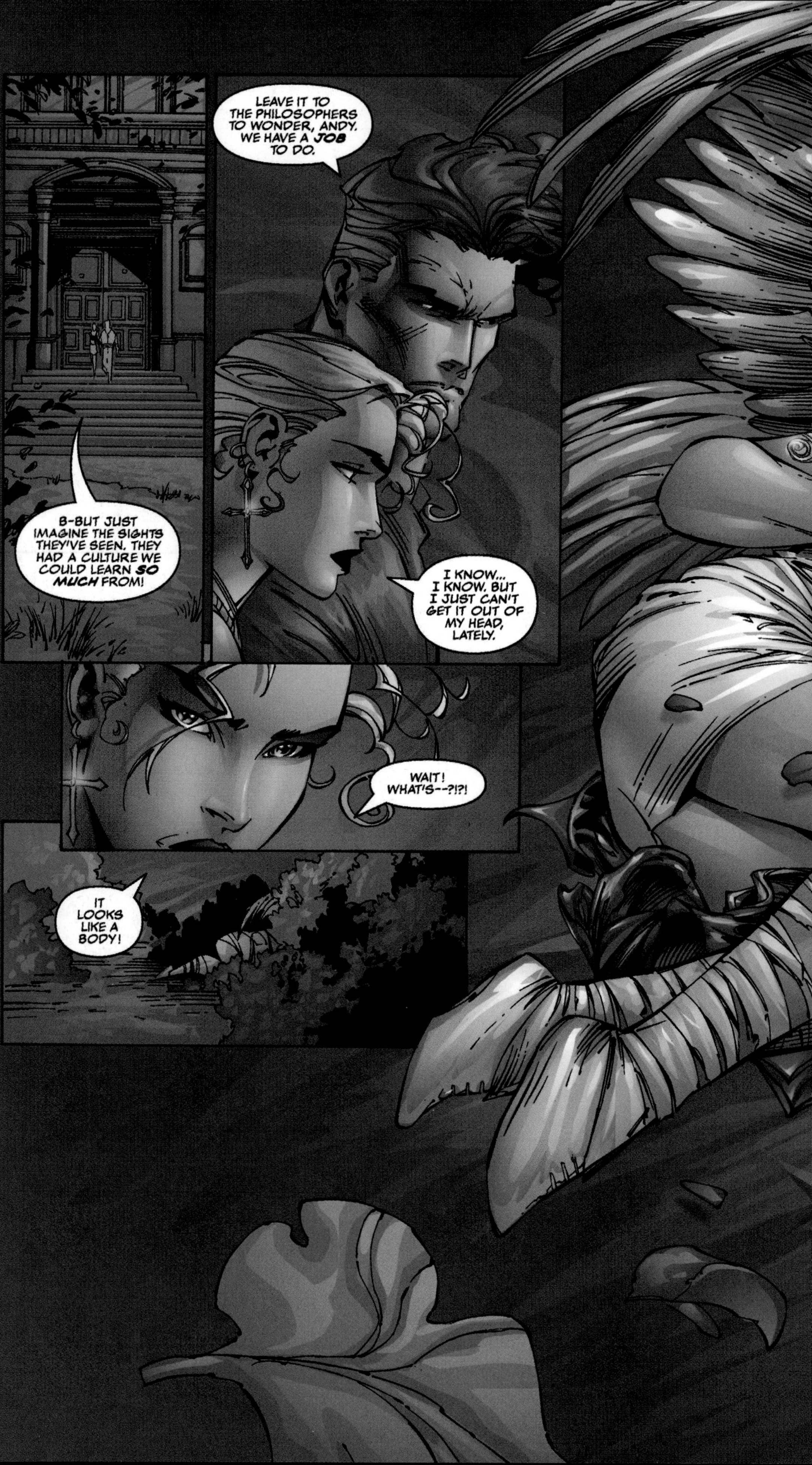

B-BUT JUST IMAGINE THE SIGHTS THEY'VE SEEN. THEY HAD A CULTURE WE COULD LEARN **SO MUCH** FROM!
LEAVE IT TO THE PHILOSOPHERS TO WONDER, ANDY. WE HAVE A **JOB** TO DO.
I KNOW... I KNOW. BUT I JUST CAN'T GET IT OUT OF MY HEAD, LATELY.
WAIT! WHAT'S--?!?!
IT LOOKS LIKE A BODY!

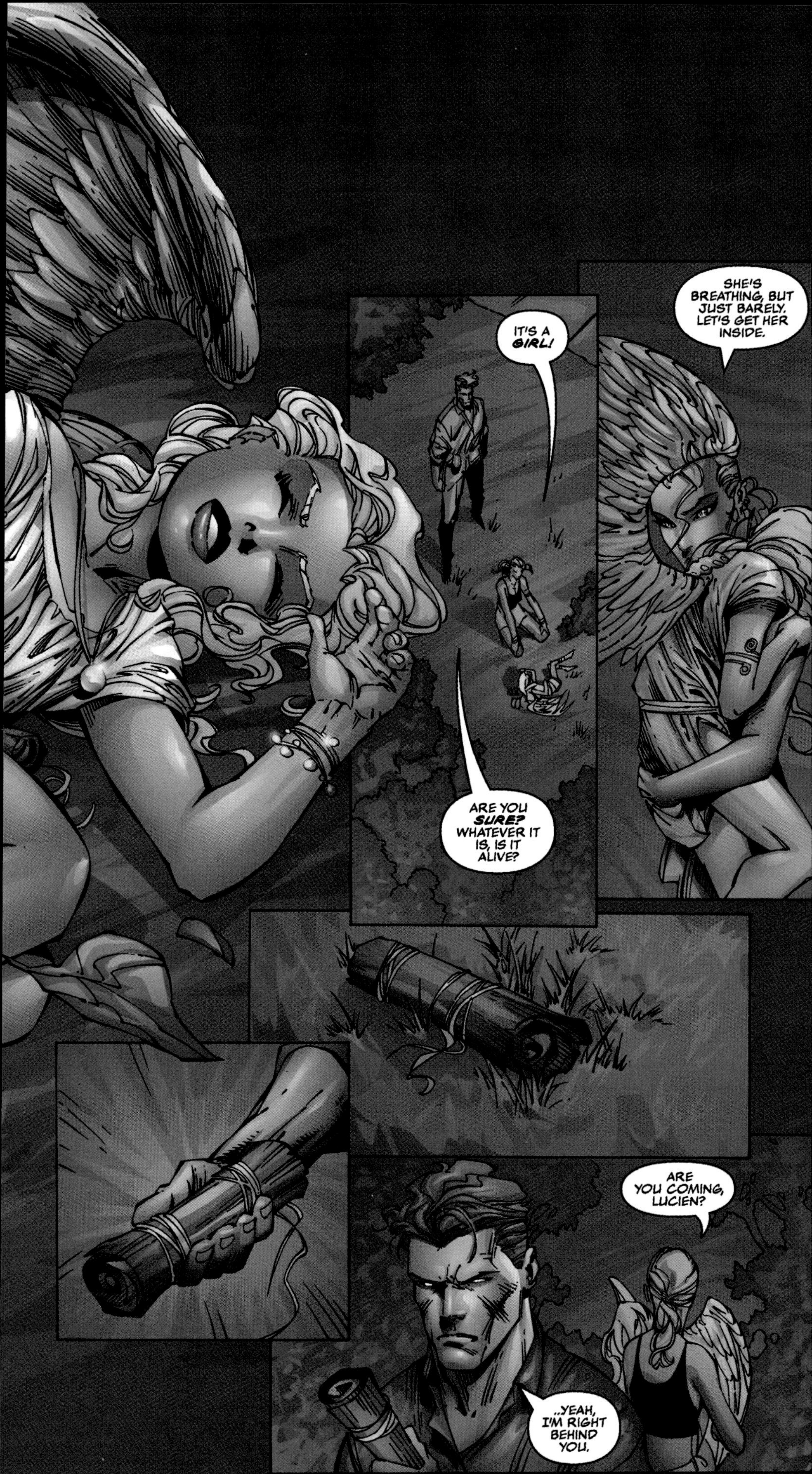

IT'S A GIRL!
ARE YOU SURE? WHATEVER IT IS, IS IT ALIVE?
SHE'S BREATHING, BUT JUST BARELY. LET'S GET HER INSIDE.
ARE YOU COMING, LUCIEN?
..YEAH, I'M RIGHT BEHIND YOU.

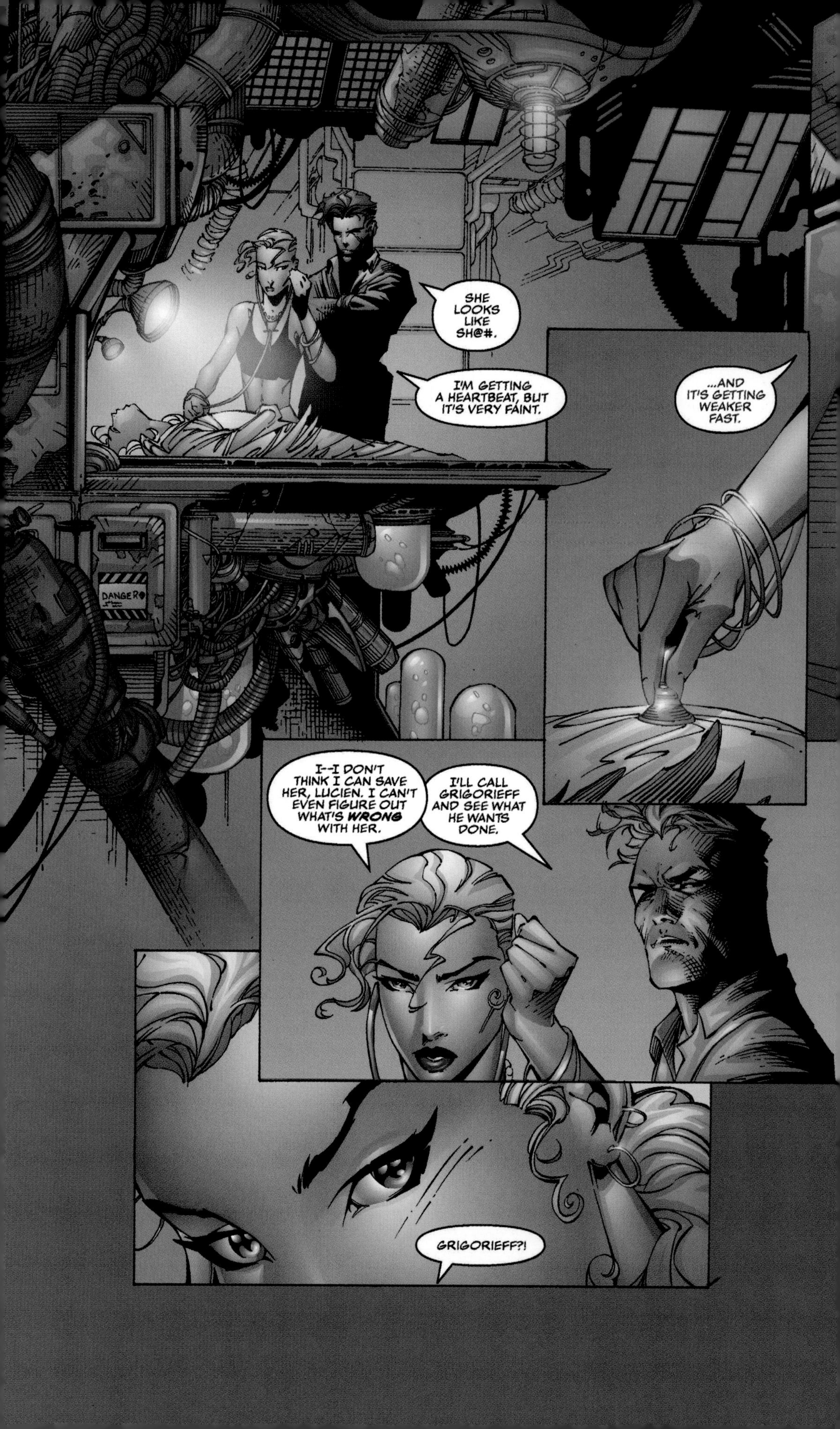
SHE LOOKS LIKE SH@#.
I'M GETTING A HEARTBEAT, BUT IT'S VERY FAINT.
...AND IT'S GETTING WEAKER FAST.
DANGER
I--I DON'T THINK I CAN SAVE HER, LUCIEN. I CAN'T EVEN FIGURE OUT WHAT'S **WRONG** WITH HER.
I'LL CALL GRIGORIEFF AND SEE WHAT HE WANTS DONE.
GRIGORIEFF?!

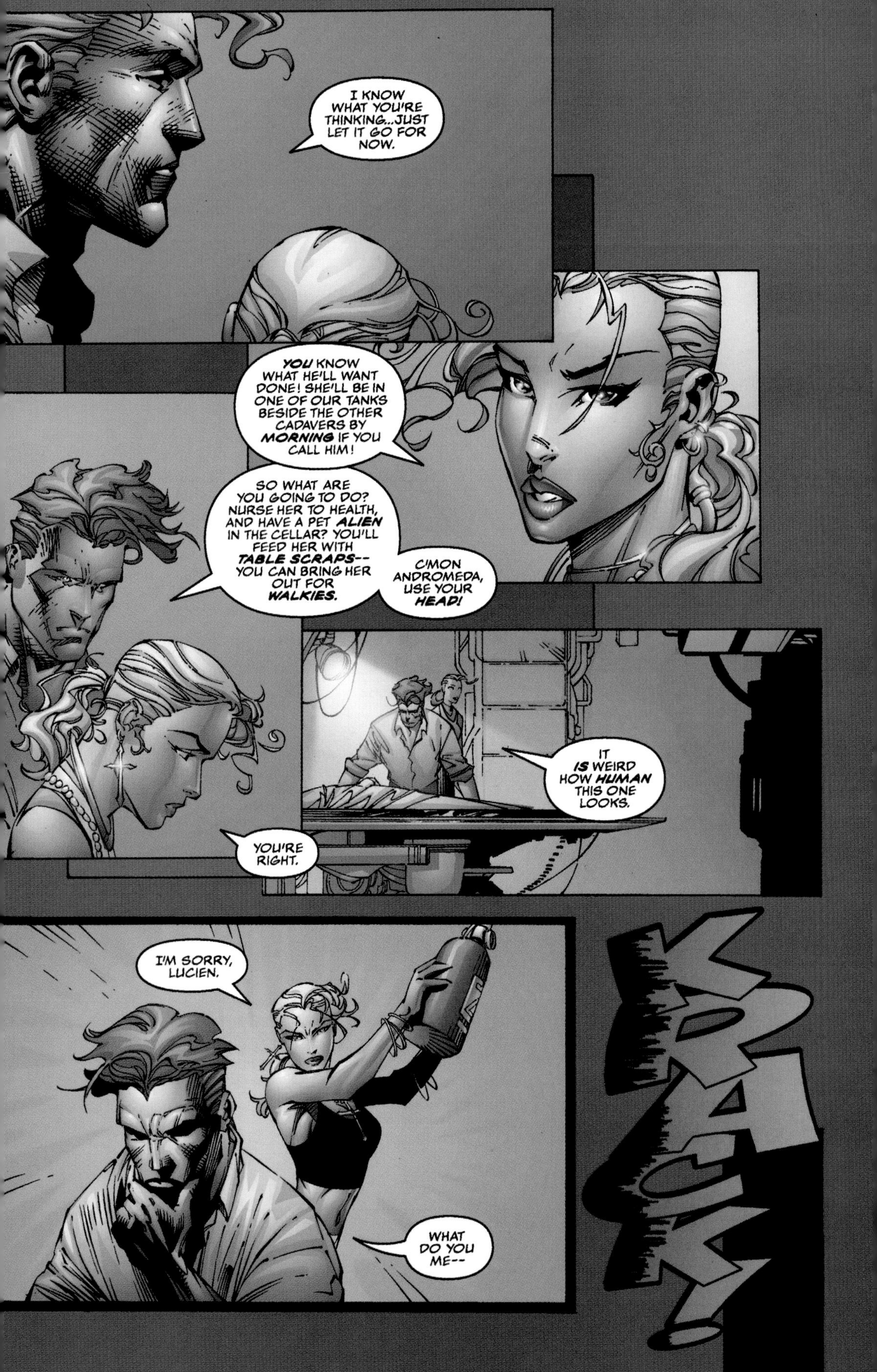
I KNOW WHAT YOU'RE THINKING...JUST LET IT GO FOR NOW.
YOU KNOW WHAT HE'LL WANT DONE! SHE'LL BE IN ONE OF OUR TANKS BESIDE THE OTHER CADAVERS BY MORNING IF YOU CALL HIM!
SO WHAT ARE YOU GOING TO DO? NURSE HER TO HEALTH, AND HAVE A PET ALIEN IN THE CELLAR? YOU'LL FEED HER WITH TABLE SCRAPS-- YOU CAN BRING HER OUT FOR WALKIES.
C'MON ANDROMEDA, USE YOUR HEAD!
YOU'RE RIGHT.
IT IS WEIRD HOW HUMAN THIS ONE LOOKS.
I'M SORRY, LUCIEN.
WHAT DO YOU ME--
KRACK

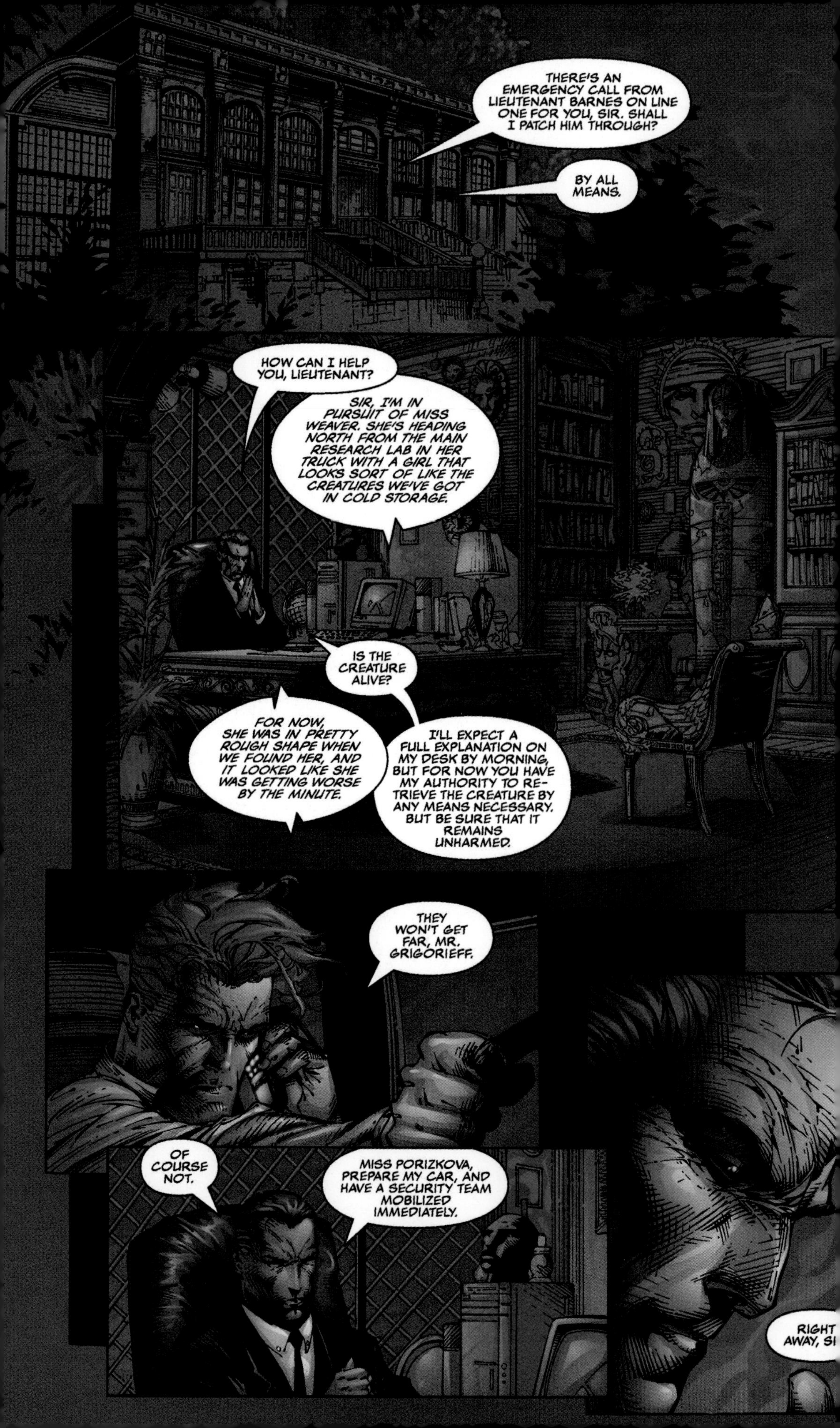
THERE'S AN EMERGENCY CALL FROM LIEUTENANT BARNES ON LINE ONE FOR YOU, SIR. SHALL I PATCH HIM THROUGH?
BY ALL MEANS.
HOW CAN I HELP YOU, LIEUTENANT?
SIR, I'M IN PURSUIT OF MISS WEAVER. SHE'S HEADING NORTH FROM THE MAIN RESEARCH LAB IN HER TRUCK WITH A GIRL THAT LOOKS SORT OF LIKE THE CREATURES WE'VE GOT IN COLD STORAGE.
IS THE CREATURE ALIVE?
FOR NOW, SHE WAS IN PRETTY ROUGH SHAPE WHEN WE FOUND HER, AND IT LOOKED LIKE SHE WAS GETTING WORSE BY THE MINUTE.
I'LL EXPECT A FULL EXPLANATION ON MY DESK BY MORNING, BUT FOR NOW YOU HAVE MY AUTHORITY TO RE-TRIEVE THE CREATURE BY ANY MEANS NECESSARY. BUT BE SURE THAT IT REMAINS UNHARMED.
THEY WON'T GET FAR, MR. GRIGORIEFF.
OF COURSE NOT.
MISS PORIZKOVA, PREPARE MY CAR, AND HAVE A SECURITY TEAM MOBILIZED IMMEDIATELY.
RIGHT AWAY, SI

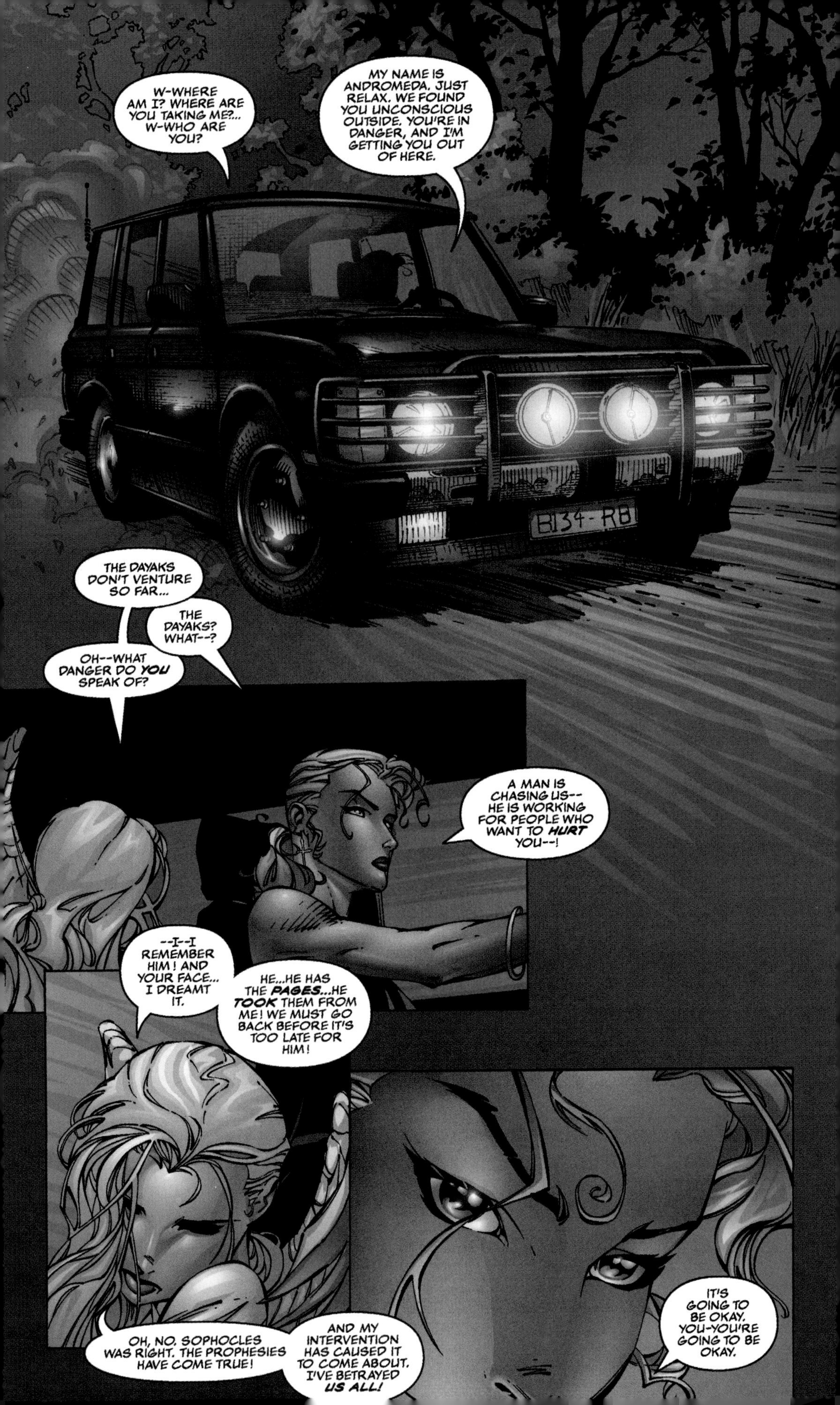
W-WHERE AM I? WHERE ARE YOU TAKING ME?... W-WHO ARE YOU?
MY NAME IS ANDROMEDA. JUST RELAX. WE FOUND YOU UNCONSCIOUS OUTSIDE. YOU'RE IN DANGER, AND I'M GETTING YOU OUT OF HERE.
B134-RB
THE DAYAKS DON'T VENTURE SO FAR...
THE DAYAKS? WHAT--?
OH--WHAT DANGER DO **YOU** SPEAK OF?
A MAN IS CHASING US-- HE IS WORKING FOR PEOPLE WHO WANT TO **HURT** YOU--!
--I--I REMEMBER HIM! AND YOUR FACE... I DREAMT IT.
HE...HE HAS THE **PAGES**...HE **TOOK** THEM FROM ME! WE MUST GO BACK BEFORE IT'S TOO LATE FOR HIM!
OH, NO. SOPHOCLES WAS RIGHT. THE PROPHESIES HAVE COME TRUE!
AND MY INTERVENTION HAS CAUSED IT TO COME ABOUT. I'VE BETRAYED **US ALL!**
IT'S GOING TO BE OKAY. YOU-YOU'RE GOING TO BE OKAY.

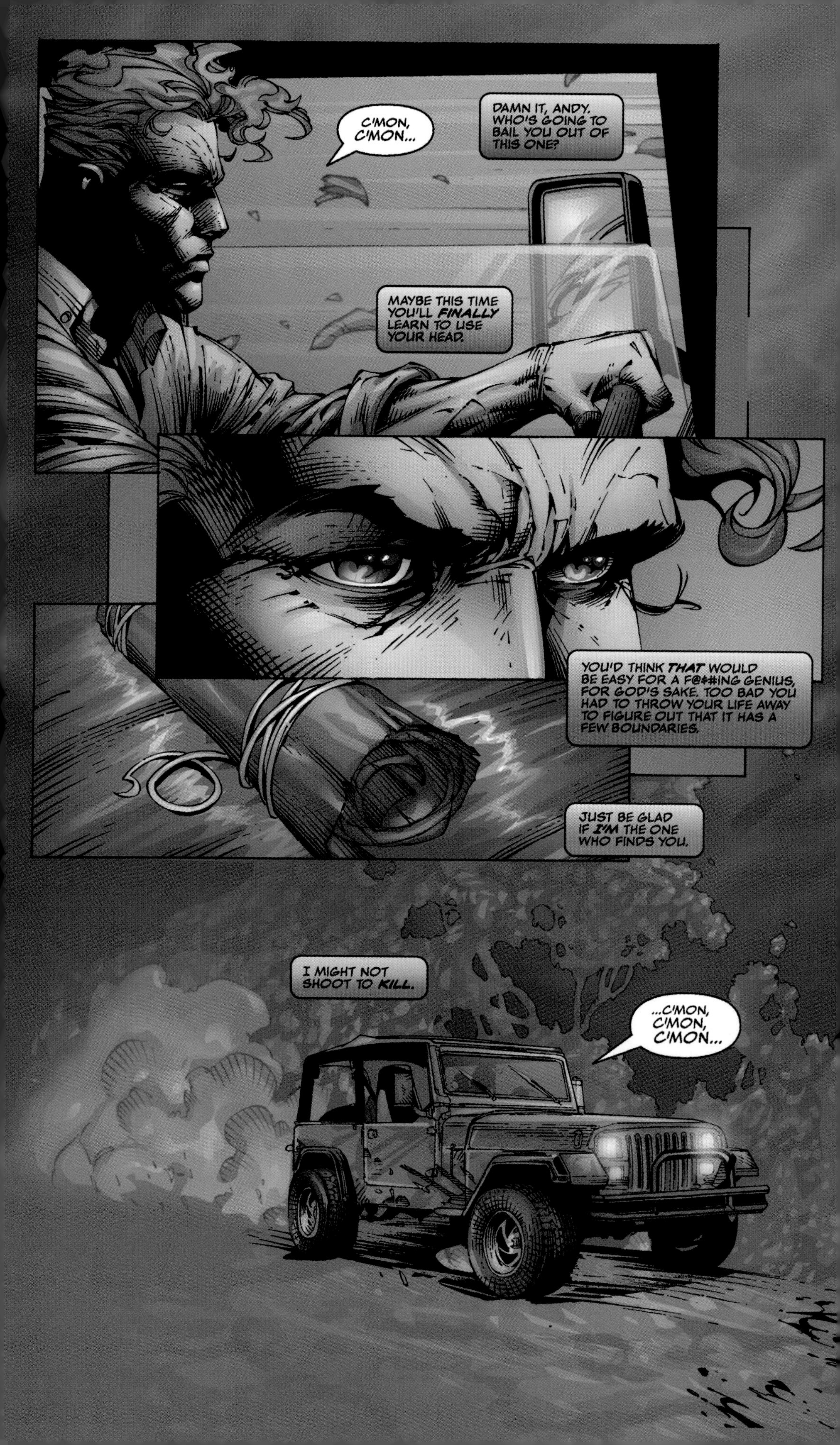
C'MON, C'MON...
DAMN IT, ANDY. WHO'S GOING TO BAIL YOU OUT OF THIS ONE?
MAYBE THIS TIME YOU'LL FINALLY LEARN TO USE YOUR HEAD.
YOU'D THINK THAT WOULD BE EASY FOR A F@$#ING GENIUS, FOR GOD'S SAKE. TOO BAD YOU HAD TO THROW YOUR LIFE AWAY TO FIGURE OUT THAT IT HAS A FEW BOUNDARIES.
JUST BE GLAD IF I'M THE ONE WHO FINDS YOU.
I MIGHT NOT SHOOT TO KILL.
...C'MON, C'MON, C'MON...

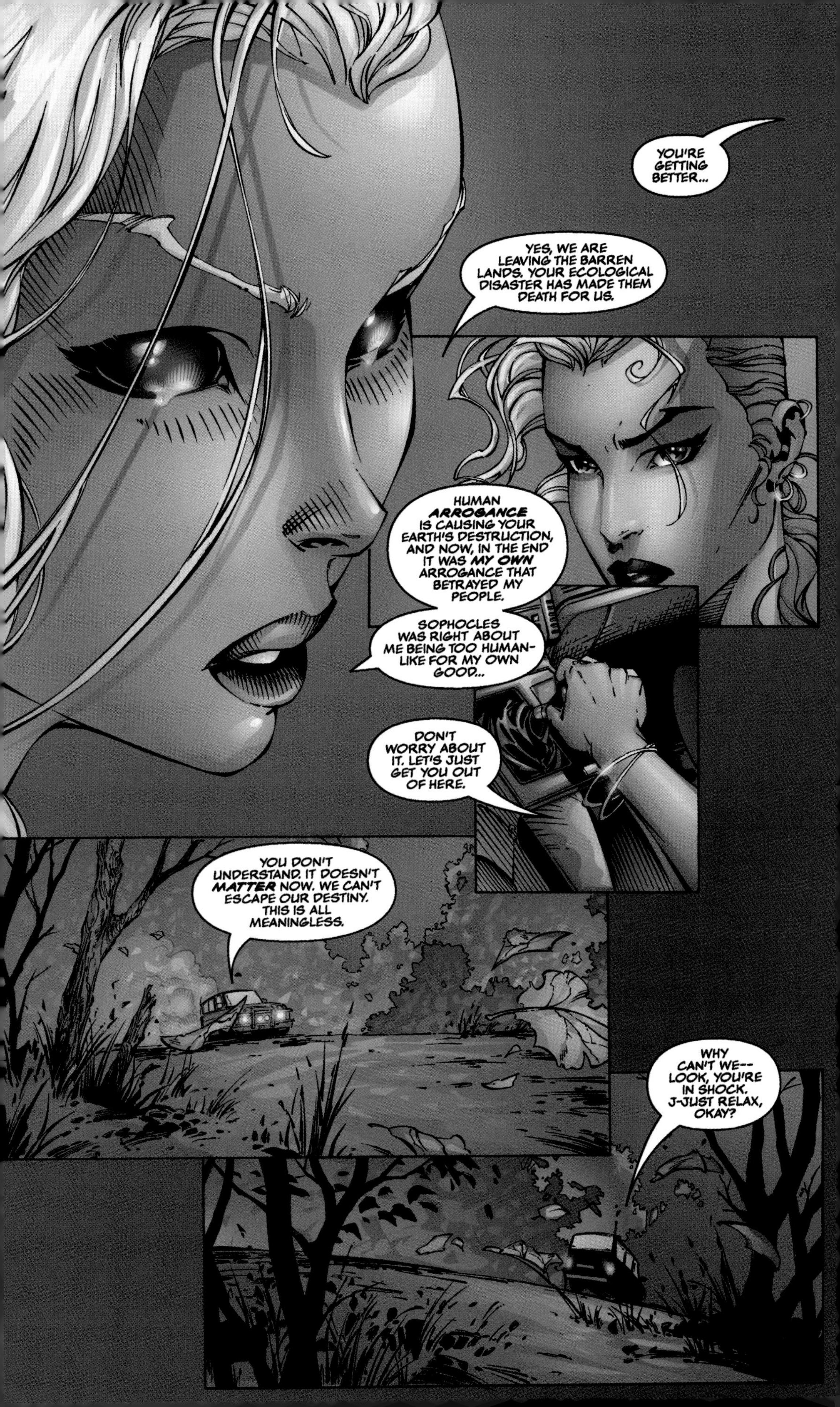

YOU'RE GETTING BETTER...
YES, WE ARE LEAVING THE BARREN LANDS. YOUR ECOLOGICAL DISASTER HAS MADE THEM DEATH FOR US.
HUMAN **ARROGANCE** IS CAUSING YOUR EARTH'S DESTRUCTION, AND NOW, IN THE END IT WAS **MY OWN** ARROGANCE THAT BETRAYED MY PEOPLE.
SOPHOCLES WAS RIGHT ABOUT ME BEING TOO HUMAN-LIKE FOR MY OWN GOOD...
DON'T WORRY ABOUT IT. LET'S JUST GET YOU OUT OF HERE.
YOU DON'T UNDERSTAND. IT DOESN'T **MATTER** NOW. WE CAN'T ESCAPE OUR DESTINY. THIS IS ALL MEANINGLESS.
WHY CAN'T WE-- LOOK, YOU'RE IN SHOCK. J-JUST RELAX, OKAY?

GODDAMMIT. SHE CAN'T KEEP PUTTING ME IN THESE SPOTS.
SHE'S THROWN HER CAREER AWAY, BUT I'LL BE DAMNED IF SHE'S GOING TO RUIN MINE!
THE GIRL GOT TO HER SOMEHOW.
ANDY SAID SHE WANTED TO SEE WHAT THEY'VE SEEN, AND THE GIRL IS GOING TO SHOW IT TO HER. THAT BITCH SOLD ME OUT FOR A TOURIST ATTRACTION!
I SHOULD HAVE SEEN THIS COMING A LONG TIME AGO--BUT IT'S NOT TOO LATE FOR ME TO--TO PUT A STOP TO IT.
ARG! WHY CAN'T I THINK?!
WHEN I'M FINISHED WITH THEM, THEY'LL WISH IT WAS SOME-ONE ELSE WHO FOUND THEM.
MY MIND JUST WON'T SHUT UP! THE CREATURE IS DOING THIS...TRYING TO CONFUSE ME.
I BET THEY'RE LAUGHING ABOUT IT NOW.
WELL THEY WON'T LAUGH LONG.

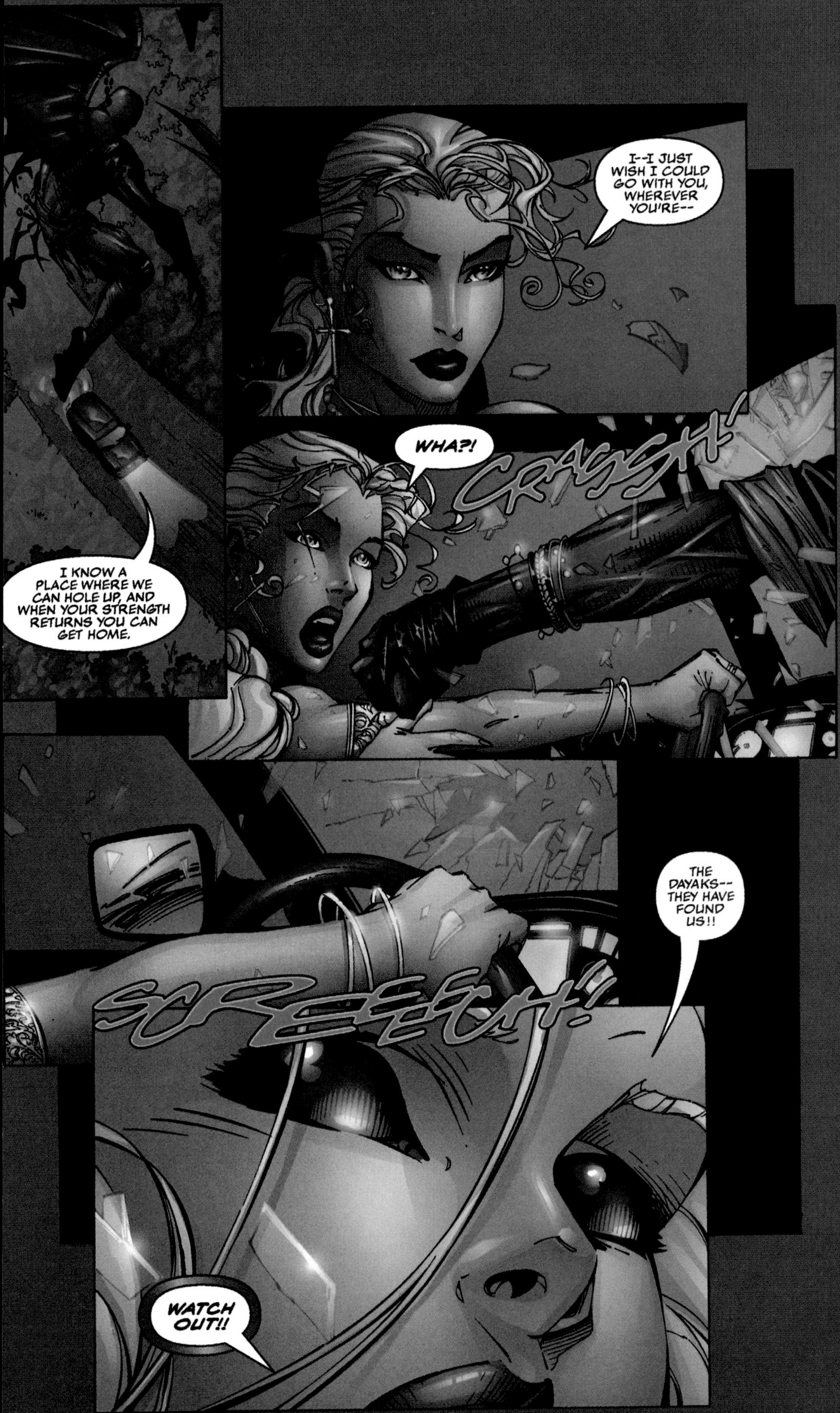
I--I JUST WISH I COULD GO WITH YOU, WHEREVER YOU'RE--
I KNOW A PLACE WHERE WE CAN HOLE UP, AND WHEN YOUR STRENGTH RETURNS YOU CAN GET HOME.
WHA?!
CRASSH!
THE DAYAKS-- THEY HAVE FOUND US!!
SCREEEECH!!
WATCH OUT!!

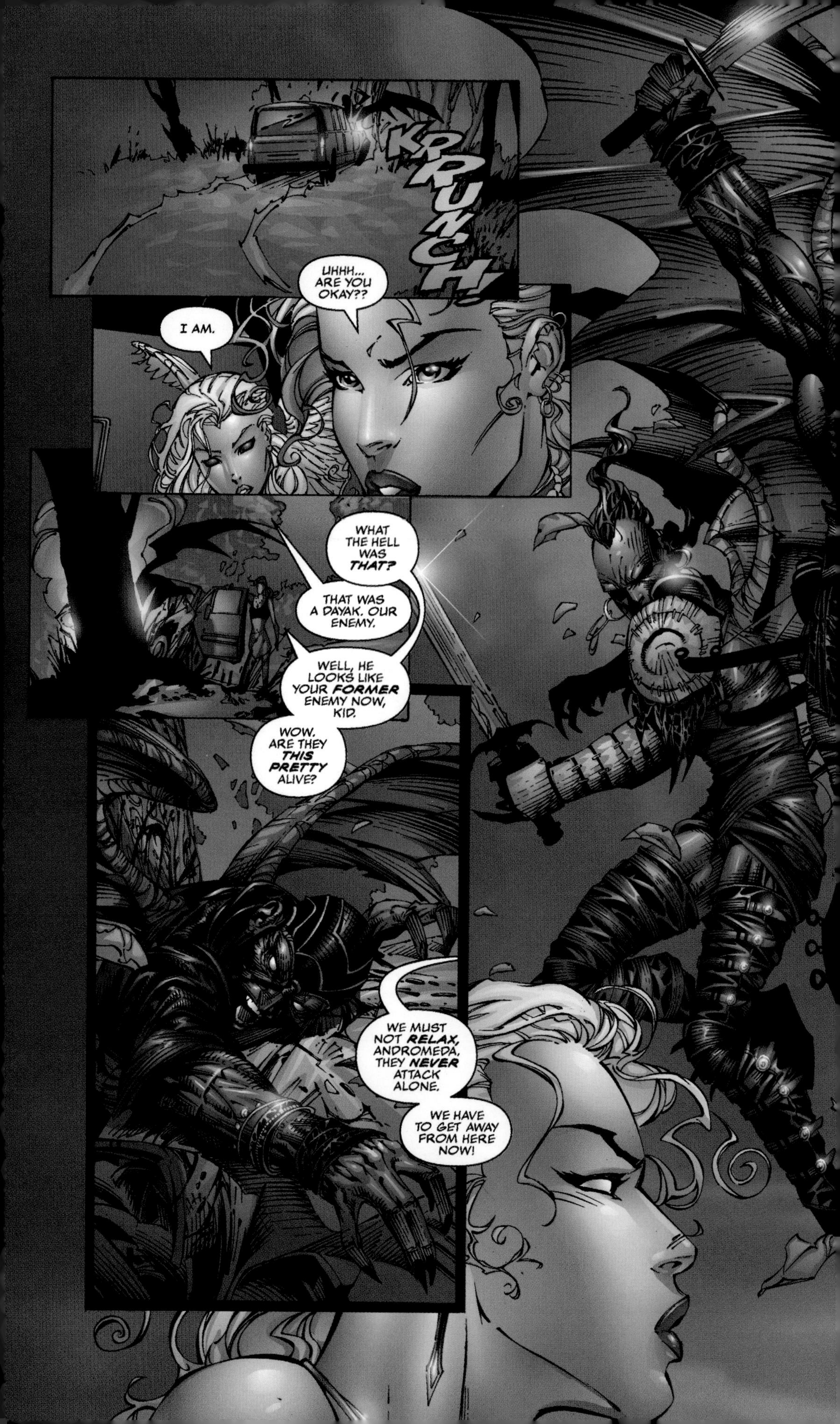
KRRUNCH!
UHHH... ARE YOU OKAY??
I AM.
WHAT THE HELL WAS THAT?
THAT WAS A DAYAK. OUR ENEMY.
WELL, HE LOOKS LIKE YOUR FORMER ENEMY NOW, KID.
WOW. ARE THEY THIS PRETTY ALIVE?
WE MUST NOT RELAX, ANDROMEDA. THEY NEVER ATTACK ALONE.
WE HAVE TO GET AWAY FROM HERE NOW!

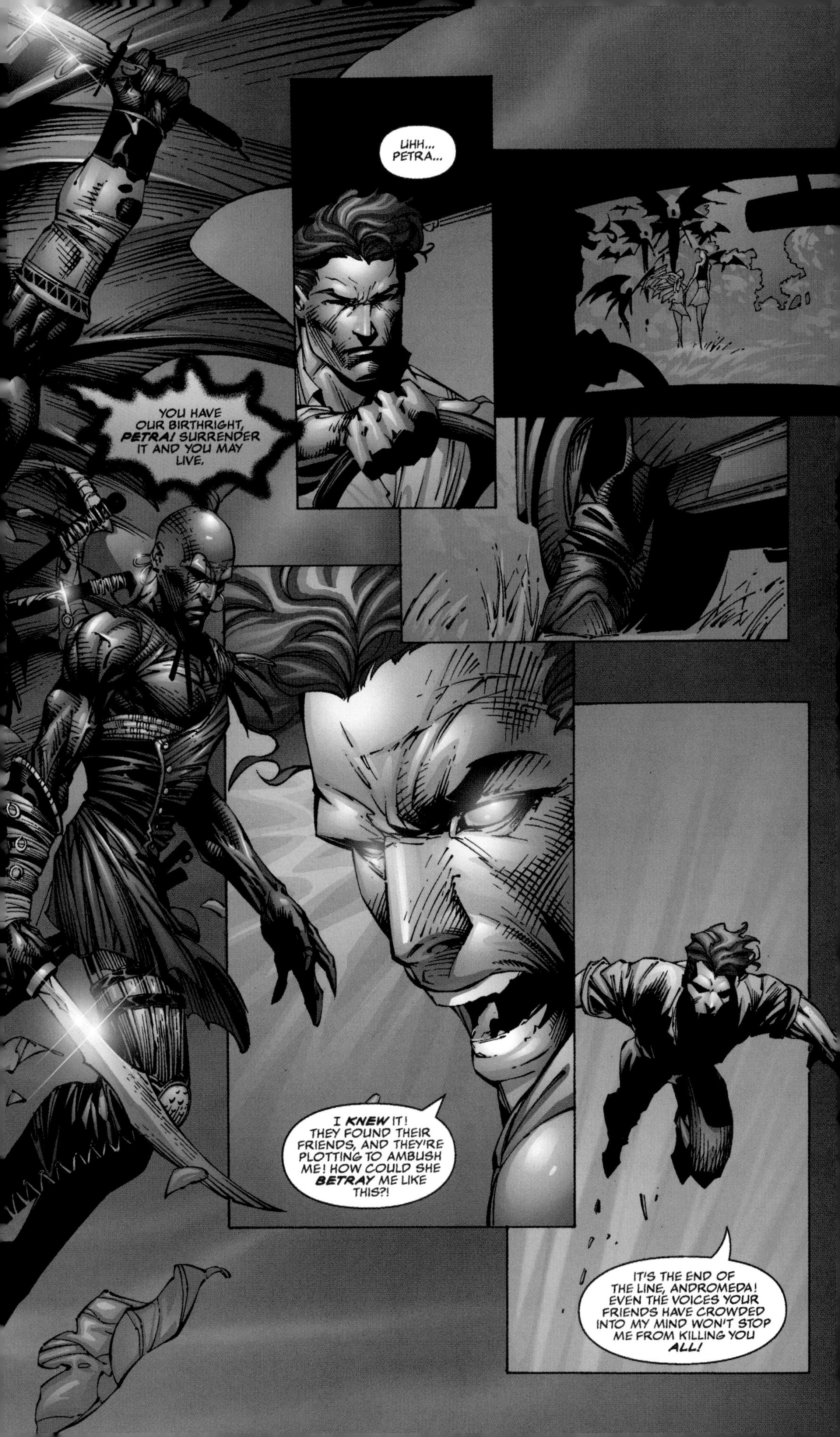

UHH... PETRA...
YOU HAVE OUR BIRTHRIGHT, PETRA! SURRENDER IT AND YOU MAY LIVE.
I KNEW IT! THEY FOUND THEIR FRIENDS, AND THEY'RE PLOTTING TO AMBUSH ME! HOW COULD SHE BETRAY ME LIKE THIS?!
IT'S THE END OF THE LINE, ANDROMEDA! EVEN THE VOICES YOUR FRIENDS HAVE CROWDED INTO MY MIND WON'T STOP ME FROM KILLING YOU ALL!

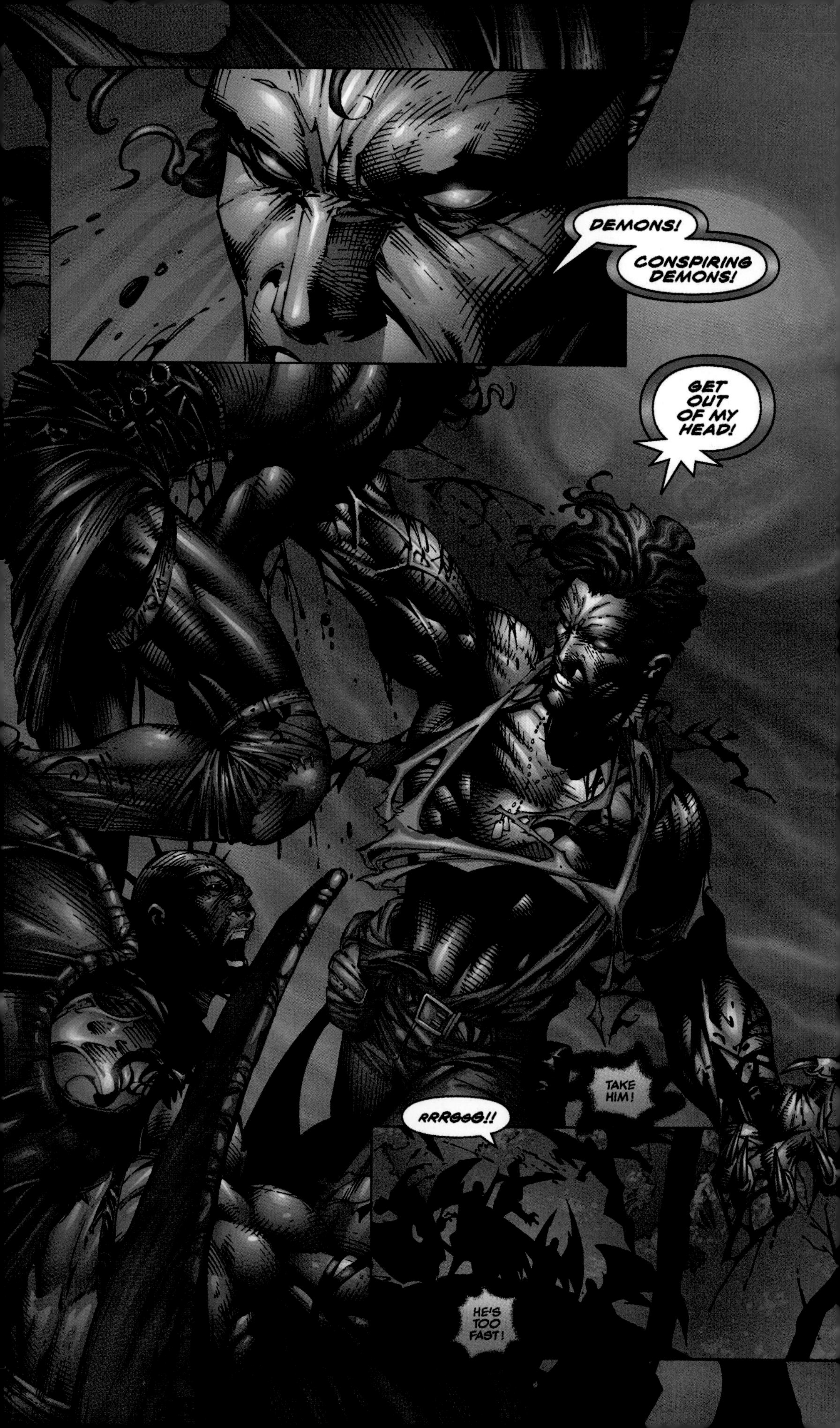
DEMONS!
CONSPIRING DEMONS!
GET OUT OF MY HEAD!
TAKE HIM!
RRRGGG!!
HE'S TOO FAST!

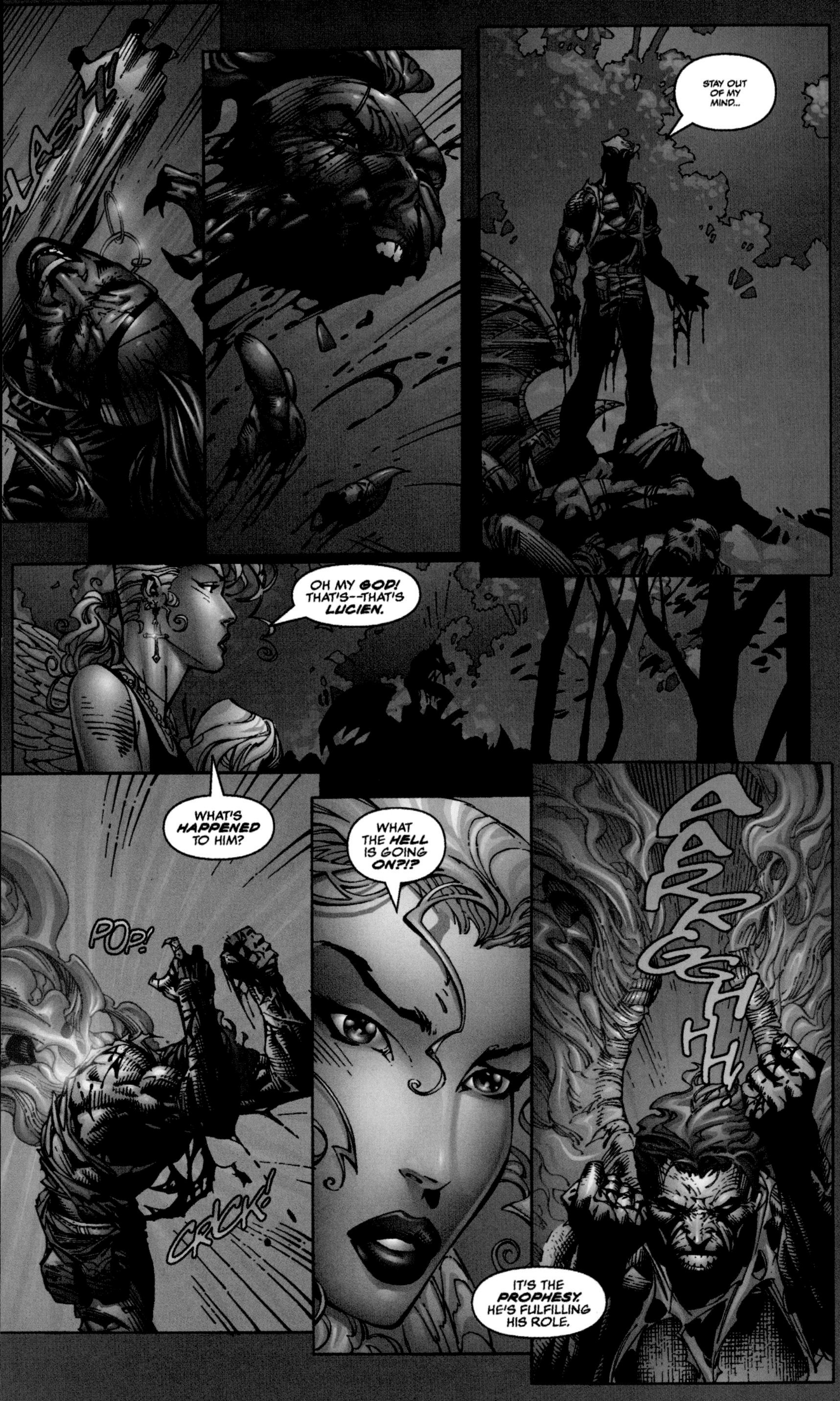
STAY OUT OF MY MIND...
OH MY GOD! THAT'S--THAT'S LUCIEN.
WHAT'S HAPPENED TO HIM?
POP!
CRACK!
WHAT THE HELL IS GOING ON?!?
AARRGGHH
IT'S THE PROPHESY. HE'S FULFILLING HIS ROLE.

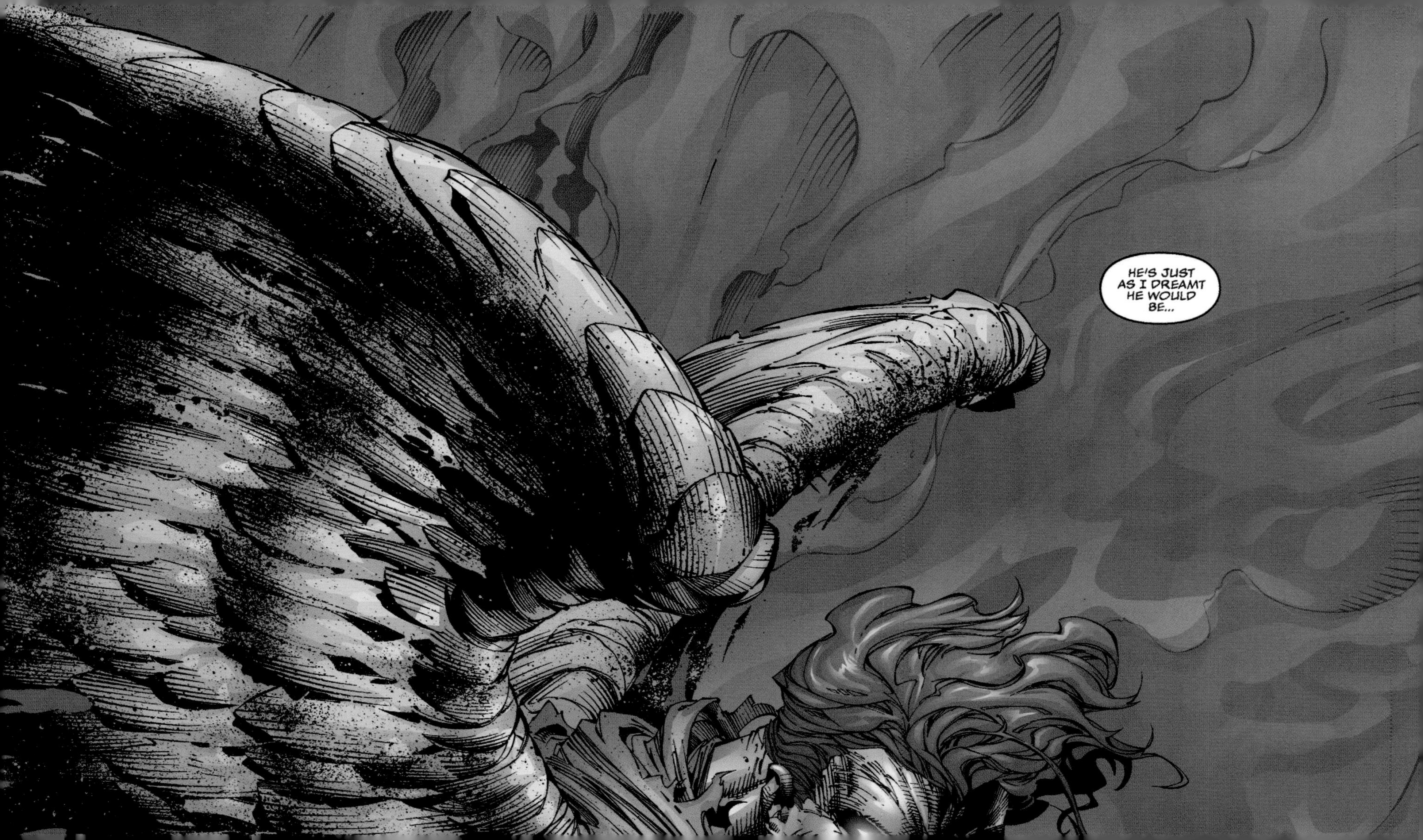
HE'S JUST AS I DREAMT HE WOULD BE...

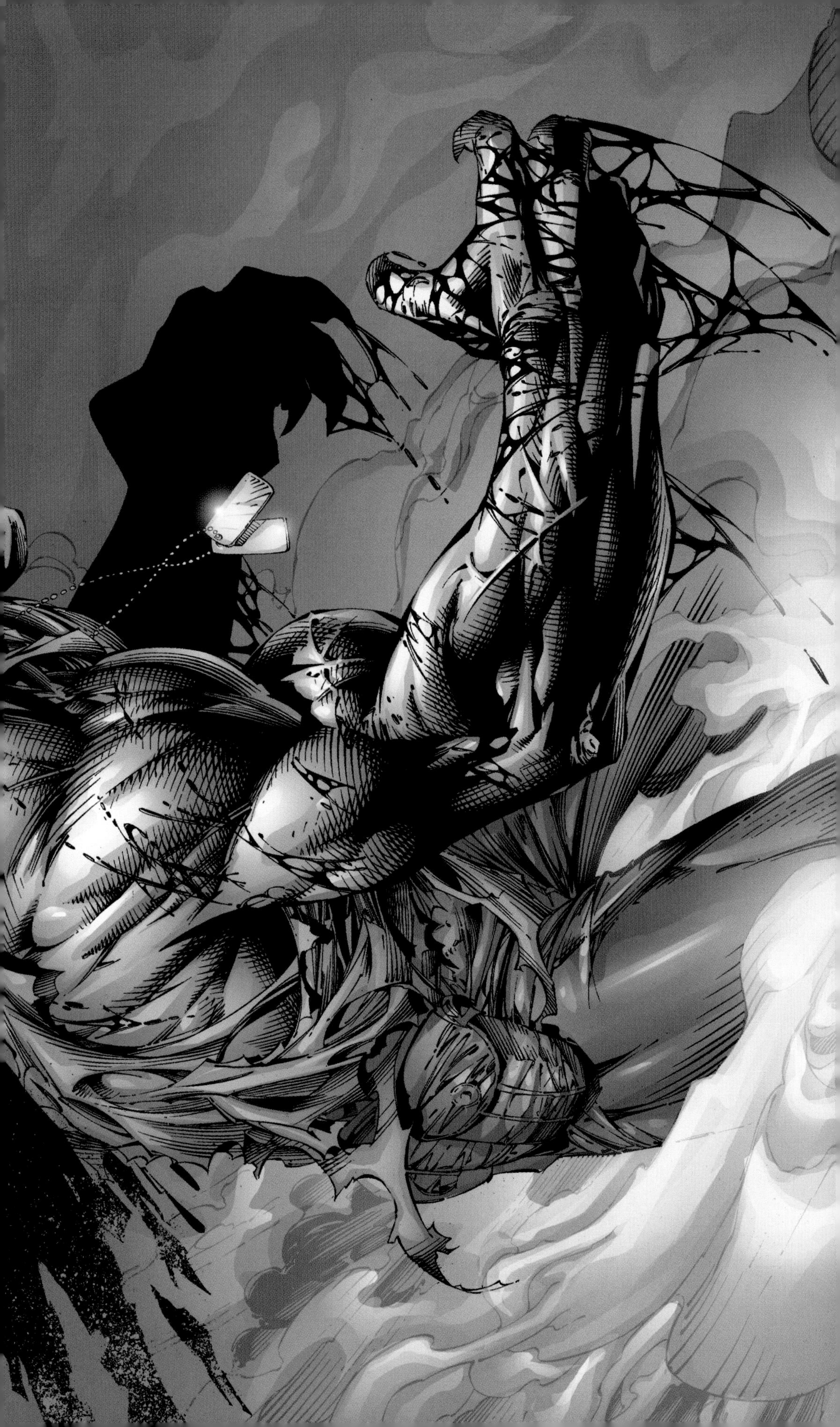

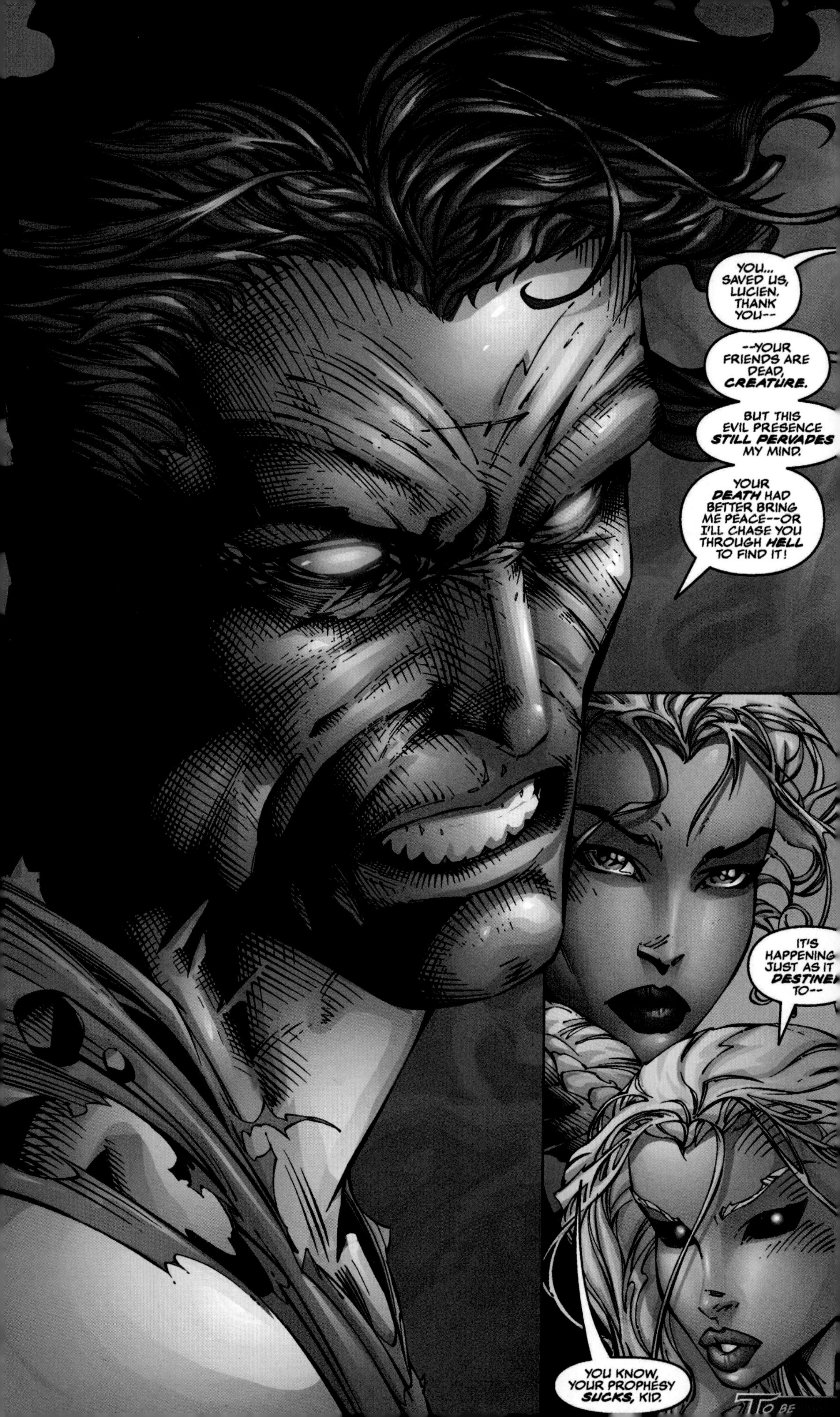
YOU... SAVED US, LUCIEN. THANK YOU--
--YOUR FRIENDS ARE DEAD, CREATURE.
BUT THIS EVIL PRESENCE STILL PERVADES MY MIND.
YOUR DEATH HAD BETTER BRING ME PEACE--OR I'LL CHASE YOU THROUGH HELL TO FIND IT!
IT'S HAPPENING JUST AS IT DESTINE TO--
YOU KNOW, YOUR PROPHESY SUCKS, KID.
TO BE

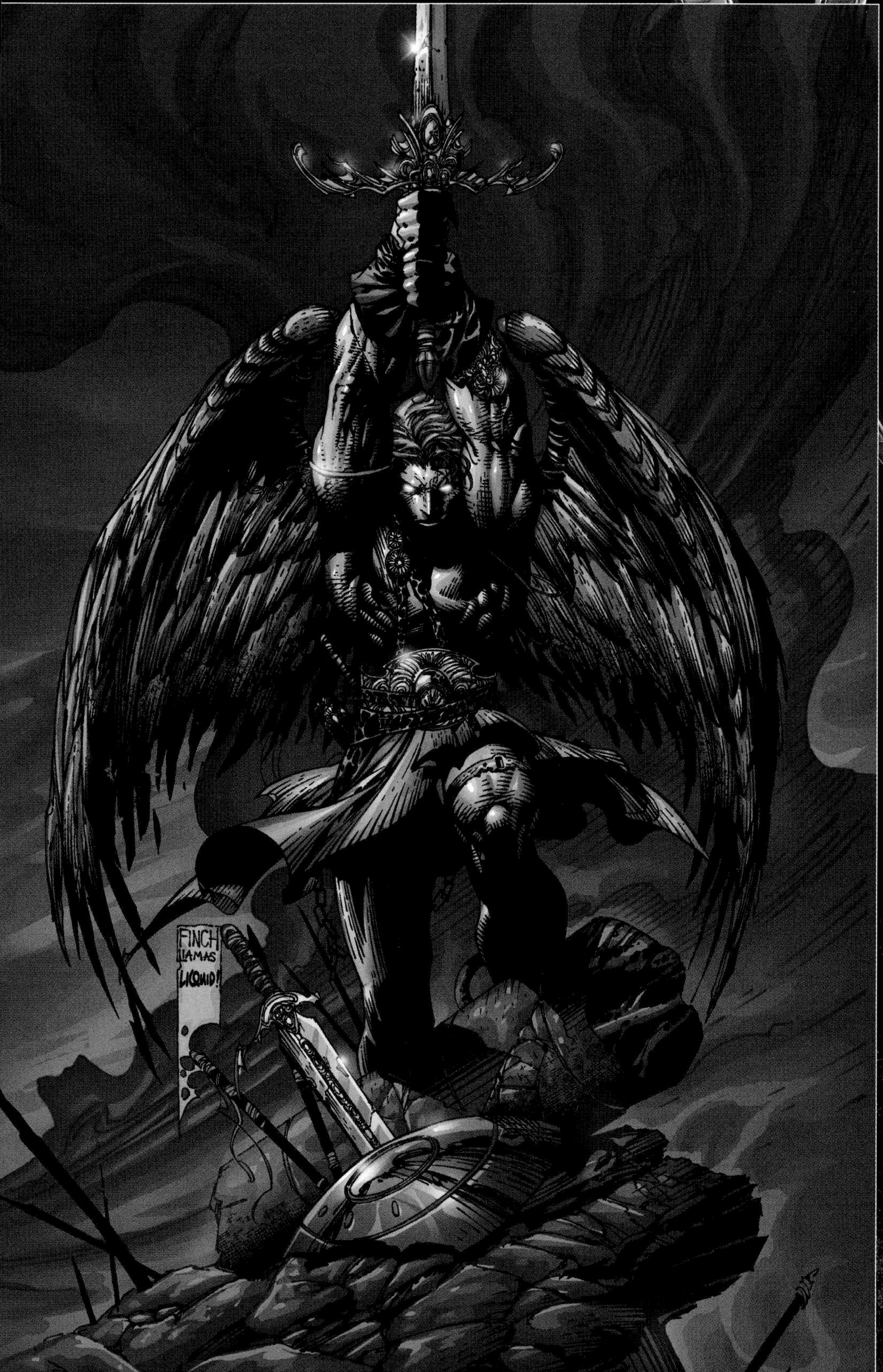
FINCH
LLAMAS
LIQUID!

Ascension issue #6 cover
art by: Dave Finch, Victor Llamas and Liquid!

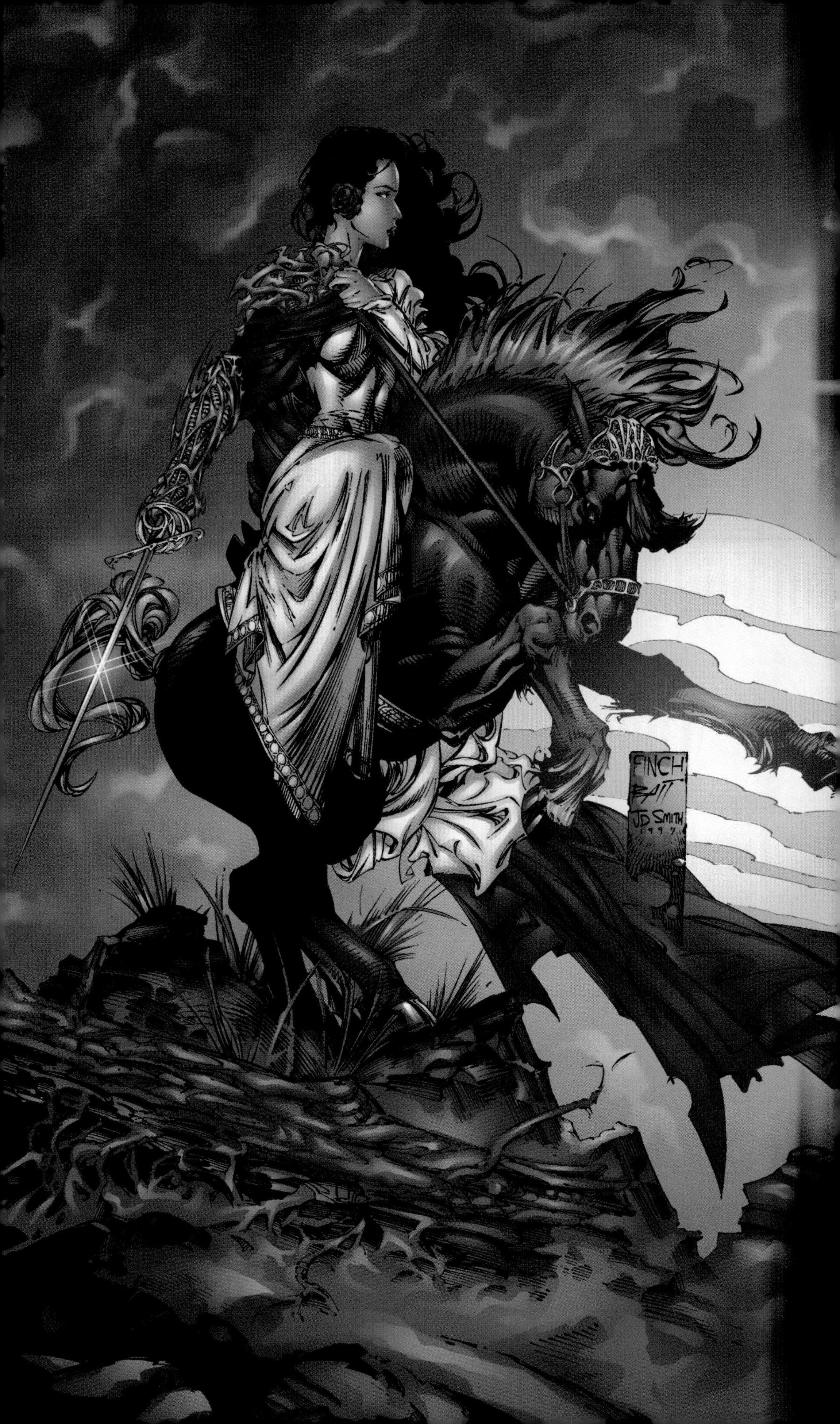
FINCH
BATT
J.D. SMITH
1997

Tales of the Witchblade

Touching every corner of the Top Cow universe, Dave Finch delivers a tale from the history of the Witchblade bearers.

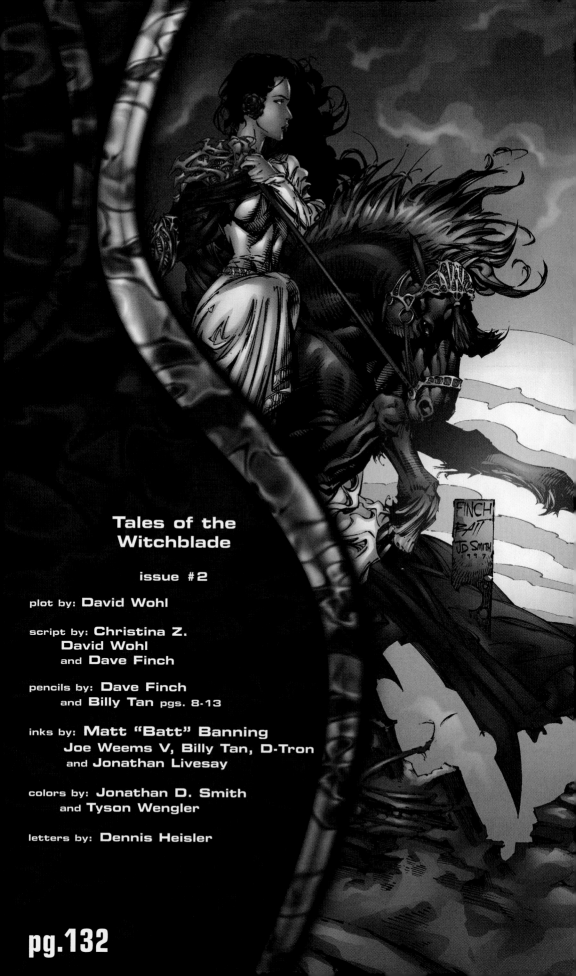

Tales of the Witchblade

issue #2

plot by: **David Wohl**

script by: **Christina Z.**
David Wohl
and **Dave Finch**

pencils by: **Dave Finch**
and **Billy Tan** pgs. 8-13

inks by: **Matt "Batt" Banning**
Joe Weems V, Billy Tan, D-Tron
and **Jonathan Livesay**

colors by: **Jonathan D. Smith**
and **Tyson Wengler**

letters by: **Dennis Heisler**

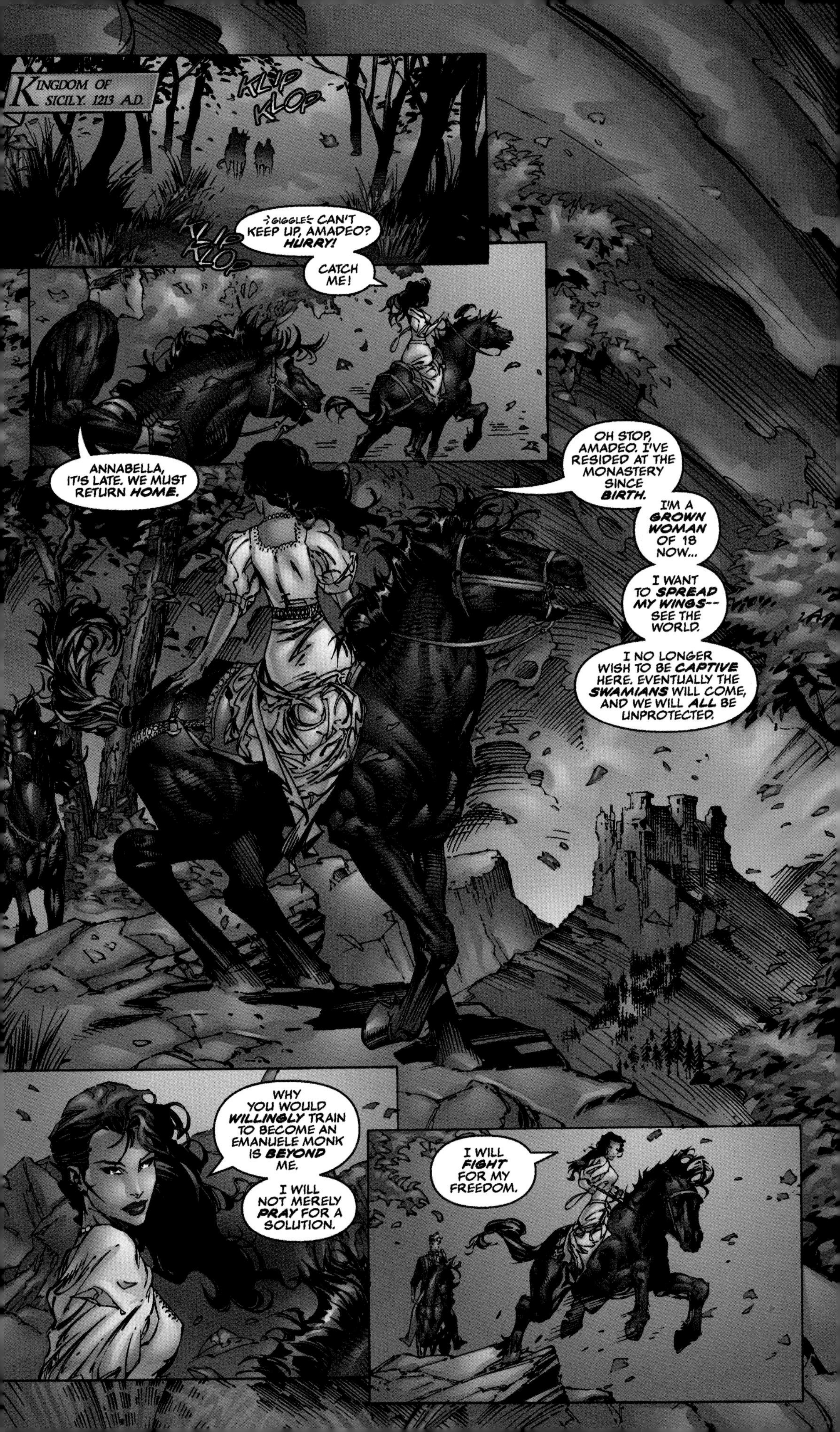
KINGDOM OF SICILY. 1213 A.D.
KLIP KLOP
KLIP KLOP
GIGGLE CAN'T KEEP UP, AMADEO? HURRY!
CATCH ME!
ANNABELLA, IT'S LATE. WE MUST RETURN HOME.
OH STOP, AMADEO. I'VE RESIDED AT THE MONASTERY SINCE BIRTH.
I'M A GROWN WOMAN OF 18 NOW...
I WANT TO SPREAD MY WINGS-- SEE THE WORLD.
I NO LONGER WISH TO BE CAPTIVE HERE. EVENTUALLY THE SWAMIANS WILL COME, AND WE WILL ALL BE UNPROTECTED.
WHY YOU WOULD WILLINGLY TRAIN TO BECOME AN EMANUELE MONK IS BEYOND ME.
I WILL NOT MERELY PRAY FOR A SOLUTION.
I WILL FIGHT FOR MY FREEDOM.

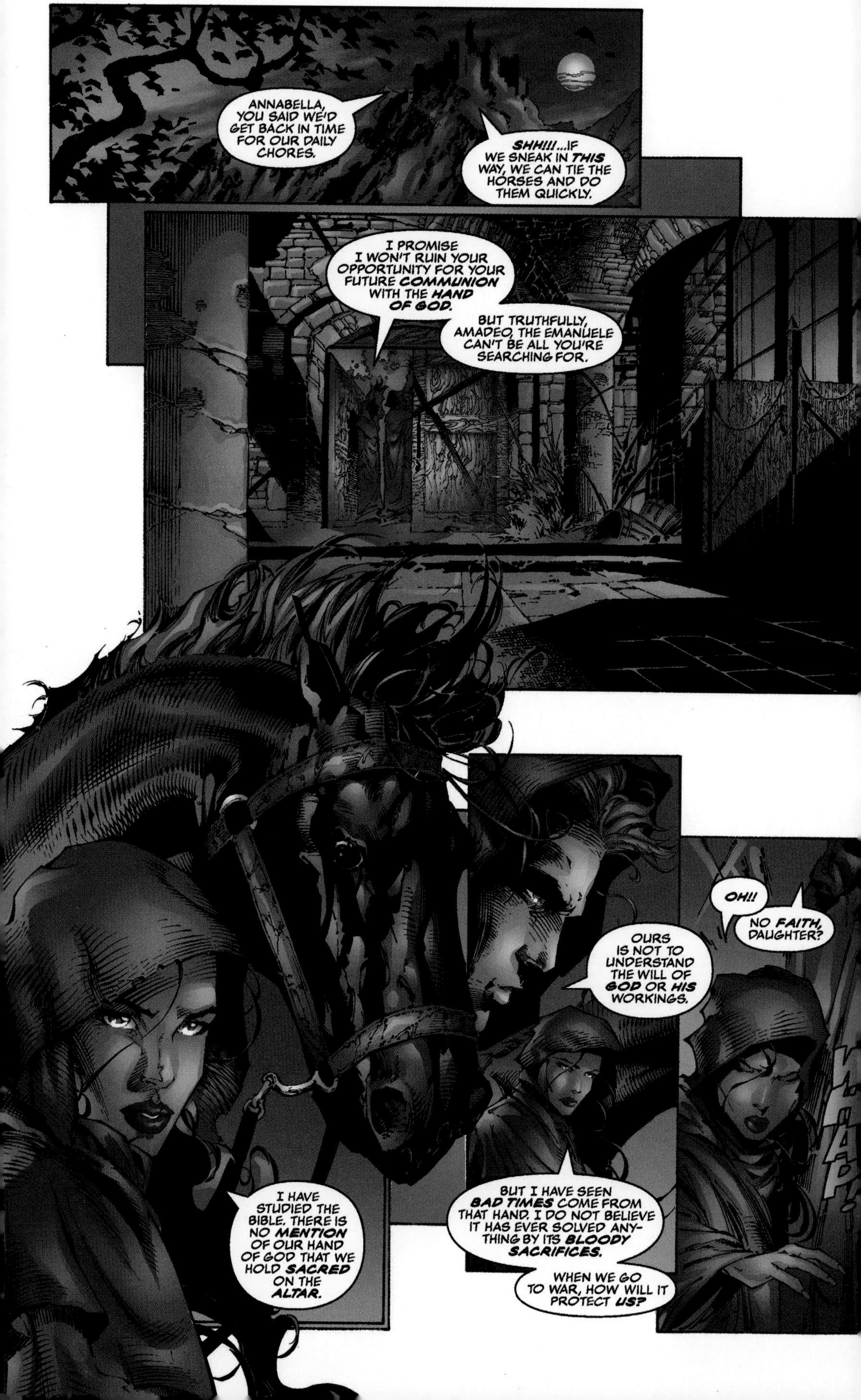

ANNABELLA, YOU SAID WE'D GET BACK IN TIME FOR OUR DAILY CHORES.
SHH!!!...IF WE SNEAK IN THIS WAY, WE CAN TIE THE HORSES AND DO THEM QUICKLY.
I PROMISE I WON'T RUIN YOUR OPPORTUNITY FOR YOUR FUTURE COMMUNION WITH THE HAND OF GOD.
BUT TRUTHFULLY, AMADEO, THE EMANUELE CAN'T BE ALL YOU'RE SEARCHING FOR.
I HAVE STUDIED THE BIBLE. THERE IS NO MENTION OF OUR HAND OF GOD THAT WE HOLD SACRED ON THE ALTAR.
OURS IS NOT TO UNDERSTAND THE WILL OF GOD OR HIS WORKINGS.
BUT I HAVE SEEN BAD TIMES COME FROM THAT HAND. I DO NOT BELIEVE IT HAS EVER SOLVED ANY-THING BY ITS BLOODY SACRIFICES.
WHEN WE GO TO WAR, HOW WILL IT PROTECT US?
OH!!
NO FAITH, DAUGHTER?
WHAP!

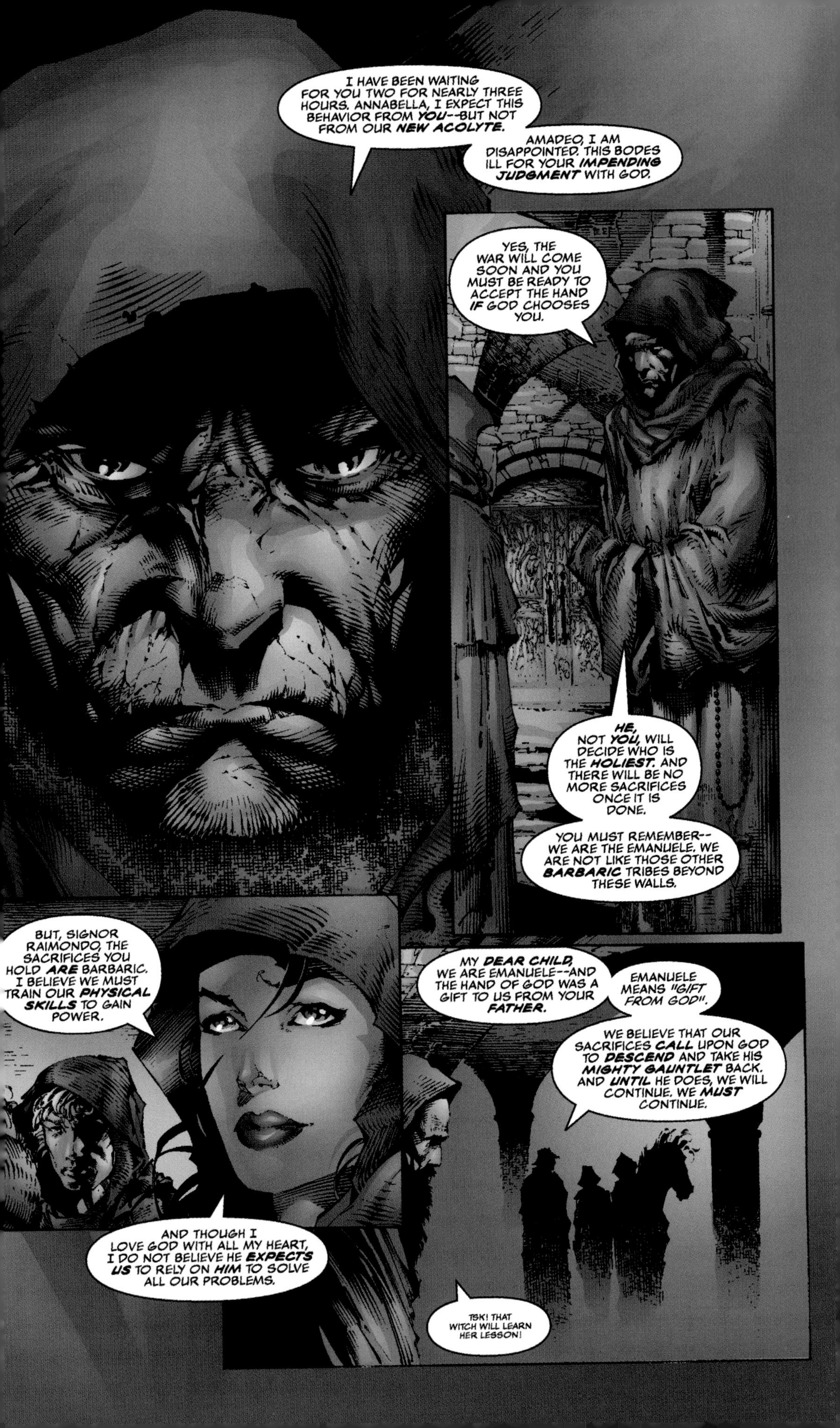
I HAVE BEEN WAITING FOR YOU TWO FOR NEARLY THREE HOURS. ANNABELLA, I EXPECT THIS BEHAVIOR FROM *YOU*--BUT NOT FROM OUR *NEW ACOLYTE*.
AMADEO, I AM DISAPPOINTED. THIS BODES ILL FOR YOUR *IMPENDING JUDGMENT* WITH GOD.
YES, THE WAR WILL COME SOON AND YOU MUST BE READY TO ACCEPT THE HAND *IF* GOD CHOOSES YOU.
HE, NOT *YOU*, WILL DECIDE WHO IS THE *HOLIEST*. AND THERE WILL BE NO MORE SACRIFICES ONCE IT IS DONE.
YOU MUST REMEMBER--WE ARE THE EMANUELE. WE ARE NOT LIKE THOSE OTHER *BARBARIC* TRIBES BEYOND THESE WALLS.
BUT, SIGNOR RAIMONDO, THE SACRIFICES YOU HOLD *ARE* BARBARIC. I BELIEVE WE MUST TRAIN OUR *PHYSICAL SKILLS* TO GAIN POWER.
AND THOUGH I LOVE GOD WITH ALL MY HEART, I DO NOT BELIEVE HE *EXPECTS US* TO RELY ON *HIM* TO SOLVE ALL OUR PROBLEMS.
MY *DEAR CHILD*, WE ARE EMANUELE--AND THE HAND OF GOD WAS A GIFT TO US FROM YOUR *FATHER*.
EMANUELE MEANS *"GIFT FROM GOD"*.
WE BELIEVE THAT OUR SACRIFICES *CALL* UPON GOD TO *DESCEND* AND TAKE HIS *MIGHTY GAUNTLET* BACK. AND *UNTIL* HE DOES, WE WILL CONTINUE. WE *MUST* CONTINUE.
TSK! THAT WITCH WILL LEARN HER LESSON!

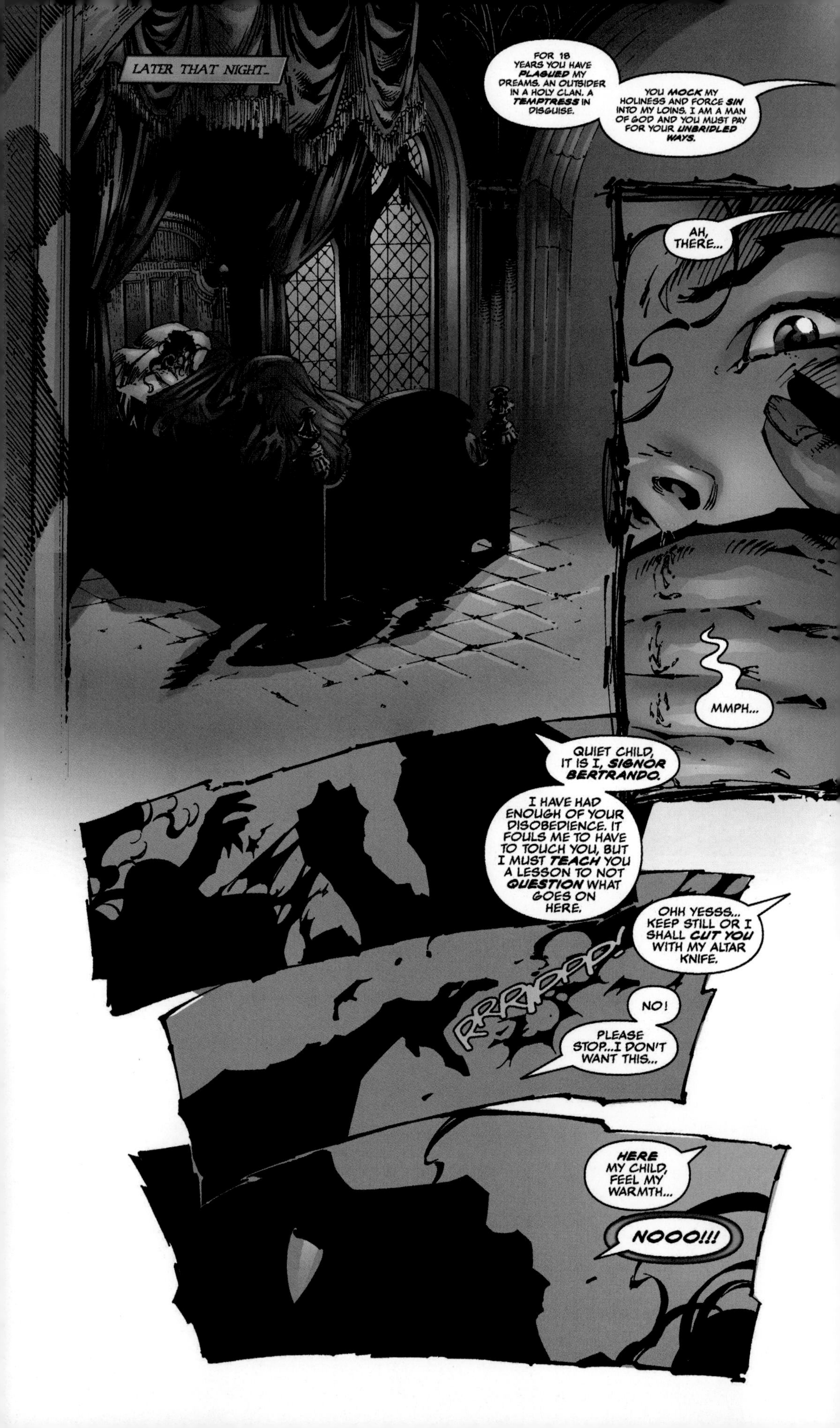
LATER THAT NIGHT...
FOR 18 YEARS YOU HAVE PLAGUED MY DREAMS. AN OUTSIDER IN A HOLY CLAN. A TEMPTRESS IN DISGUISE.
YOU MOCK MY HOLINESS AND FORCE SIN INTO MY LOINS. I AM A MAN OF GOD AND YOU MUST PAY FOR YOUR UNBRIDLED WAYS.
AH, THERE...
MMPH...
QUIET CHILD, IT IS I, SIGNOR BERTRANDO.
I HAVE HAD ENOUGH OF YOUR DISOBEDIENCE. IT FOULS ME TO HAVE TO TOUCH YOU, BUT I MUST TEACH YOU A LESSON TO NOT QUESTION WHAT GOES ON HERE.
OHH YESSS... KEEP STILL OR I SHALL CUT YOU WITH MY ALTAR KNIFE.
NO!
PLEASE STOP...I DON'T WANT THIS...
HERE MY CHILD, FEEL MY WARMTH...
NOOO!!!

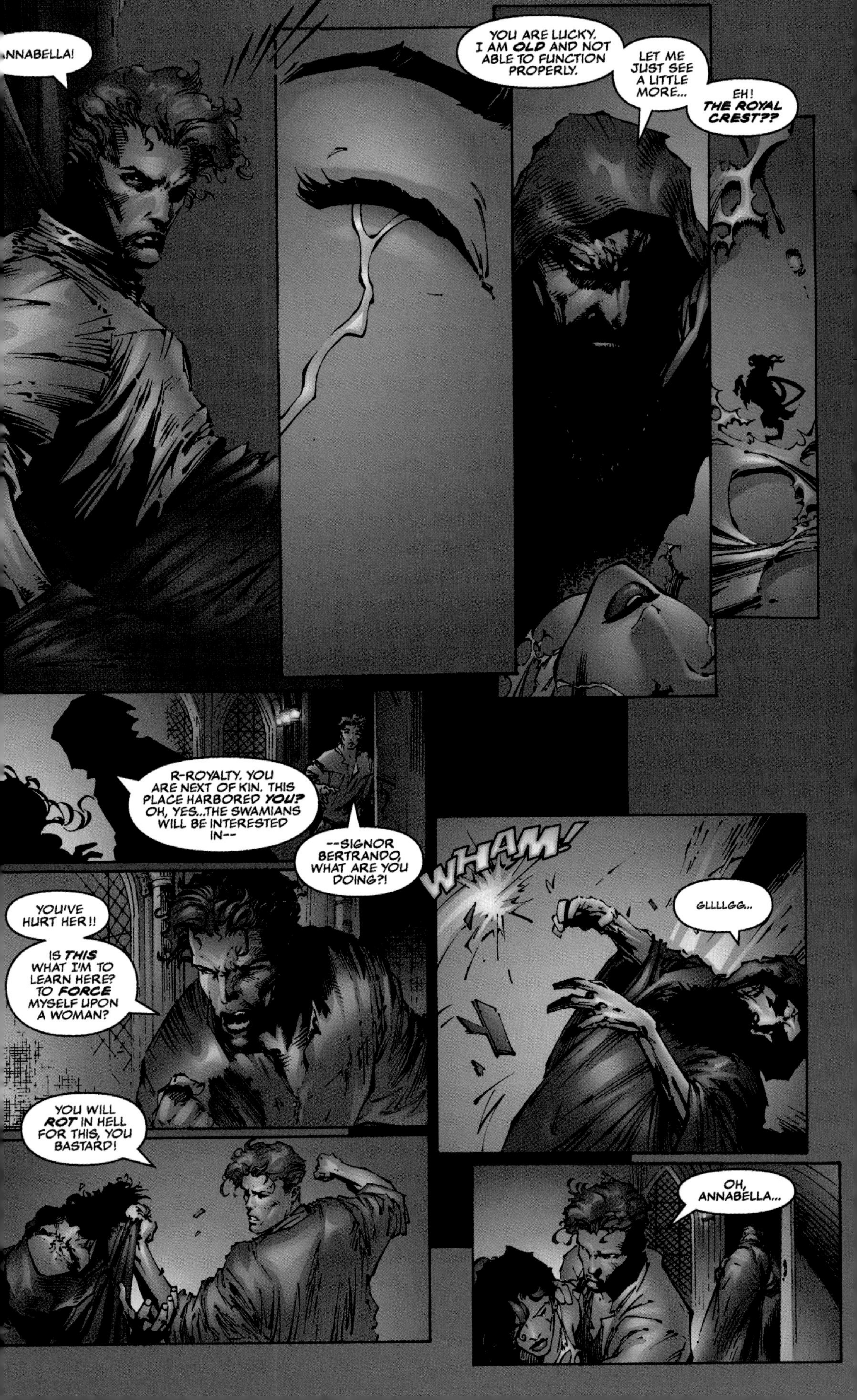

ANNABELLA!
YOU ARE LUCKY. I AM OLD AND NOT ABLE TO FUNCTION PROPERLY.
LET ME JUST SEE A LITTLE MORE...
EH! THE ROYAL CREST??
R-ROYALTY. YOU ARE NEXT OF KIN. THIS PLACE HARBORED YOU? OH, YES...THE SWAMIANS WILL BE INTERESTED IN--
--SIGNOR BERTRANDO, WHAT ARE YOU DOING?!
YOU'VE HURT HER!!
IS THIS WHAT I'M TO LEARN HERE? TO FORCE MYSELF UPON A WOMAN?
WHAM!
GLLLLGG...
YOU WILL ROT IN HELL FOR THIS, YOU BASTARD!
OH, ANNABELLA...

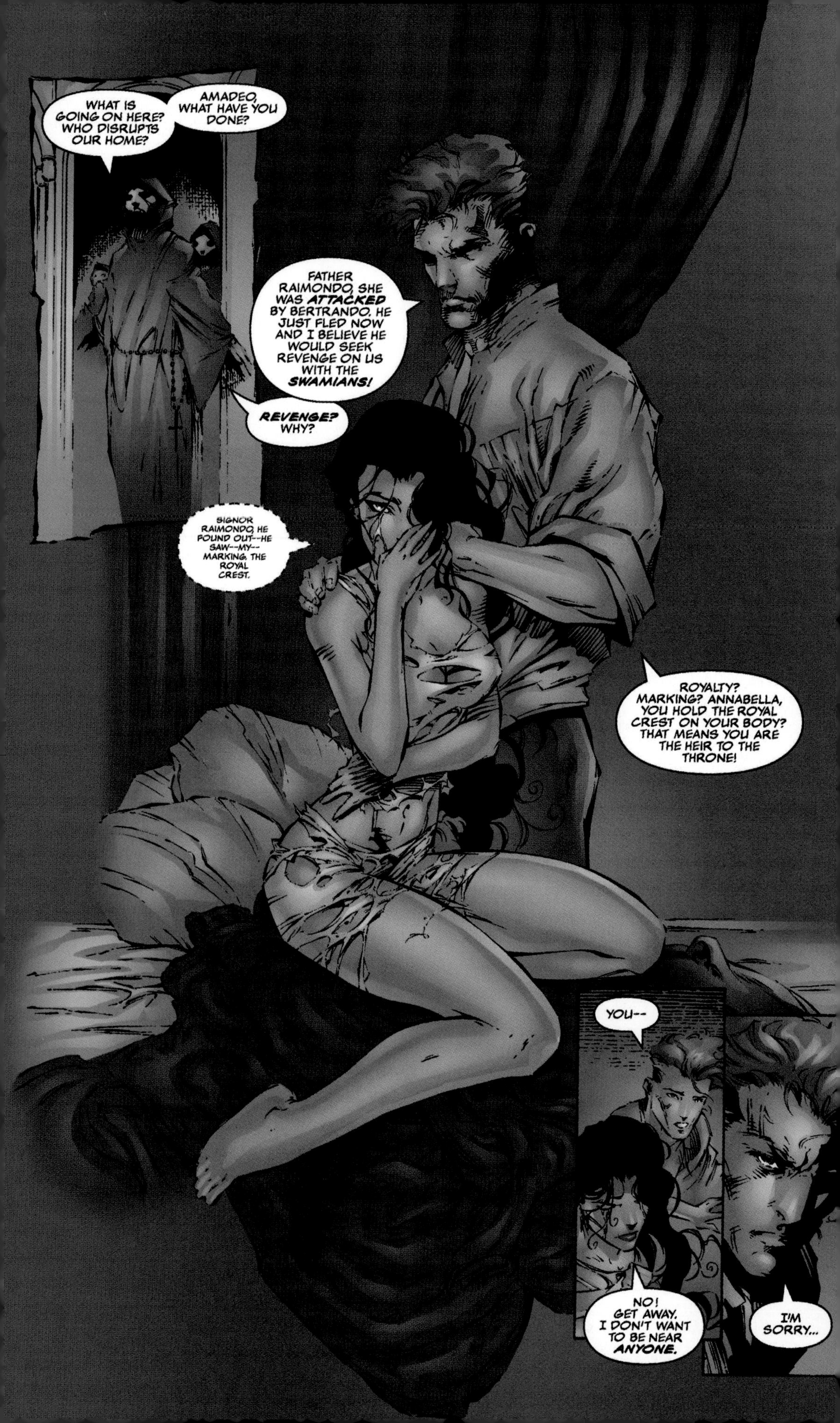
WHAT IS GOING ON HERE? WHO DISRUPTS OUR HOME?
AMADEO, WHAT HAVE YOU DONE?
FATHER RAIMONDO, SHE WAS ATTACKED BY BERTRANDO. HE JUST FLED NOW AND I BELIEVE HE WOULD SEEK REVENGE ON US WITH THE SWAMIANS!
REVENGE? WHY?
SIGNOR RAIMONDO, HE FOUND OUT--HE SAW--MY--MARKING. THE ROYAL CREST.
ROYALTY? MARKING? ANNABELLA, YOU HOLD THE ROYAL CREST ON YOUR BODY? THAT MEANS YOU ARE THE HEIR TO THE THRONE!
YOU--
NO! GET AWAY. I DON'T WANT TO BE NEAR ANYONE.
I'M SORRY...

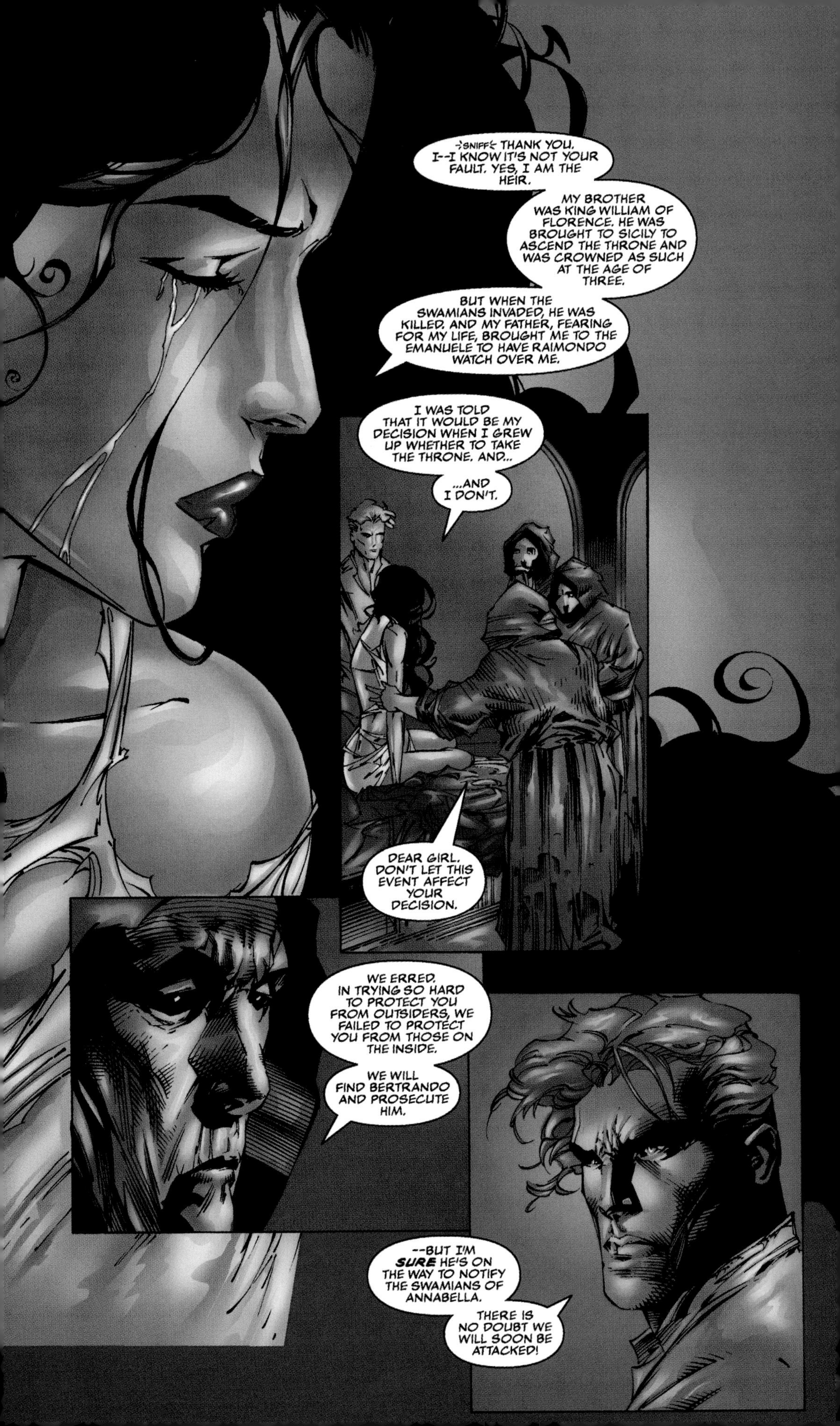

-SNIFF- THANK YOU. I--I KNOW IT'S NOT YOUR FAULT. YES, I AM THE HEIR.
MY BROTHER WAS KING WILLIAM OF FLORENCE. HE WAS BROUGHT TO SICILY TO ASCEND THE THRONE AND WAS CROWNED AS SUCH AT THE AGE OF THREE.
BUT WHEN THE SWAMIANS INVADED, HE WAS KILLED. AND MY FATHER, FEARING FOR MY LIFE, BROUGHT ME TO THE EMANUELE TO HAVE RAIMONDO WATCH OVER ME.
I WAS TOLD THAT IT WOULD BE MY DECISION WHEN I GREW UP WHETHER TO TAKE THE THRONE. AND...
...AND I DON'T.
DEAR GIRL. DON'T LET THIS EVENT AFFECT YOUR DECISION.
WE ERRED. IN TRYING SO HARD TO PROTECT YOU FROM OUTSIDERS, WE FAILED TO PROTECT YOU FROM THOSE ON THE INSIDE.
WE WILL FIND BERTRANDO AND PROSECUTE HIM.
--BUT I'M SURE HE'S ON THE WAY TO NOTIFY THE SWAMIANS OF ANNABELLA.
THERE IS NO DOUBT WE WILL SOON BE ATTACKED!

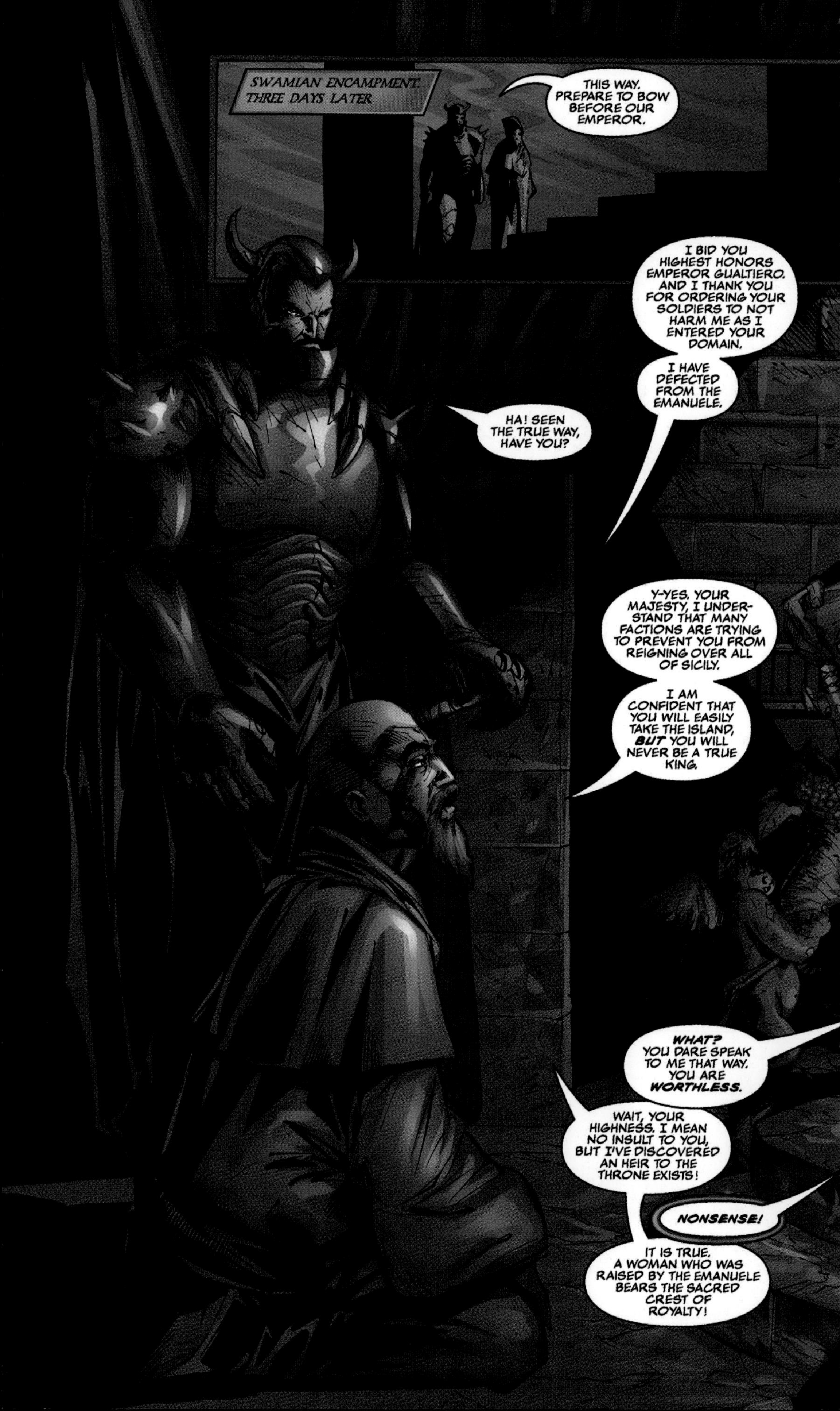
SWAMIAN ENCAMPMENT. THREE DAYS LATER
THIS WAY. PREPARE TO BOW BEFORE OUR EMPEROR.
I BID YOU HIGHEST HONORS EMPEROR GUALTIERO. AND I THANK YOU FOR ORDERING YOUR SOLDIERS TO NOT HARM ME AS I ENTERED YOUR DOMAIN.
I HAVE DEFECTED FROM THE EMANUELE.
HA! SEEN THE TRUE WAY, HAVE YOU?
Y-YES, YOUR MAJESTY, I UNDERSTAND THAT MANY FACTIONS ARE TRYING TO PREVENT YOU FROM REIGNING OVER ALL OF SICILY.
I AM CONFIDENT THAT YOU WILL EASILY TAKE THE ISLAND, *BUT* YOU WILL NEVER BE A TRUE KING.
WHAT? YOU DARE SPEAK TO ME THAT WAY. YOU ARE *WORTHLESS.*
WAIT, YOUR HIGHNESS. I MEAN NO INSULT TO YOU, BUT I'VE DISCOVERED AN HEIR TO THE THRONE EXISTS!
NONSENSE!
IT IS TRUE. A WOMAN WHO WAS RAISED BY THE EMANUELE BEARS THE SACRED CREST OF ROYALTY!

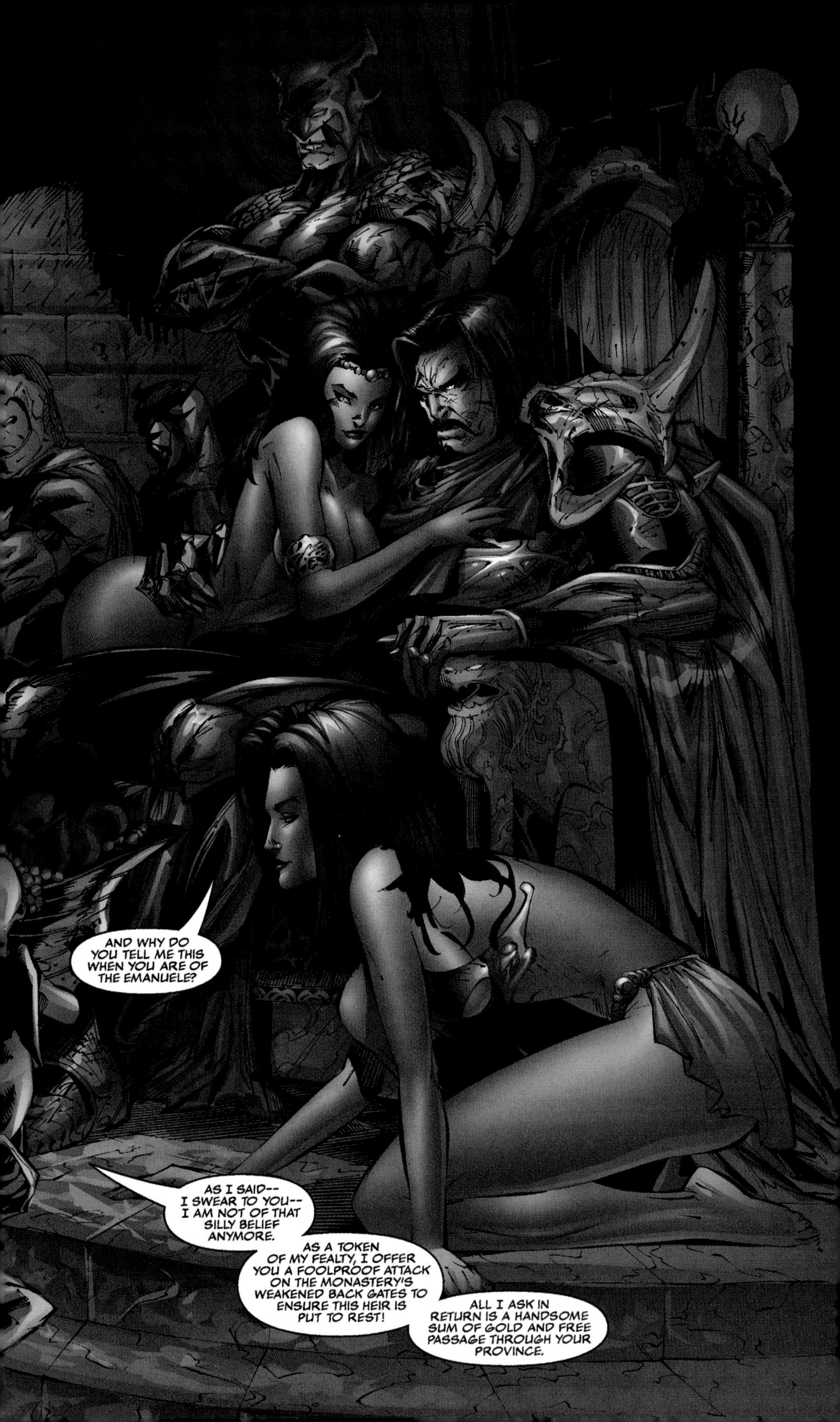
AND WHY DO YOU TELL ME THIS WHEN YOU ARE OF THE EMANUELE?
AS I SAID-- I SWEAR TO YOU-- I AM NOT OF THAT SILLY BELIEF ANYMORE.
AS A TOKEN OF MY FEALTY, I OFFER YOU A FOOLPROOF ATTACK ON THE MONASTERY'S WEAKENED BACK GATES TO ENSURE THIS HEIR IS PUT TO REST!
ALL I ASK IN RETURN IS A HANDSOME SUM OF GOLD AND FREE PASSAGE THROUGH YOUR PROVINCE.

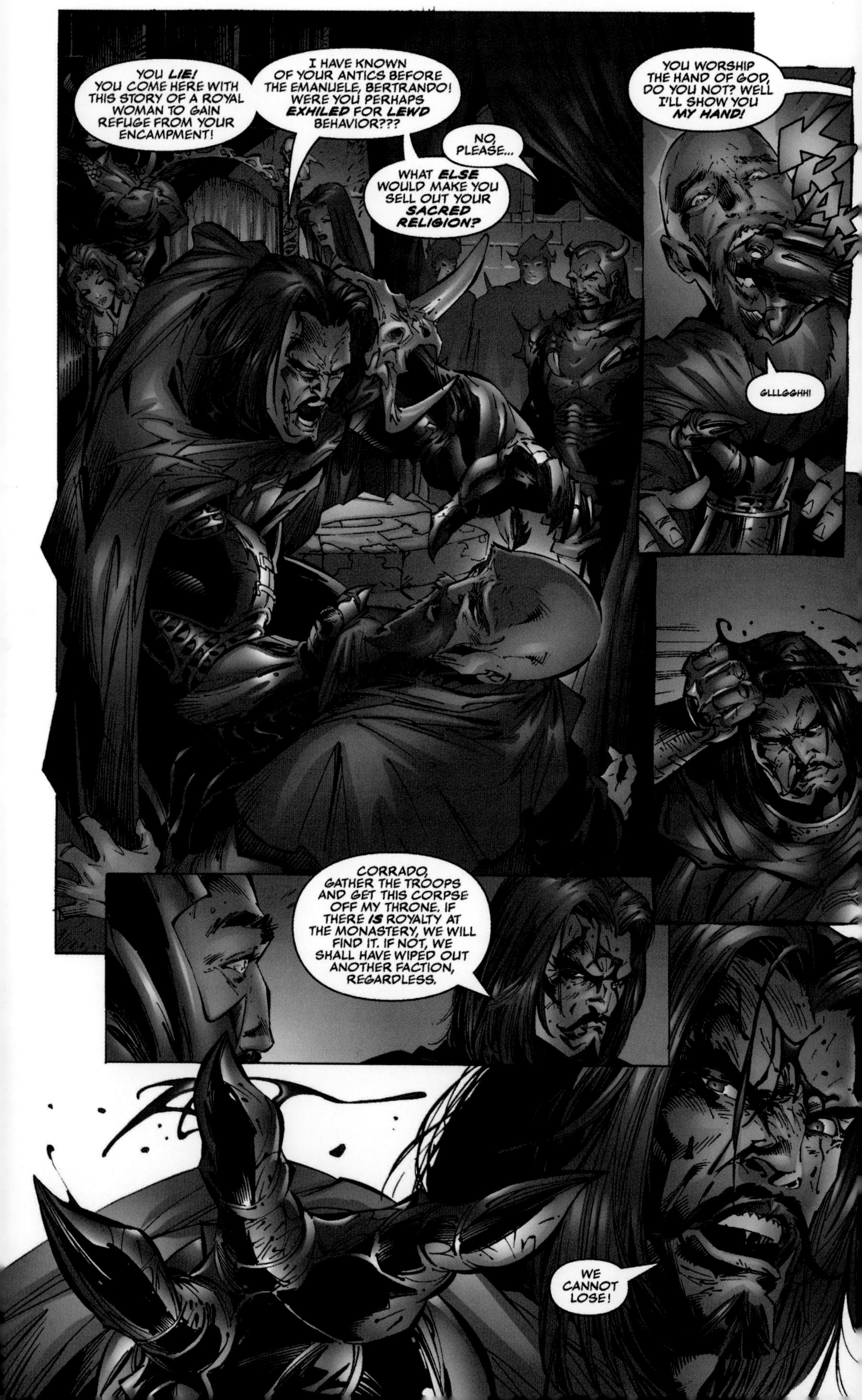
YOU LIE! YOU COME HERE WITH THIS STORY OF A ROYAL WOMAN TO GAIN REFUGE FROM YOUR ENCAMPMENT!
I HAVE KNOWN OF YOUR ANTICS BEFORE THE EMANUELE, BERTRANDO! WERE YOU PERHAPS EXHILED FOR LEWD BEHAVIOR???
NO, PLEASE...
WHAT ELSE WOULD MAKE YOU SELL OUT YOUR SACRED RELIGION?
YOU WORSHIP THE HAND OF GOD, DO YOU NOT? WELL I'LL SHOW YOU MY HAND!
GLLLGGHH!
CORRADO, GATHER THE TROOPS AND GET THIS CORPSE OFF MY THRONE. IF THERE IS ROYALTY AT THE MONASTERY, WE WILL FIND IT. IF NOT, WE SHALL HAVE WIPED OUT ANOTHER FACTION, REGARDLESS.
WE CANNOT LOSE!

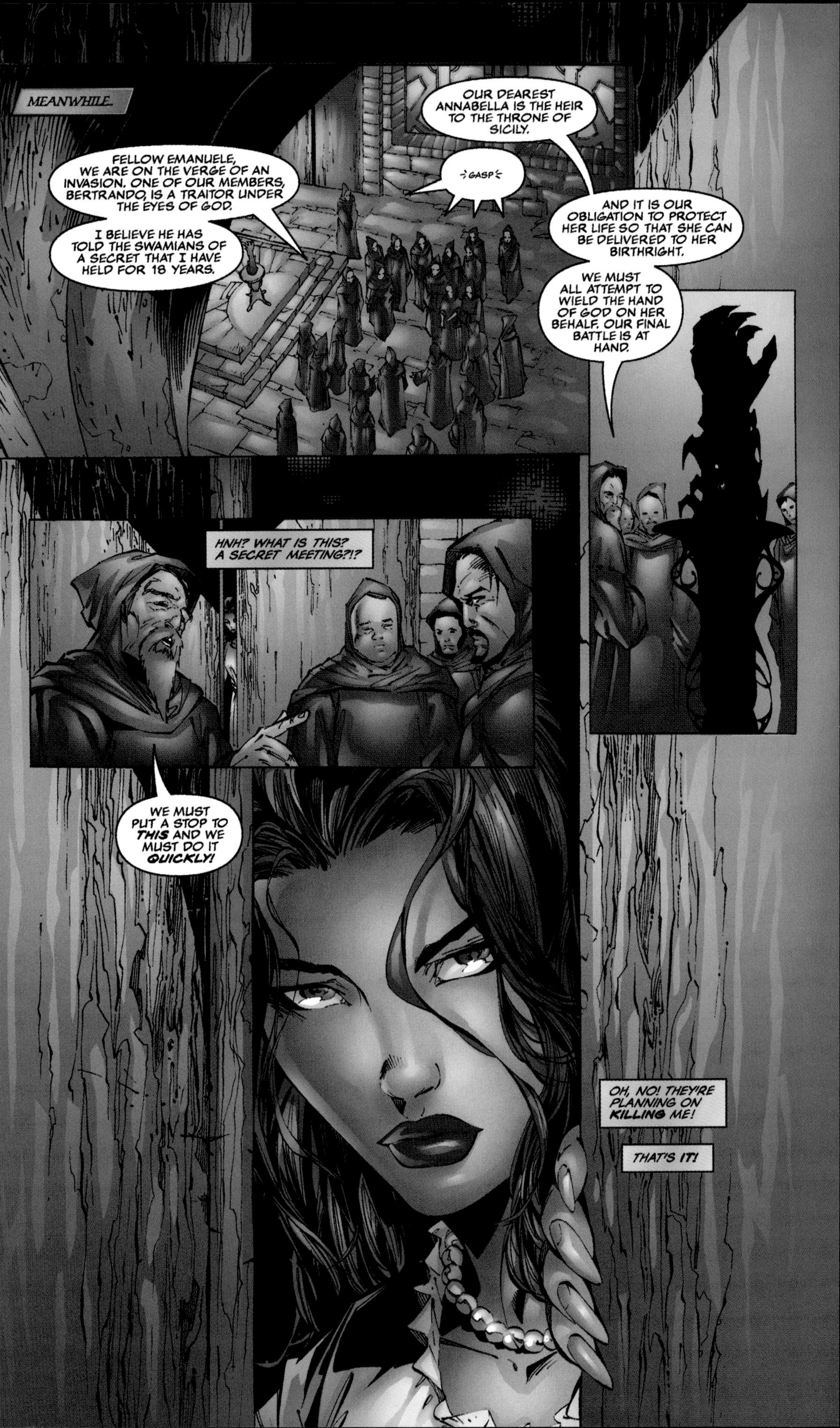
MEANWHILE...
FELLOW EMANUELE, WE ARE ON THE VERGE OF AN INVASION. ONE OF OUR MEMBERS, BERTRANDO, IS A TRAITOR UNDER THE EYES OF GOD.
I BELIEVE HE HAS TOLD THE SWAMIANS OF A SECRET THAT I HAVE HELD FOR 18 YEARS.
GASP
OUR DEAREST ANNABELLA IS THE HEIR TO THE THRONE OF SICILY.
AND IT IS OUR OBLIGATION TO PROTECT HER LIFE SO THAT SHE CAN BE DELIVERED TO HER BIRTHRIGHT.
WE MUST ALL ATTEMPT TO WIELD THE HAND OF GOD ON HER BEHALF. OUR FINAL BATTLE IS AT HAND.
HNH? WHAT IS THIS? A SECRET MEETING?!?
WE MUST PUT A STOP TO THIS AND WE MUST DO IT QUICKLY!
OH, NO! THEY'RE PLANNING ON KILLING ME!
THAT'S IT!

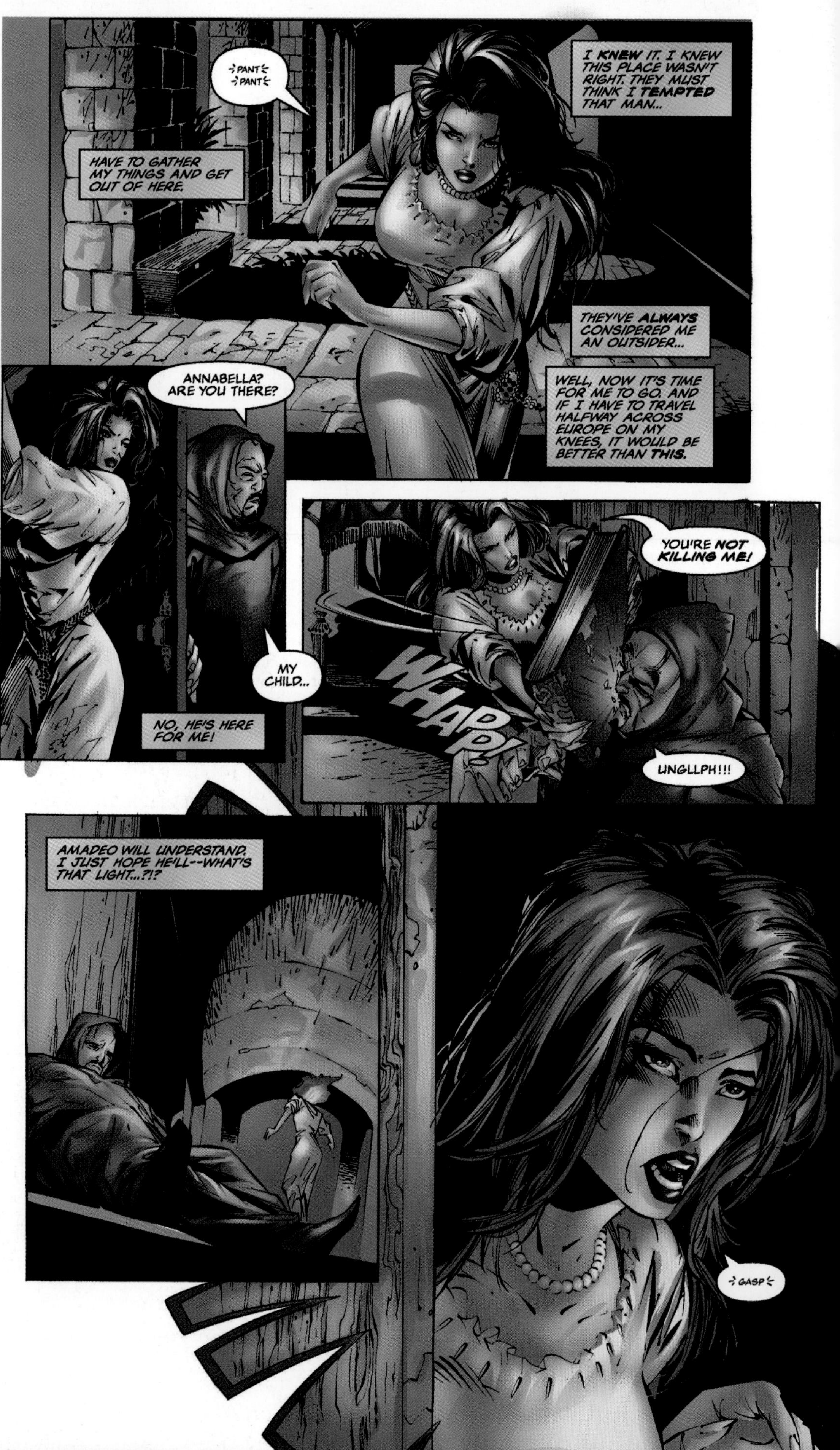
PANT
PANT
I KNEW IT. I KNEW THIS PLACE WASN'T RIGHT. THEY MUST THINK I TEMPTED THAT MAN...
HAVE TO GATHER MY THINGS AND GET OUT OF HERE.
THEY'VE ALWAYS CONSIDERED ME AN OUTSIDER...
WELL, NOW IT'S TIME FOR ME TO GO. AND IF I HAVE TO TRAVEL HALFWAY ACROSS EUROPE ON MY KNEES, IT WOULD BE BETTER THAN THIS.
ANNABELLA? ARE YOU THERE?
MY CHILD...
NO, HE'S HERE FOR ME!
YOU'RE NOT KILLING ME!
WHAP!
UNGLLPH!!!
AMADEO WILL UNDERSTAND. I JUST HOPE HE'LL--WHAT'S THAT LIGHT...?!?
GASP

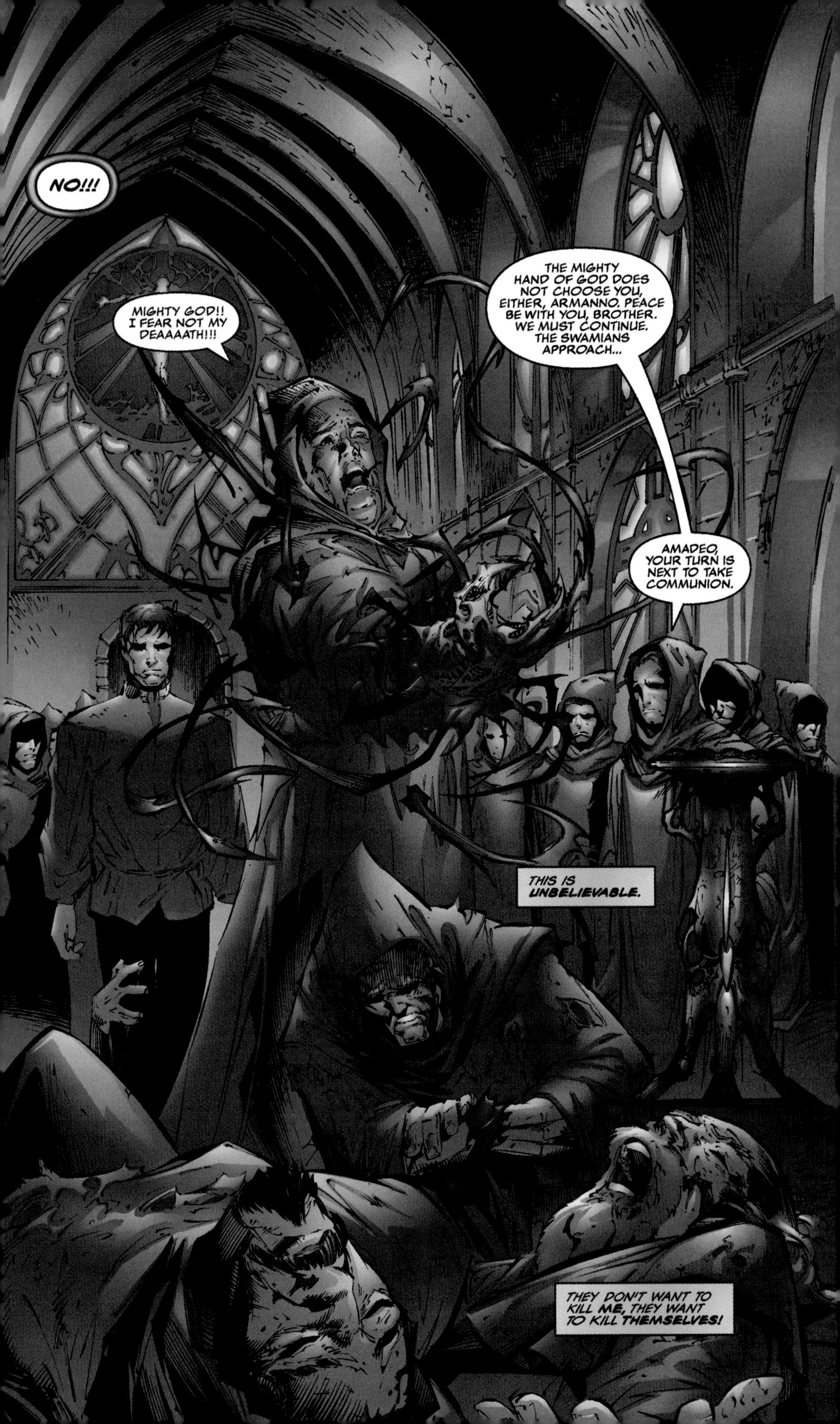
NO!!!
MIGHTY GOD!! I FEAR NOT MY DEAAAATH!!!
THE MIGHTY HAND OF GOD DOES NOT CHOOSE YOU, EITHER, ARMANNO. PEACE BE WITH YOU, BROTHER. WE MUST CONTINUE. THE SWAMIANS APPROACH...
AMADEO, YOUR TURN IS NEXT TO TAKE COMMUNION.
THIS IS UNBELIEVABLE.
THEY DON'T WANT TO KILL ME, THEY WANT TO KILL THEMSELVES!

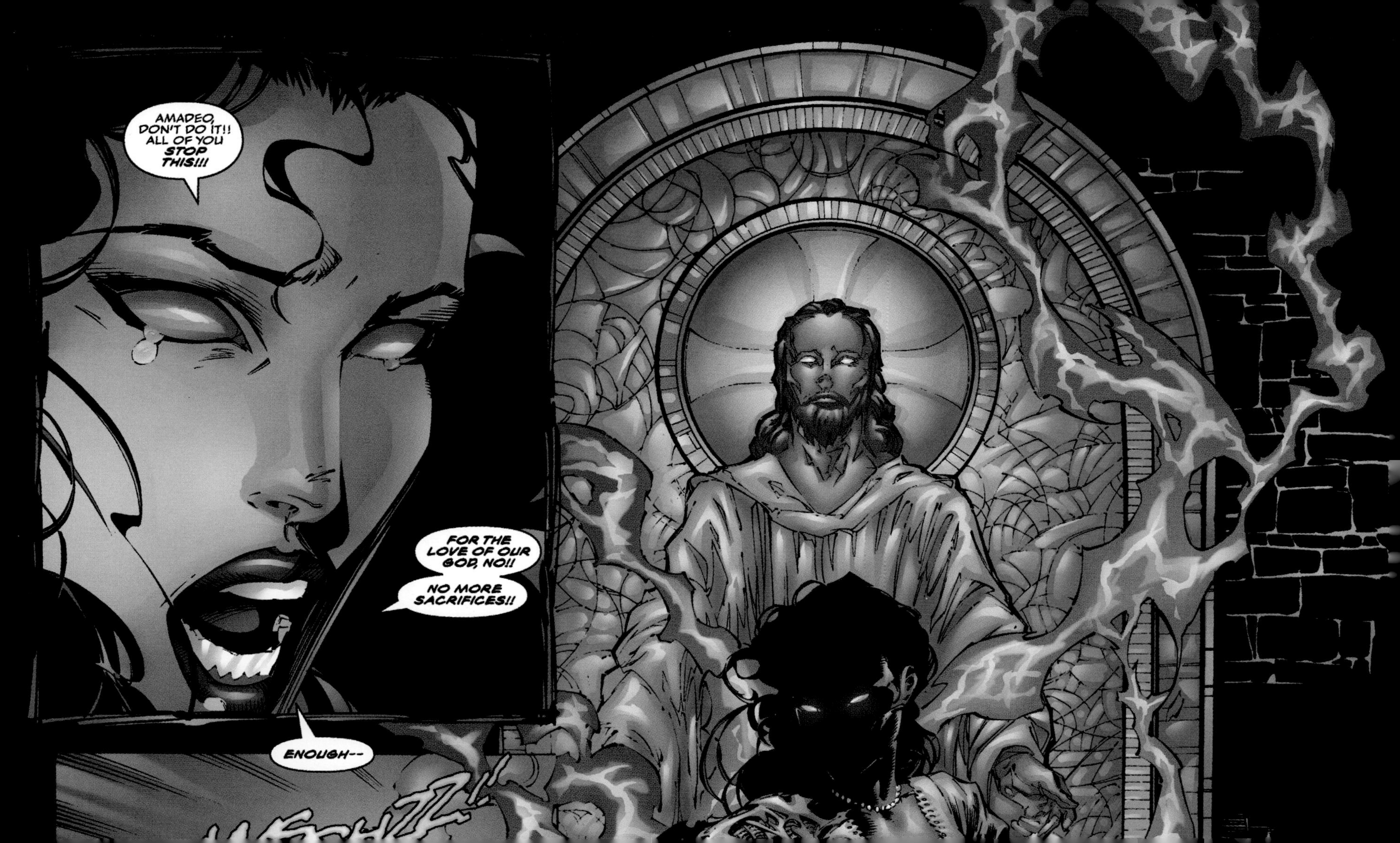
AMADEO, DON'T DO IT!! ALL OF YOU STOP THIS!!!
FOR THE LOVE OF OUR GOD, NO!!
NO MORE SACRIFICES!!
ENOUGH--

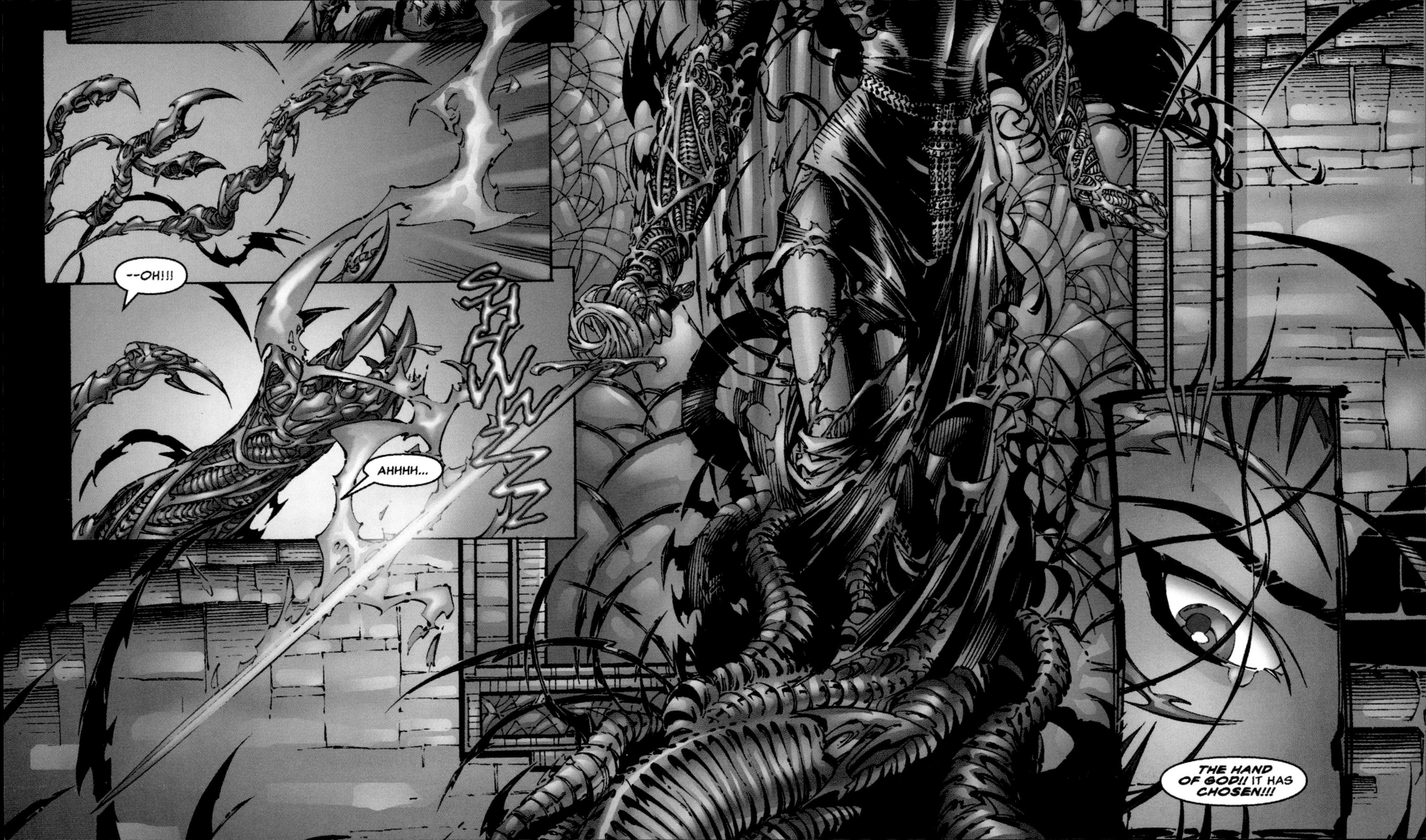
--OH!!!
AHHHH...
SHWNNZ
THE HAND OF GOD!! IT HAS CHOSEN!!!

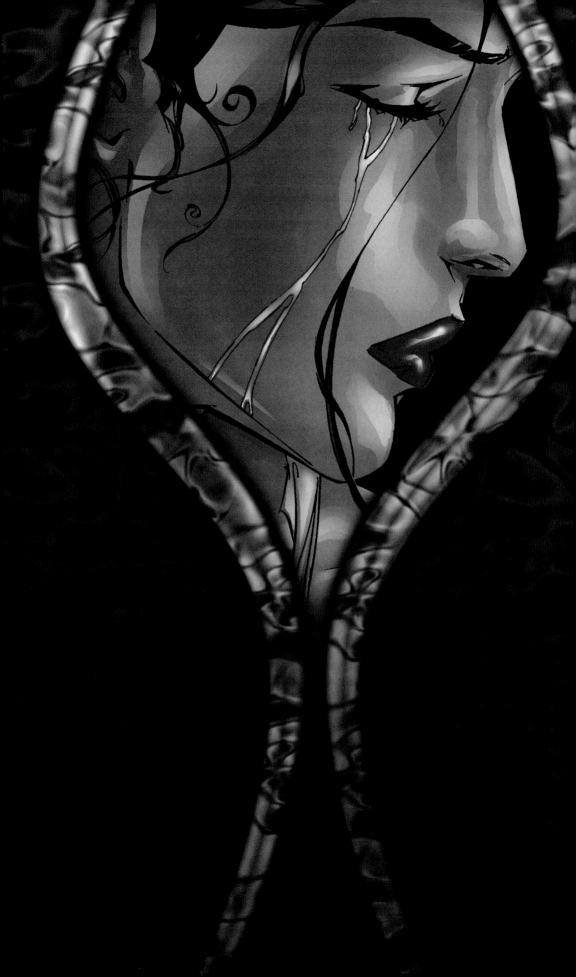

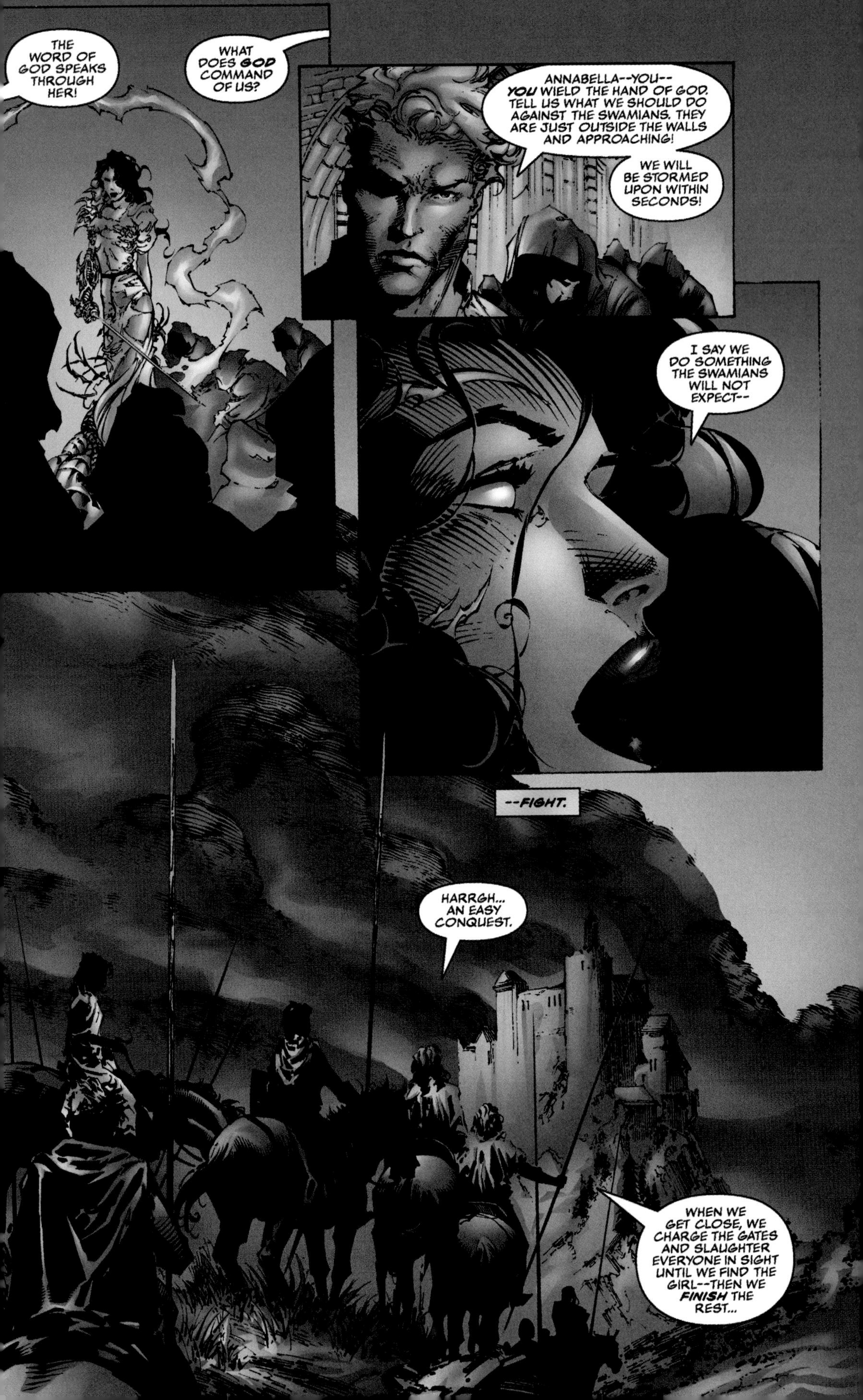
THE WORD OF GOD SPEAKS THROUGH HER!
WHAT DOES GOD COMMAND OF US?
ANNABELLA--YOU-- YOU WIELD THE HAND OF GOD. TELL US WHAT WE SHOULD DO AGAINST THE SWAMIANS. THEY ARE JUST OUTSIDE THE WALLS AND APPROACHING!
WE WILL BE STORMED UPON WITHIN SECONDS!
I SAY WE DO SOMETHING THE SWAMIANS WILL NOT EXPECT--
--FIGHT.
HARRGH... AN EASY CONQUEST.
WHEN WE GET CLOSE, WE CHARGE THE GATES AND SLAUGHTER EVERYONE IN SIGHT UNTIL WE FIND THE GIRL--THEN WE FINISH THE REST...

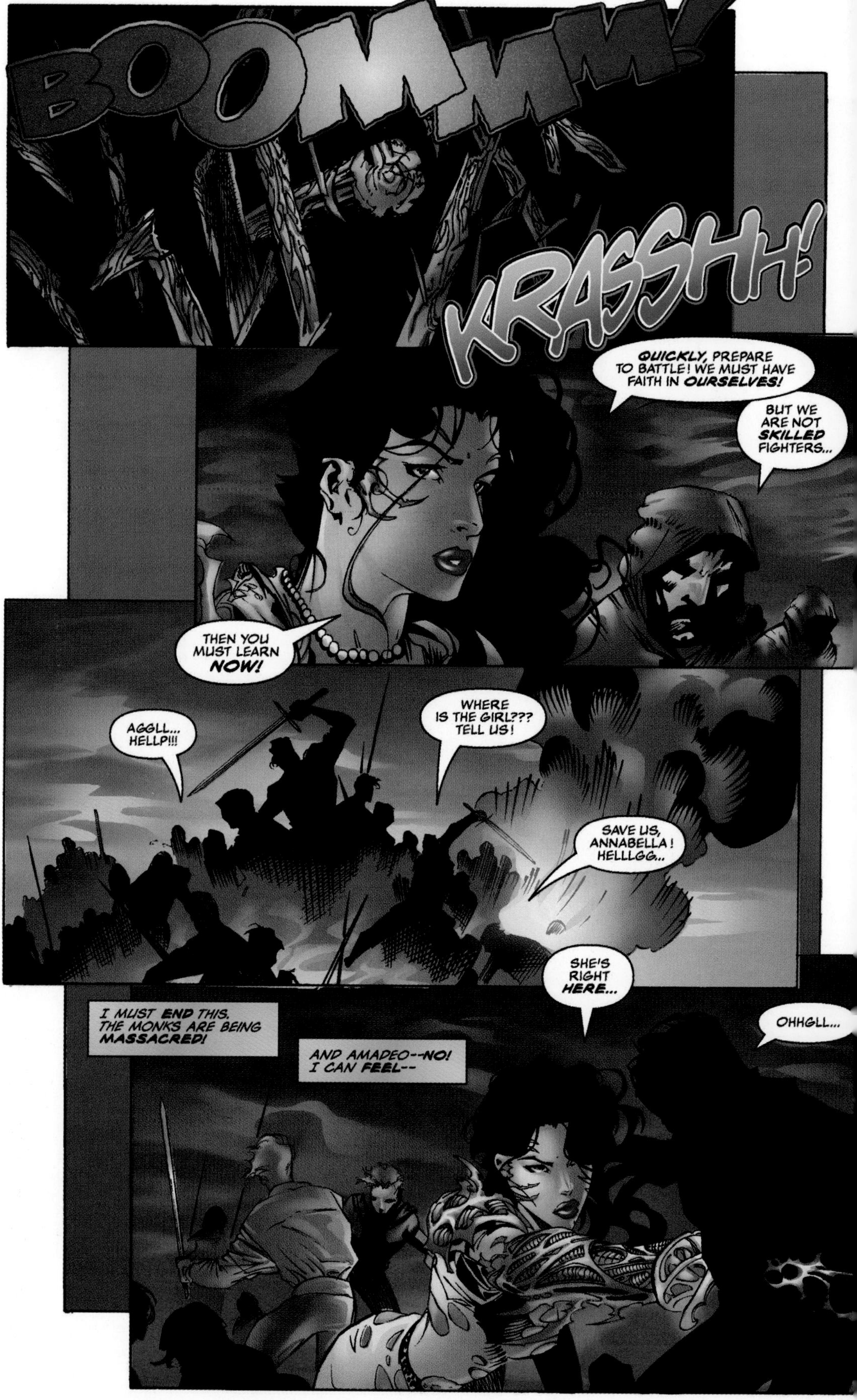
BOOMMM!
KRASSHH!
QUICKLY, PREPARE TO BATTLE! WE MUST HAVE FAITH IN OURSELVES!
BUT WE ARE NOT SKILLED FIGHTERS...
THEN YOU MUST LEARN NOW!
AGGLL... HELLP!!!
WHERE IS THE GIRL??? TELL US!
SAVE US, ANNABELLA! HELLLGG...
SHE'S RIGHT HERE...
OHHGLL...
I MUST END THIS. THE MONKS ARE BEING MASSACRED!
AND AMADEO--NO! I CAN FEEL--

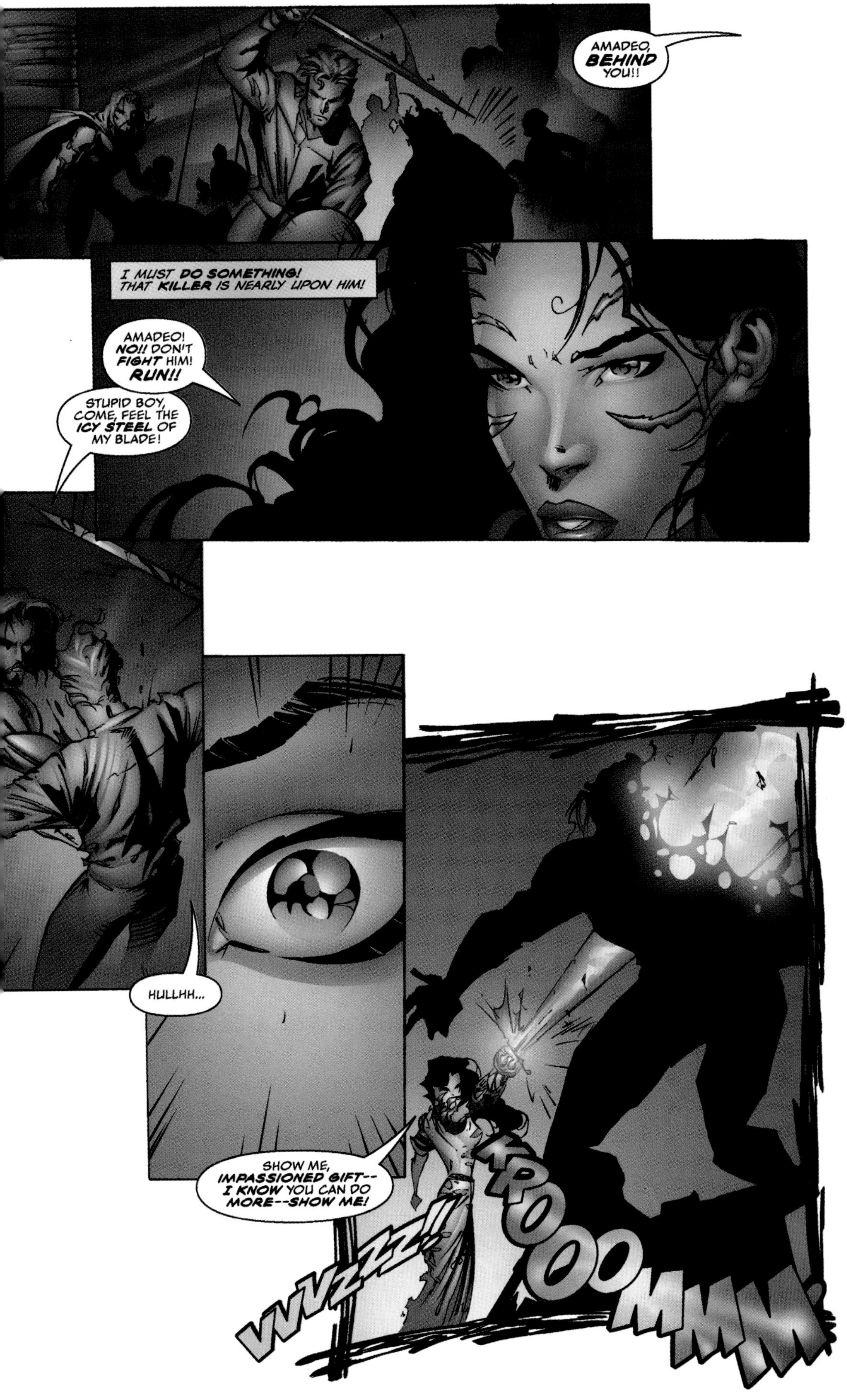
AMADEO, BEHIND YOU!!
I MUST DO SOMETHING! THAT KILLER IS NEARLY UPON HIM!
AMADEO! NO!! DON'T FIGHT HIM! RUN!!
STUPID BOY, COME, FEEL THE ICY STEEL OF MY BLADE!
HULLHH...
SHOW ME, IMPASSIONED GIFT-- I KNOW YOU CAN DO MORE--SHOW ME!
VVVZZZ!!
KROOOMMMM!

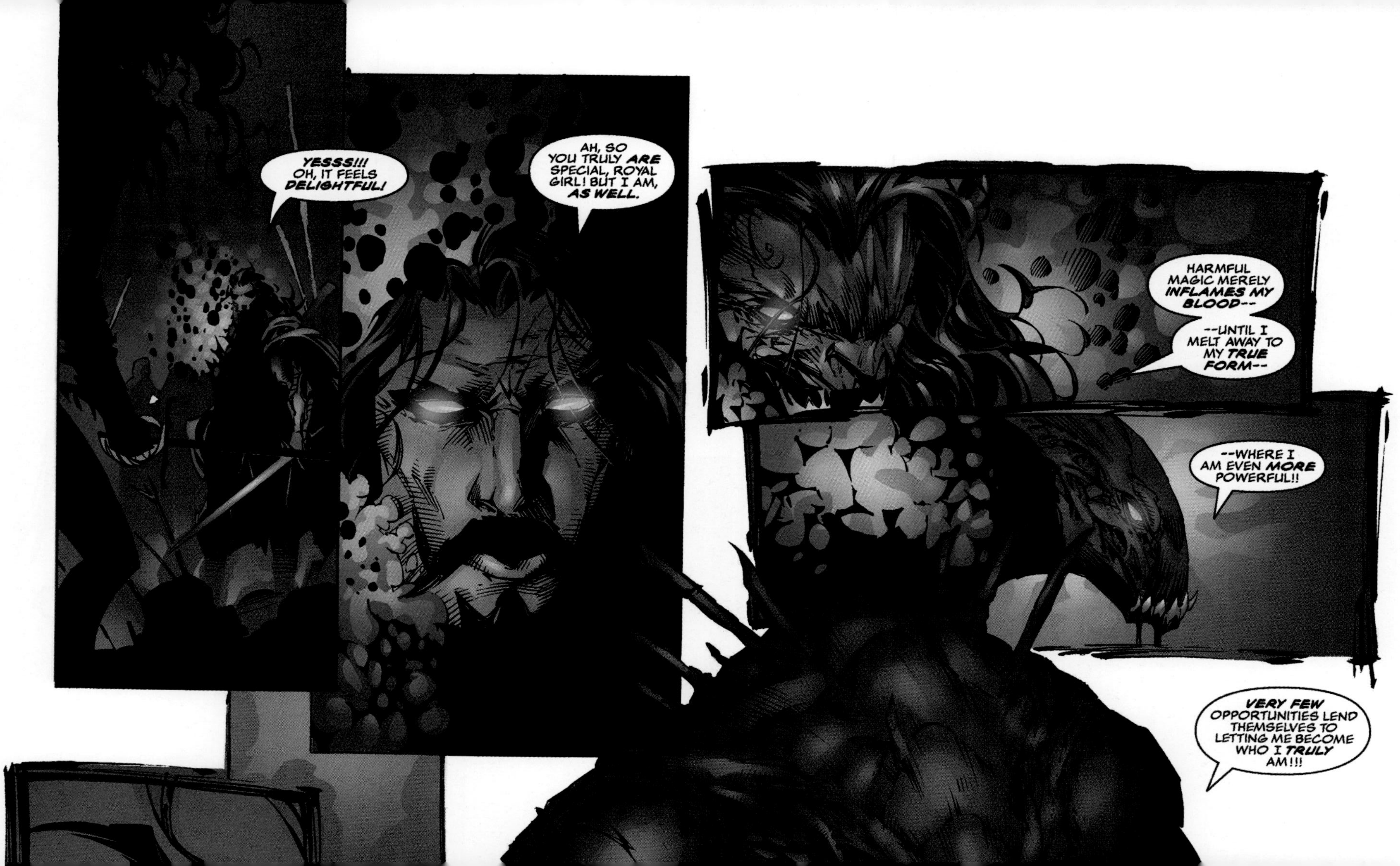
YESSS!!! OH, IT FEELS DELIGHTFUL!
AH, SO YOU TRULY ARE SPECIAL, ROYAL GIRL! BUT I AM, AS WELL.
HARMFUL MAGIC MERELY INFLAMES MY BLOOD--
--UNTIL I MELT AWAY TO MY TRUE FORM--
--WHERE I AM EVEN MORE POWERFUL!!
VERY FEW OPPORTUNITIES LEND THEMSELVES TO LETTING ME BECOME WHO I TRULY AM!!!

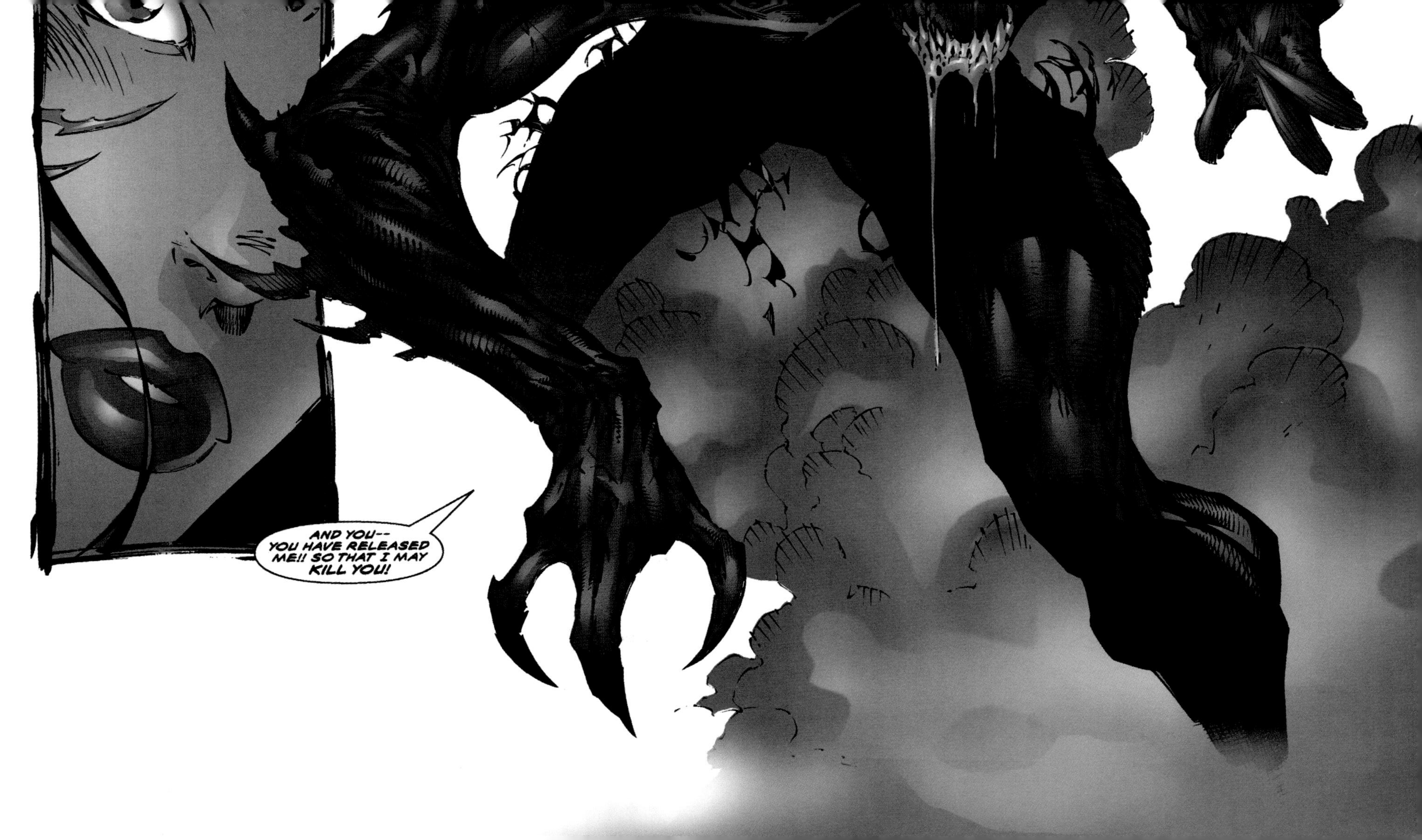
AND YOU-- YOU HAVE RELEASED ME!! SO THAT I MAY KILL YOU!

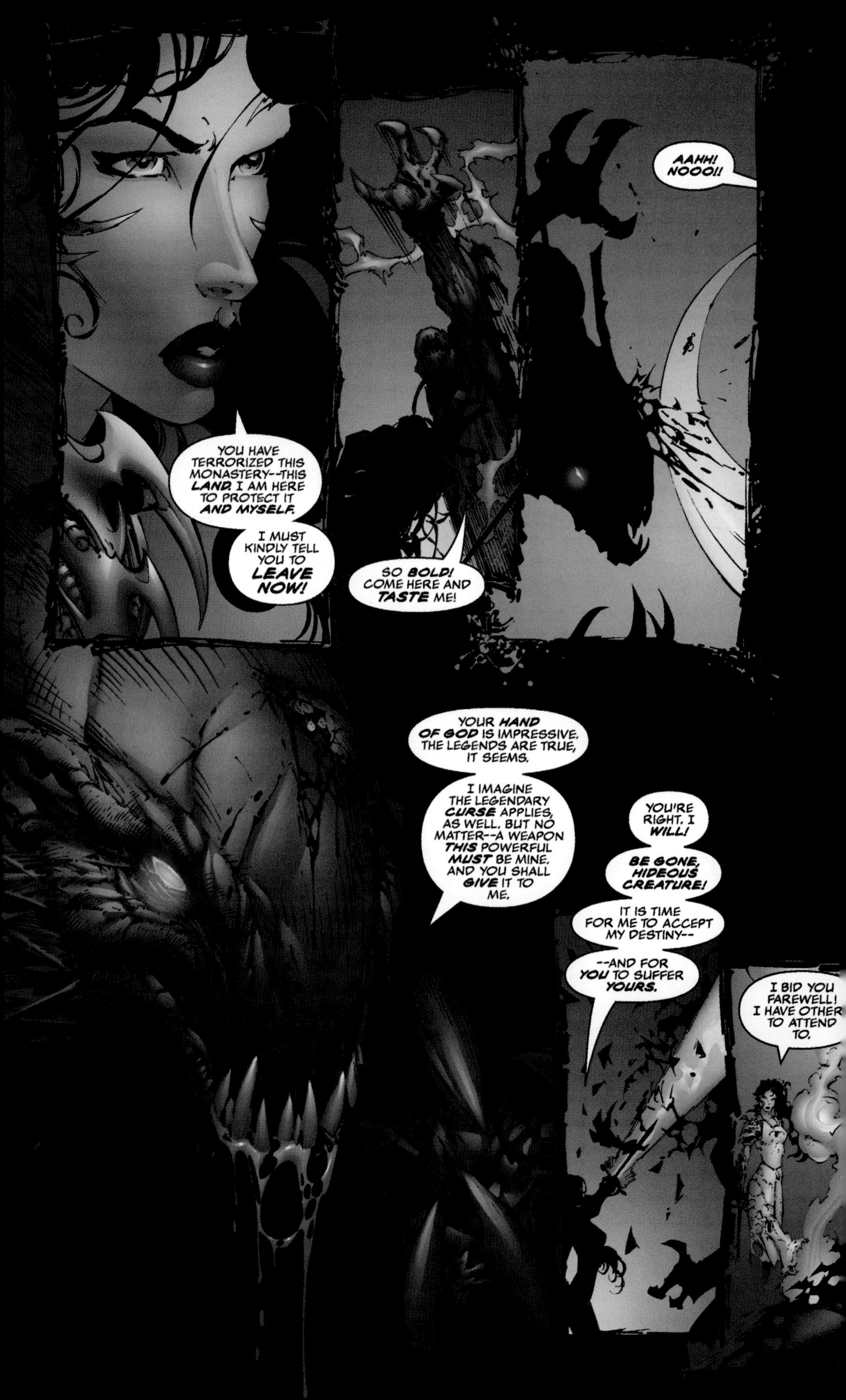
YOU HAVE TERRORIZED THIS MONASTERY--THIS LAND. I AM HERE TO PROTECT IT AND MYSELF.
I MUST KINDLY TELL YOU TO LEAVE NOW!
SO BOLD! COME HERE AND TASTE ME!
AAHH! NOOO!!
YOUR HAND OF GOD IS IMPRESSIVE. THE LEGENDS ARE TRUE, IT SEEMS.
I IMAGINE THE LEGENDARY CURSE APPLIES, AS WELL. BUT NO MATTER--A WEAPON THIS POWERFUL MUST BE MINE. AND YOU SHALL GIVE IT TO ME.
YOU'RE RIGHT. I WILL!
BE GONE, HIDEOUS CREATURE!
IT IS TIME FOR ME TO ACCEPT MY DESTINY--
--AND FOR YOU TO SUFFER YOURS.
I BID YOU FAREWELL! I HAVE OTHER TO ATTEND TO.

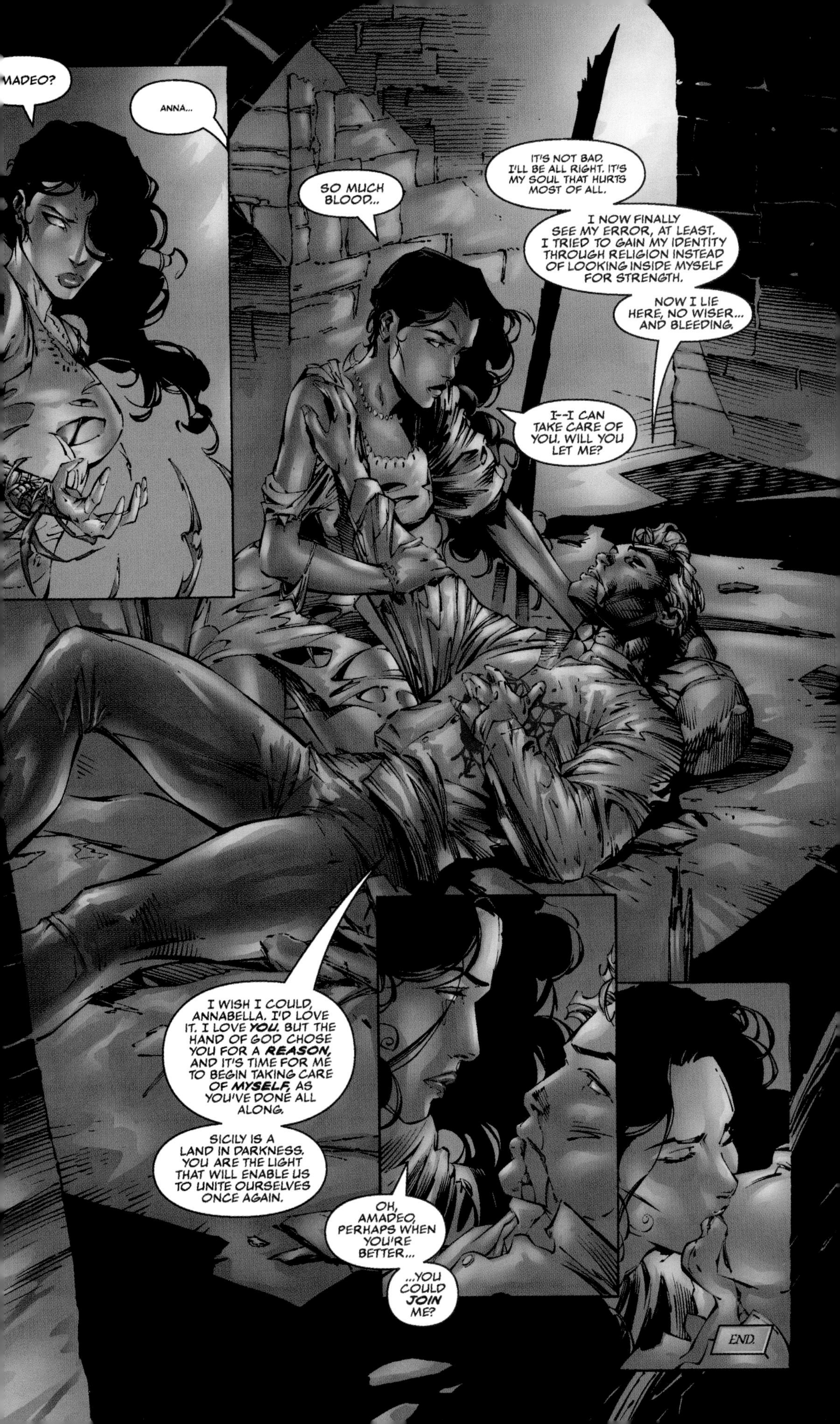
MADEO?
ANNA...
SO MUCH BLOOD...
IT'S NOT BAD. I'LL BE ALL RIGHT. IT'S MY SOUL THAT HURTS MOST OF ALL.
I NOW FINALLY SEE MY ERROR, AT LEAST. I TRIED TO GAIN MY IDENTITY THROUGH RELIGION INSTEAD OF LOOKING INSIDE MYSELF FOR STRENGTH.
NOW I LIE HERE, NO WISER... AND BLEEDING.
I--I CAN TAKE CARE OF YOU. WILL YOU LET ME?
I WISH I COULD, ANNABELLA. I'D LOVE IT. I LOVE YOU. BUT THE HAND OF GOD CHOSE YOU FOR A REASON, AND IT'S TIME FOR ME TO BEGIN TAKING CARE OF MYSELF, AS YOU'VE DONE ALL ALONG.
SICILY IS A LAND IN DARKNESS. YOU ARE THE LIGHT THAT WILL ENABLE US TO UNITE OURSELVES ONCE AGAIN.
OH, AMADEO, PERHAPS WHEN YOU'RE BETTER...
...YOU COULD JOIN ME?
END.

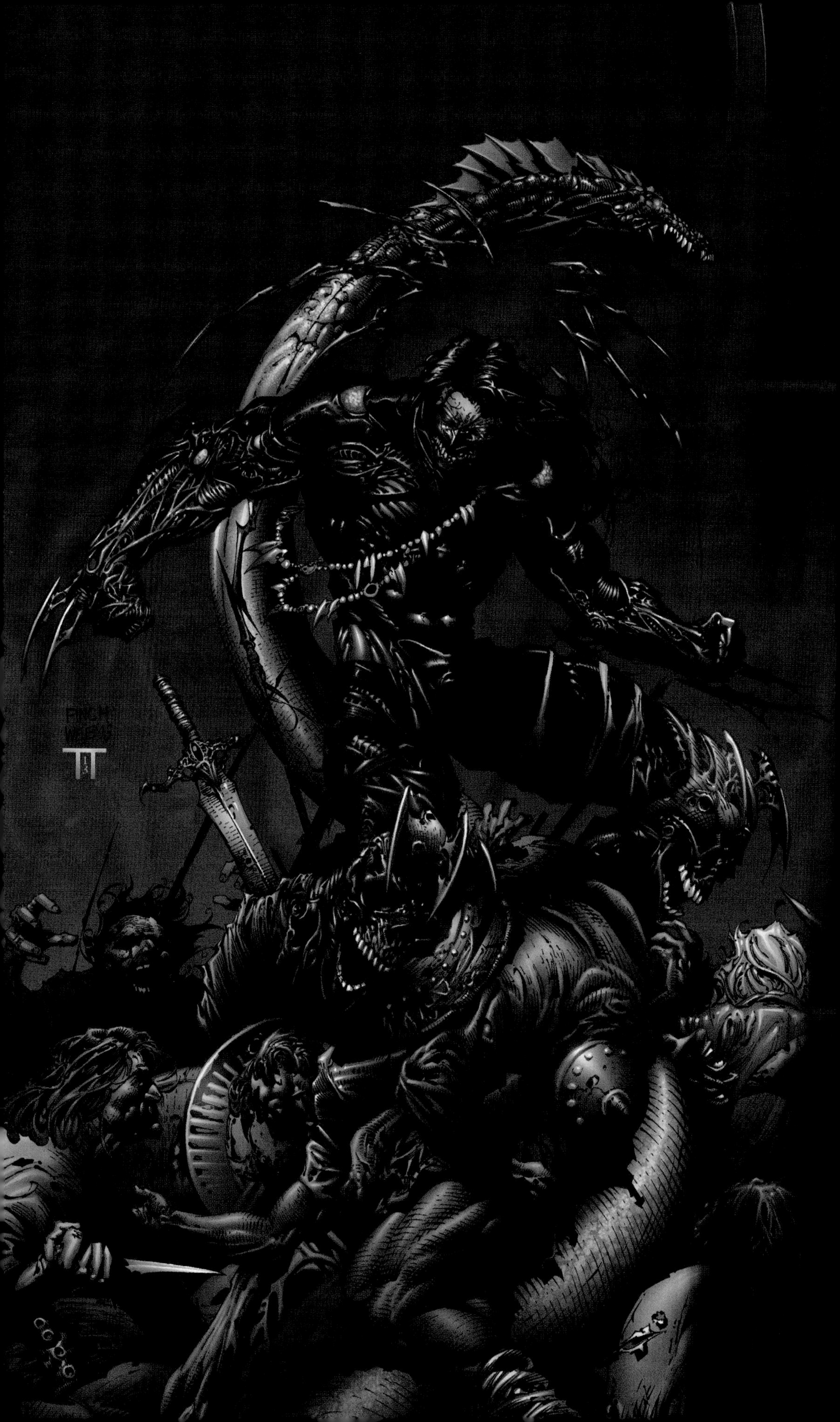

THE DARKNESS

The following story was originally
slated as a *Tales of the Darkness* story
but was moved as a fill-in issue on
the regular series. The pencils for
page 2 and 3 are so detailed they
were once used as a test for
prospective inkers.

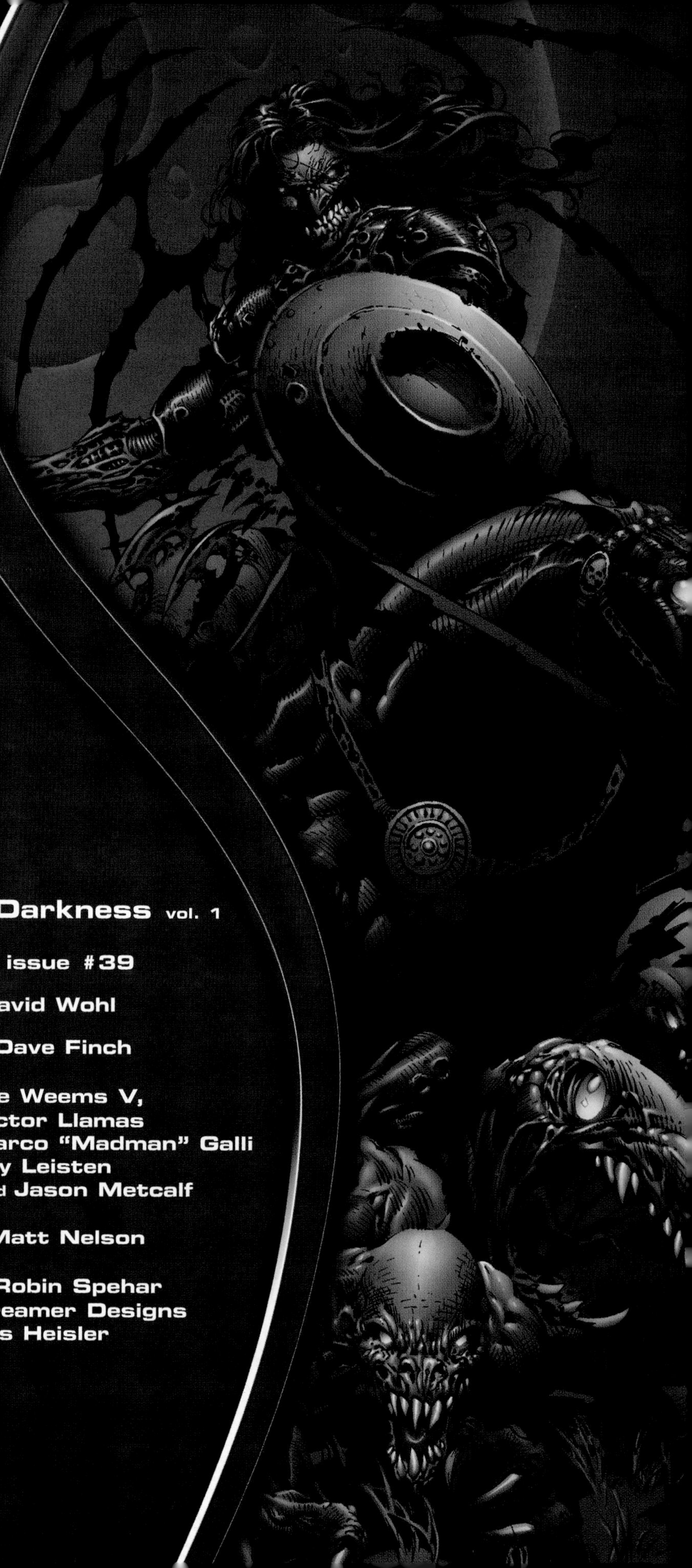

The Darkness vol. 1

issue #39

story by: **David Wohl**

pencils by: **Dave Finch**

inks by: **Joe Weems V,**
Victor Llamas
Marco "Madman" Galli
Jay Leisten
and **Jason Metcalf**

colors by: **Matt Nelson**

letters by: **Robin Spehar**
and **Dreamer Designs**
Dennis Heisler

LADIES AND GENTLEMEN...
...BOYS AND GIRLS...
...PLEASE ALLOW ME THE INDULGENCE OF A LITTLE OF YOUR TIME...
...SO THAT I MAY TELL YOU A STORY...
...A CAUTIONARY TALE, IF YOU W--
C'MON, CORNBALL -- LET'S HEAR IT!!!
EXCUSE ME, SIR. IT'S JUST THAT THESE PEOPLE THINK THEY KNOW ABOUT THE DARK --
SO *TELL* 'EM, ALREADY!!!
ALL RIGHT, ALL RIGHT...
WHERE WAS I?
OH YES...

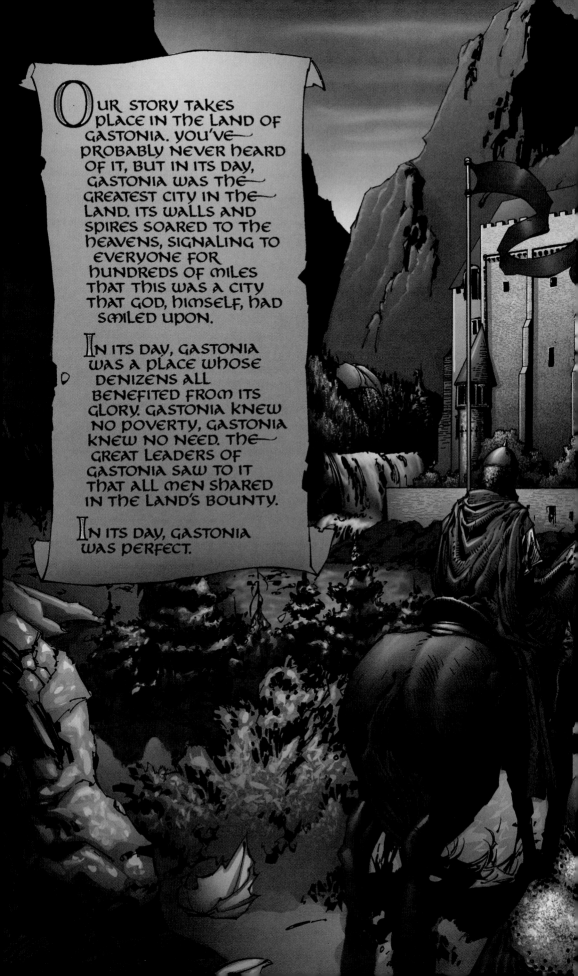

OUR STORY TAKES PLACE IN THE LAND OF GASTONIA. YOU'VE PROBABLY NEVER HEARD OF IT, BUT IN ITS DAY, GASTONIA WAS THE GREATEST CITY IN THE LAND. ITS WALLS AND SPIRES SOARED TO THE HEAVENS, SIGNALING TO EVERYONE FOR HUNDREDS OF MILES THAT THIS WAS A CITY THAT GOD, HIMSELF, HAD SMILED UPON.

IN ITS DAY, GASTONIA WAS A PLACE WHOSE DENIZENS ALL BENEFITED FROM ITS GLORY. GASTONIA KNEW NO POVERTY, GASTONIA KNEW NO NEED. THE GREAT LEADERS OF GASTONIA SAW TO IT THAT ALL MEN SHARED IN THE LAND'S BOUNTY.

IN ITS DAY, GASTONIA WAS PERFECT.

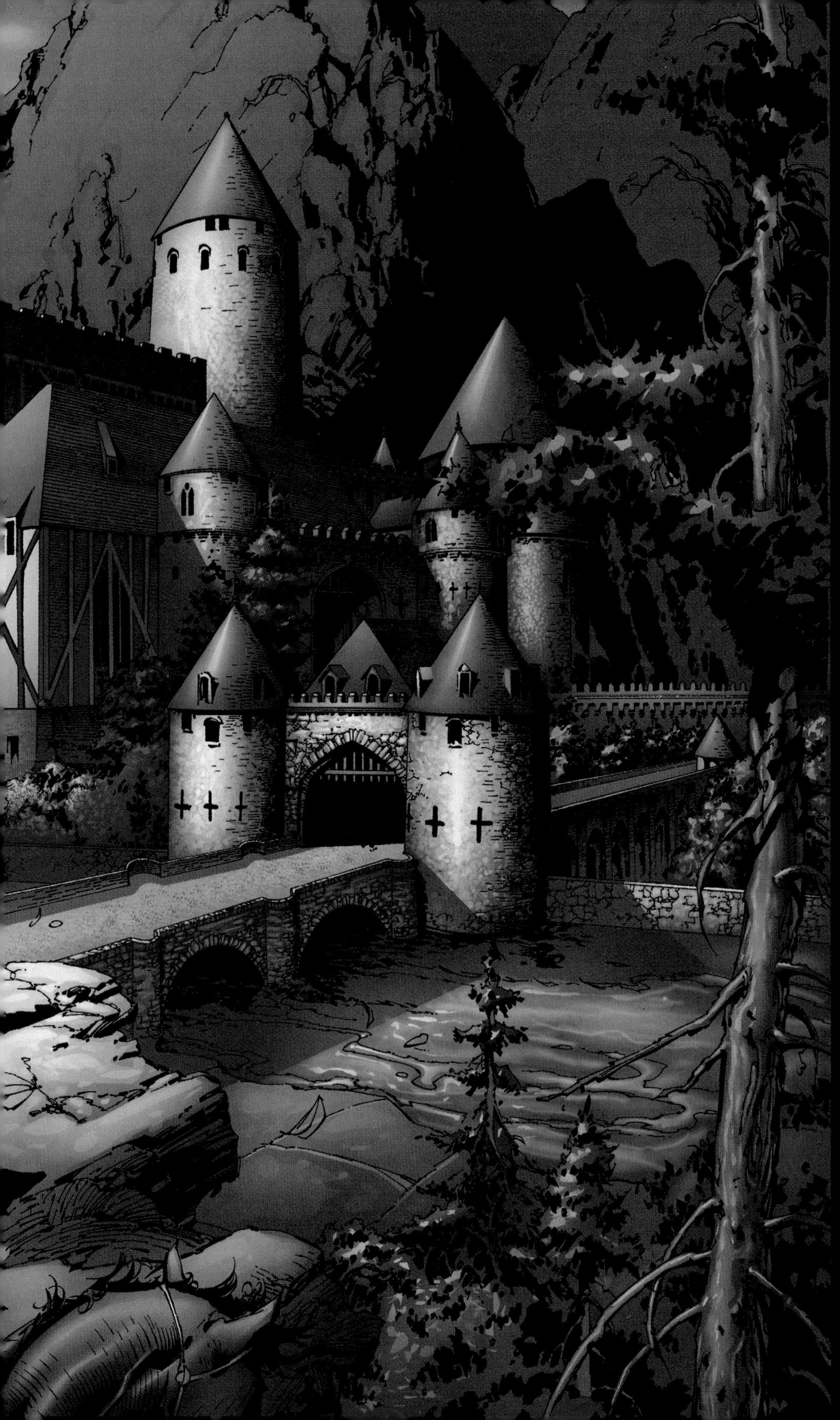

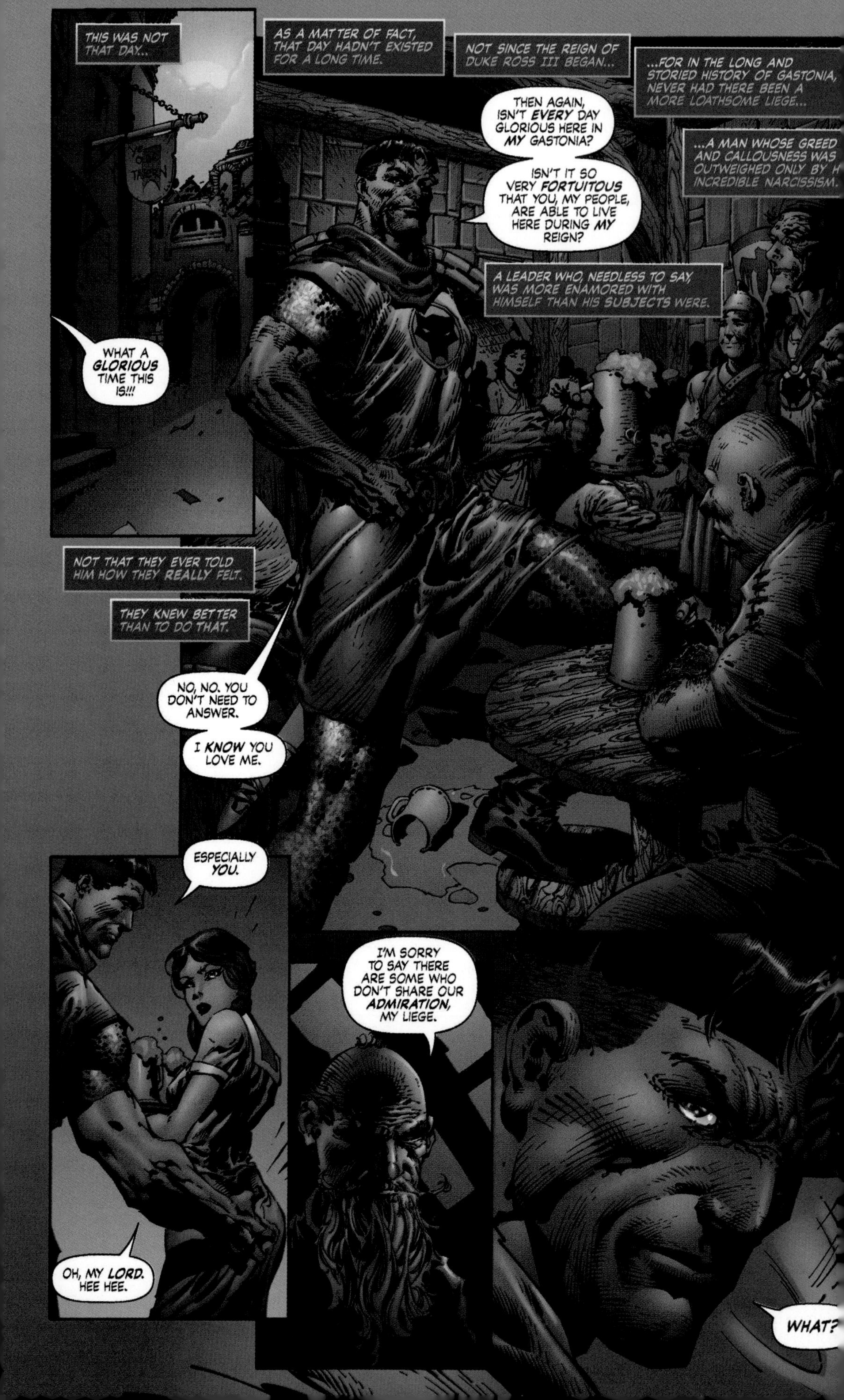
THIS WAS NOT THAT DAY...
AS A MATTER OF FACT, THAT DAY HADN'T EXISTED FOR A LONG TIME.
NOT SINCE THE REIGN OF DUKE ROSS III BEGAN...
...FOR IN THE LONG AND STORIED HISTORY OF GASTONIA, NEVER HAD THERE BEEN A MORE LOATHSOME LIEGE...
...A MAN WHOSE GREED AND CALLOUSNESS WAS OUTWEIGHED ONLY BY H INCREDIBLE NARCISSISM.
WHAT A GLORIOUS TIME THIS IS!!!
THEN AGAIN, ISN'T EVERY DAY GLORIOUS HERE IN MY GASTONIA?
ISN'T IT SO VERY FORTUITOUS THAT YOU, MY PEOPLE, ARE ABLE TO LIVE HERE DURING MY REIGN?
A LEADER WHO, NEEDLESS TO SAY, WAS MORE ENAMORED WITH HIMSELF THAN HIS SUBJECTS WERE.
NOT THAT THEY EVER TOLD HIM HOW THEY REALLY FELT.
THEY KNEW BETTER THAN TO DO THAT.
NO, NO. YOU DON'T NEED TO ANSWER.
I KNOW YOU LOVE ME.
ESPECIALLY YOU.
OH, MY LORD. HEE HEE.
I'M SORRY TO SAY THERE ARE SOME WHO DON'T SHARE OUR ADMIRATION, MY LIEGE.
WHAT?

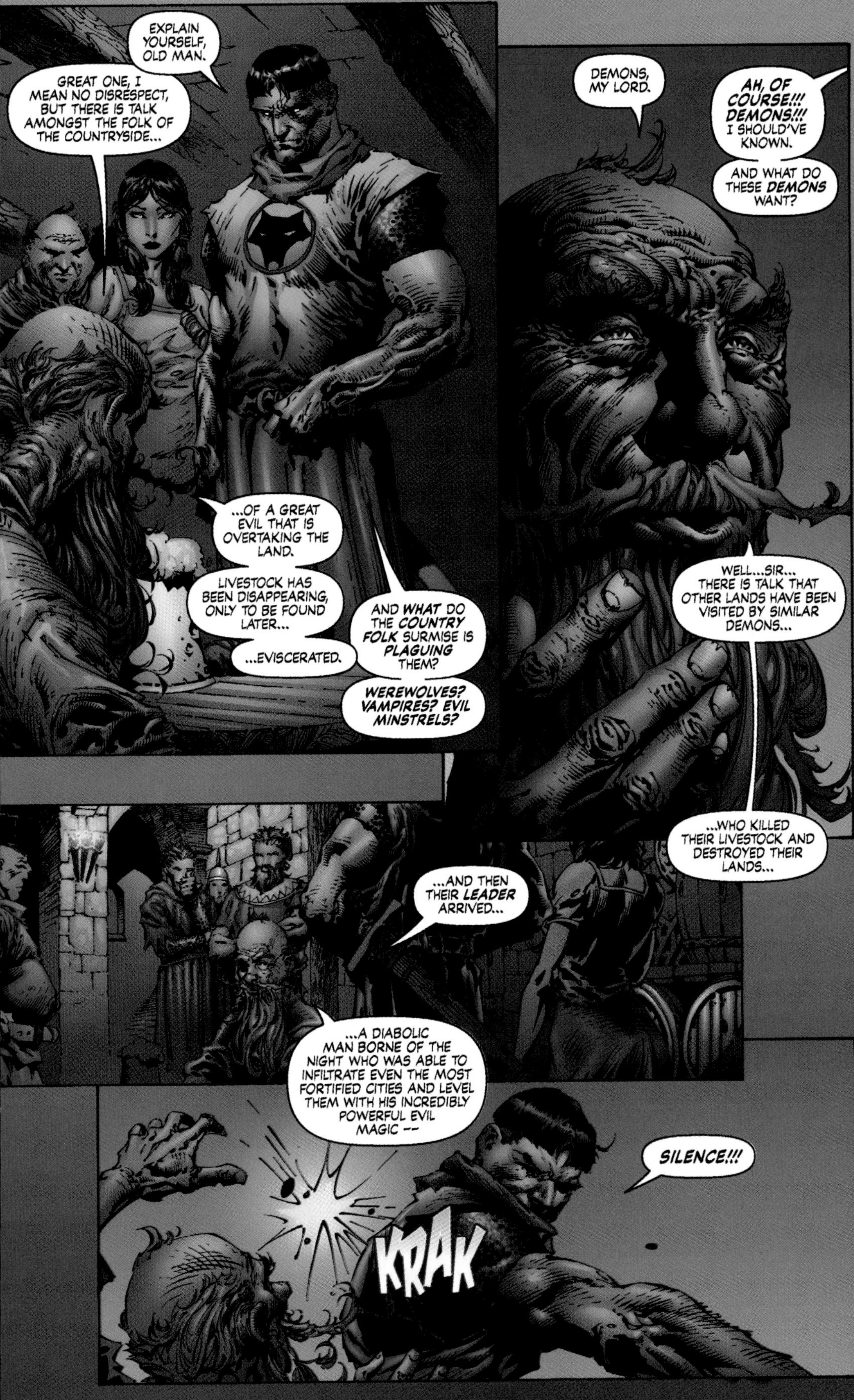
EXPLAIN YOURSELF, OLD MAN.
GREAT ONE, I MEAN NO DISRESPECT, BUT THERE IS TALK AMONGST THE FOLK OF THE COUNTRYSIDE...
...OF A GREAT EVIL THAT IS OVERTAKING THE LAND.
LIVESTOCK HAS BEEN DISAPPEARING, ONLY TO BE FOUND LATER...
...EVISCERATED.
AND WHAT DO THE COUNTRY FOLK SURMISE IS PLAGUING THEM?
WEREWOLVES? VAMPIRES? EVIL MINSTRELS?
DEMONS, MY LORD.
AH, OF COURSE!!! DEMONS!!! I SHOULD'VE KNOWN.
AND WHAT DO THESE DEMONS WANT?
WELL...SIR... THERE IS TALK THAT OTHER LANDS HAVE BEEN VISITED BY SIMILAR DEMONS...
...WHO KILLED THEIR LIVESTOCK AND DESTROYED THEIR LANDS...
...AND THEN THEIR LEADER ARRIVED...
...A DIABOLIC MAN BORNE OF THE NIGHT WHO WAS ABLE TO INFILTRATE EVEN THE MOST FORTIFIED CITIES AND LEVEL THEM WITH HIS INCREDIBLY POWERFUL EVIL MAGIC --
SILENCE!!!
KRAK

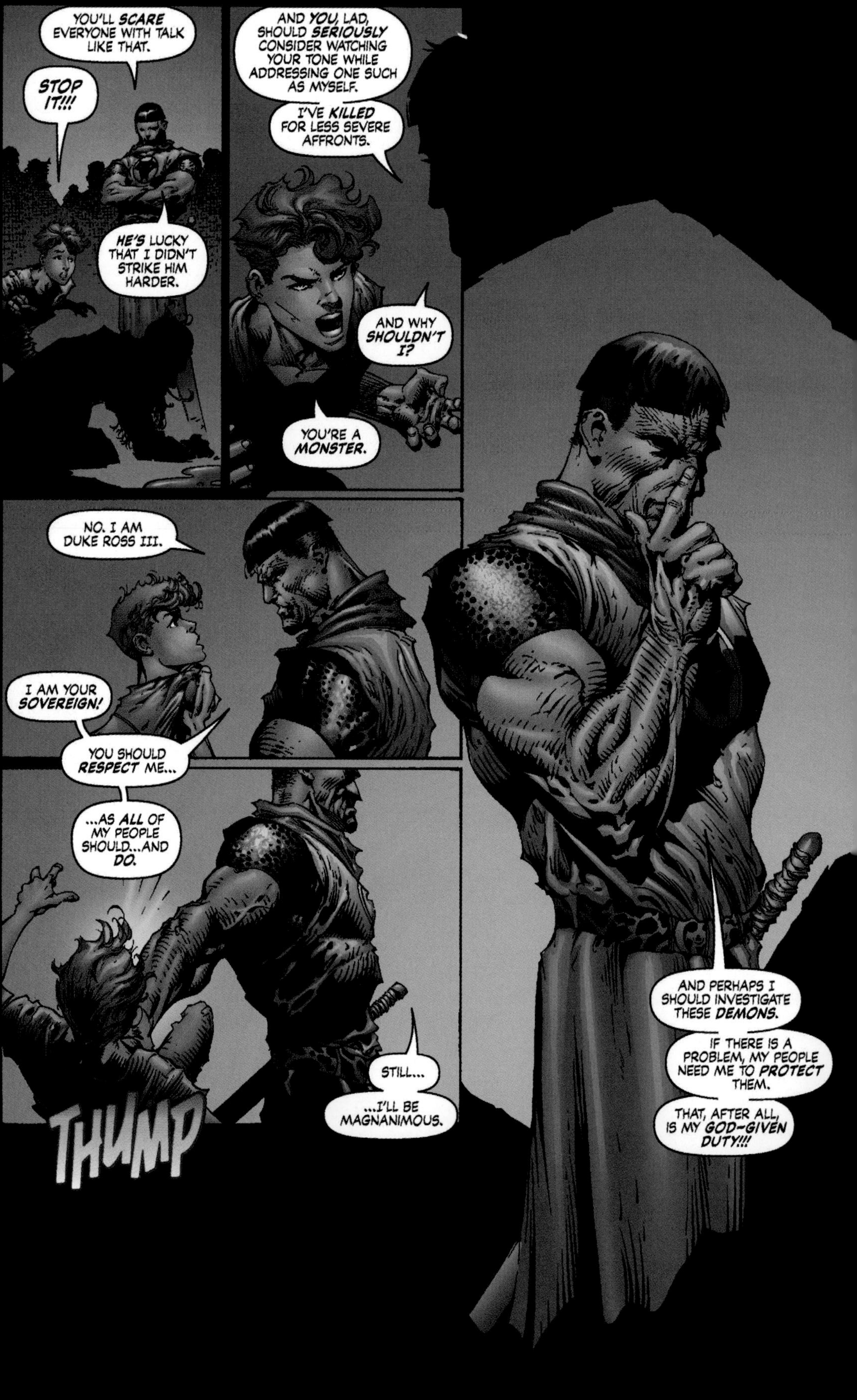
YOU'LL SCARE EVERYONE WITH TALK LIKE THAT.
STOP IT!!!
HE'S LUCKY THAT I DIDN'T STRIKE HIM HARDER.
AND YOU, LAD, SHOULD SERIOUSLY CONSIDER WATCHING YOUR TONE WHILE ADDRESSING ONE SUCH AS MYSELF.
I'VE KILLED FOR LESS SEVERE AFFRONTS.
AND WHY SHOULDN'T I?
YOU'RE A MONSTER.
NO. I AM DUKE ROSS III.
I AM YOUR SOVEREIGN!
YOU SHOULD RESPECT ME...
...AS ALL OF MY PEOPLE SHOULD...AND DO.
THUMP
STILL...
...I'LL BE MAGNANIMOUS.
AND PERHAPS I SHOULD INVESTIGATE THESE DEMONS.
IF THERE IS A PROBLEM, MY PEOPLE NEED ME TO PROTECT THEM.
THAT, AFTER ALL, IS MY GOD-GIVEN DUTY!!!

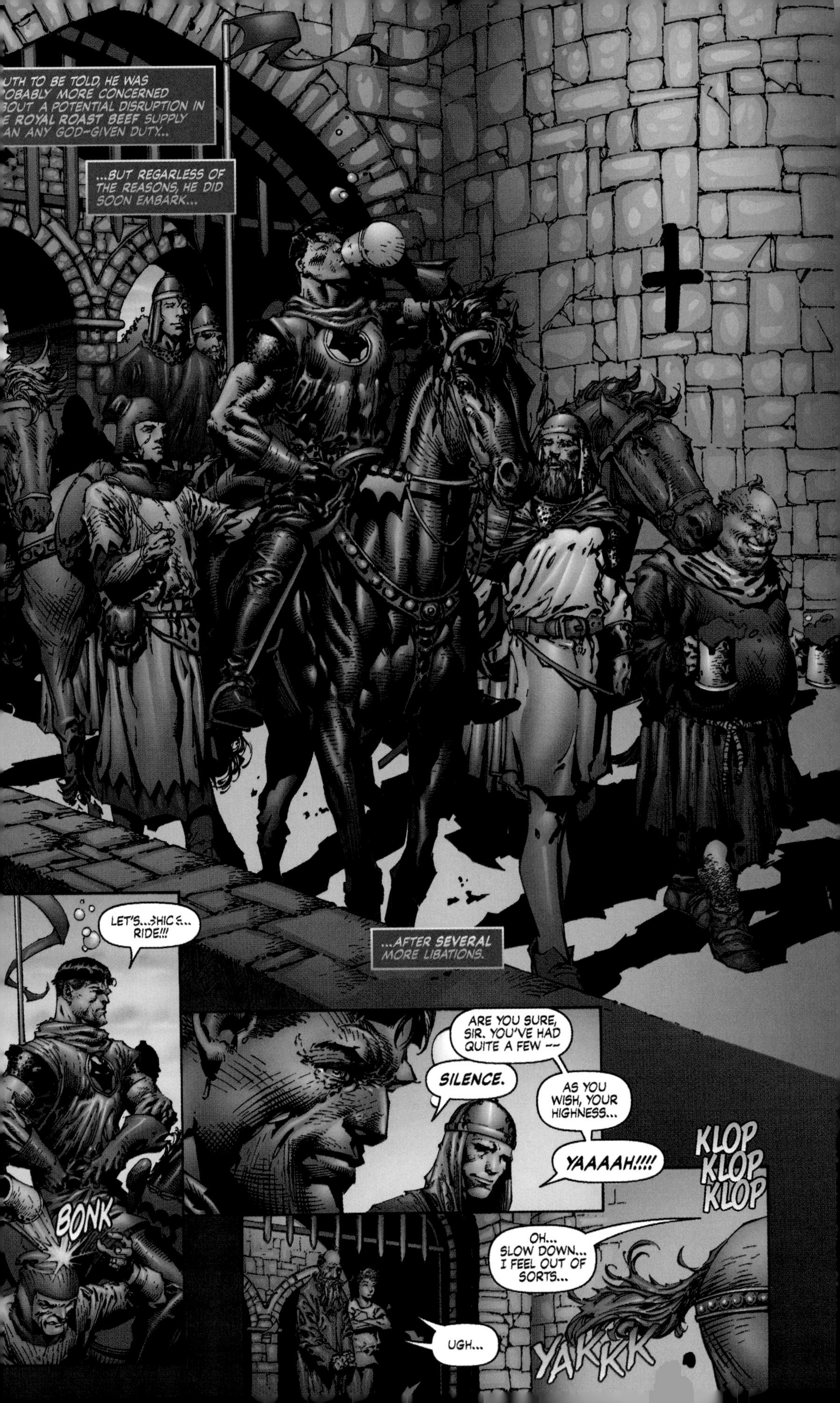
UTH TO BE TOLD, HE WAS OBABLY MORE CONCERNED BOUT A POTENTIAL DISRUPTION IN E ROYAL ROAST BEEF SUPPLY AN ANY GOD-GIVEN DUTY...
...BUT REGARLESS OF THE REASONS, HE DID SOON EMBARK...
...AFTER SEVERAL MORE LIBATIONS.
LET'S...*HIC*... RIDE!!!
ARE YOU SURE, SIR. YOU'VE HAD QUITE A FEW --
SILENCE.
AS YOU WISH, YOUR HIGHNESS...
YAAAAH!!!!
KLOP KLOP KLOP
BONK
OH... SLOW DOWN... I FEEL OUT OF SORTS...
UGH...
YAKKK

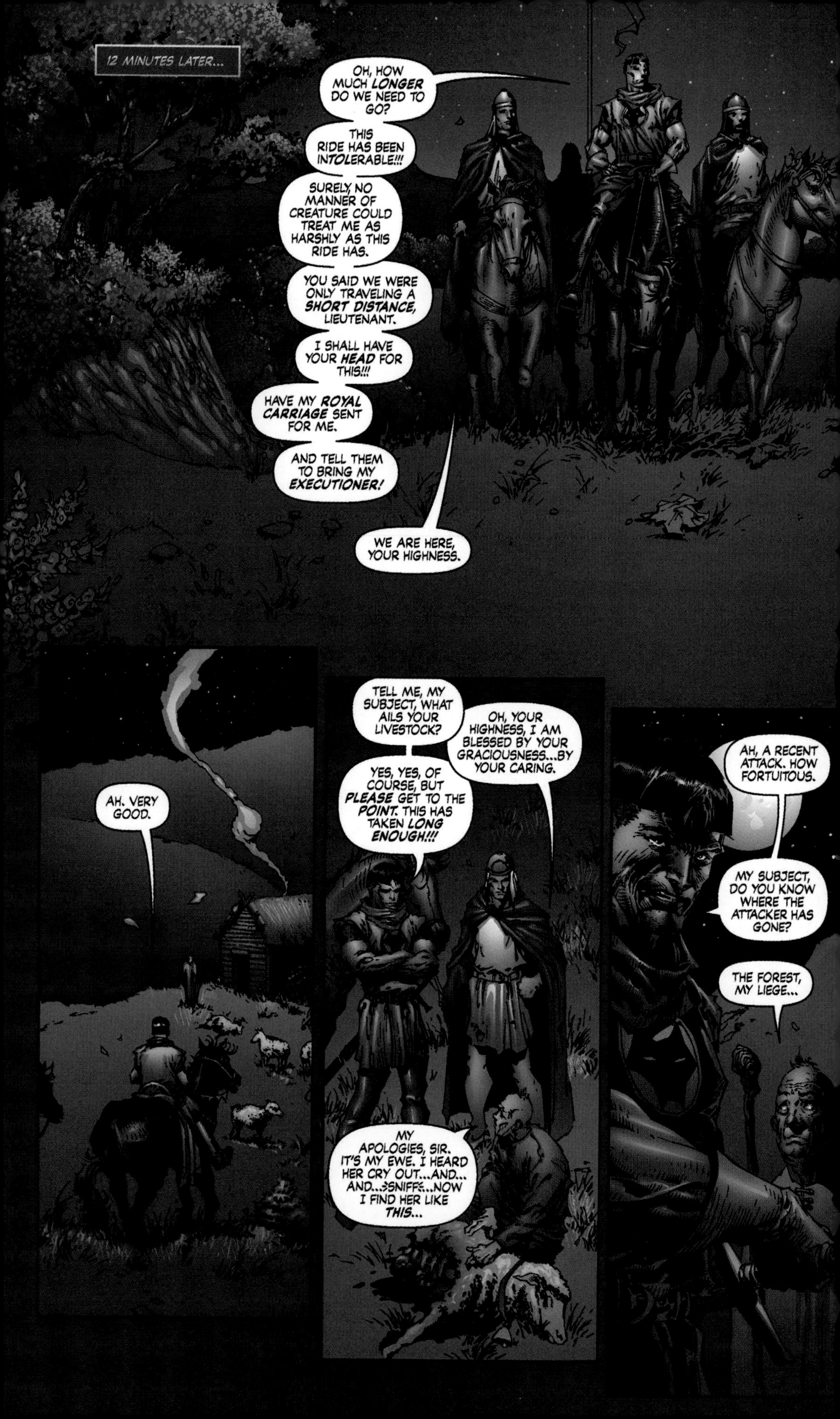
12 MINUTES LATER...
OH, HOW MUCH LONGER DO WE NEED TO GO?
THIS RIDE HAS BEEN INTOLERABLE!!!
SURELY, NO MANNER OF CREATURE COULD TREAT ME AS HARSHLY AS THIS RIDE HAS.
YOU SAID WE WERE ONLY TRAVELING A SHORT DISTANCE, LIEUTENANT.
I SHALL HAVE YOUR HEAD FOR THIS!!!
HAVE MY ROYAL CARRIAGE SENT FOR ME.
AND TELL THEM TO BRING MY EXECUTIONER!
WE ARE HERE, YOUR HIGHNESS.
AH. VERY GOOD.
TELL ME, MY SUBJECT, WHAT AILS YOUR LIVESTOCK?
OH, YOUR HIGHNESS, I AM BLESSED BY YOUR GRACIOUSNESS...BY YOUR CARING.
YES, YES, OF COURSE, BUT PLEASE GET TO THE POINT. THIS HAS TAKEN LONG ENOUGH!!!
MY APOLOGIES, SIR. IT'S MY EWE. I HEARD HER CRY OUT...AND... AND...SNIFF...NOW I FIND HER LIKE THIS...
AH, A RECENT ATTACK. HOW FORTUITOUS.
MY SUBJECT, DO YOU KNOW WHERE THE ATTACKER HAS GONE?
THE FOREST, MY LIEGE...

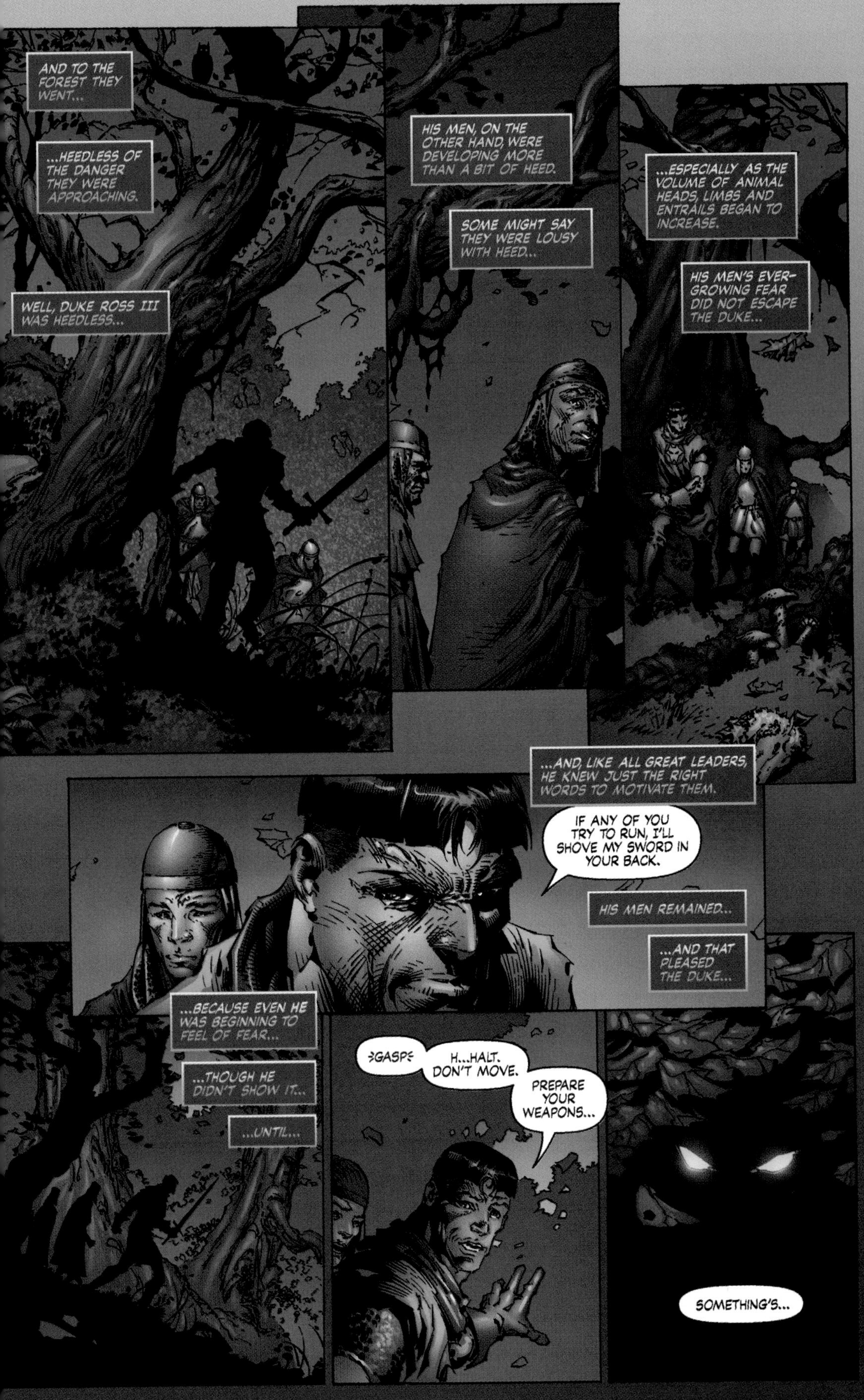
AND TO THE FOREST THEY WENT...
...HEEDLESS OF THE DANGER THEY WERE APPROACHING.
WELL, DUKE ROSS III WAS HEEDLESS...
HIS MEN, ON THE OTHER HAND, WERE DEVELOPING MORE THAN A BIT OF HEED.
SOME MIGHT SAY THEY WERE LOUSY WITH HEED...
...ESPECIALLY AS THE VOLUME OF ANIMAL HEADS, LIMBS AND ENTRAILS BEGAN TO INCREASE.
HIS MEN'S EVER-GROWING FEAR DID NOT ESCAPE THE DUKE...
...AND, LIKE ALL GREAT LEADERS, HE KNEW JUST THE RIGHT WORDS TO MOTIVATE THEM.
IF ANY OF YOU TRY TO RUN, I'LL SHOVE MY SWORD IN YOUR BACK.
HIS MEN REMAINED...
...AND THAT PLEASED THE DUKE...
...BECAUSE EVEN HE WAS BEGINNING TO FEEL OF FEAR...
...THOUGH HE DIDN'T SHOW IT...
...UNTIL...
GASP
H...HALT. DON'T MOVE.
PREPARE YOUR WEAPONS...
SOMETHING'S...

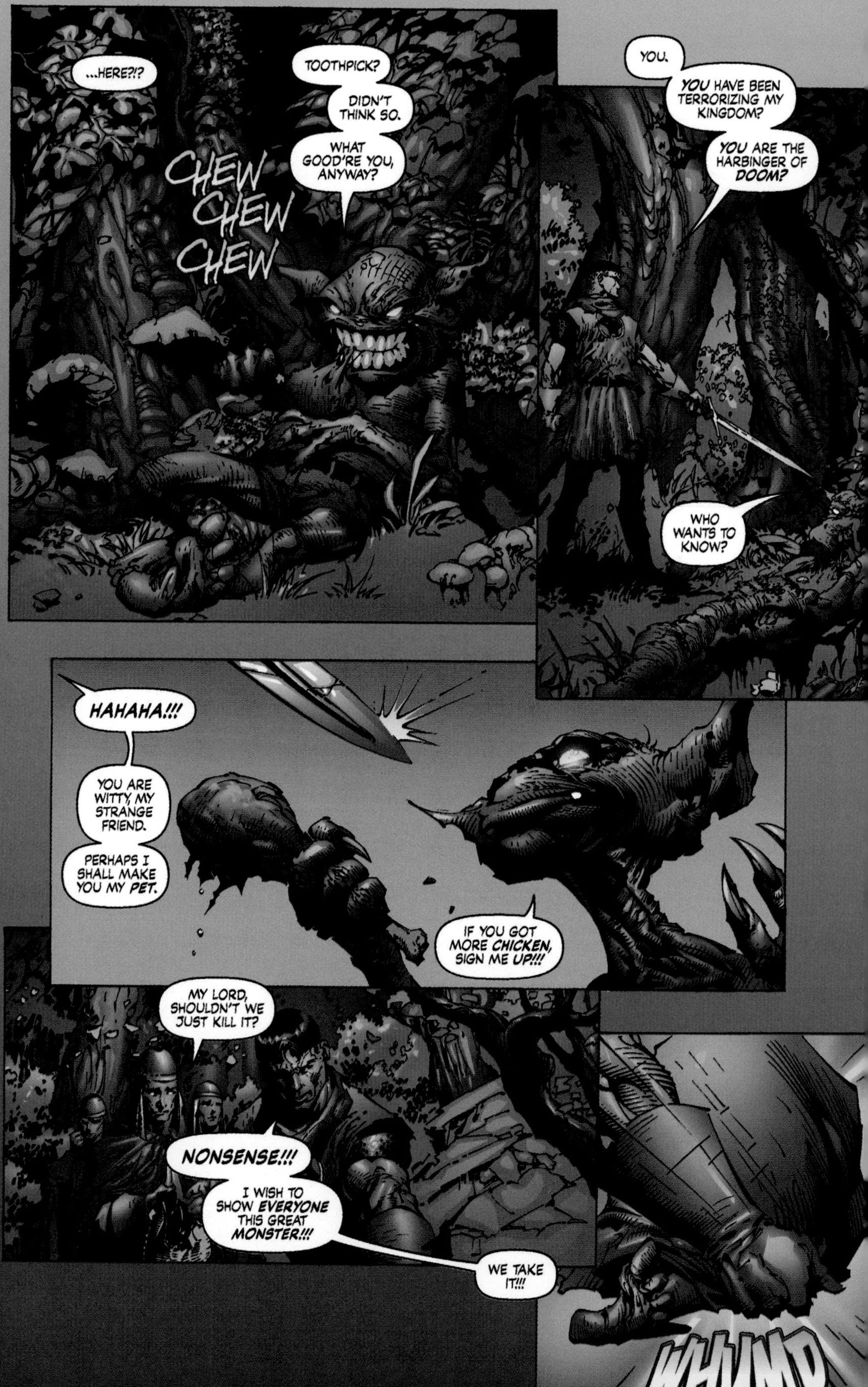
...HERE?!?
TOOTHPICK?
DIDN'T THINK SO.
WHAT GOOD'RE YOU, ANYWAY?
CHEW CHEW CHEW
YOU.
YOU HAVE BEEN TERRORIZING MY KINGDOM?
YOU ARE THE HARBINGER OF DOOM?
WHO WANTS TO KNOW?
HAHAHA!!!
YOU ARE WITTY, MY STRANGE FRIEND.
PERHAPS I SHALL MAKE YOU MY PET.
IF YOU GOT MORE CHICKEN, SIGN ME UP!!!
MY LORD, SHOULDN'T WE JUST KILL IT?
NONSENSE!!!
I WISH TO SHOW EVERYONE THIS GREAT MONSTER!!!
WE TAKE IT!!!
WHUMP

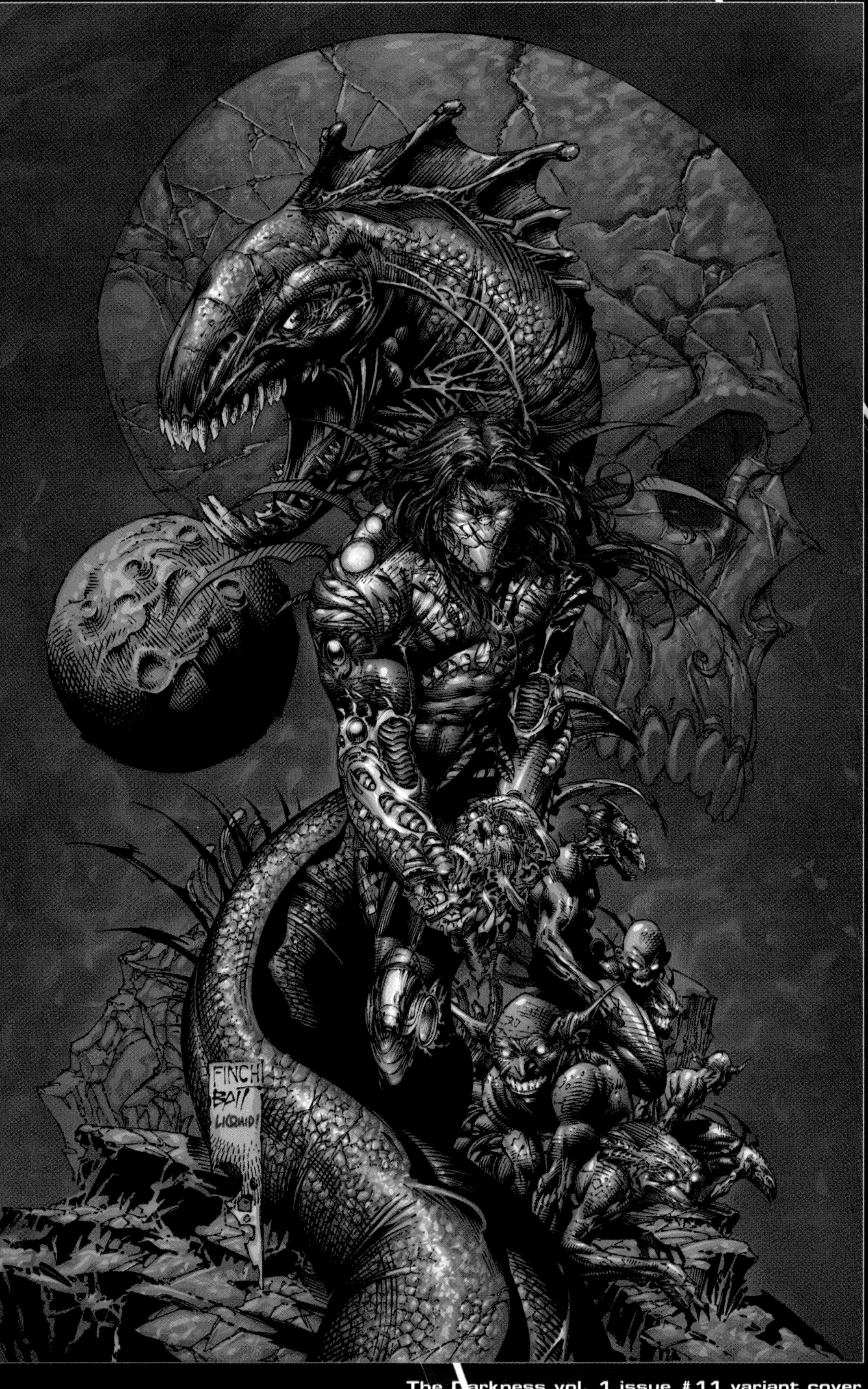
FINCH
BATT
LIQUID!

The Darkness vol. 1 issue #11 variant cover
art by: **Dave Finch, Matt "Batt" Banning and Liquid!**

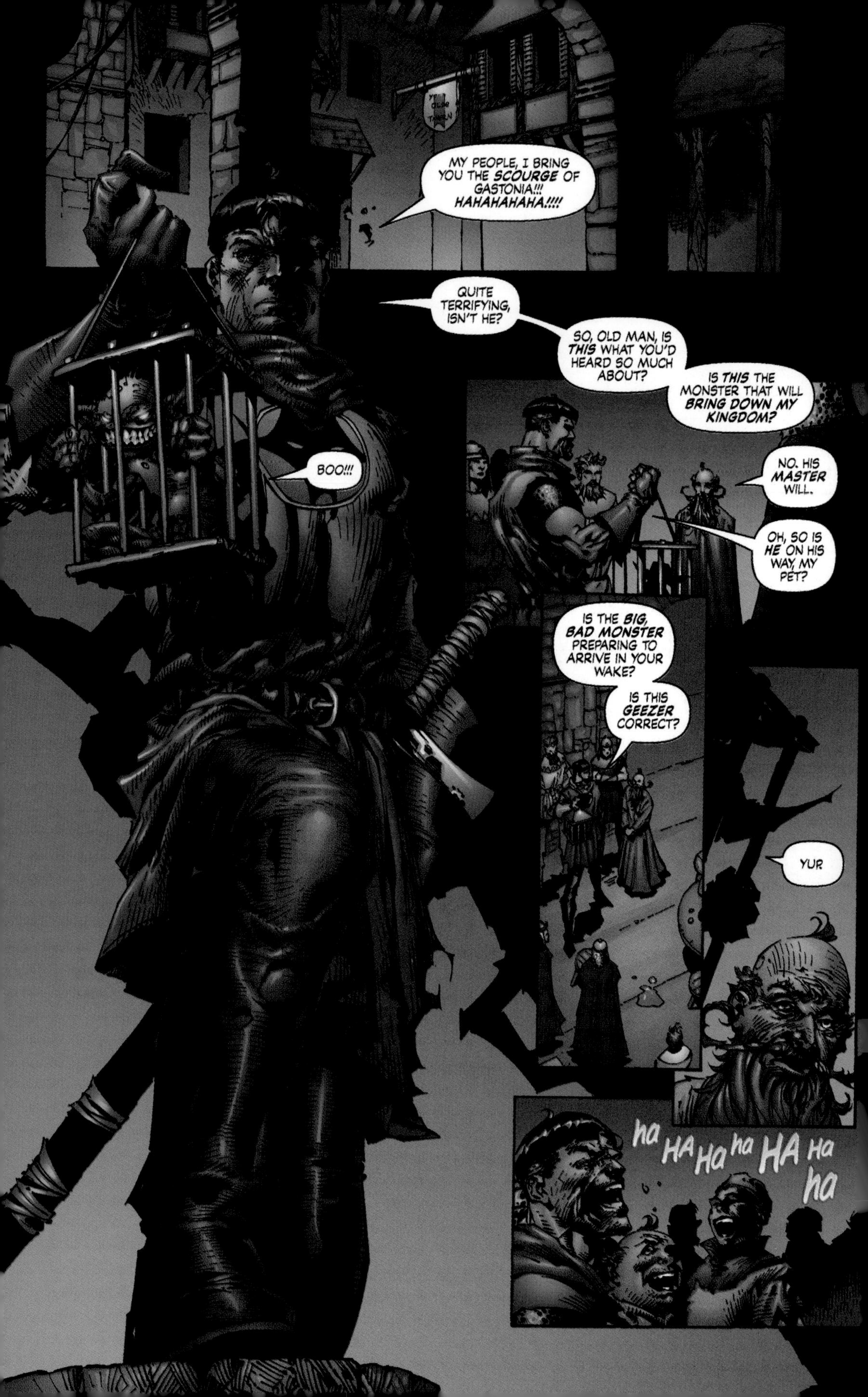

MY PEOPLE, I BRING YOU THE SCOURGE OF GASTONIA!!! HAHAHAHAHA!!!!
QUITE TERRIFYING, ISN'T HE?
SO, OLD MAN, IS THIS WHAT YOU'D HEARD SO MUCH ABOUT?
IS THIS THE MONSTER THAT WILL BRING DOWN MY KINGDOM?
BOO!!!
NO. HIS MASTER WILL.
OH, SO IS HE ON HIS WAY, MY PET?
IS THE BIG, BAD MONSTER PREPARING TO ARRIVE IN YOUR WAKE?
IS THIS GEEZER CORRECT?
YUR
ha HA Ha ha HA Ha ha

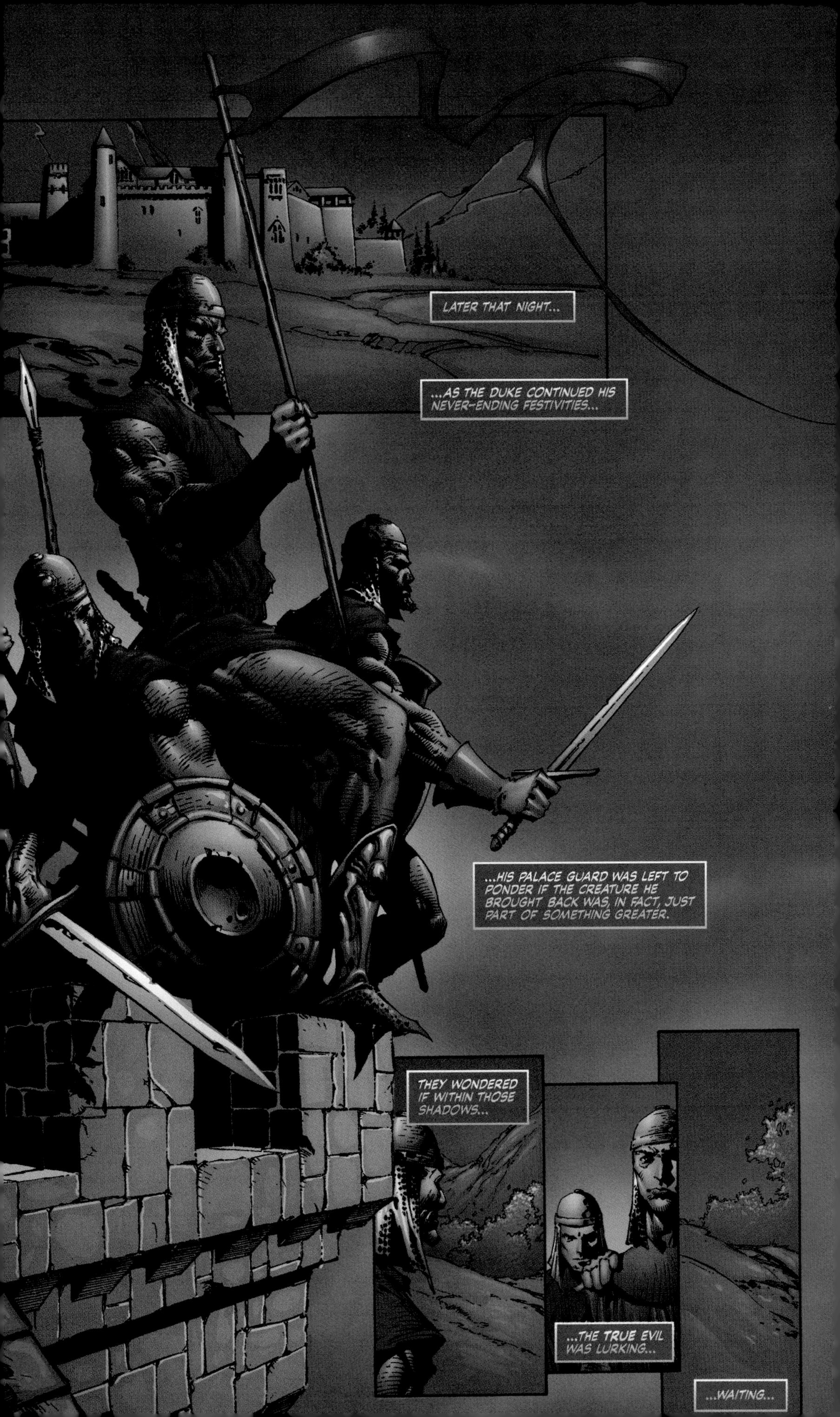
LATER THAT NIGHT...
...AS THE DUKE CONTINUED HIS NEVER-ENDING FESTIVITIES...
...HIS PALACE GUARD WAS LEFT TO PONDER IF THE CREATURE HE BROUGHT BACK WAS, IN FACT, JUST PART OF SOMETHING GREATER.
THEY WONDERED IF WITHIN THOSE SHADOWS...
...THE TRUE EVIL WAS LURKING...
...WAITING...

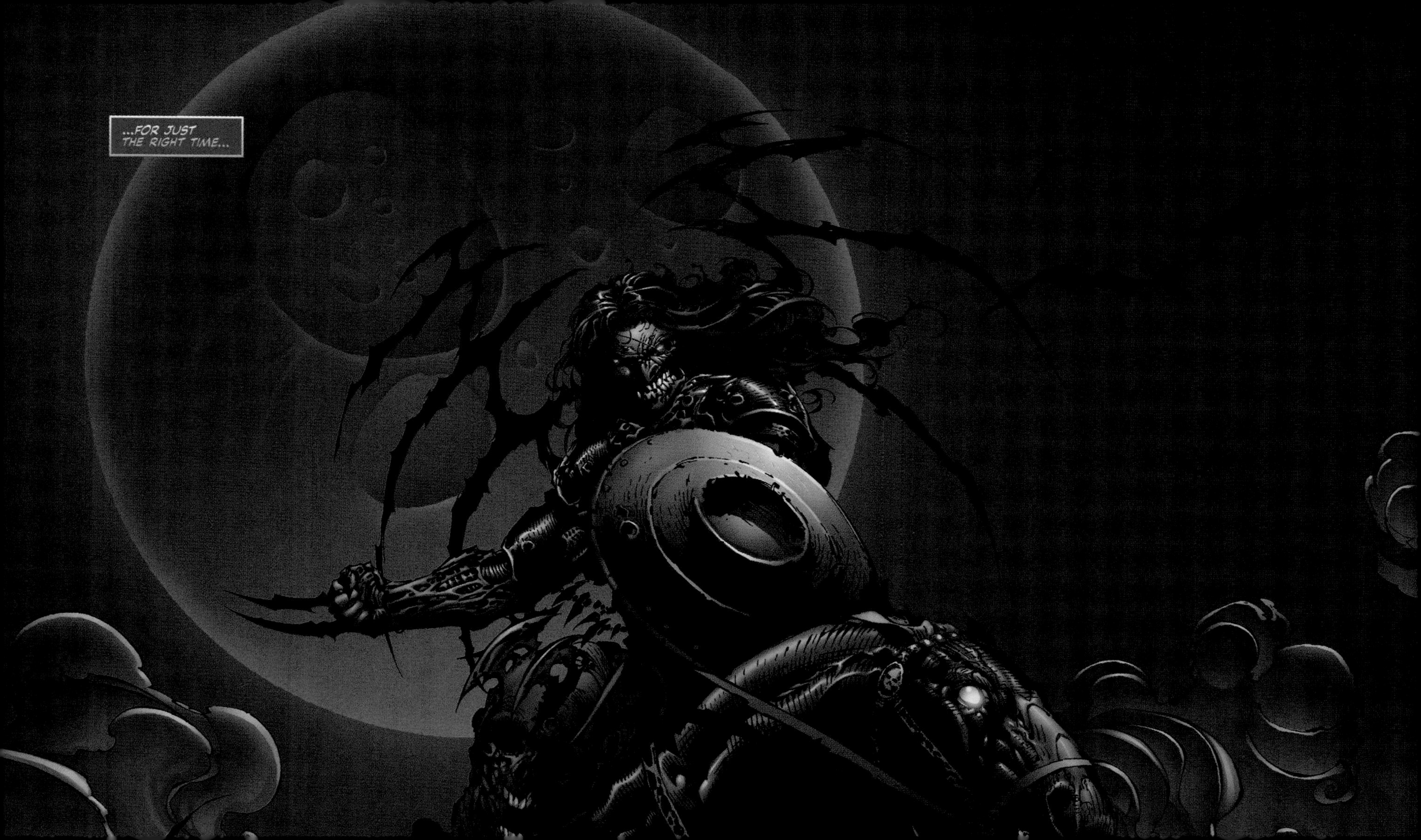
...FOR JUST THE RIGHT TIME...

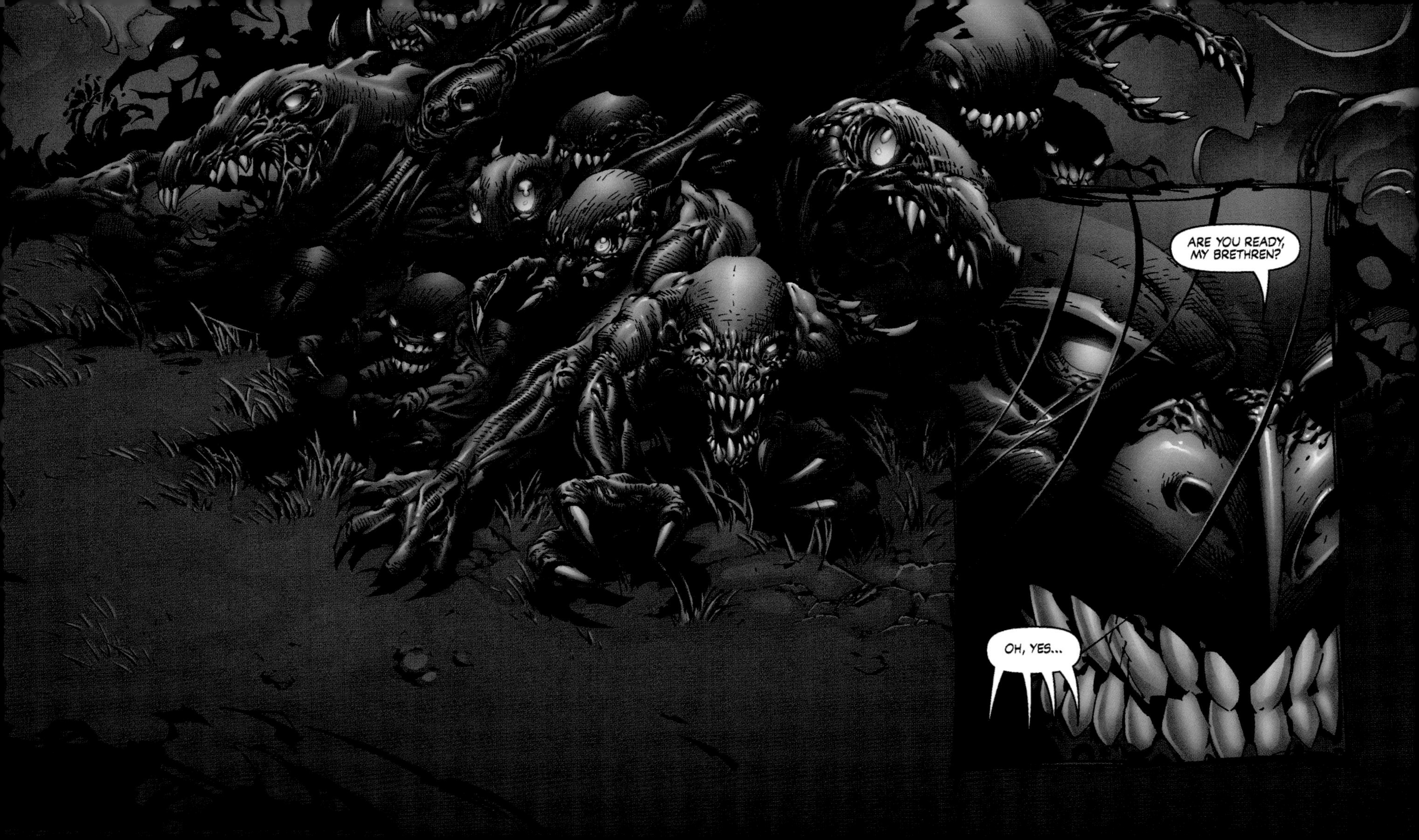
ARE YOU READY, MY BRETHREN?
OH, YES...

MY FRIENDS, THE ONLY WIZARDRY *I'M* WITNESSING TONIGHT...

...IS RIGHT HERE...

...IN MY *HANDS!!!*

LOOKS LIKE I'VE WON AGAIN. SORRY...

MUST BE *MY NIGHT!!!*

NOBODY IS *THAT* LUCKY.

YOU'RE *CHEATING* AGAIN.

SSSSSSSLLLLRRRRRRPPPPP

BUT I *ASSURE* YOU, THIS WILL BE THE *LAST* --

OH, NO... SOUND THE --

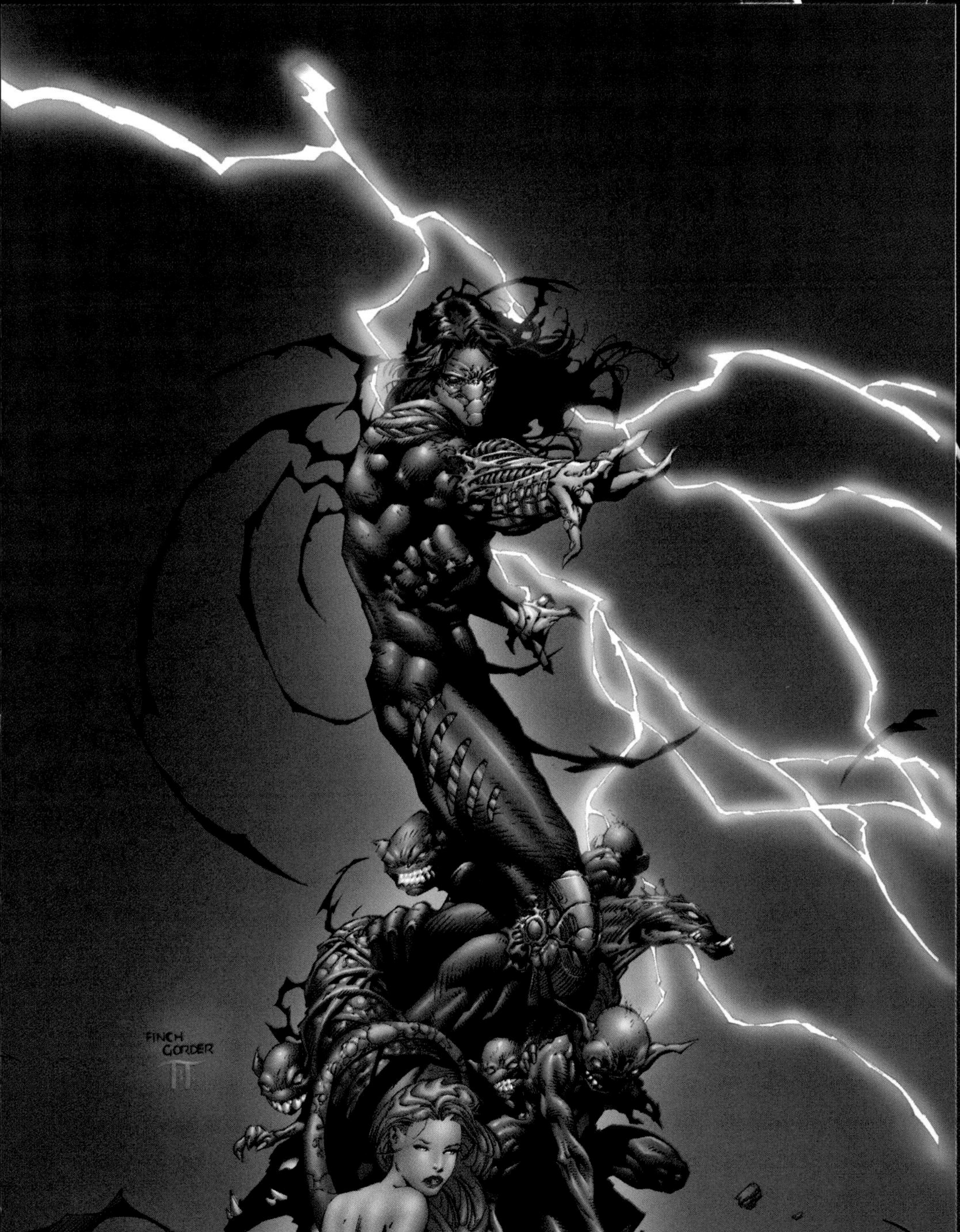
FINCH
GORDER

The Darkness vol. 1 issue #32 variant cover
art by: Dave Finch, Jason Gorder and Tyson Wengler

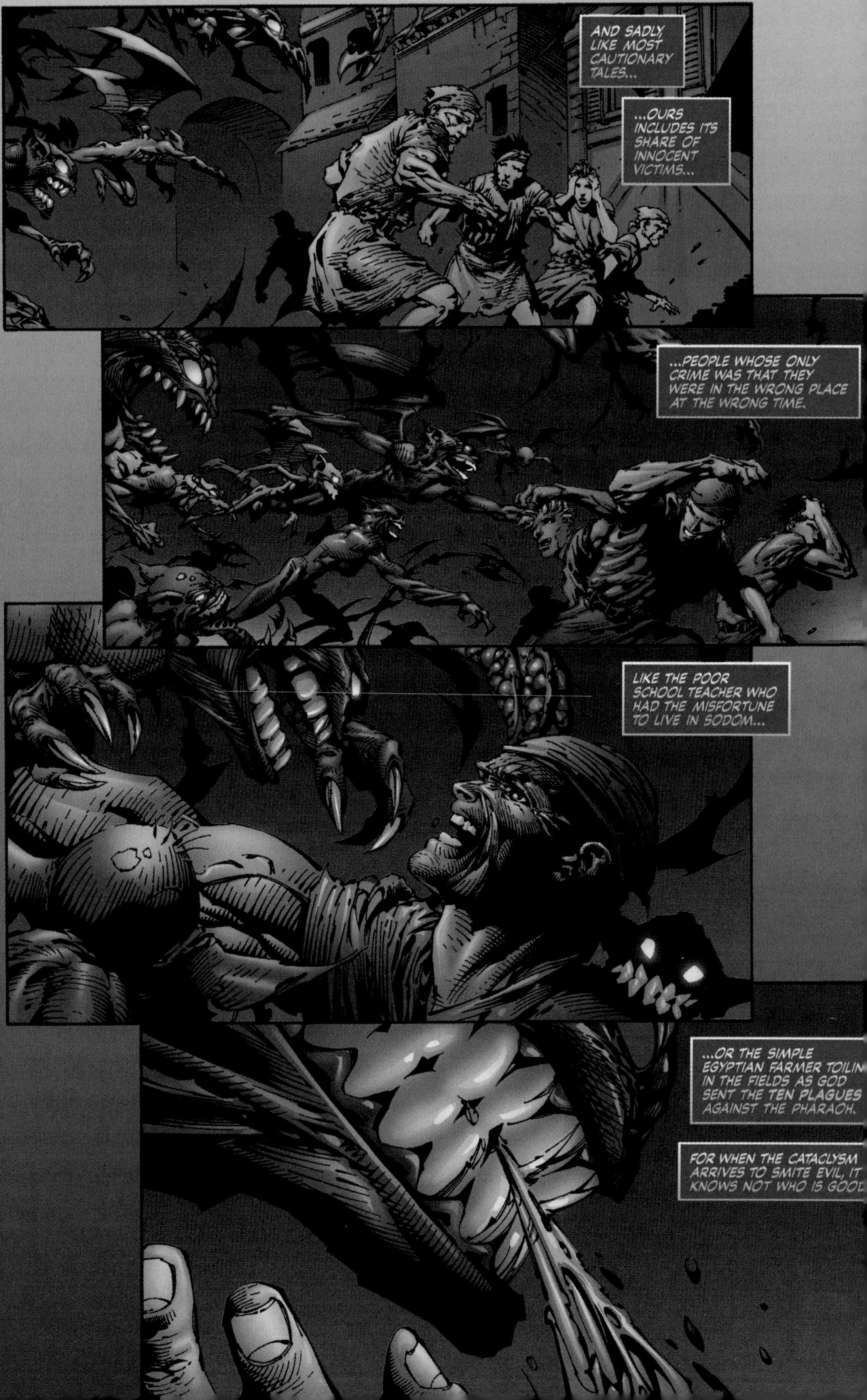
AND SADLY, LIKE MOST CAUTIONARY TALES...
...OURS INCLUDES ITS SHARE OF INNOCENT VICTIMS...
...PEOPLE WHOSE ONLY CRIME WAS THAT THEY WERE IN THE WRONG PLACE AT THE WRONG TIME.
LIKE THE POOR SCHOOL TEACHER WHO HAD THE MISFORTUNE TO LIVE IN SODOM...
...OR THE SIMPLE EGYPTIAN FARMER TOILIN IN THE FIELDS AS GOD SENT THE TEN PLAGUES AGAINST THE PHARAOH.
FOR WHEN THE CATACLYSM ARRIVES TO SMITE EVIL, IT KNOWS NOT WHO IS GOOD

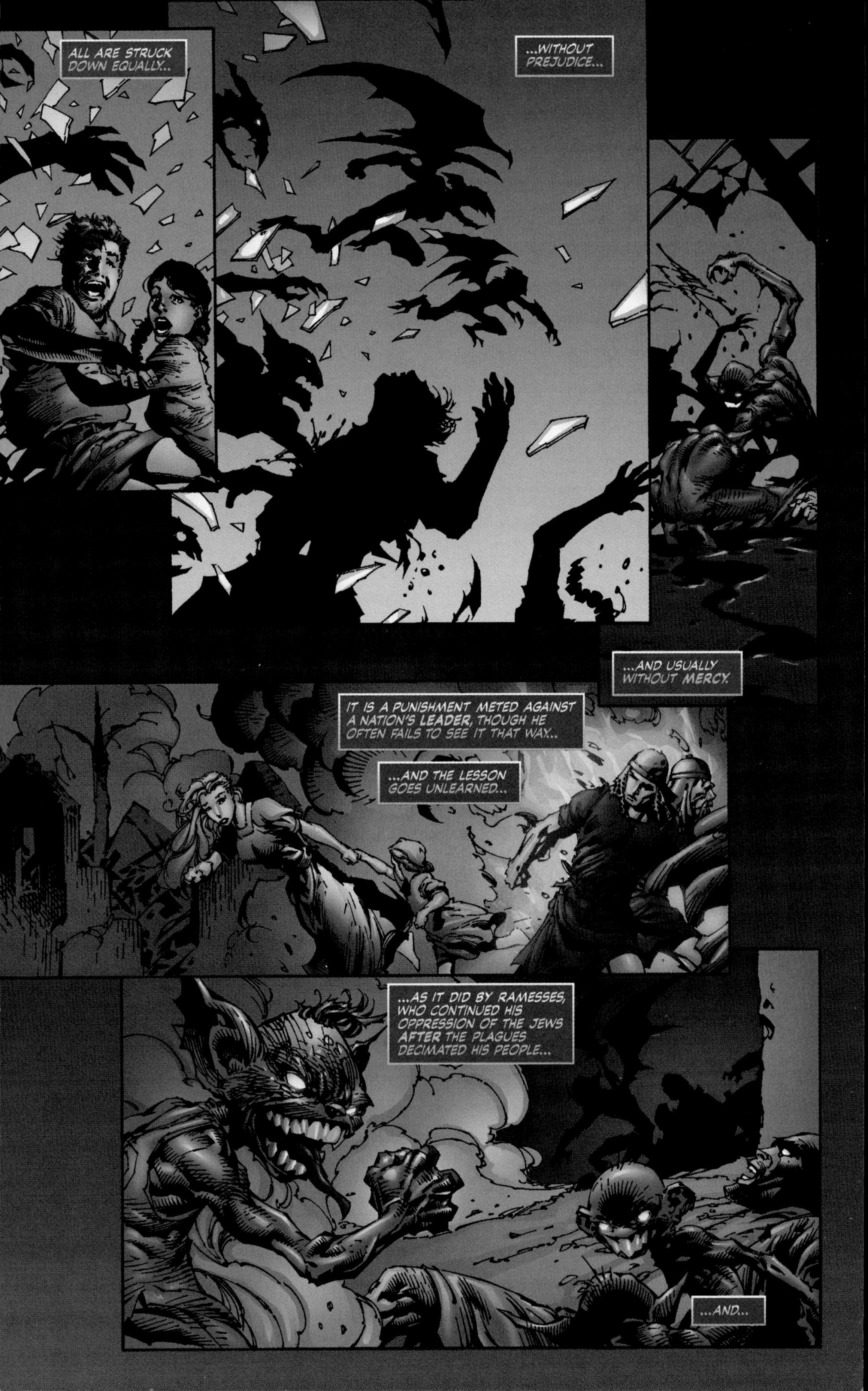
ALL ARE STRUCK DOWN EQUALLY...
...WITHOUT PREJUDICE...
...AND USUALLY WITHOUT MERCY.
IT IS A PUNISHMENT METED AGAINST A NATION'S LEADER, THOUGH HE OFTEN FAILS TO SEE IT THAT WAY..
...AND THE LESSON GOES UNLEARNED...
...AS IT DID BY RAMESSES, WHO CONTINUED HIS OPPRESSION OF THE JEWS AFTER THE PLAGUES DECIMATED HIS PEOPLE...
...AND...

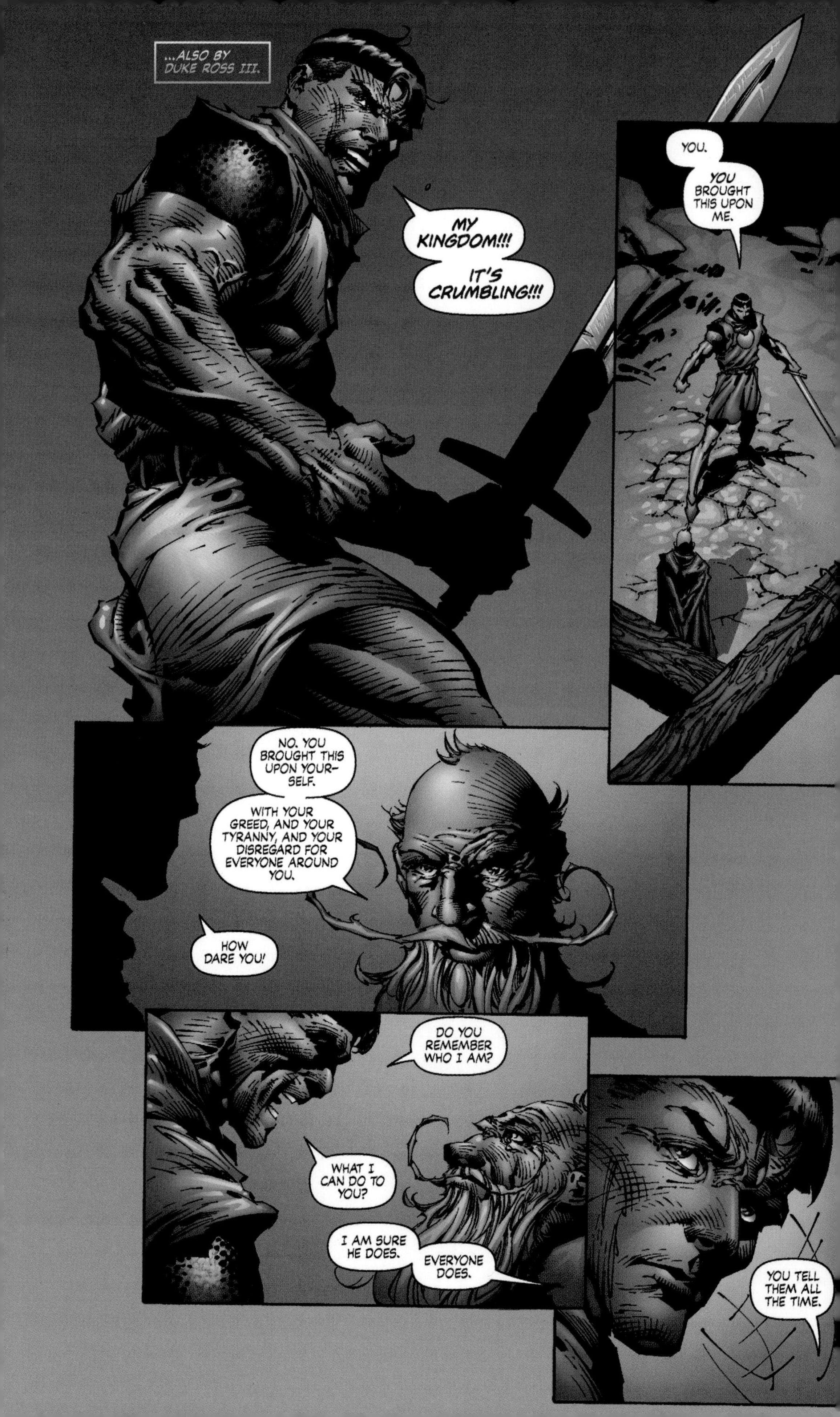
...ALSO BY DUKE ROSS III.
MY KINGDOM!!!
IT'S CRUMBLING!!!
YOU.
YOU BROUGHT THIS UPON ME.
NO. YOU BROUGHT THIS UPON YOURSELF.
WITH YOUR GREED, AND YOUR TYRANNY, AND YOUR DISREGARD FOR EVERYONE AROUND YOU.
HOW DARE YOU!
DO YOU REMEMBER WHO I AM?
WHAT I CAN DO TO YOU?
I AM SURE HE DOES.
EVERYONE DOES.
YOU TELL THEM ALL THE TIME.

BUT MY QUESTION FOR YOU IS...
...DO YOU KNOW THE NAMES OF *ANYONE* IN YOUR KINGDOM?
YOU KNOW -- *YOUR* PEOPLE. *YOUR* SUBJECTS.
THE PEOPLE THAT *YOU* SHOULD HAVE BEEN SERVING?
ANYONE?
WELL...I...
I THINK...
COULD...UH... YOU GIVE ME A MOMENT?
NO.
SLRRRRRRRR

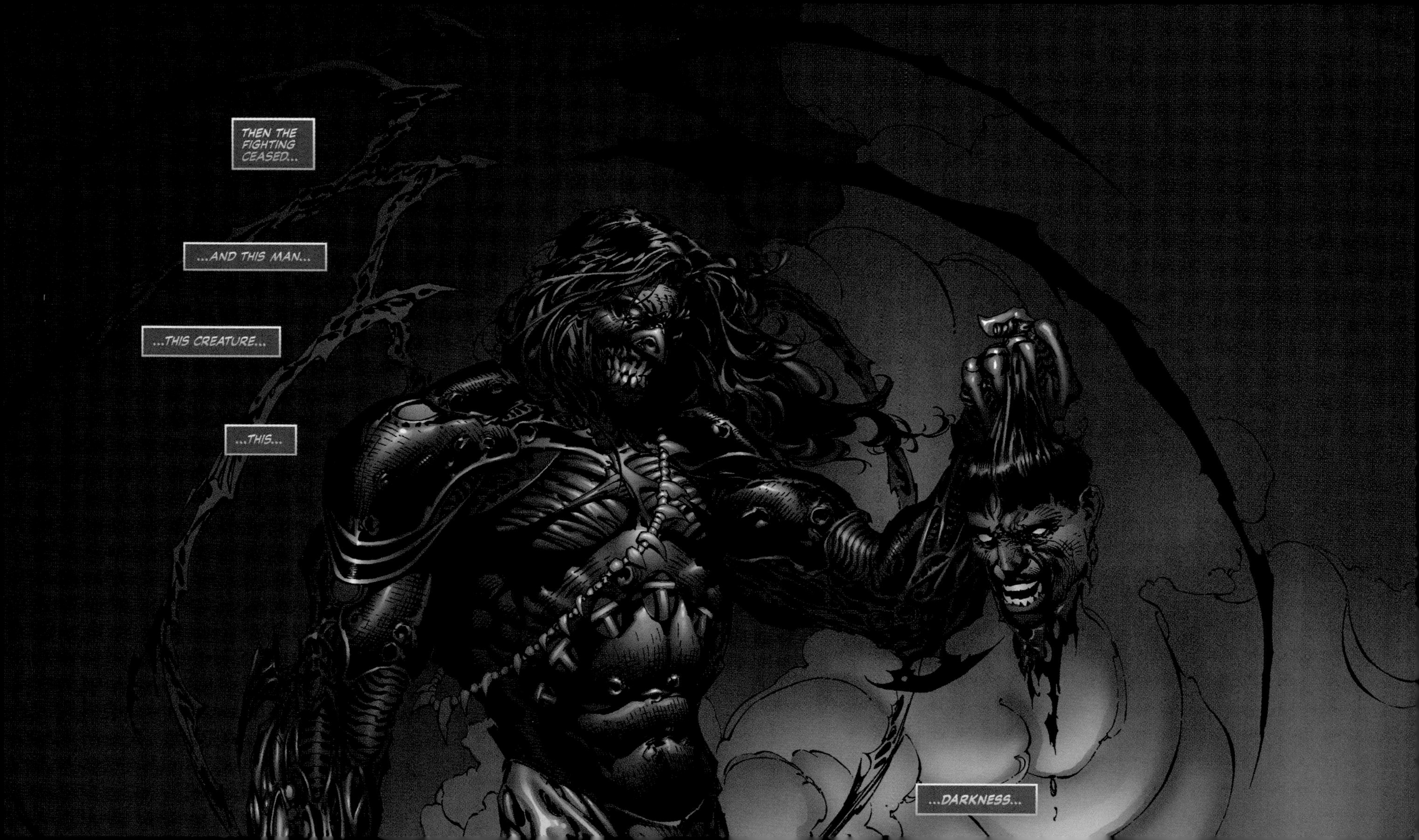
THEN THE FIGHTING CEASED...
...AND THIS MAN...
...THIS CREATURE...
...THIS...
...DARKNESS...

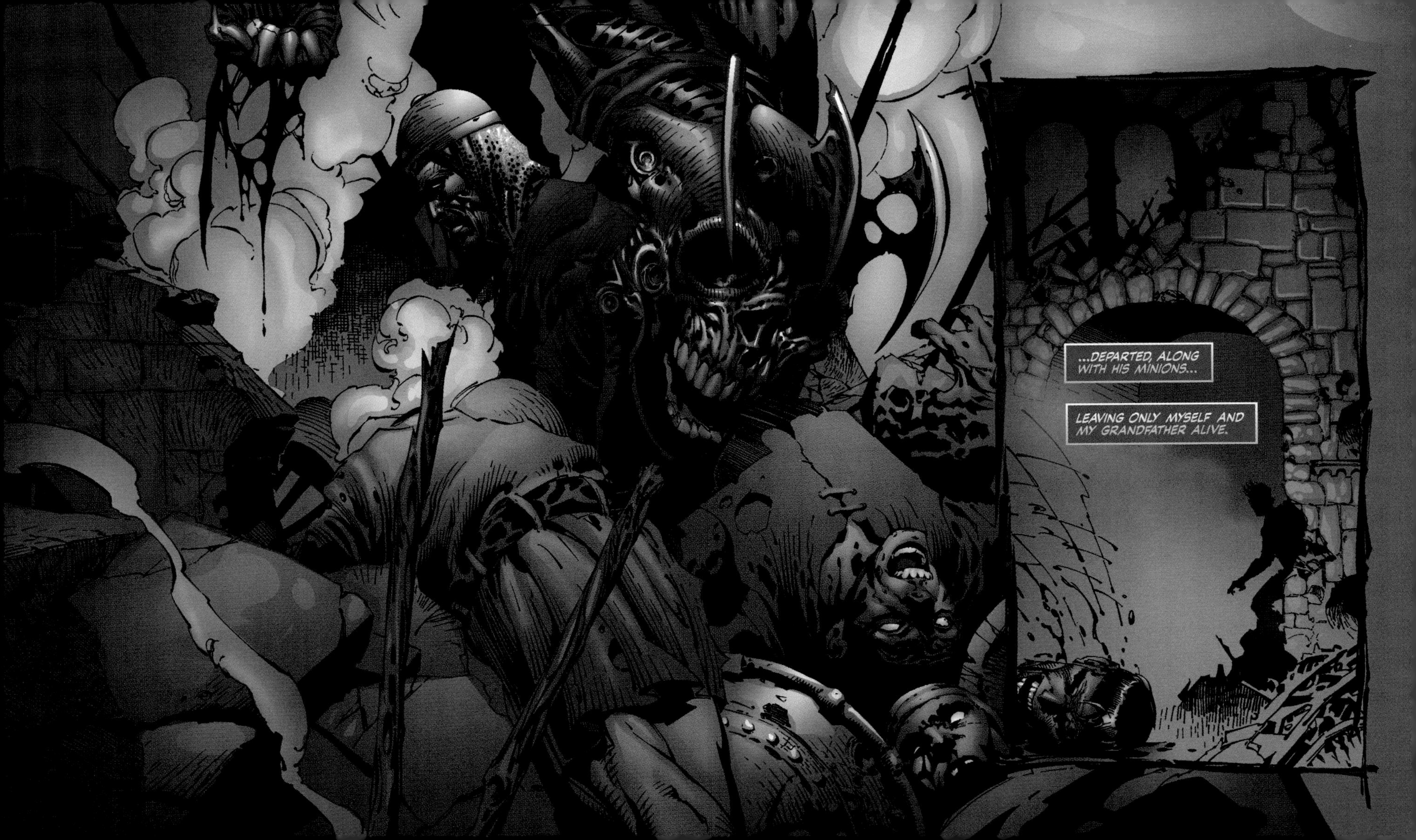
...DEPARTED, ALONG WITH HIS MINIONS...
LEAVING ONLY MYSELF AND MY GRANDFATHER ALIVE.

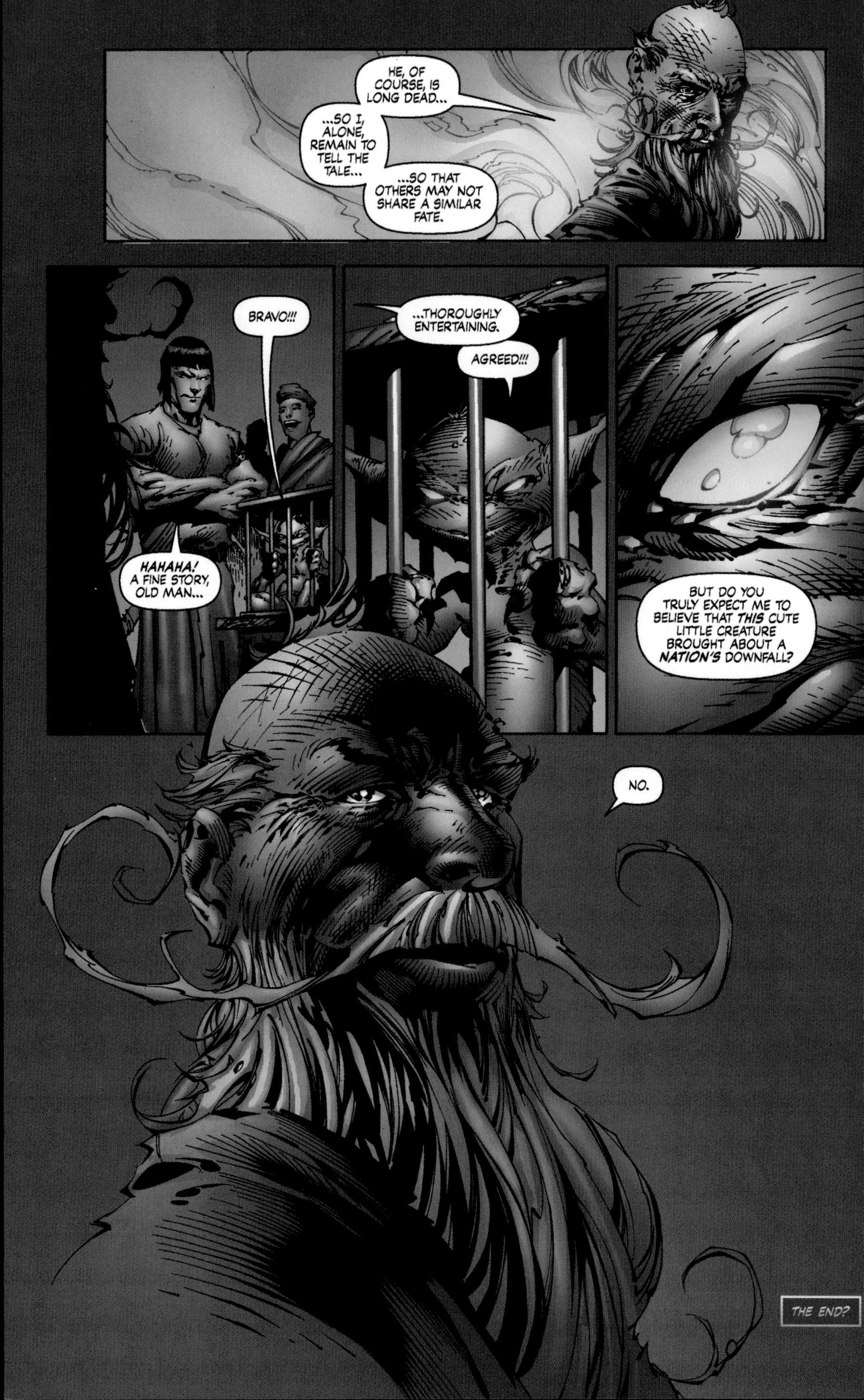
HE, OF COURSE, IS LONG DEAD...
...SO I, ALONE, REMAIN TO TELL THE TALE...
...SO THAT OTHERS MAY NOT SHARE A SIMILAR FATE.
BRAVO!!!
HAHAHA! A FINE STORY, OLD MAN...
...THOROUGHLY ENTERTAINING.
AGREED!!!
BUT DO YOU TRULY EXPECT ME TO BELIEVE THAT THIS CUTE LITTLE CREATURE BROUGHT ABOUT A NATION'S DOWNFALL?
NO.
THE END?

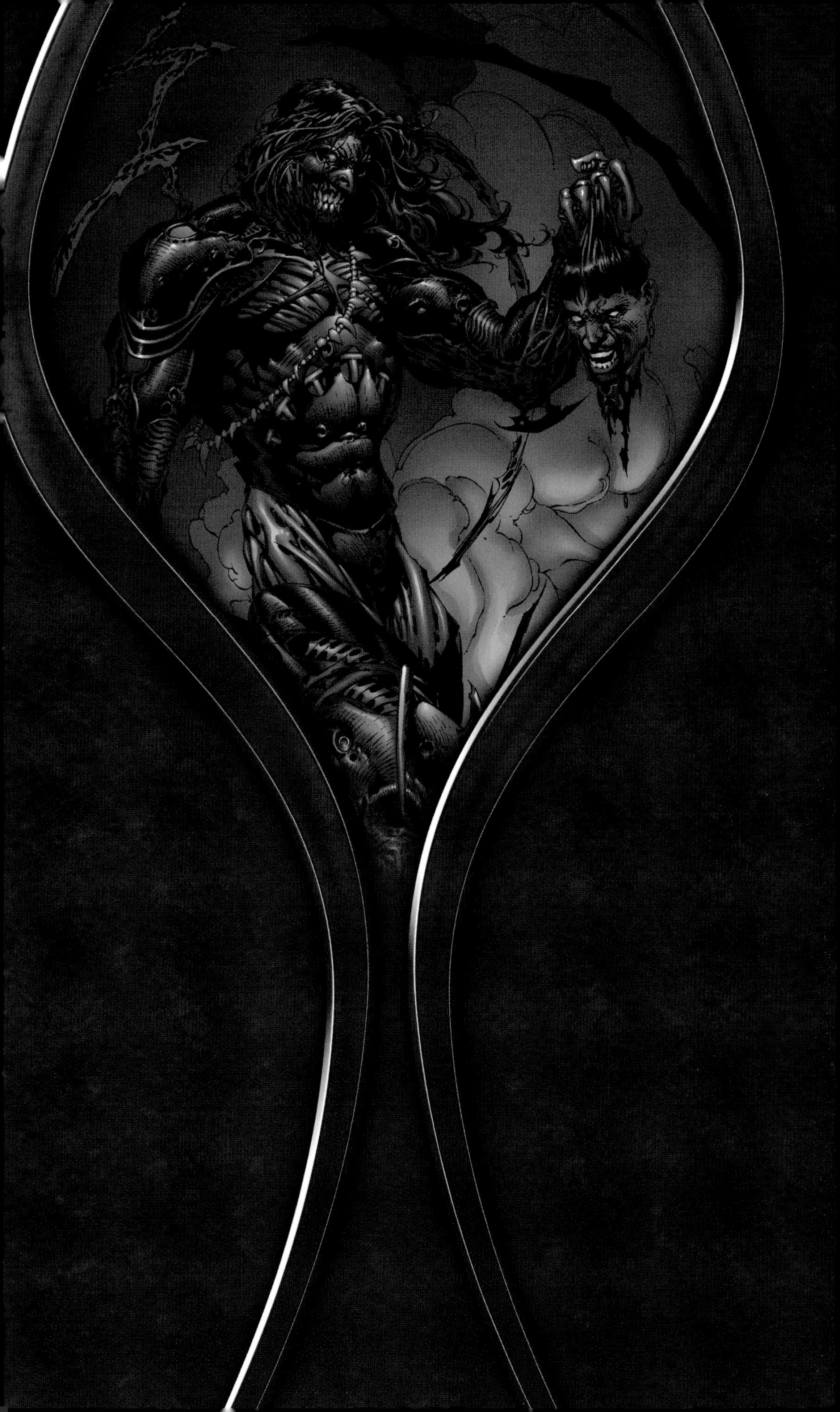

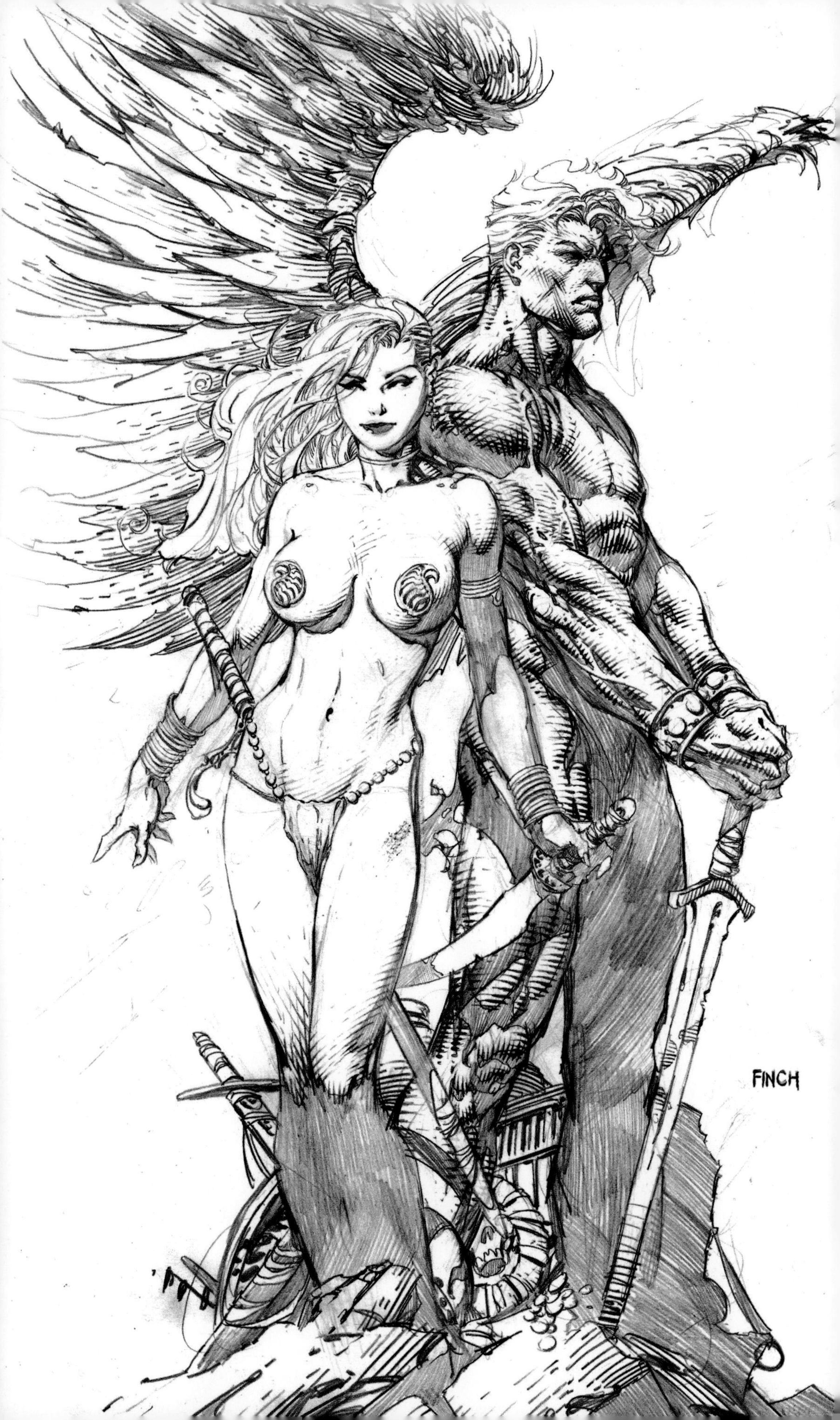
FINCH

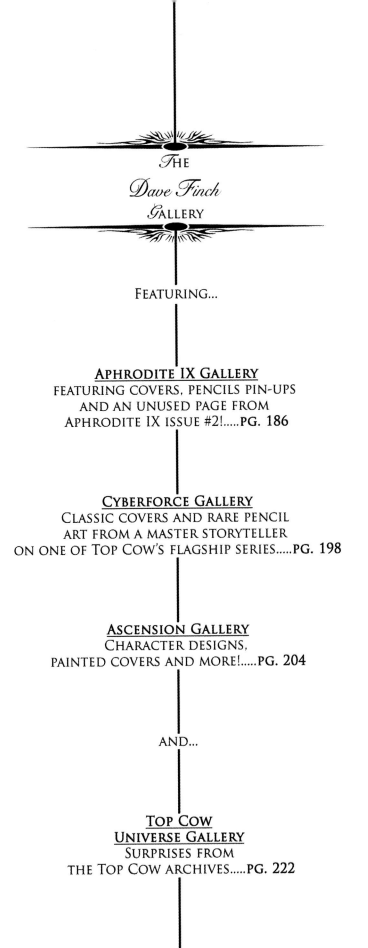

The
Dave Finch
GALLERY

FEATURING...

APHRODITE IX GALLERY
FEATURING COVERS, PENCILS PIN-UPS
AND AN UNUSED PAGE FROM
APHRODITE IX ISSUE #2!.....PG. 186

CYBERFORCE GALLERY
CLASSIC COVERS AND RARE PENCIL
ART FROM A MASTER STORYTELLER
ON ONE OF TOP COW'S FLAGSHIP SERIES.....PG. 198

ASCENSION GALLERY
CHARACTER DESIGNS,
PAINTED COVERS AND MORE!.....PG. 204

AND...

TOP COW
UNIVERSE GALLERY
SURPRISES FROM
THE TOP COW ARCHIVES.....PG. 222

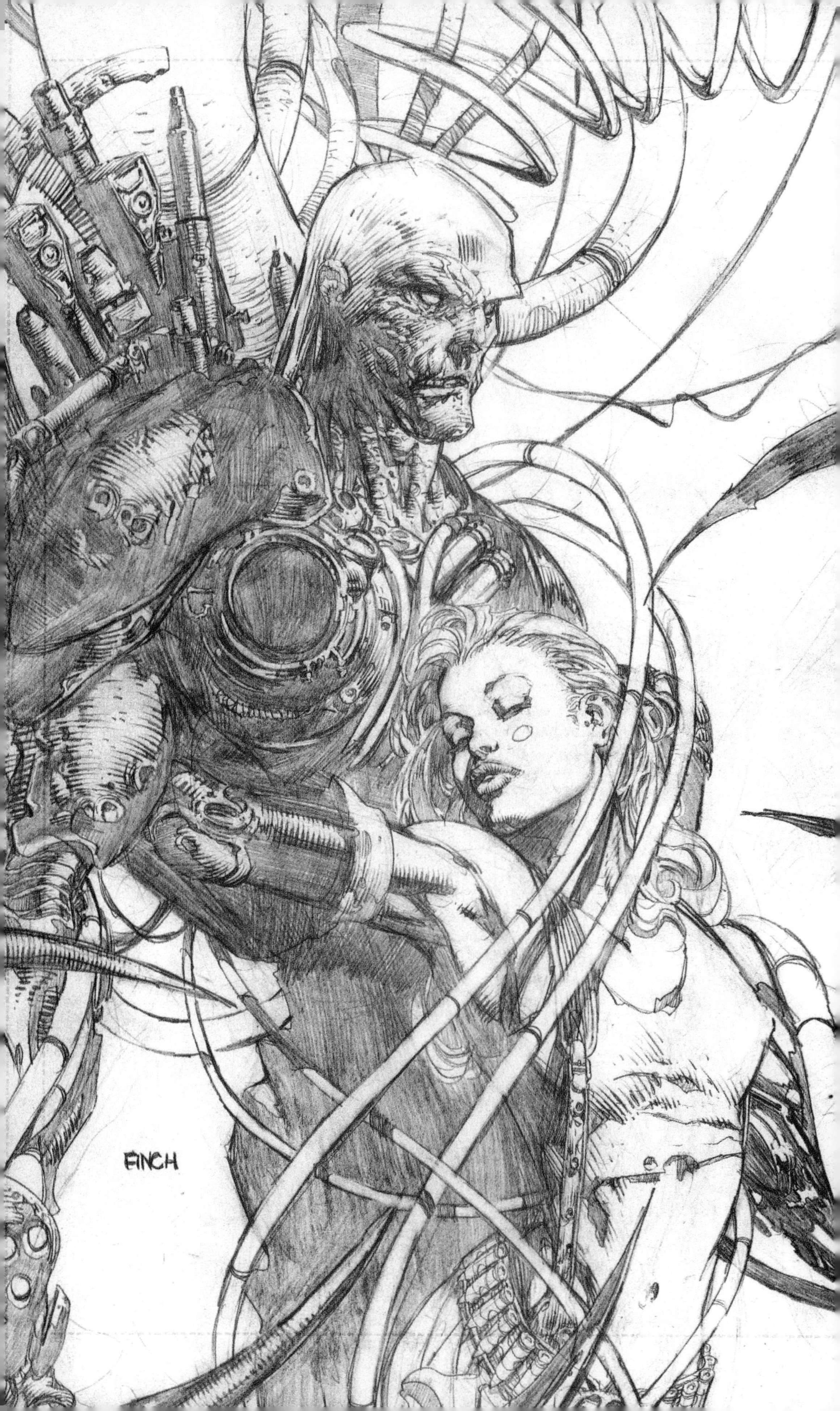
FINCH

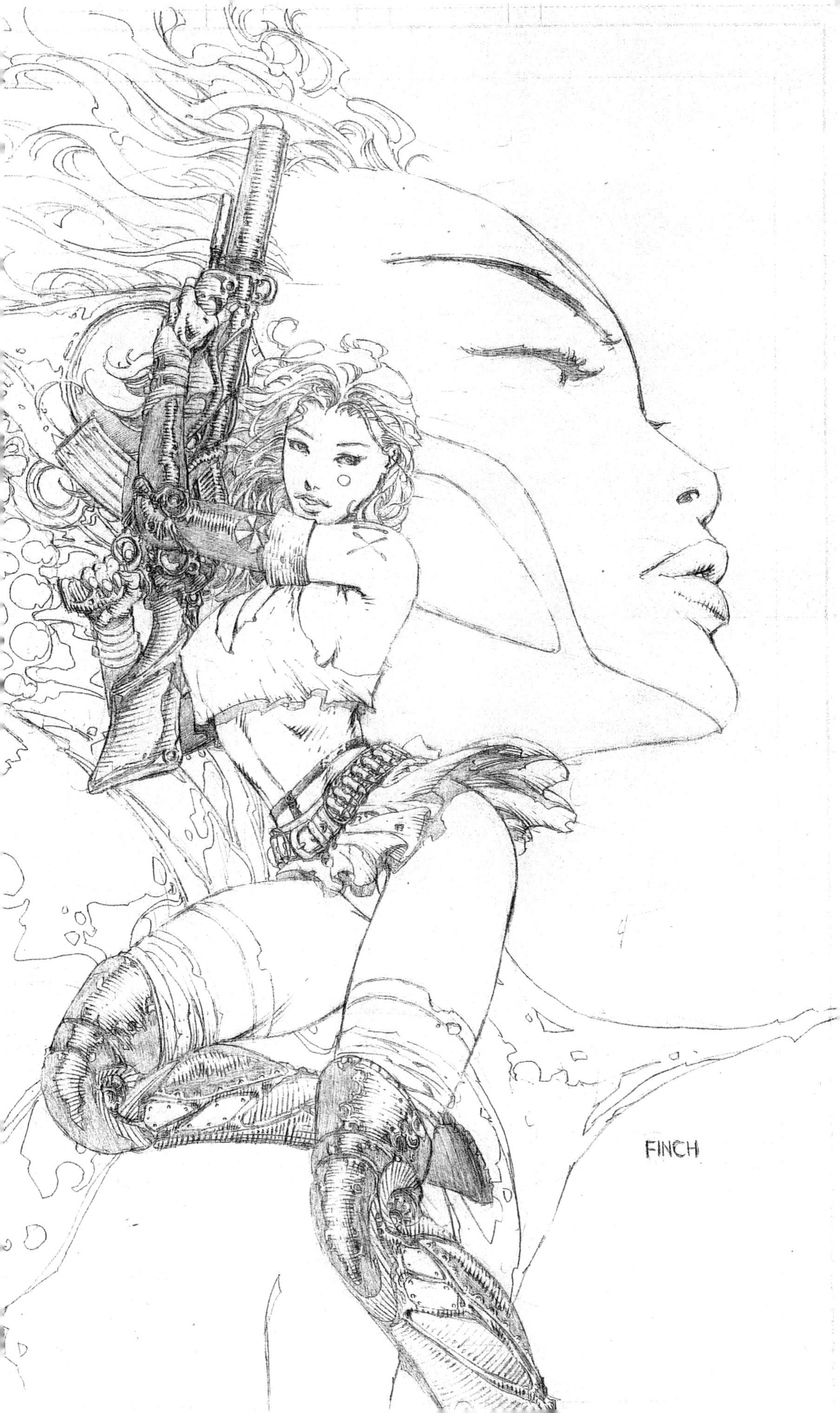
FINCH

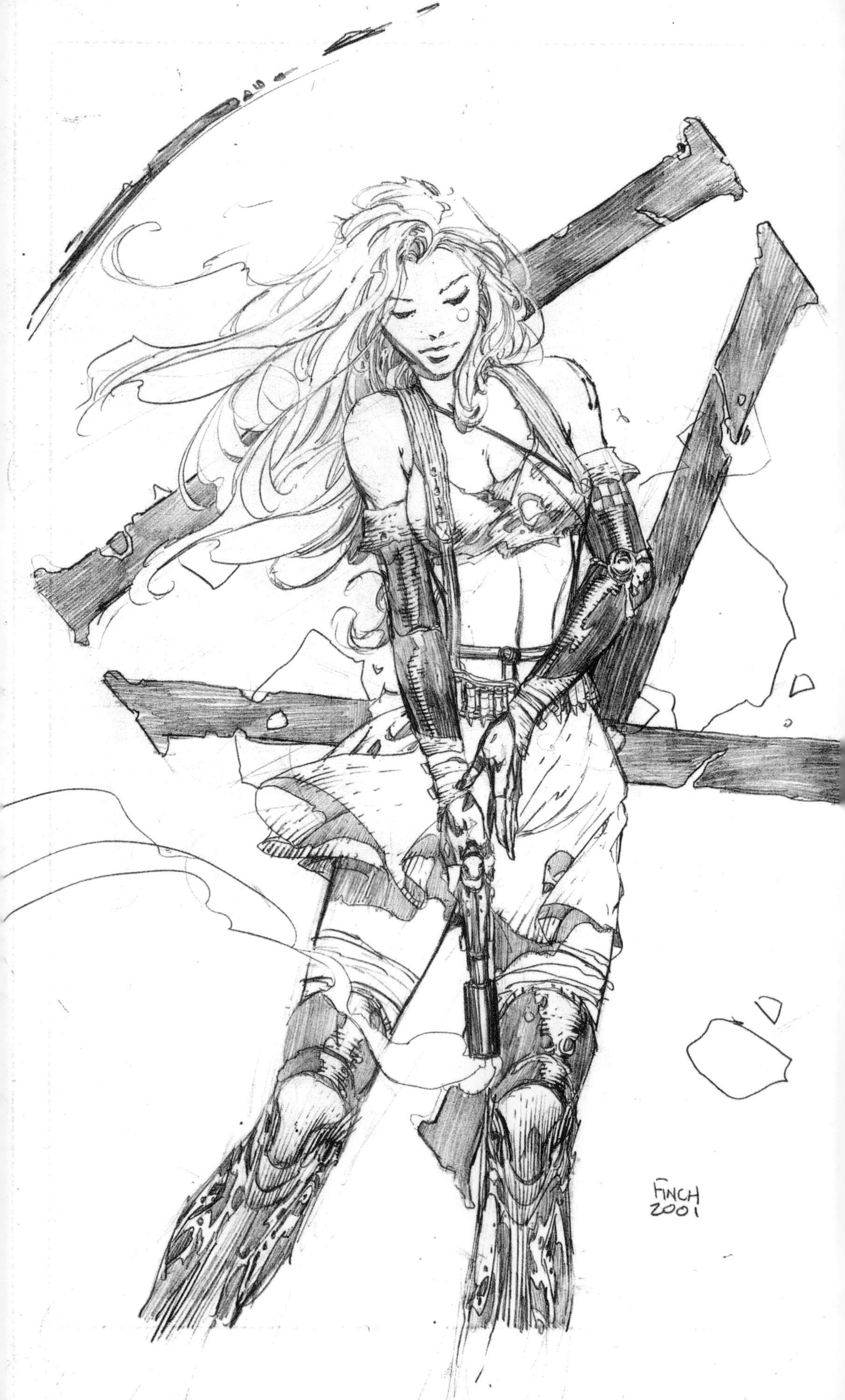
FINCH
2001

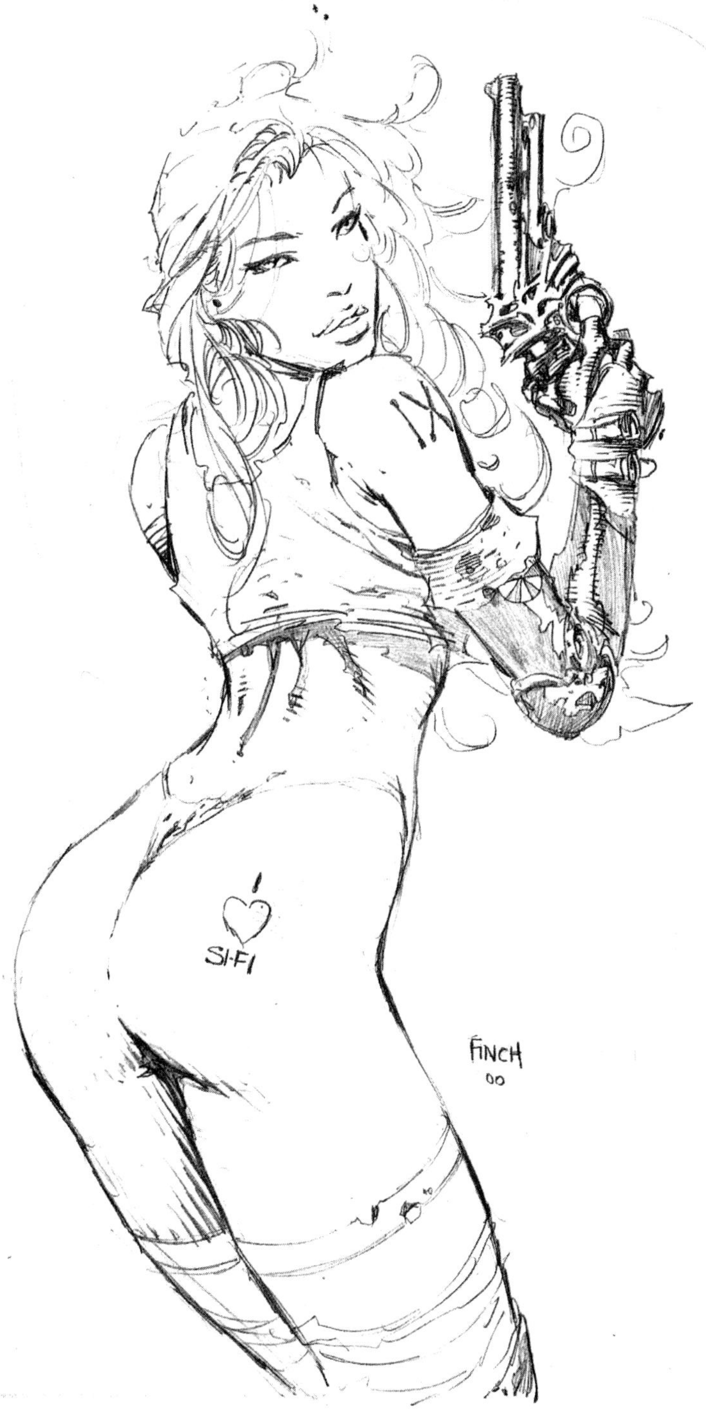
SI-FI
FINCH
00

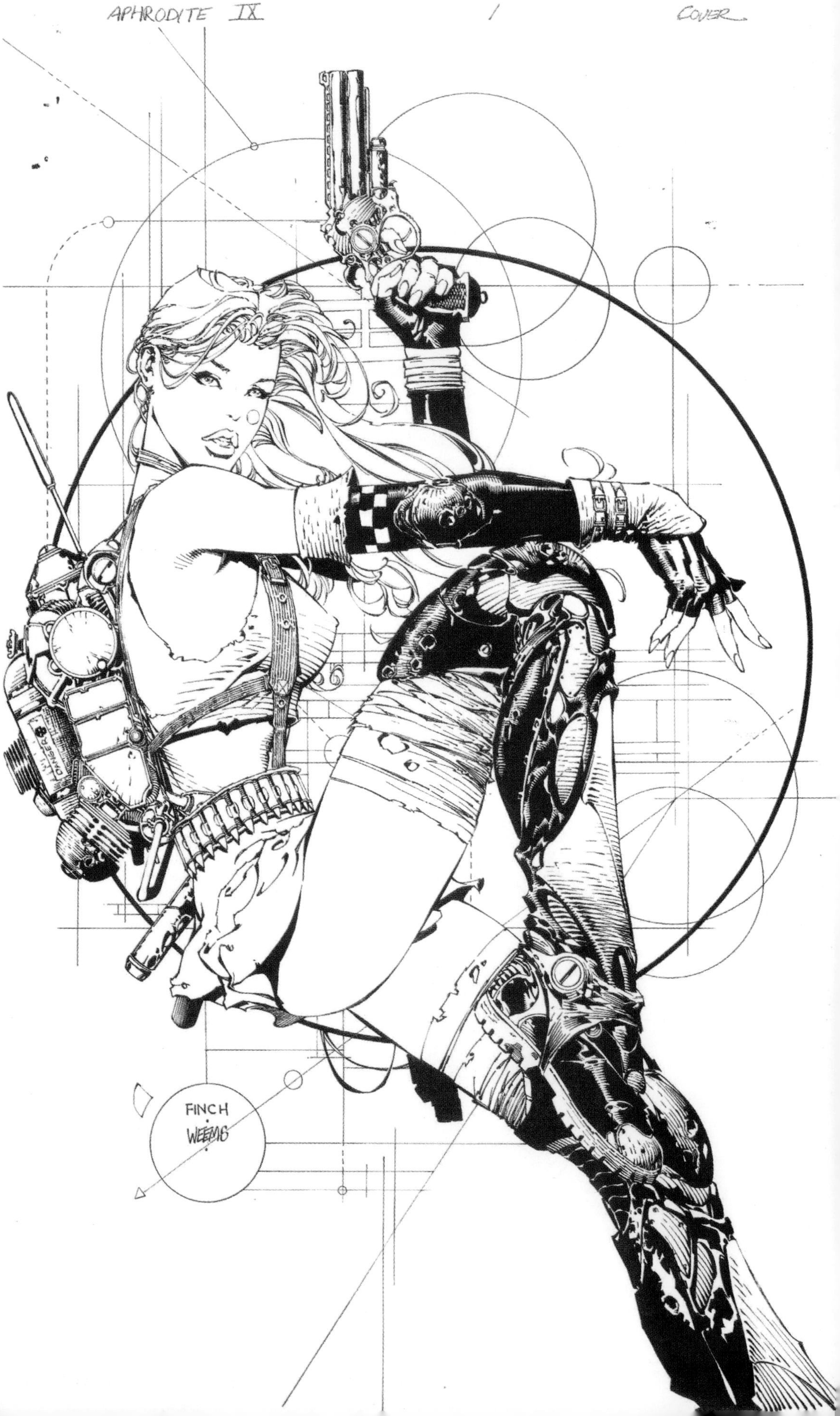
APHRODITE IX
1
COVER
DANGER
FINCH
WEEMS

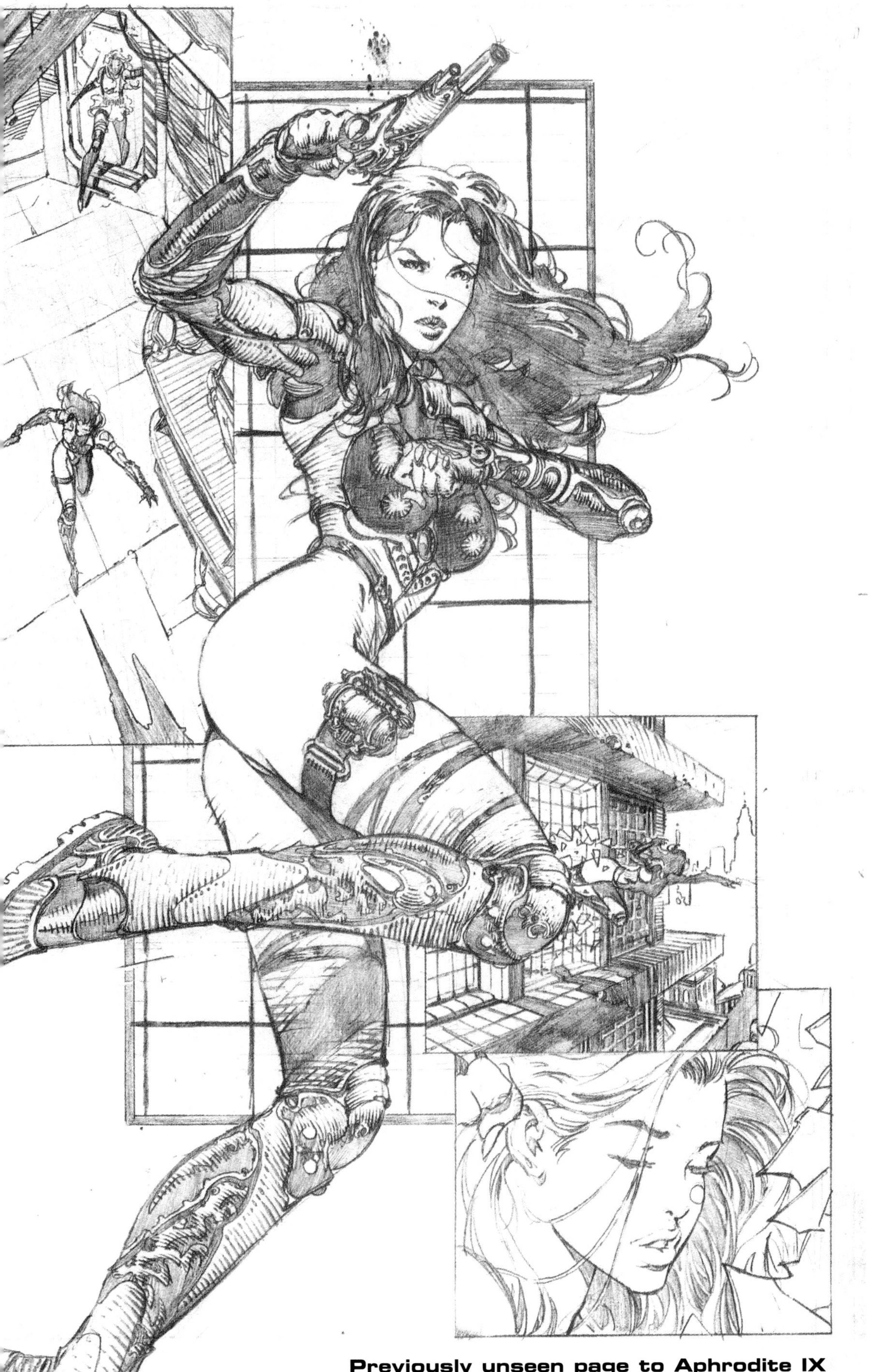

Previously unseen page to Aphrodite IX

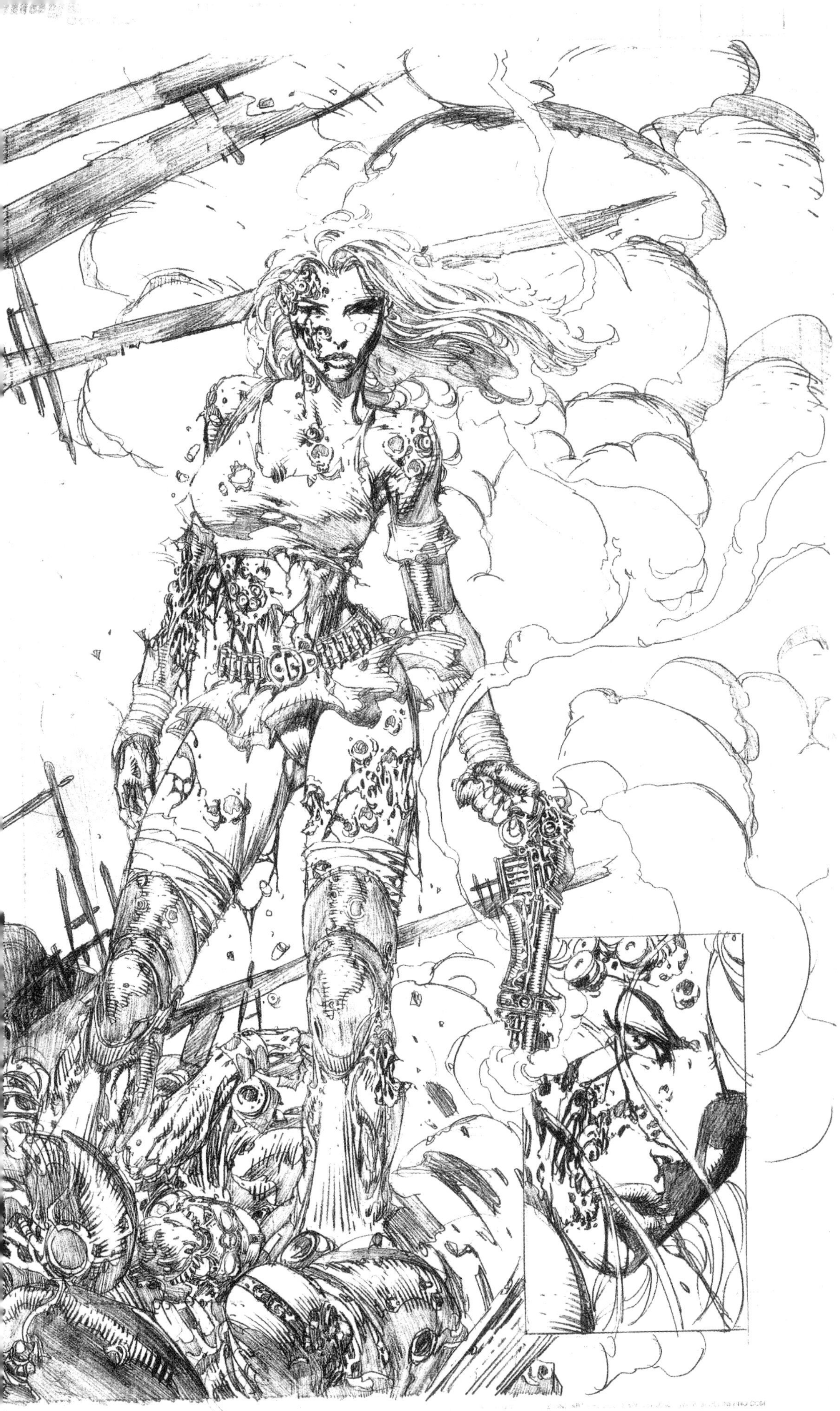

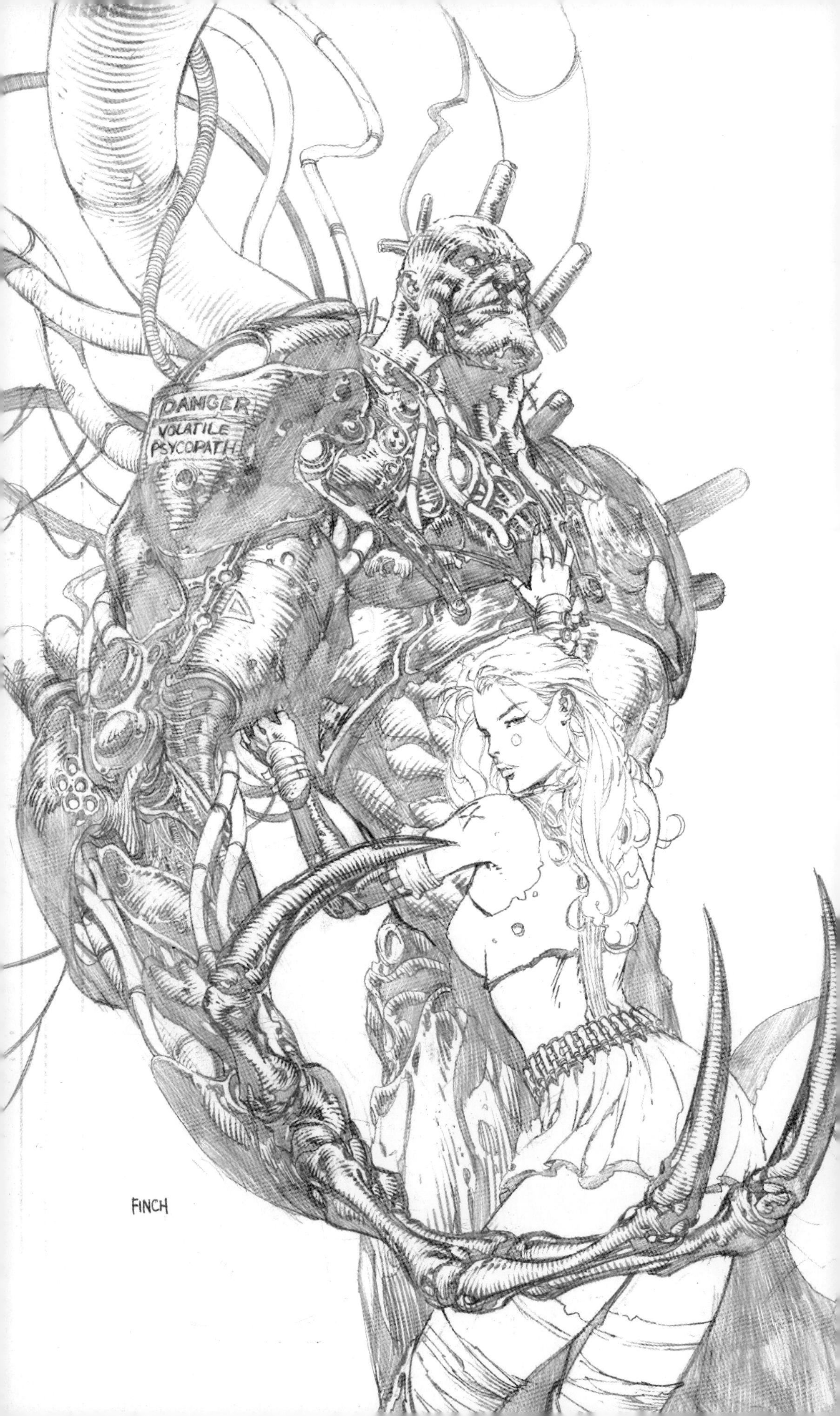
DANGER
VOLATILE
PSYCOPATH
FINCH

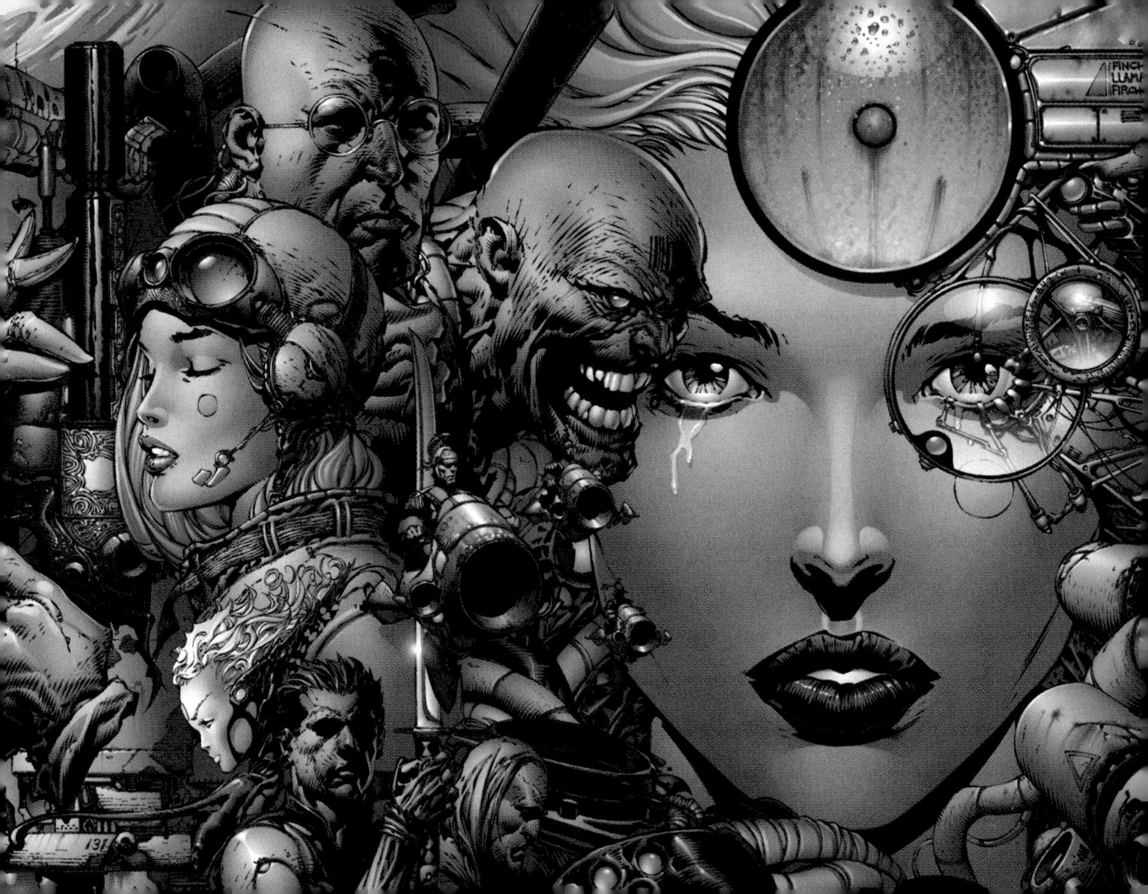

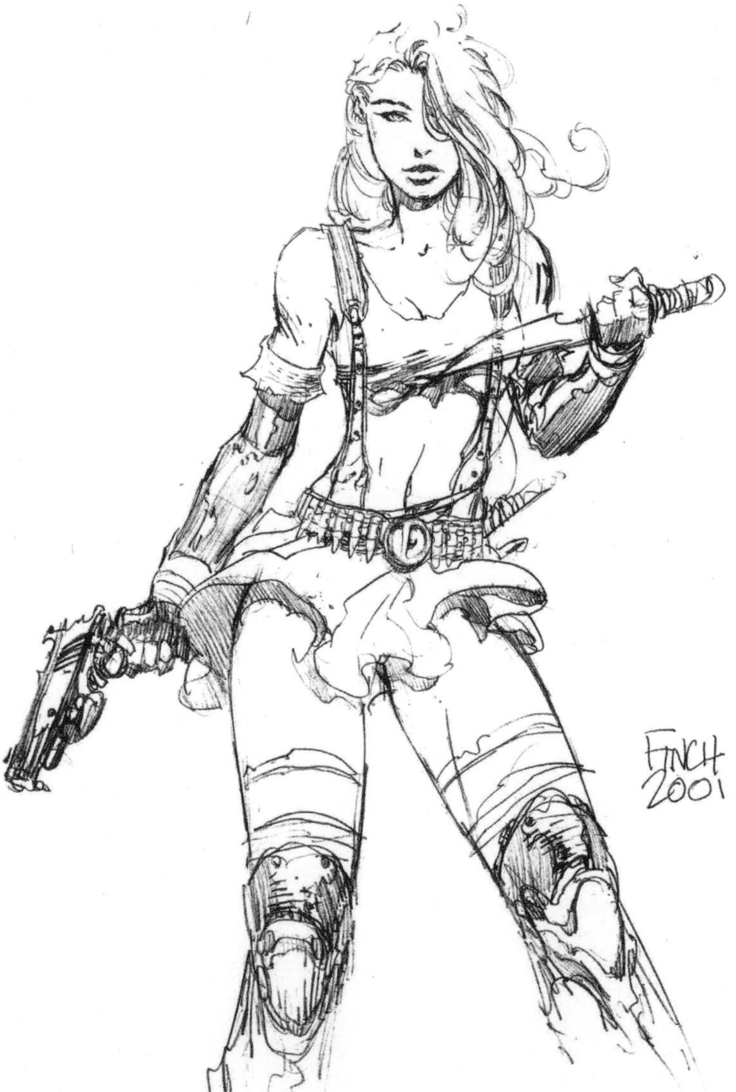
FINCH
2001

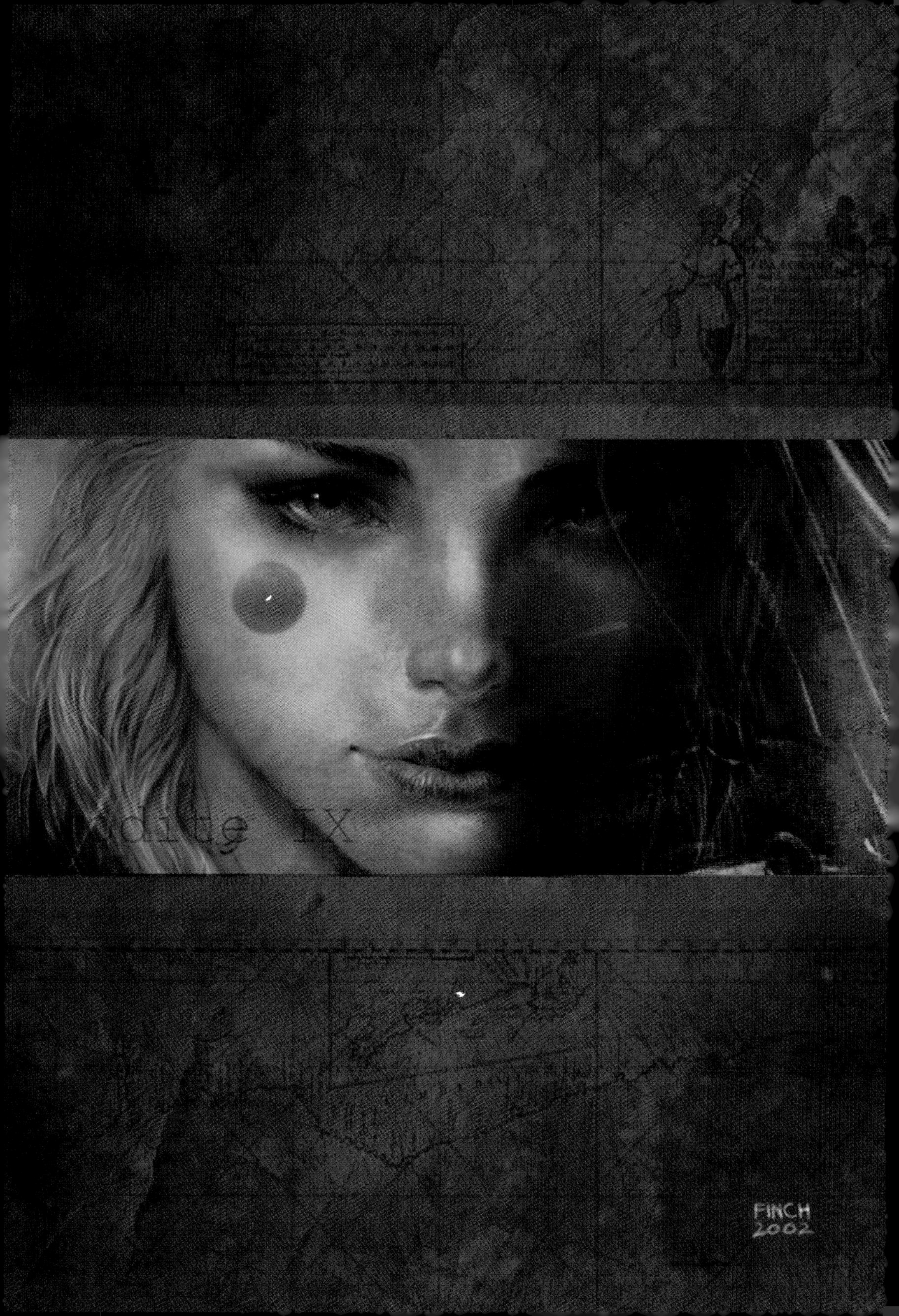
FINCH
2002

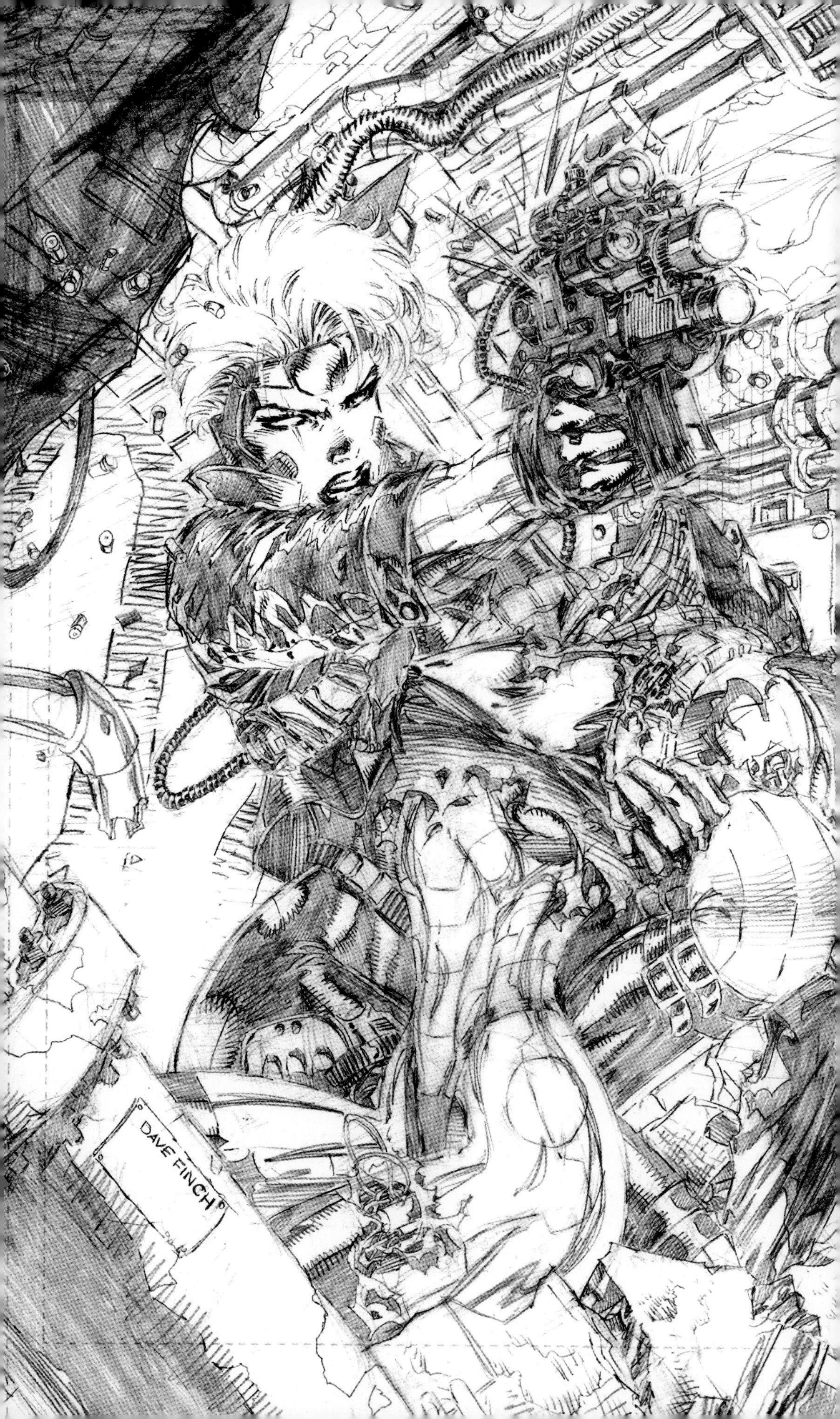
DAVE FINCH

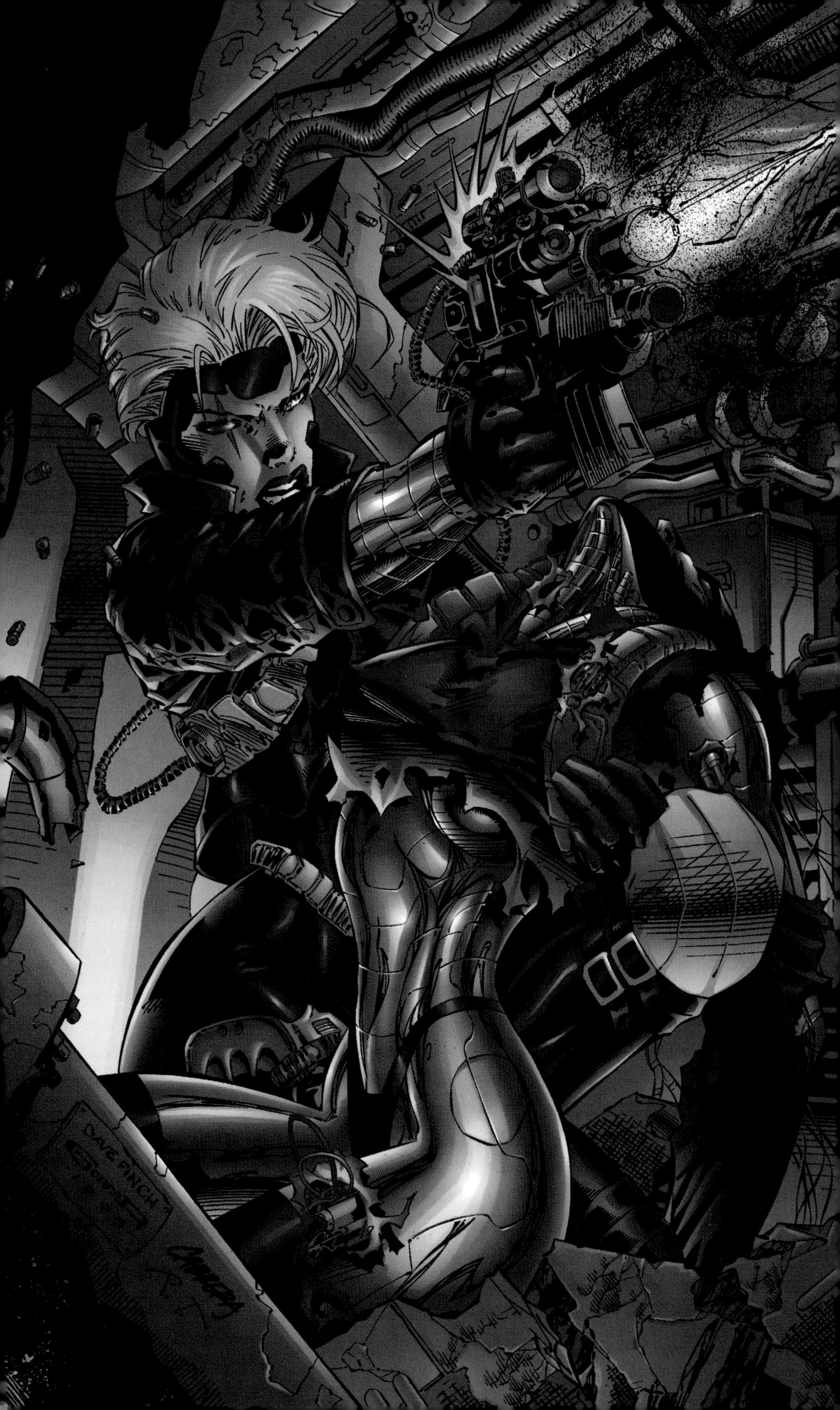
DAVE FINCH

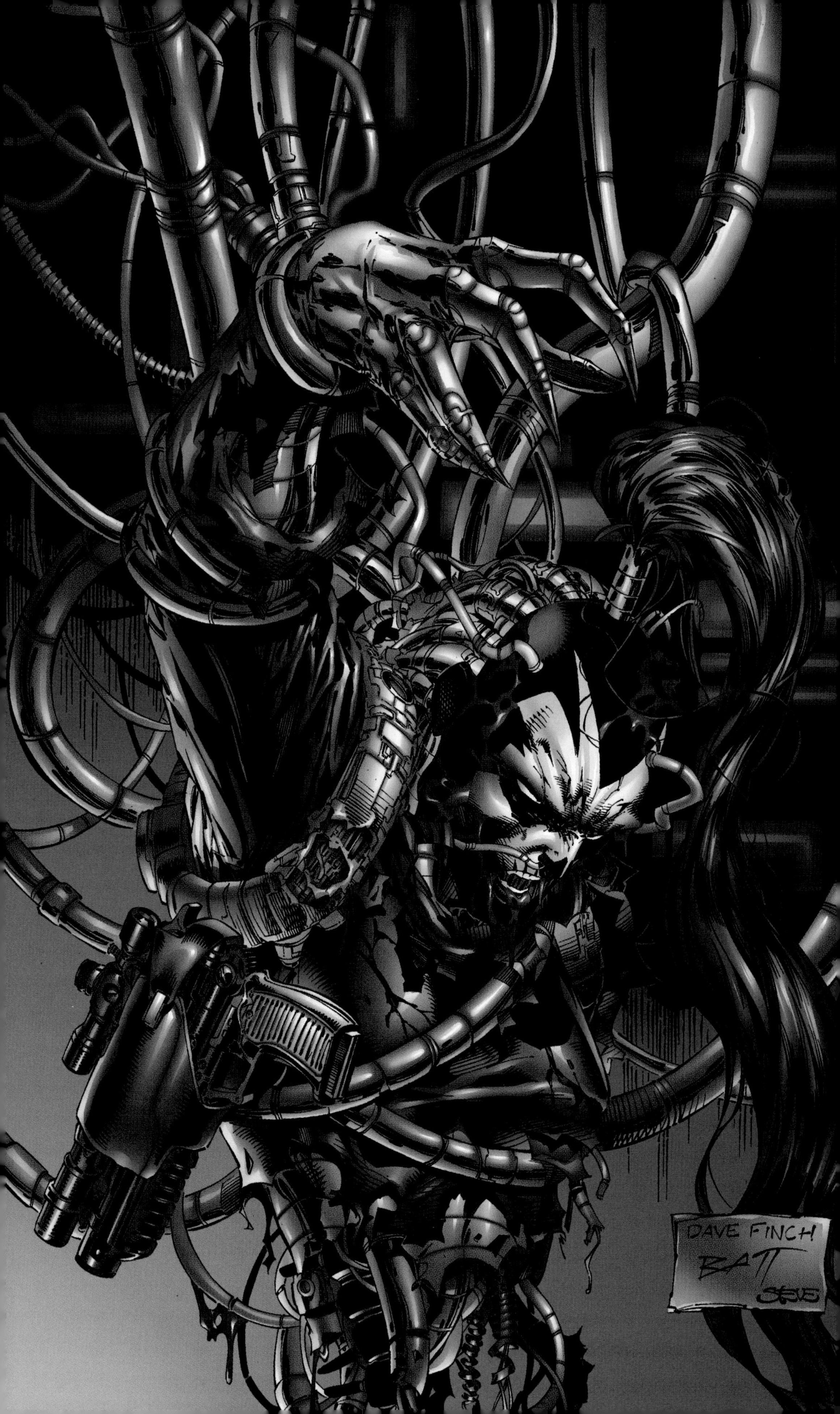
DAVE FINCH
BATT

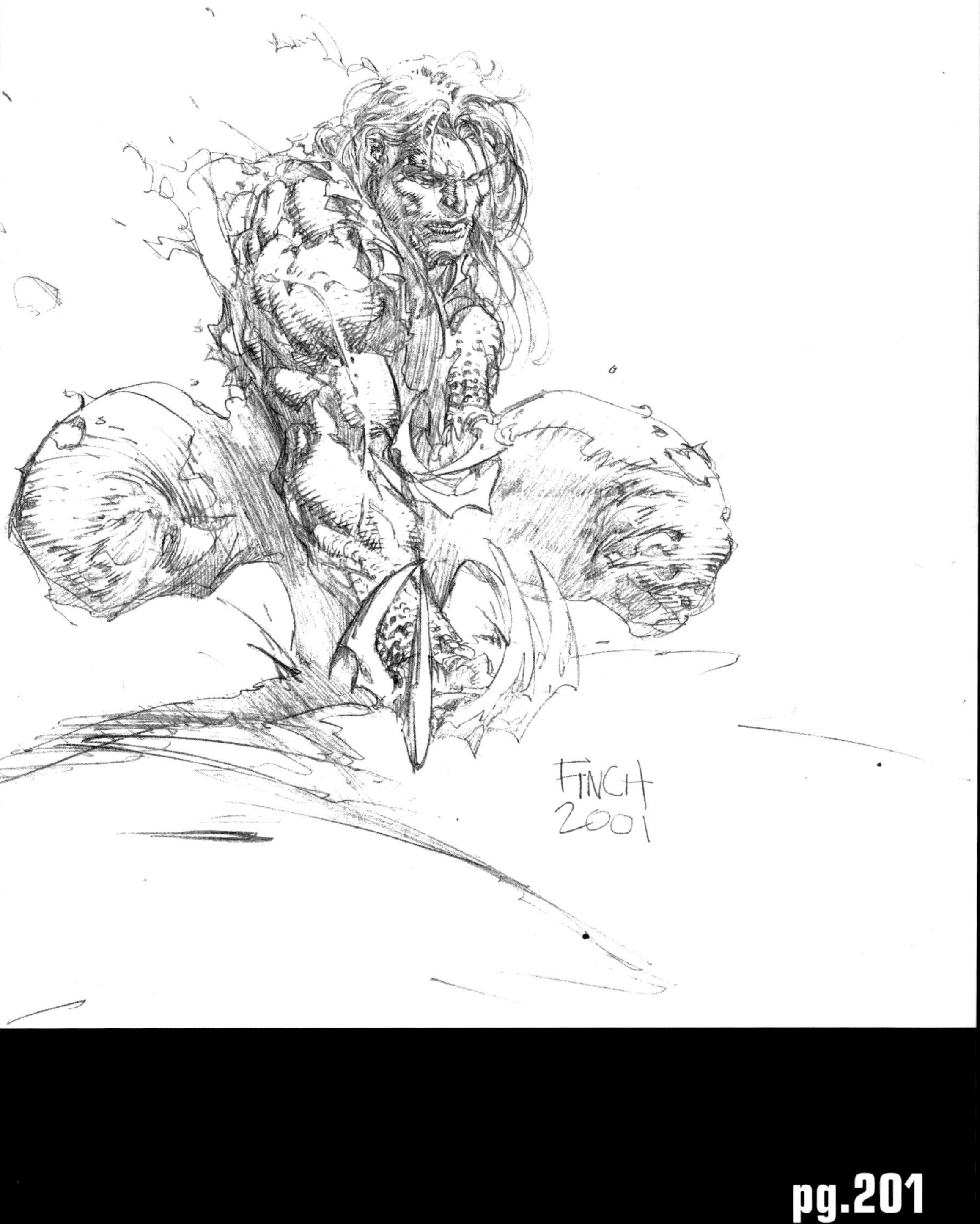
FINCH
2001

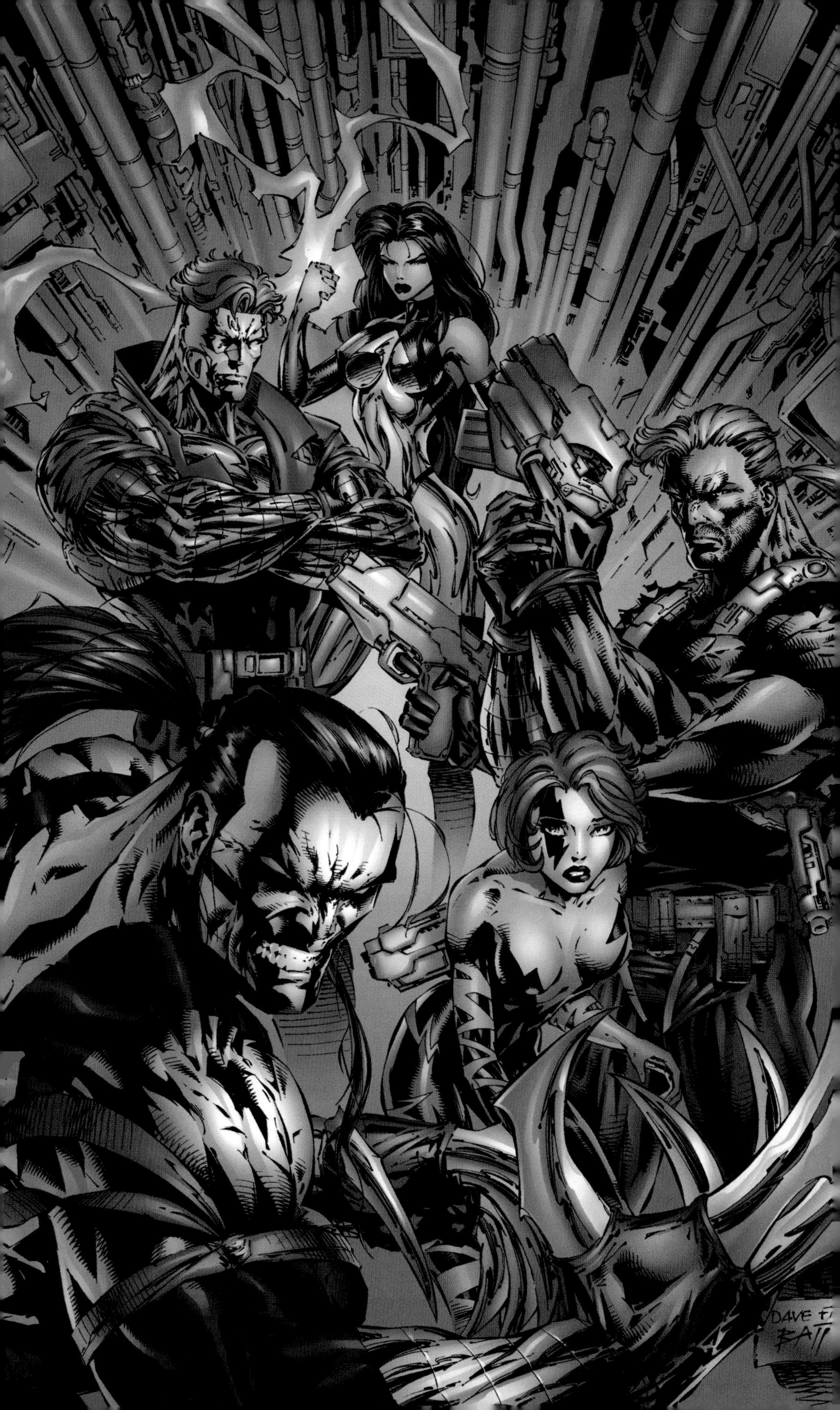

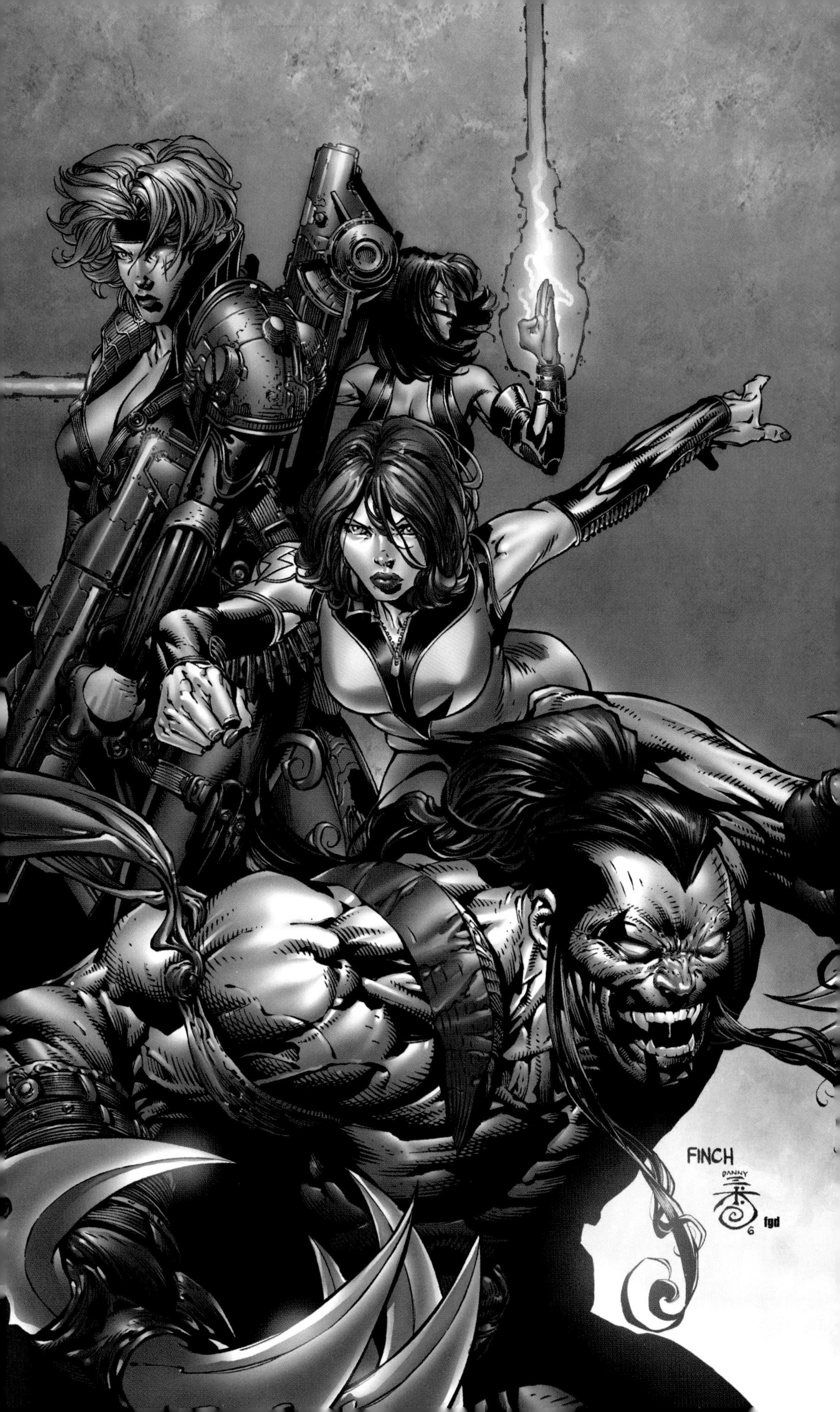
FINCH
DANNY
fgd

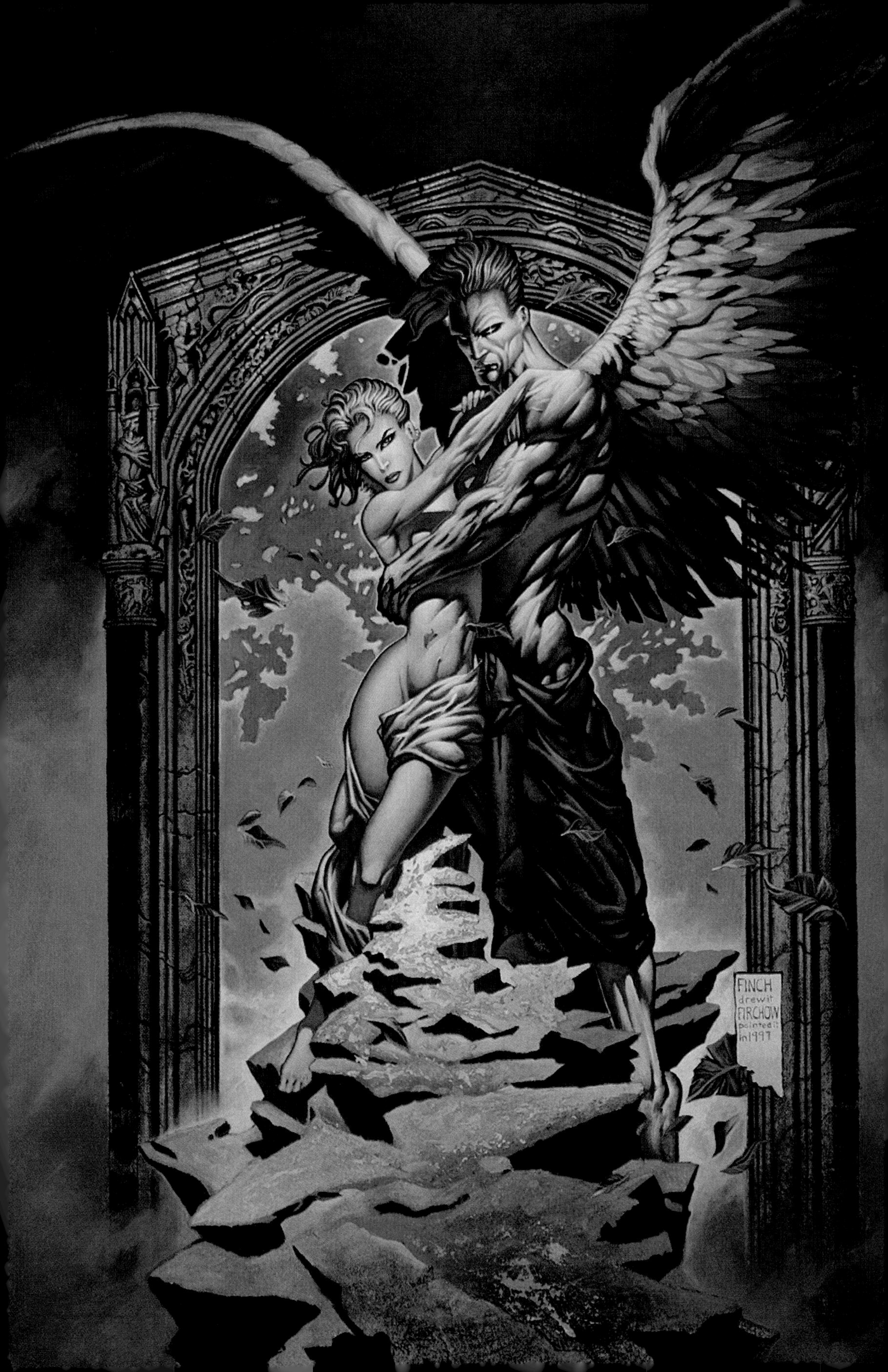
FINCH
drew it
FIRCHOW
painted it
in 1997

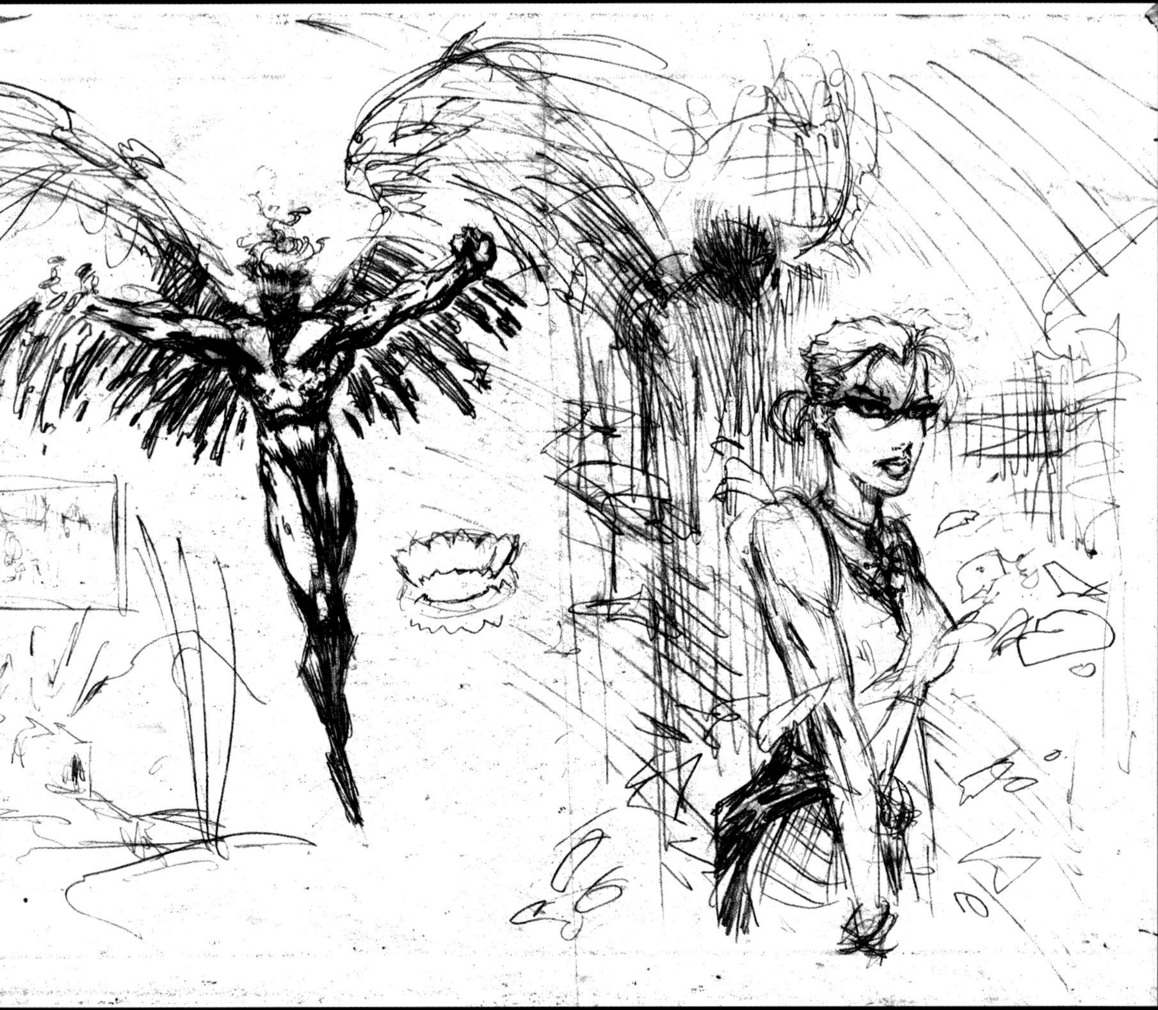

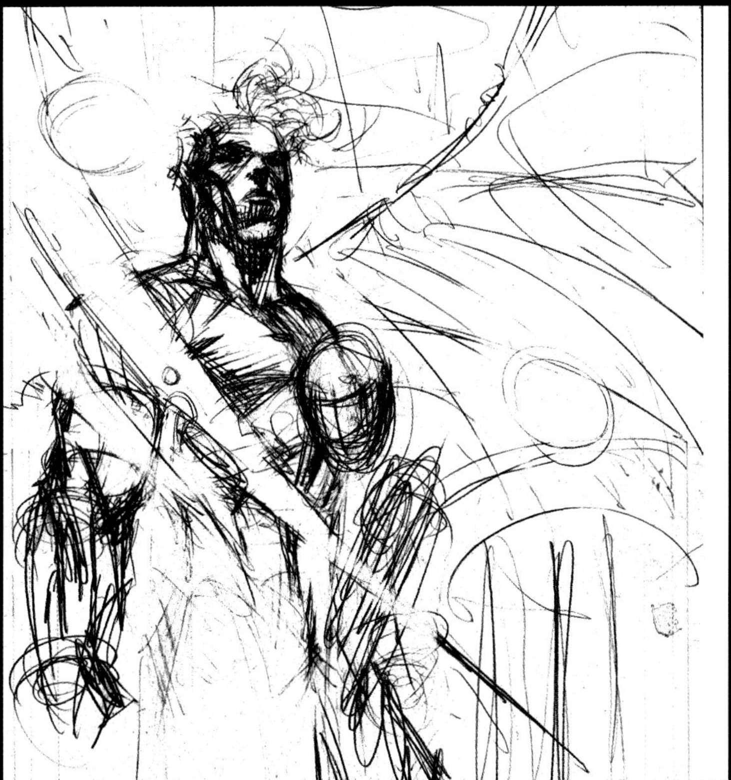

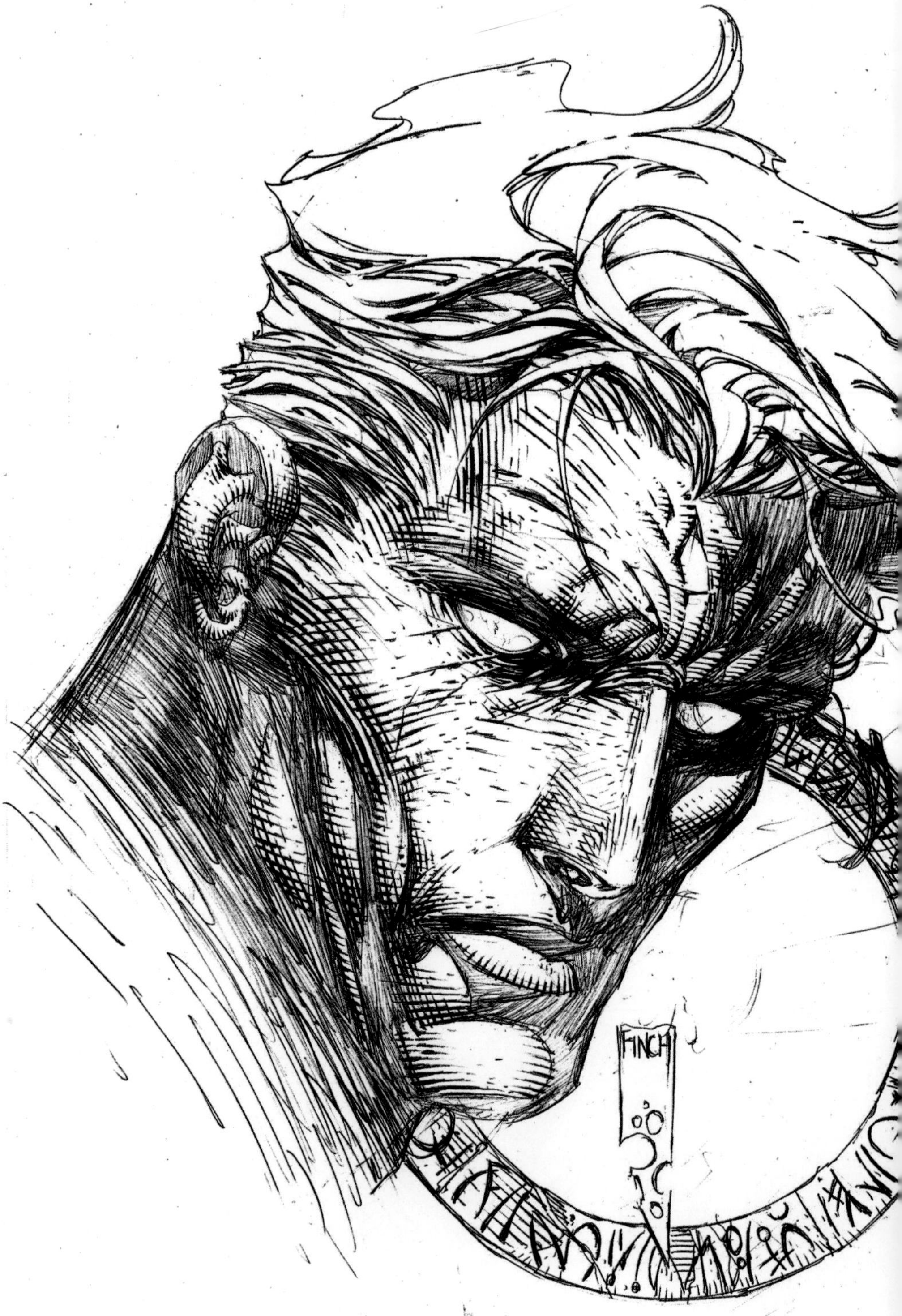
FINCH

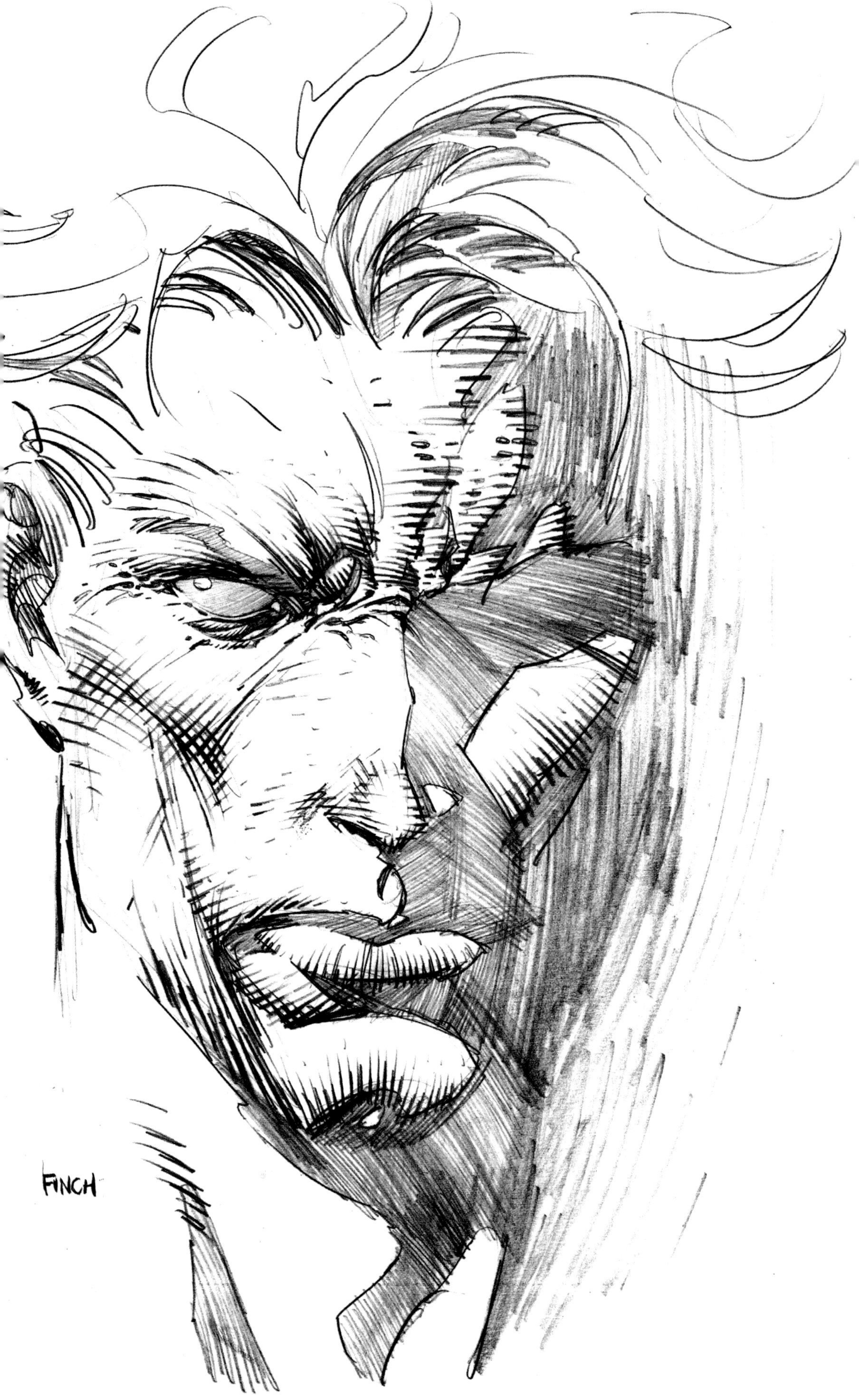
FINCH

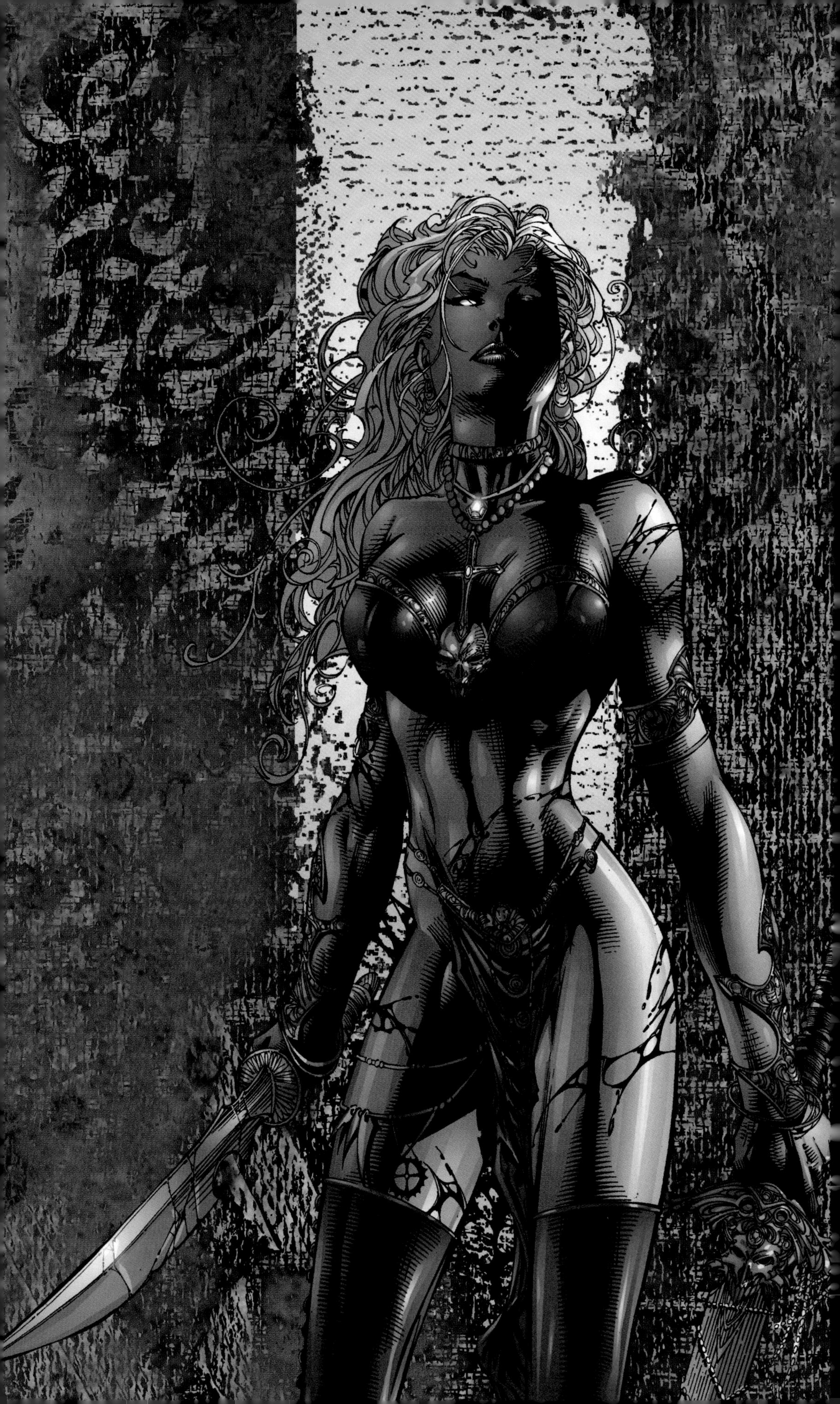

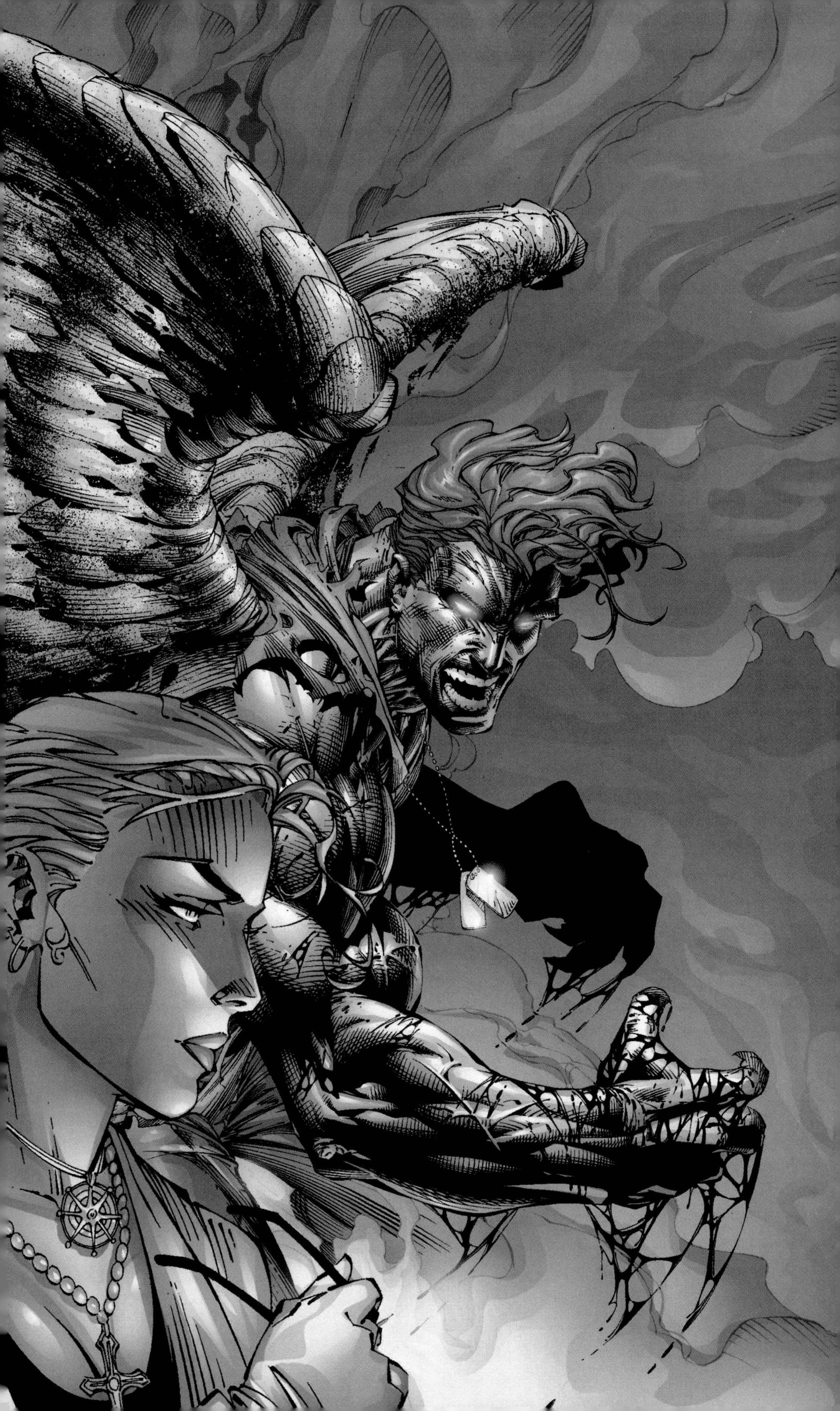

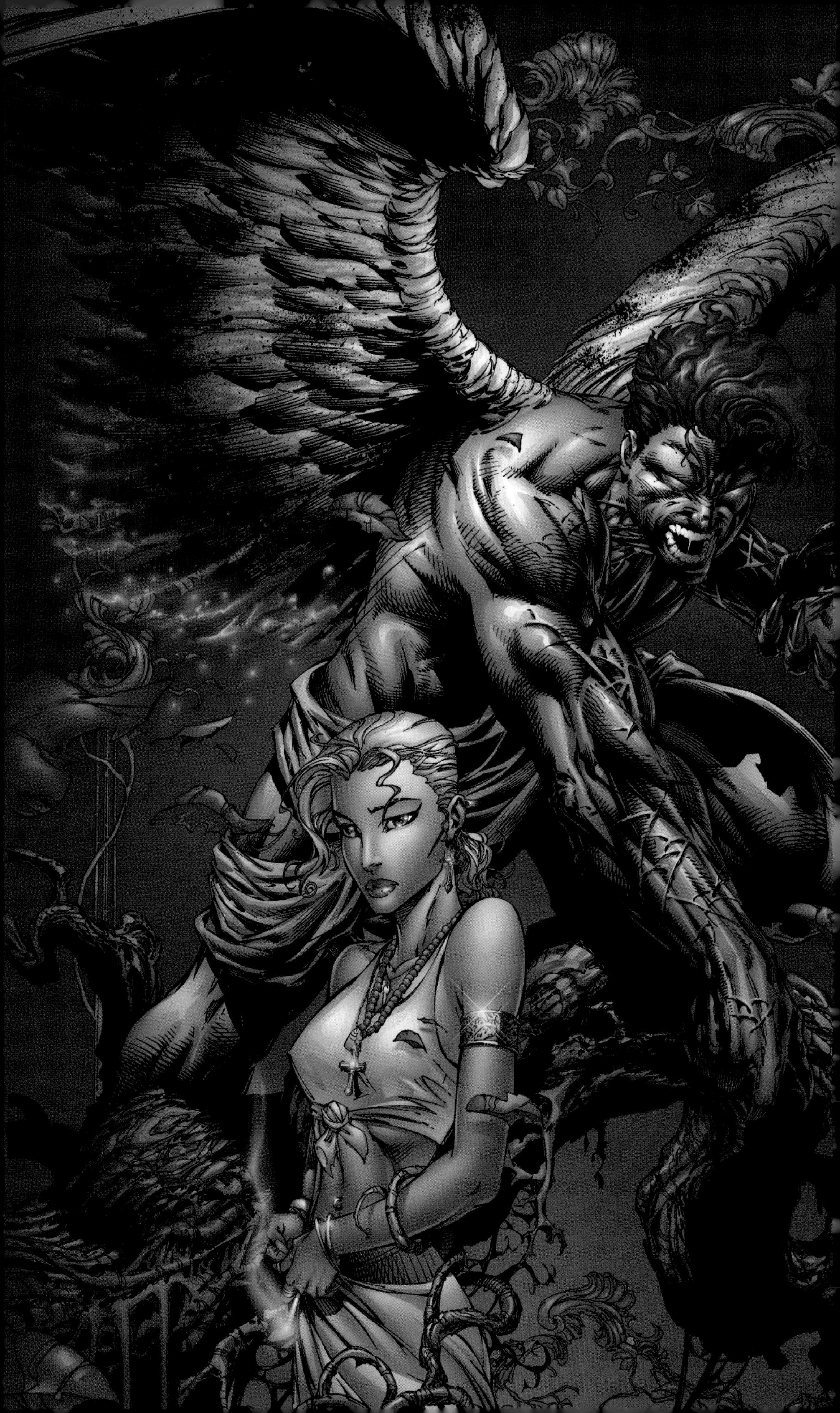

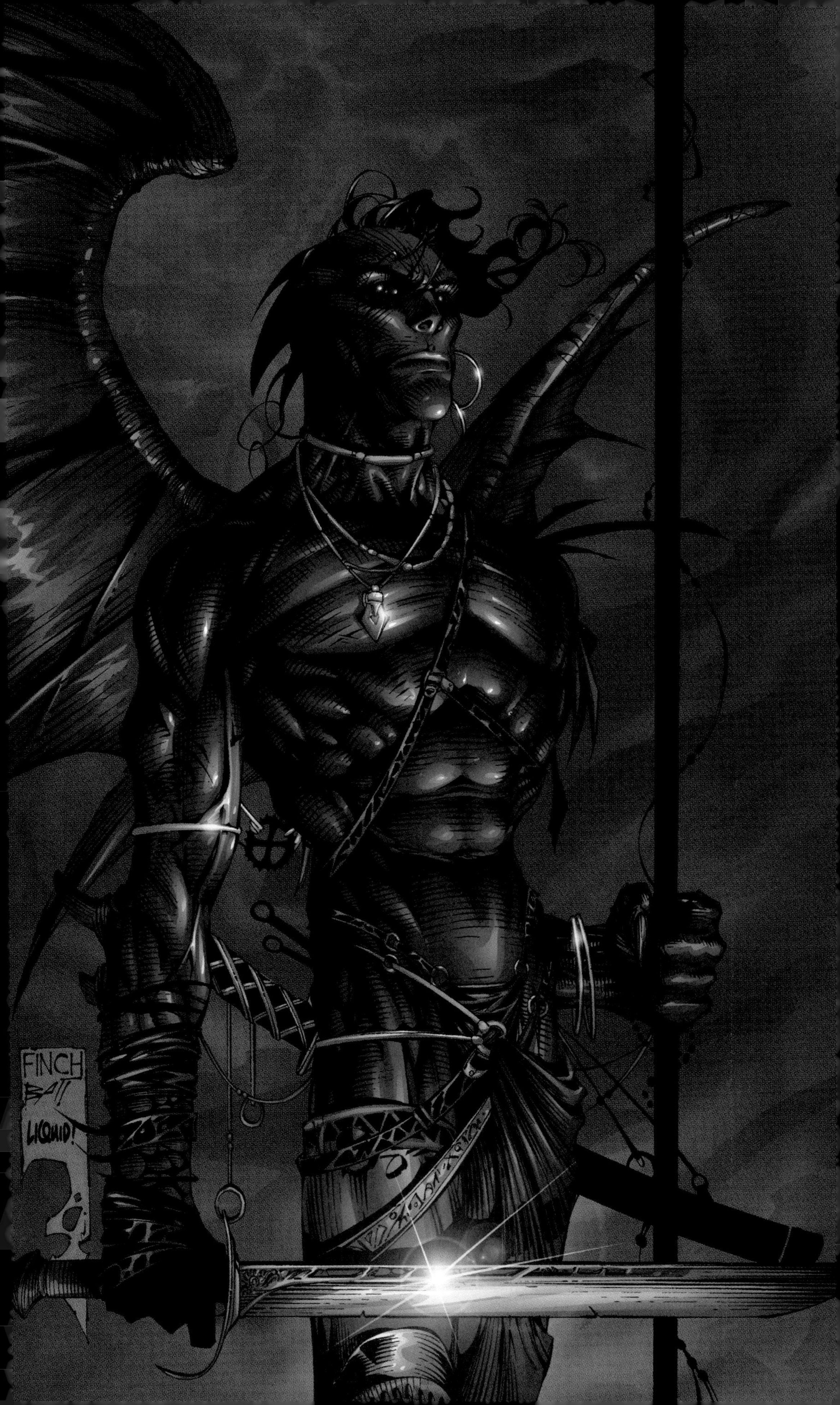
FINCH
BATT
LIQUID!

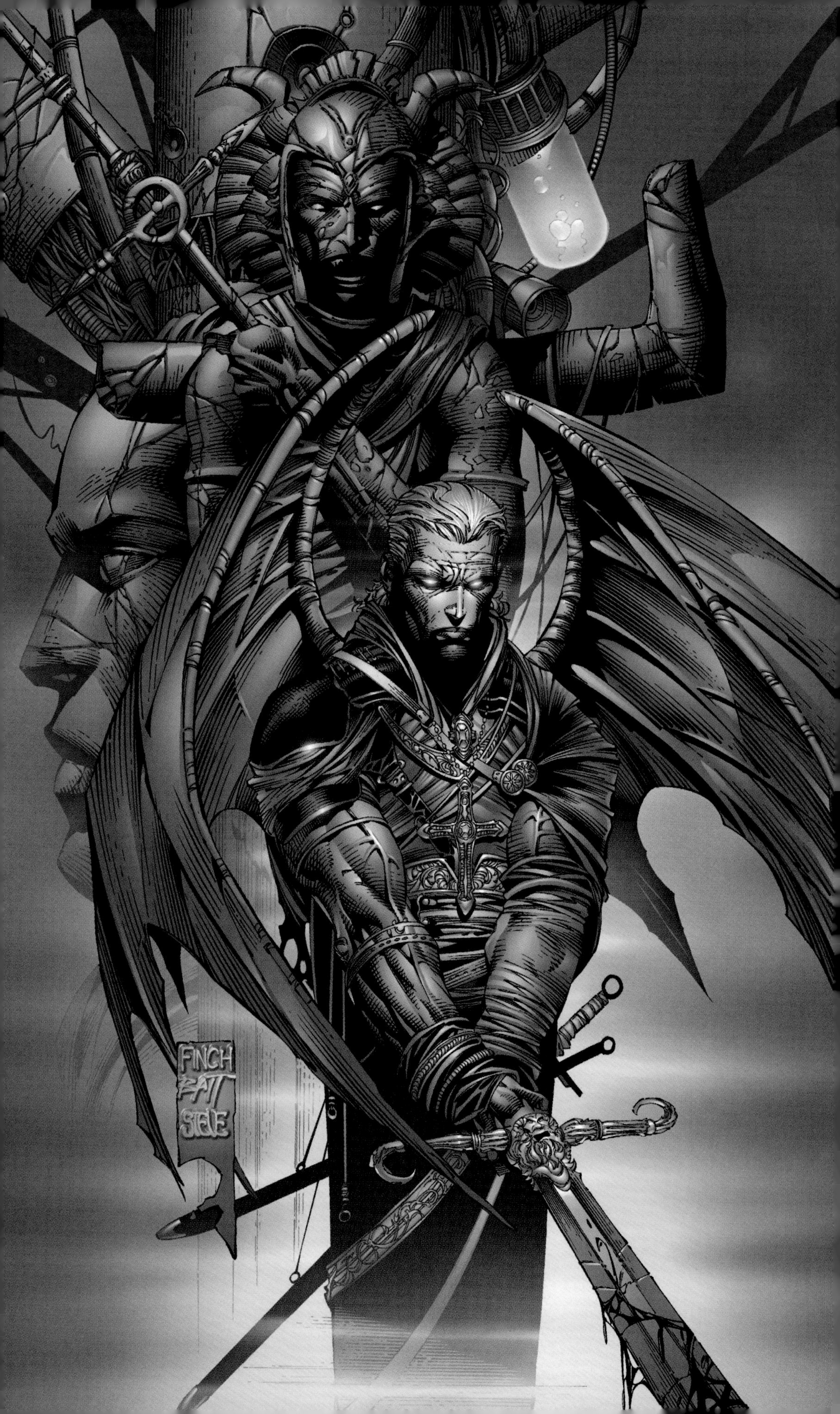
FINCH

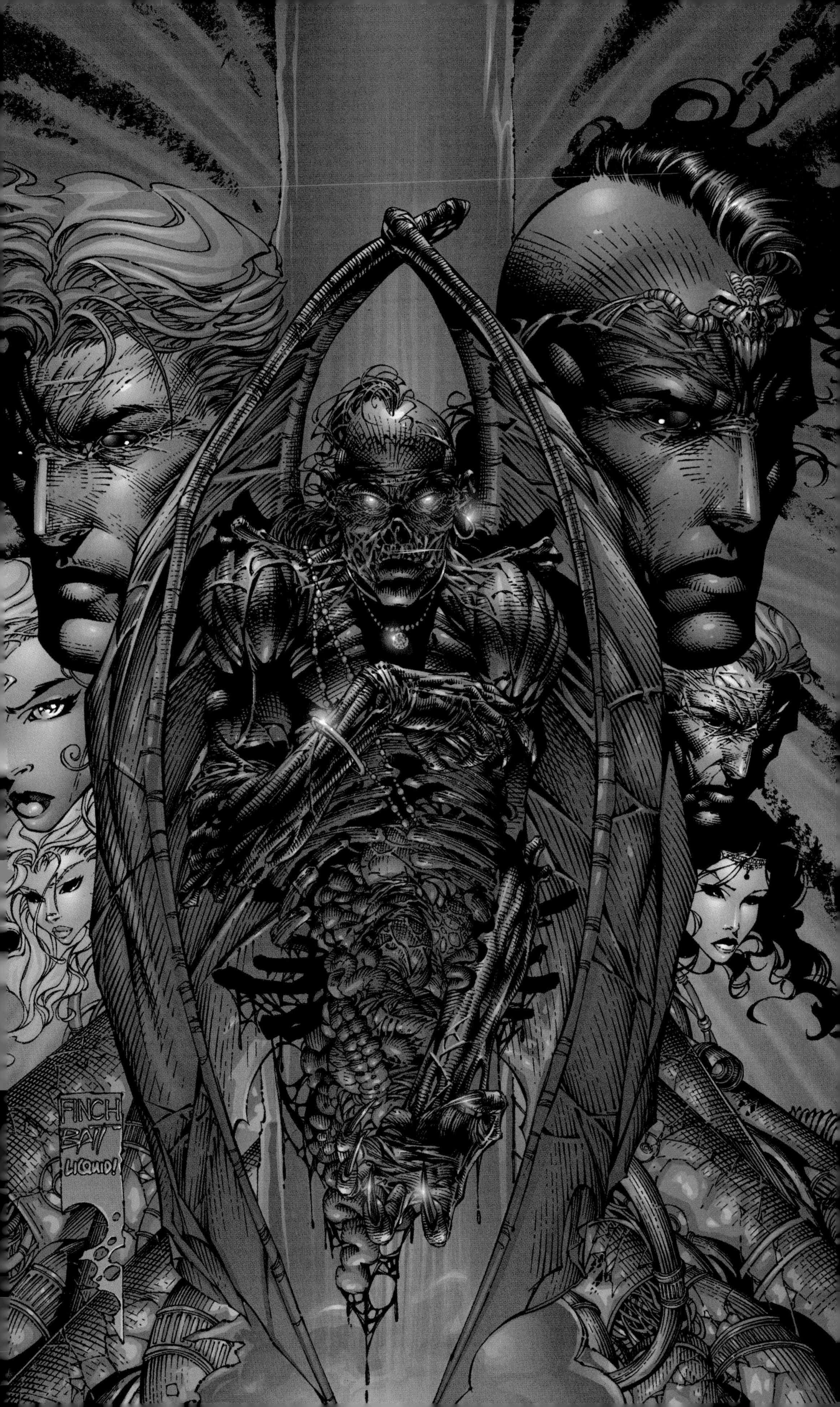
FINCH
BATT
LIQUID!

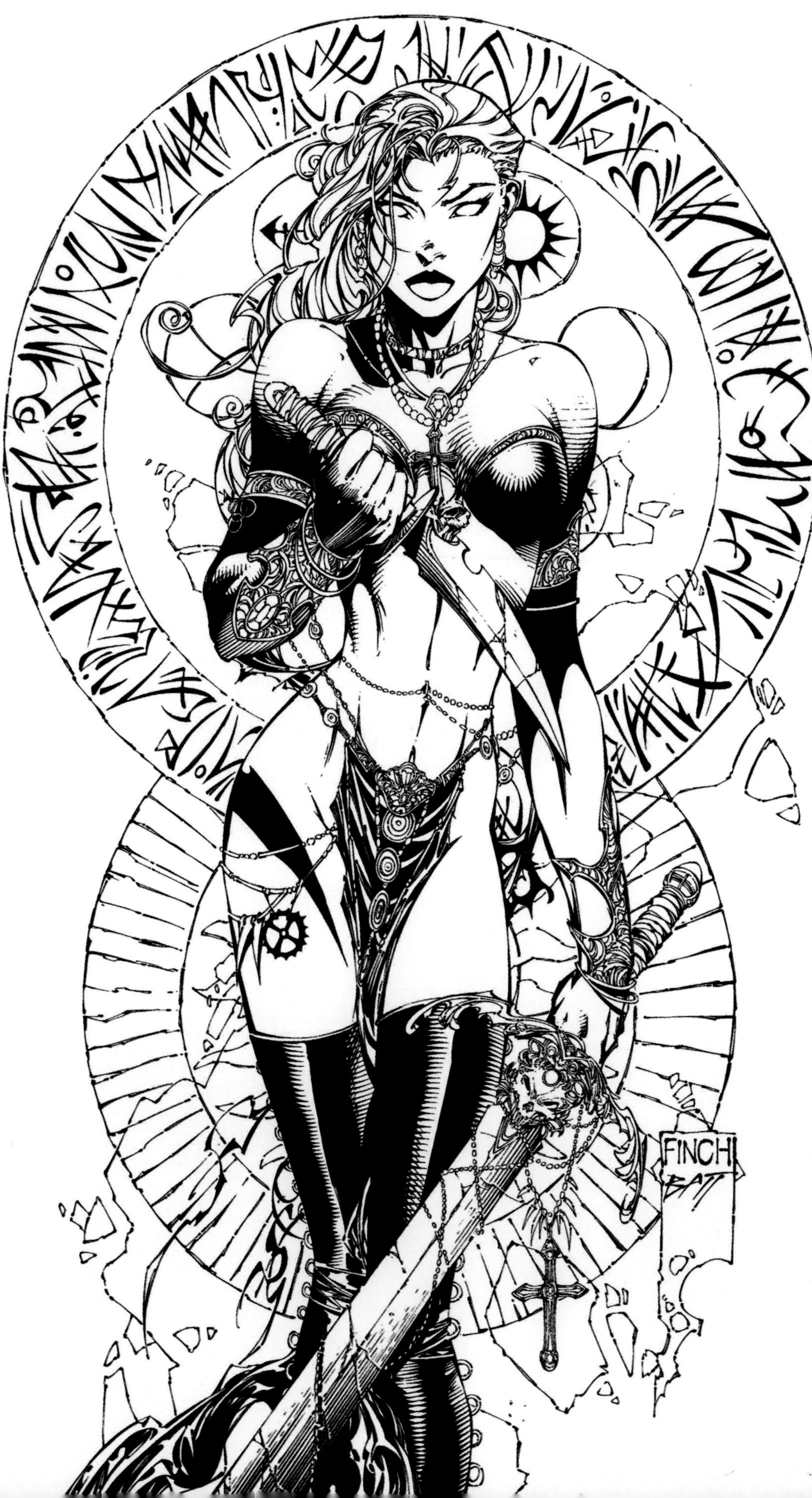
FINCH
BAT

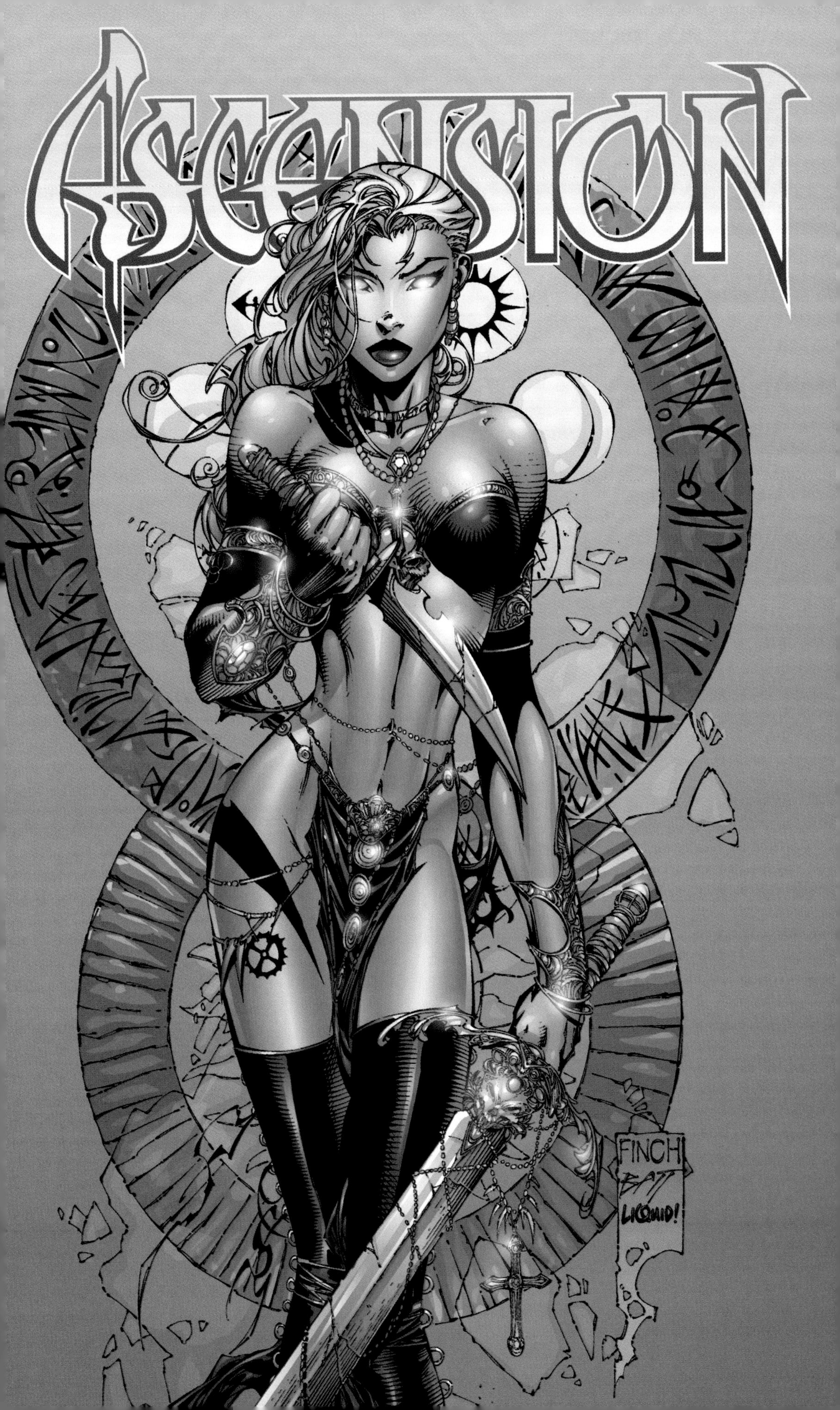
ASCENSION
FINCH
BATT
LIQUID!

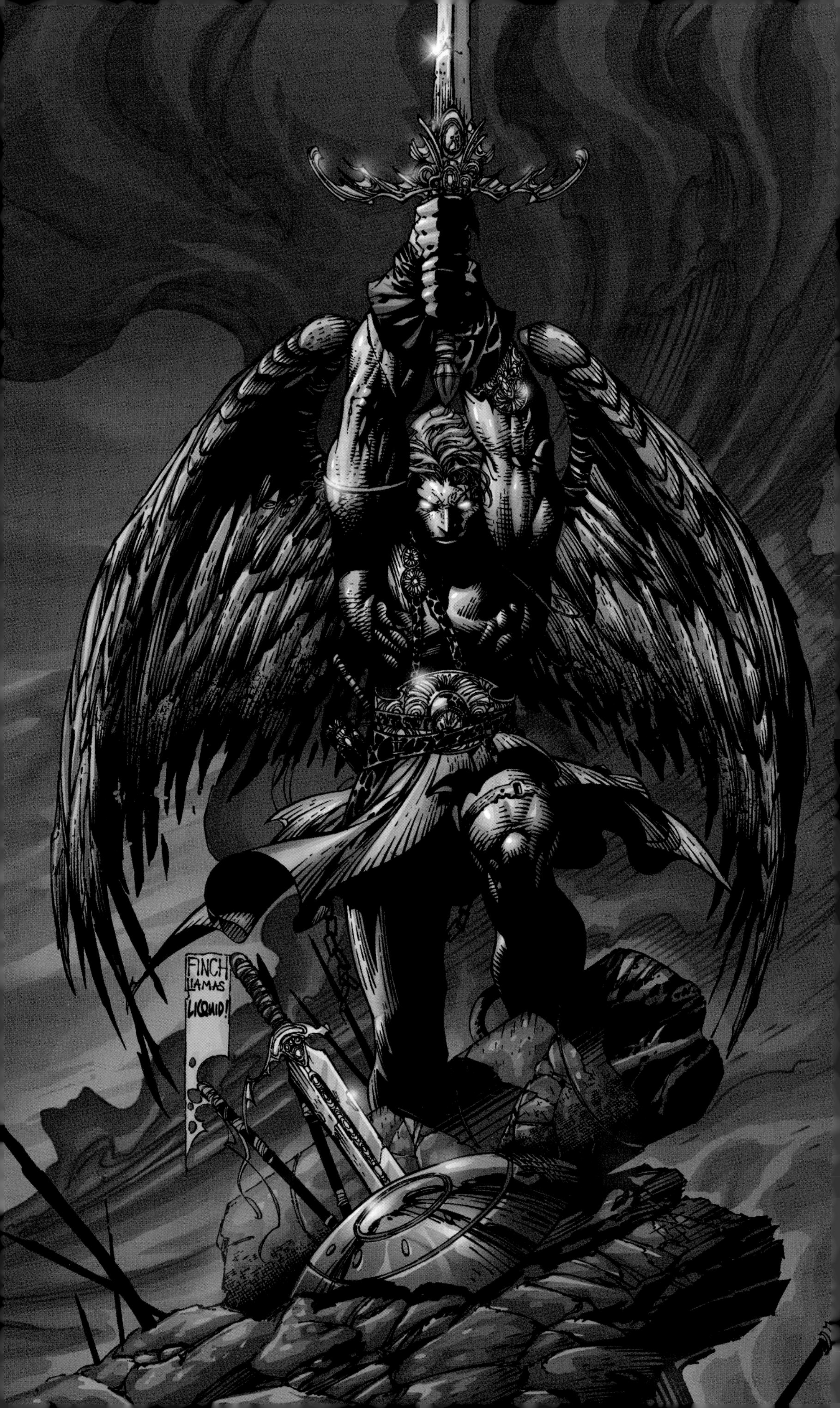
FINCH
LLAMAS
LIQUID!

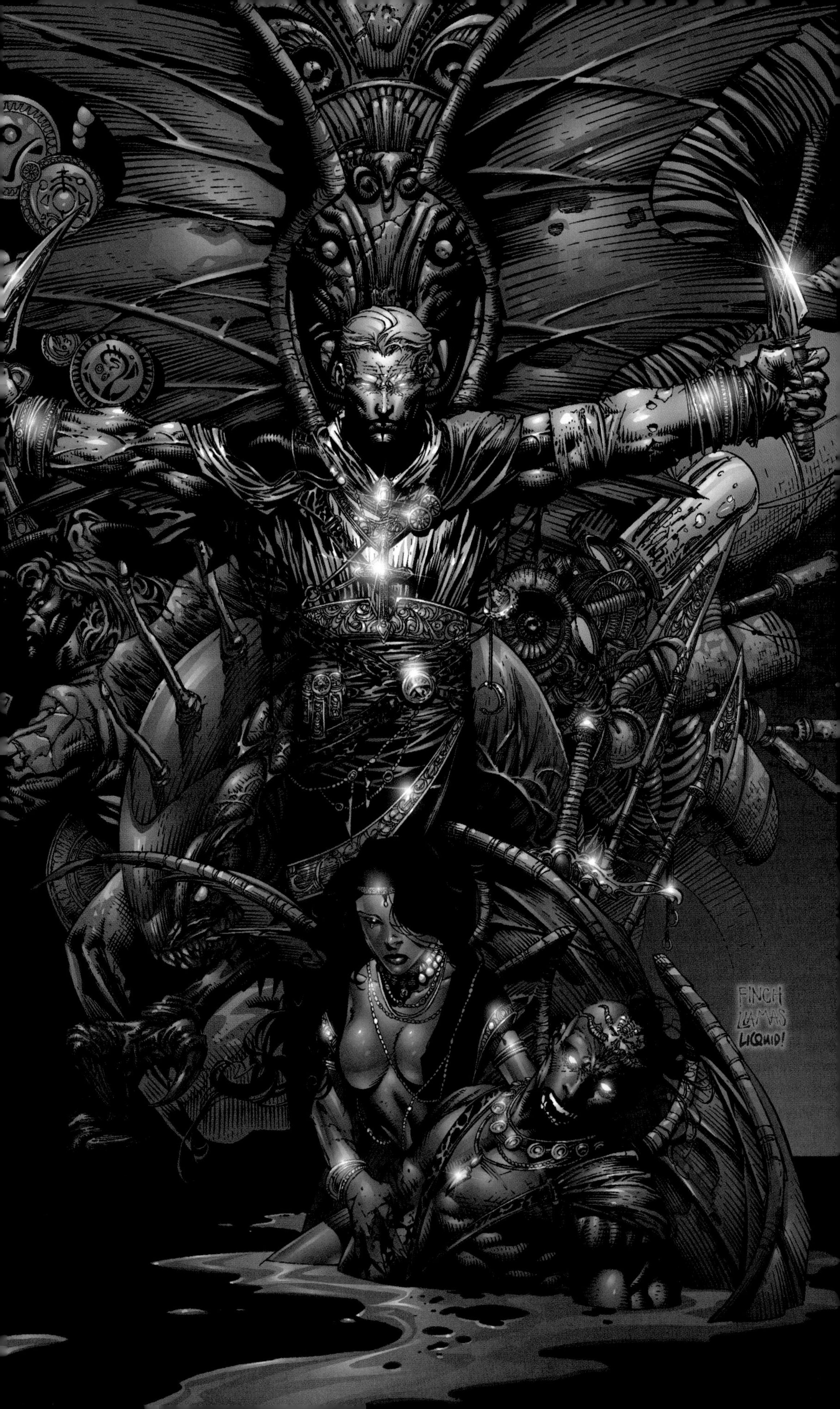
FINCH
LLAMAS
LIQUID!

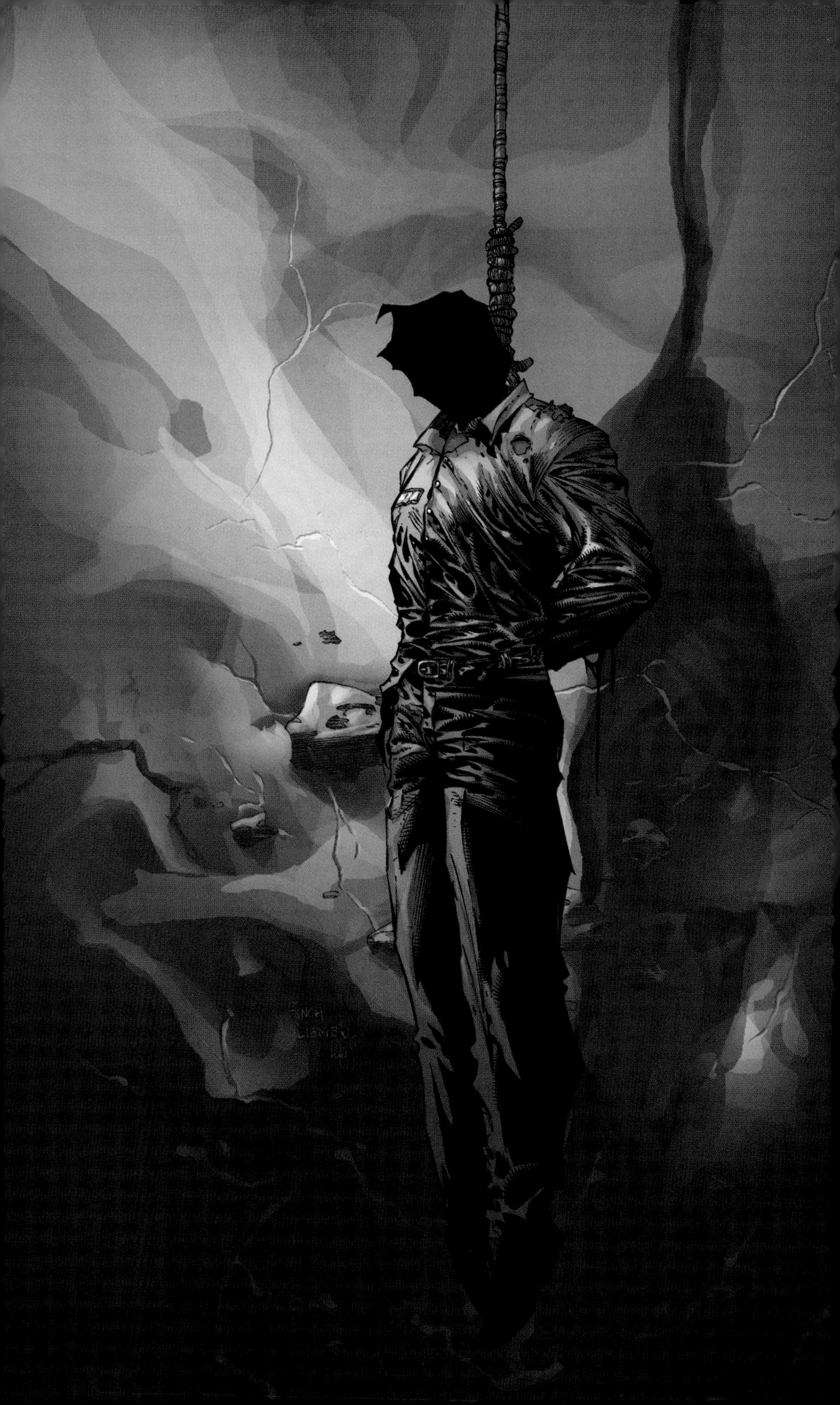

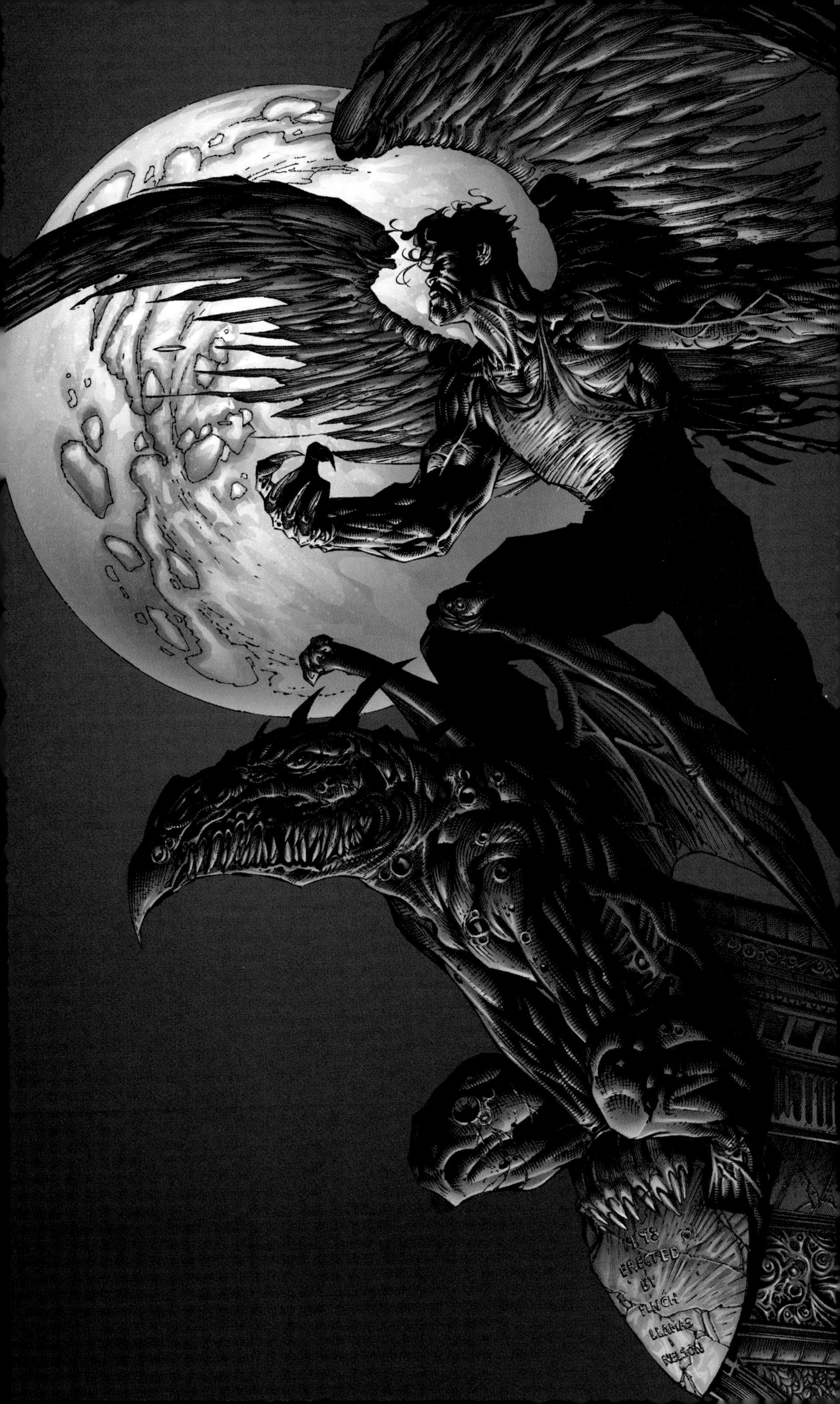
98
ERECTED
BY
FINCH
LLAMAS
NELSON

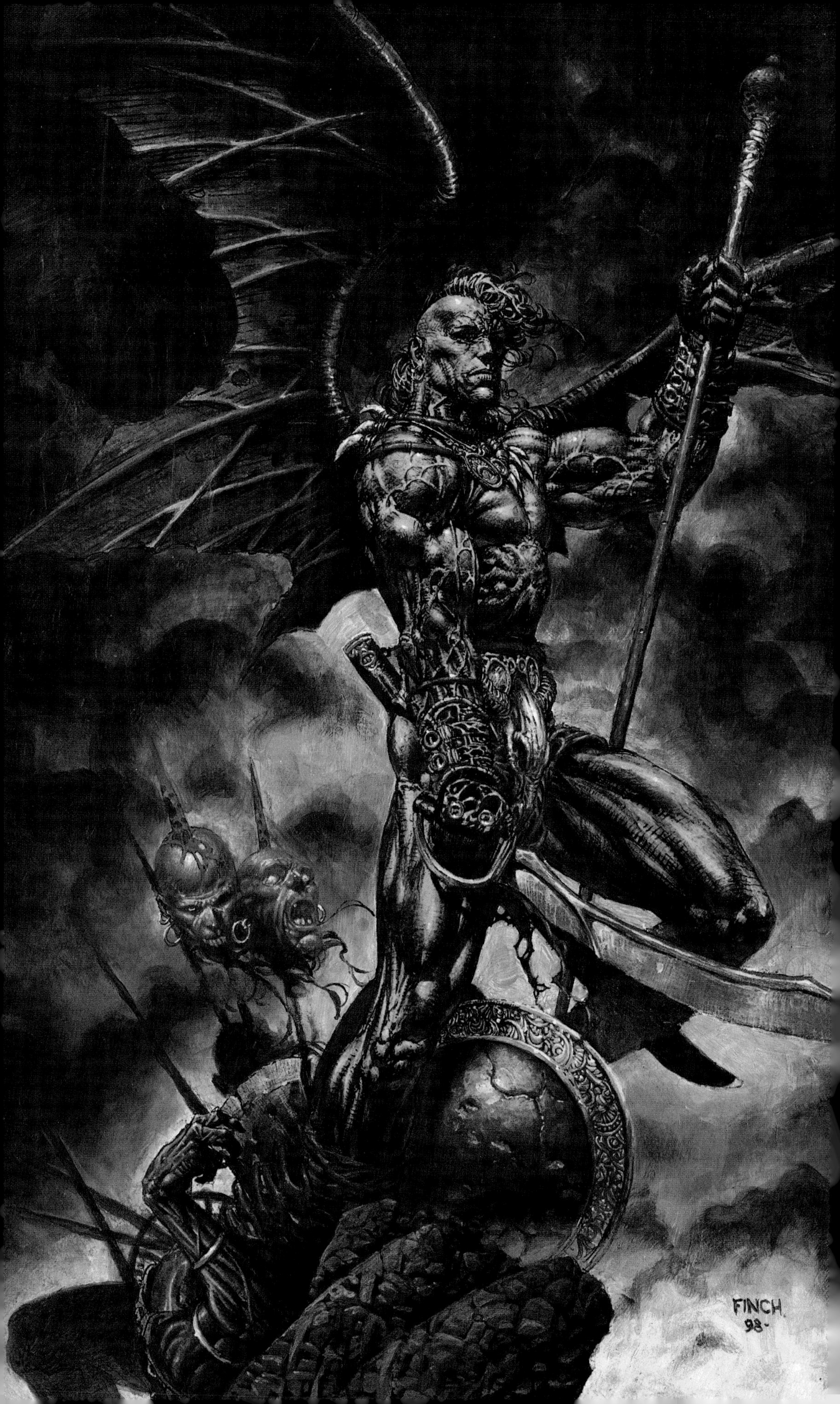
FINCH
98-

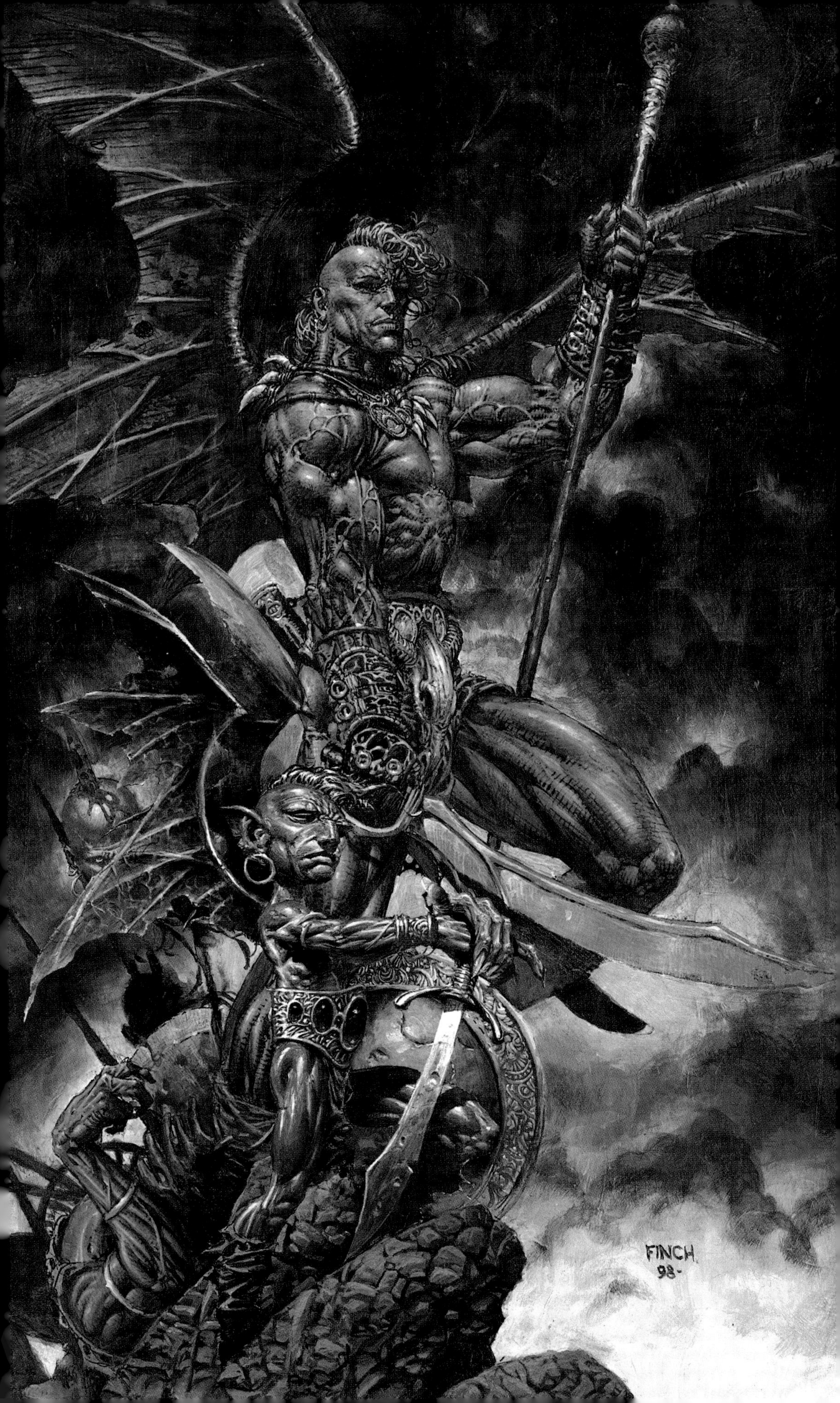
FINCH
98

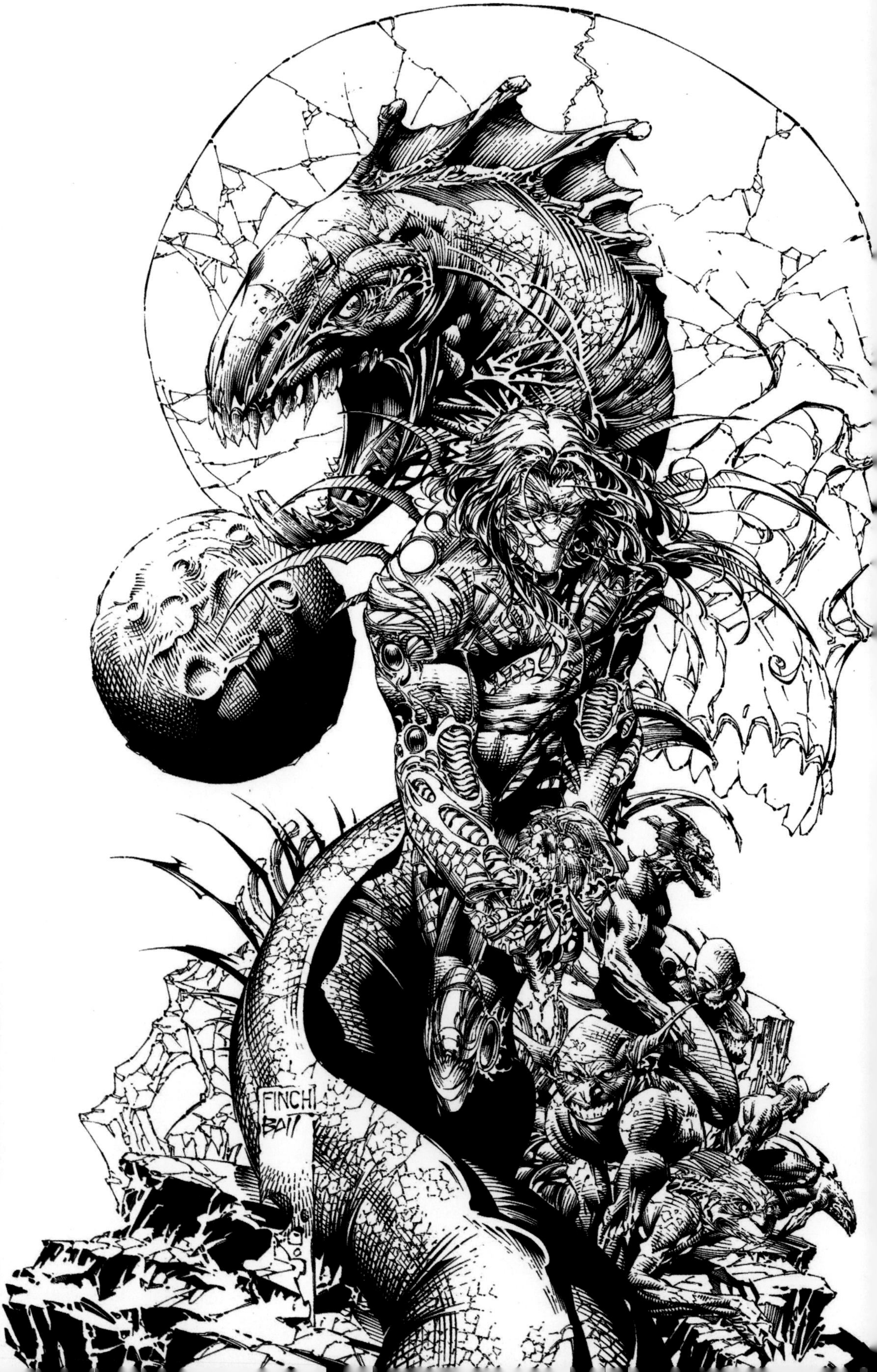
FINCH
BATT

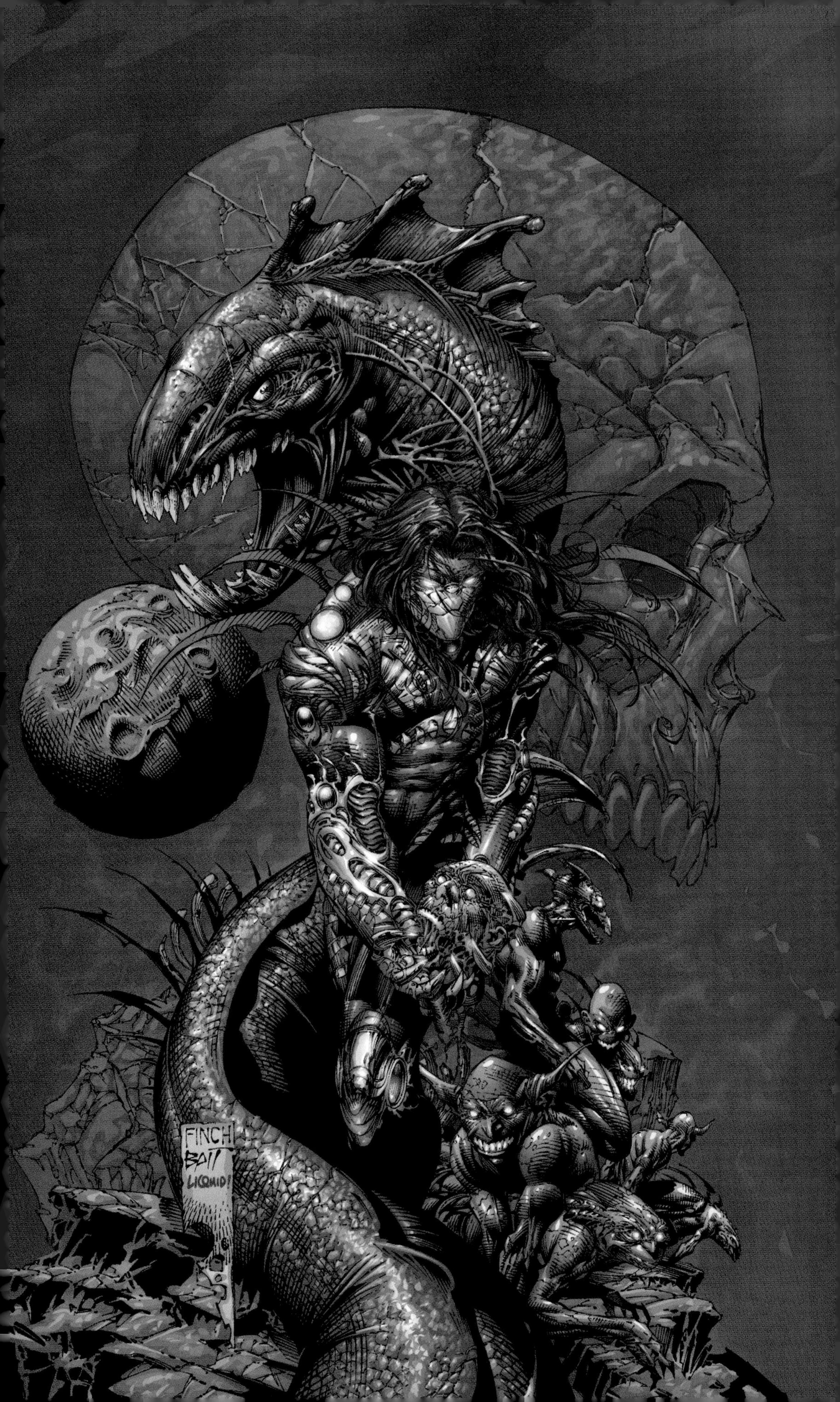
FINCH
LIQUID!

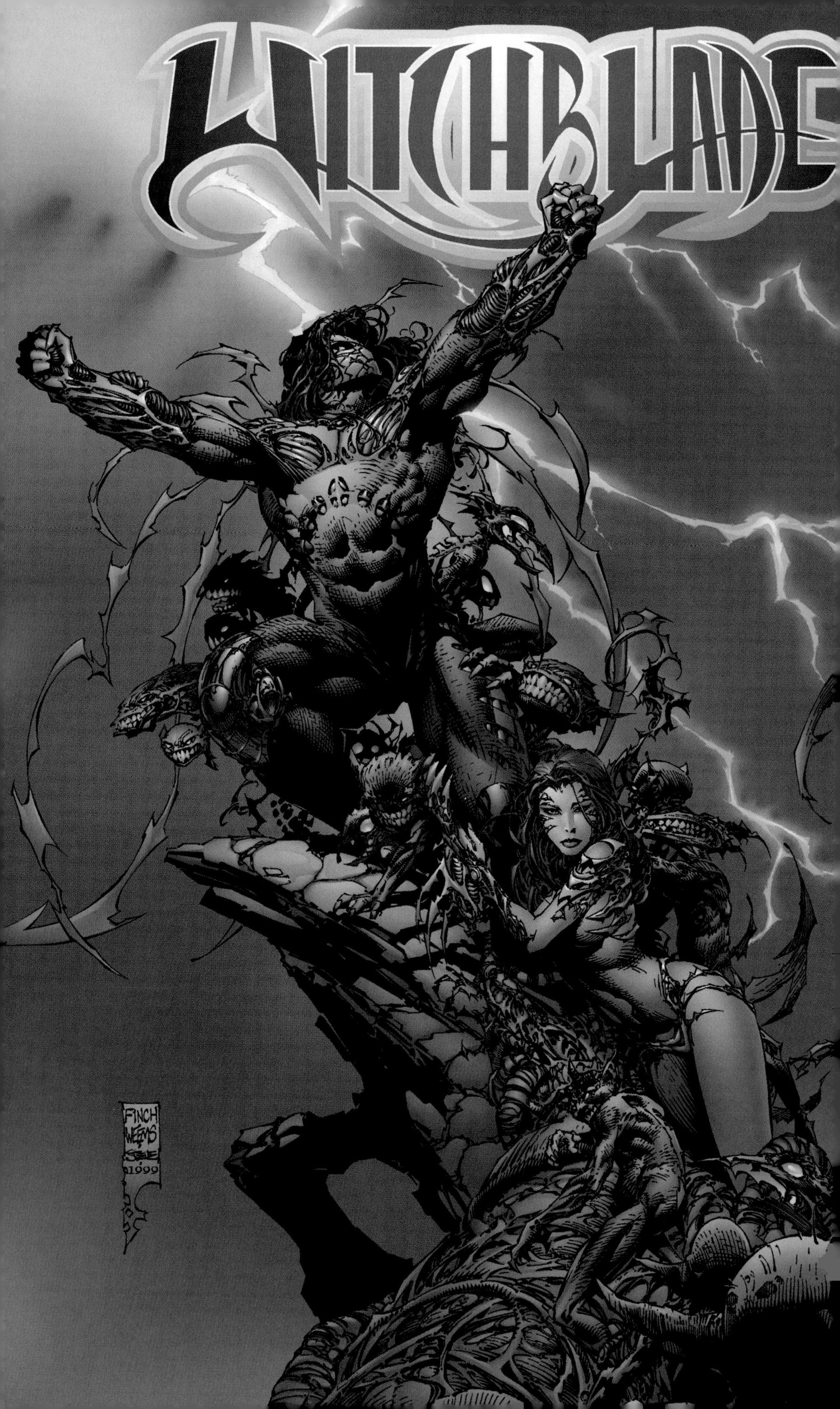
WITCHBLADE
FINCH
WEEMS

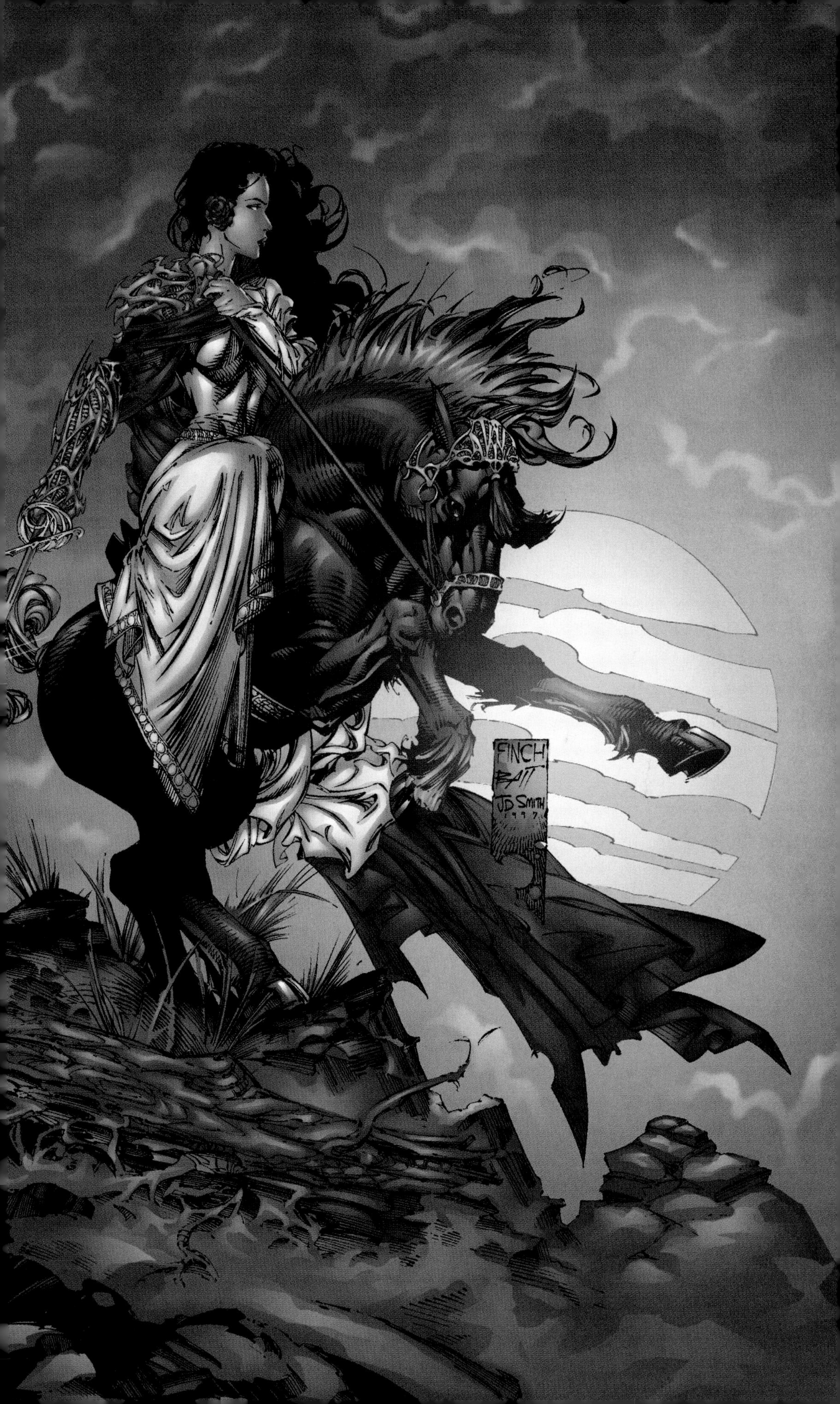
FINCH
BATT
JD SMITH
1997

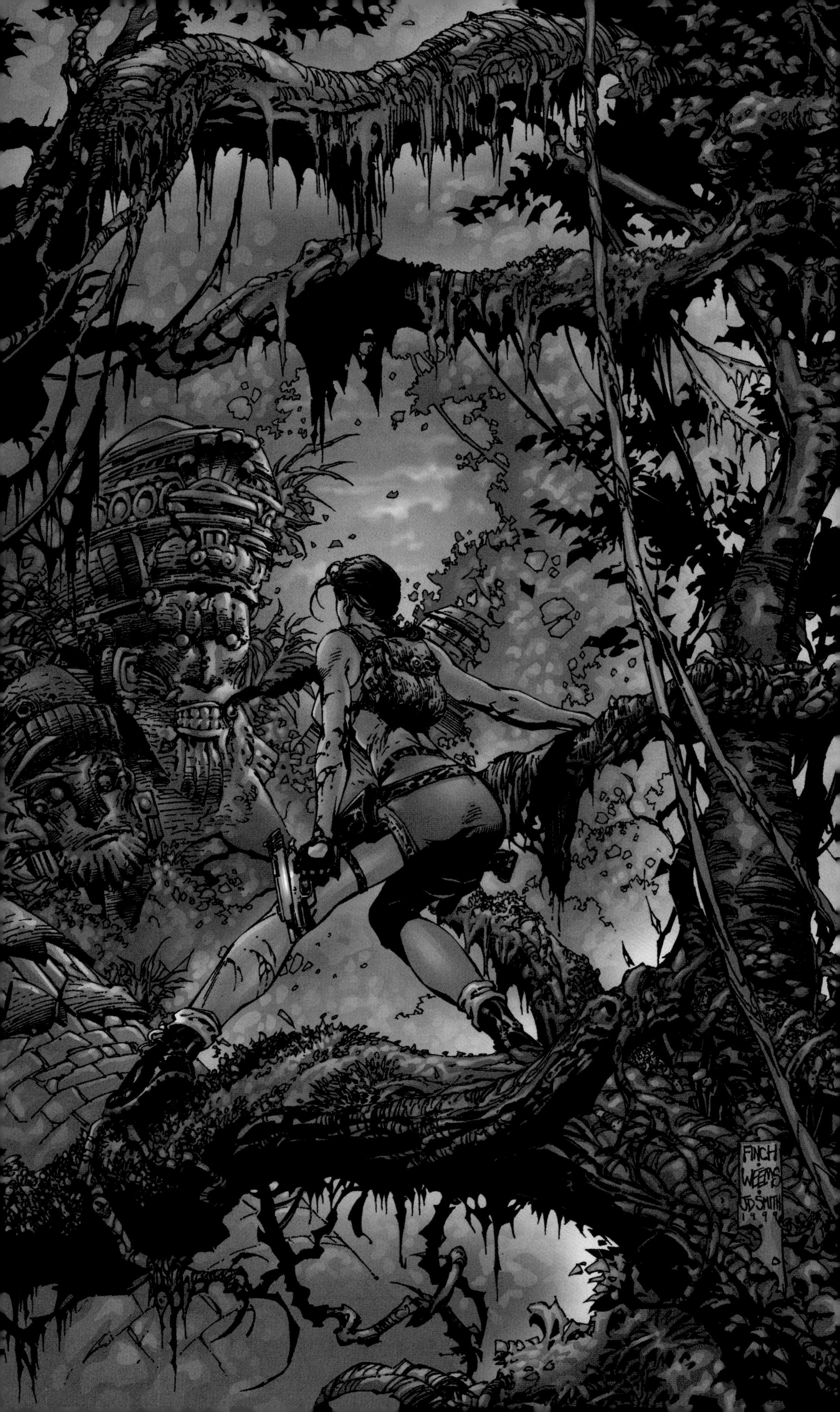
FINCH
WEEMS
JD SMITH
1999

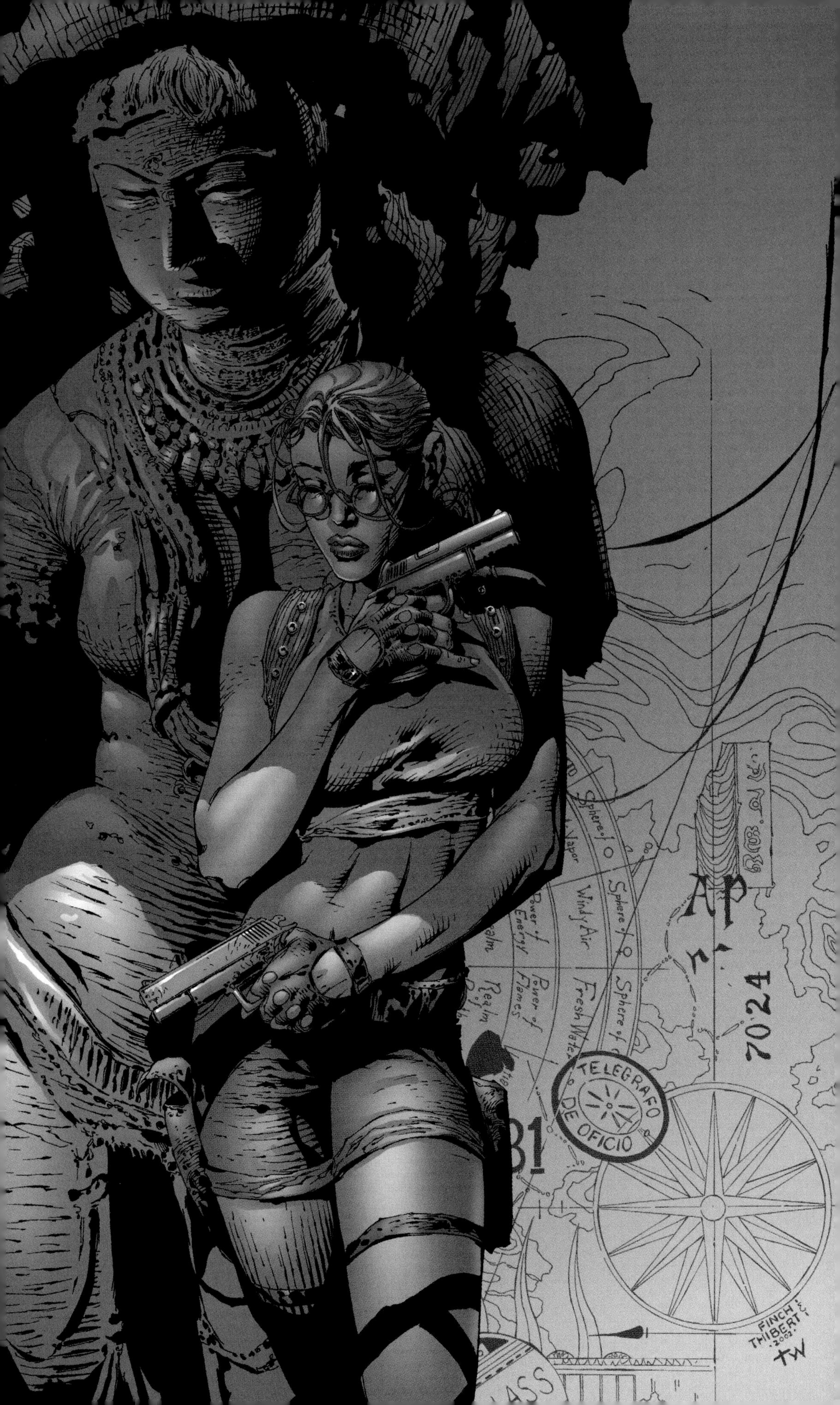
TELEGRAFO
DE OFICIO
70'24
AP
Sphere of
Windy Air
Fresh Water
Power of Flames
Power of Energy
Realm
FINCH
THIBERT
2002
TW

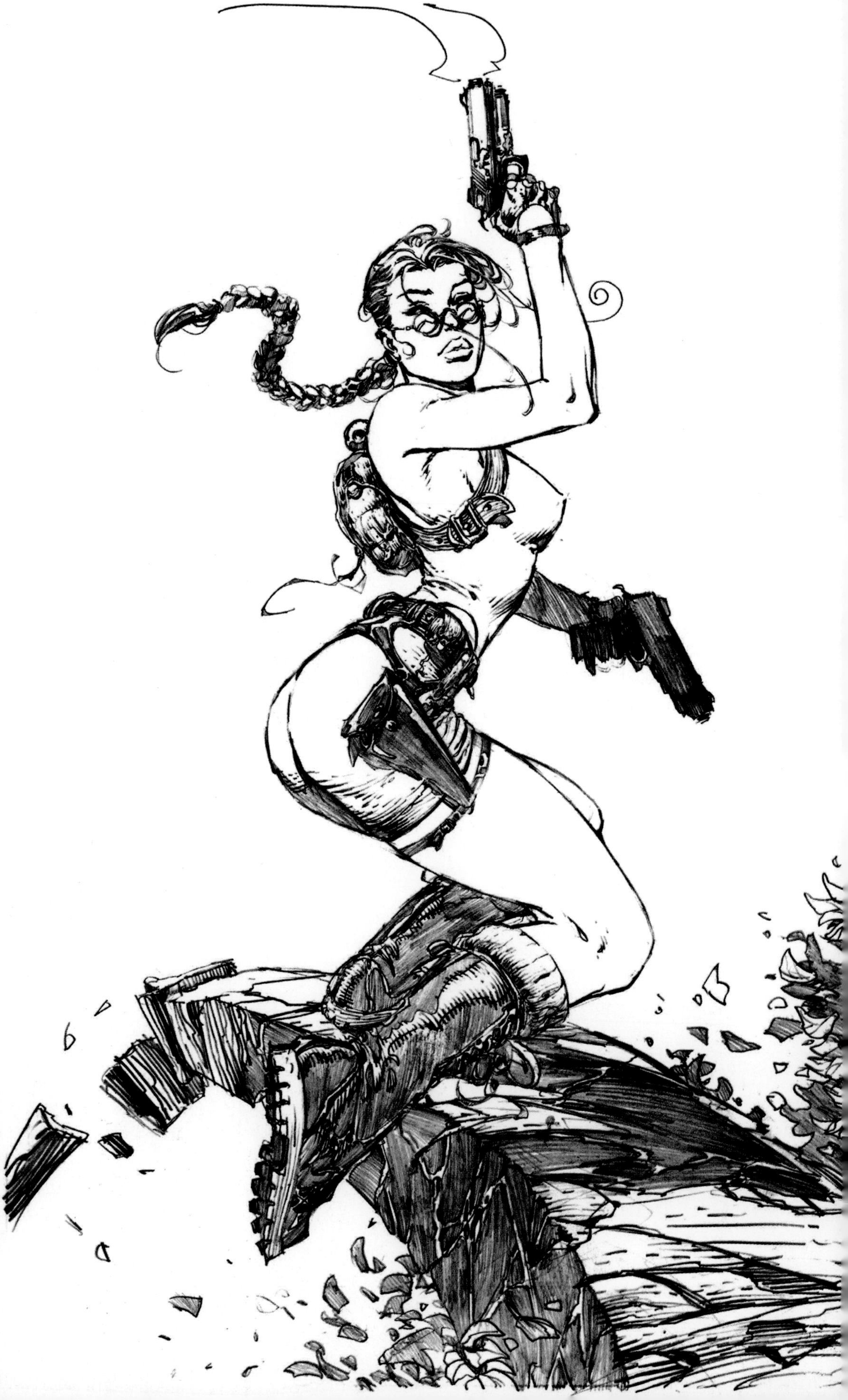

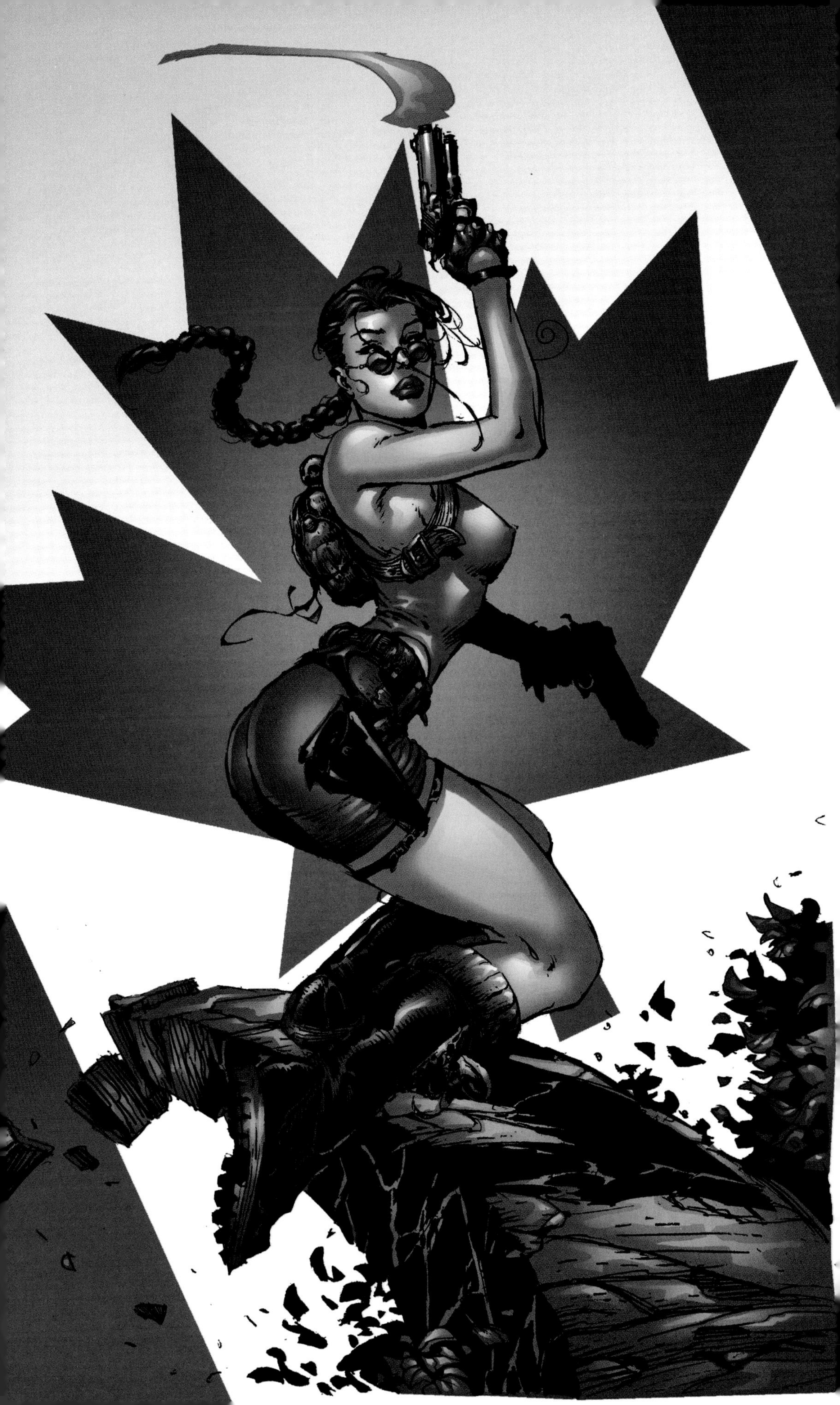

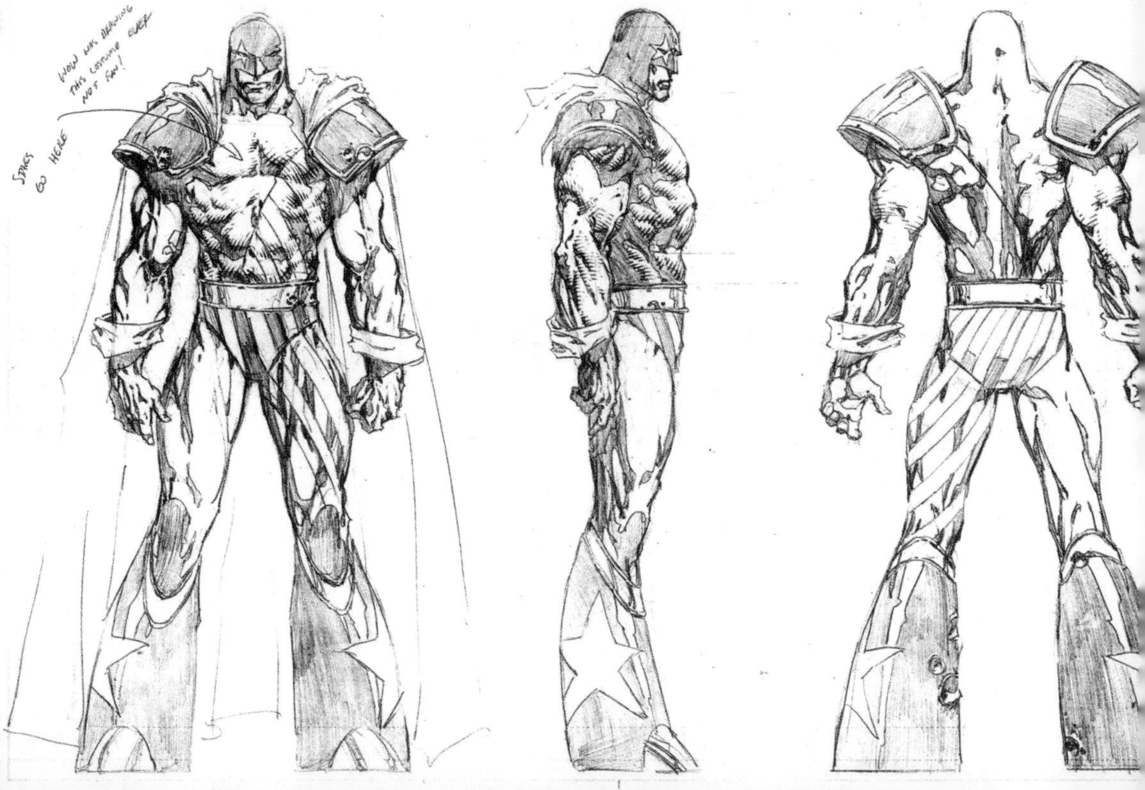
WOW WAS DRAWING THIS COSTUME EVER NOT FUN!
STARS GO HERE

ILLUSTRATED QUALITY PAPER FULL BLEED COMIC PAGES

xerox	stats	code

RISING STARS. 2 COVER

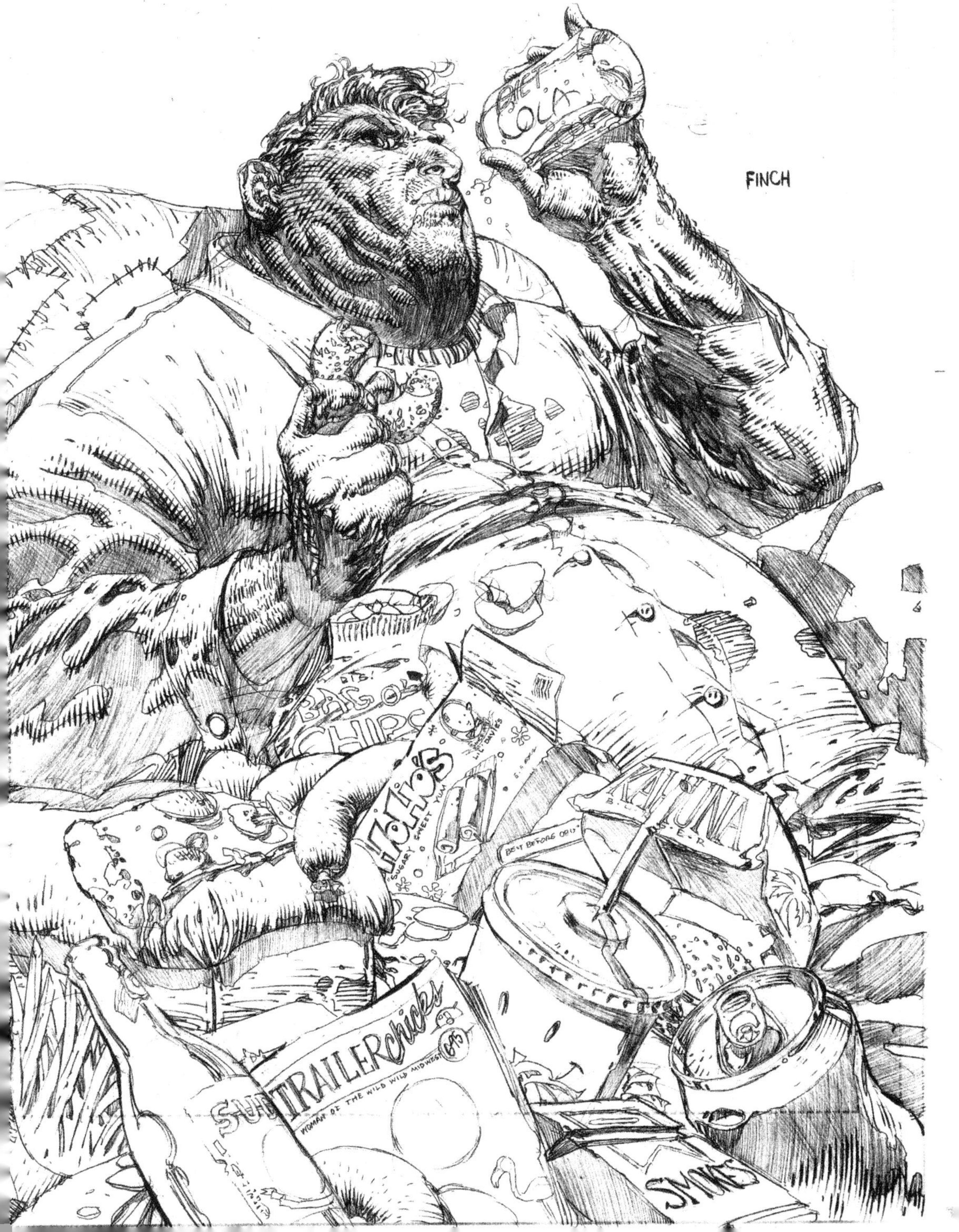
DIET COLA
FINCH
BAG O' CHIPS
KAHUNA
BEST BEFORE
TRAILER chicks
WOMAN OF THE WILD WILD MIDWEST
SMOKES

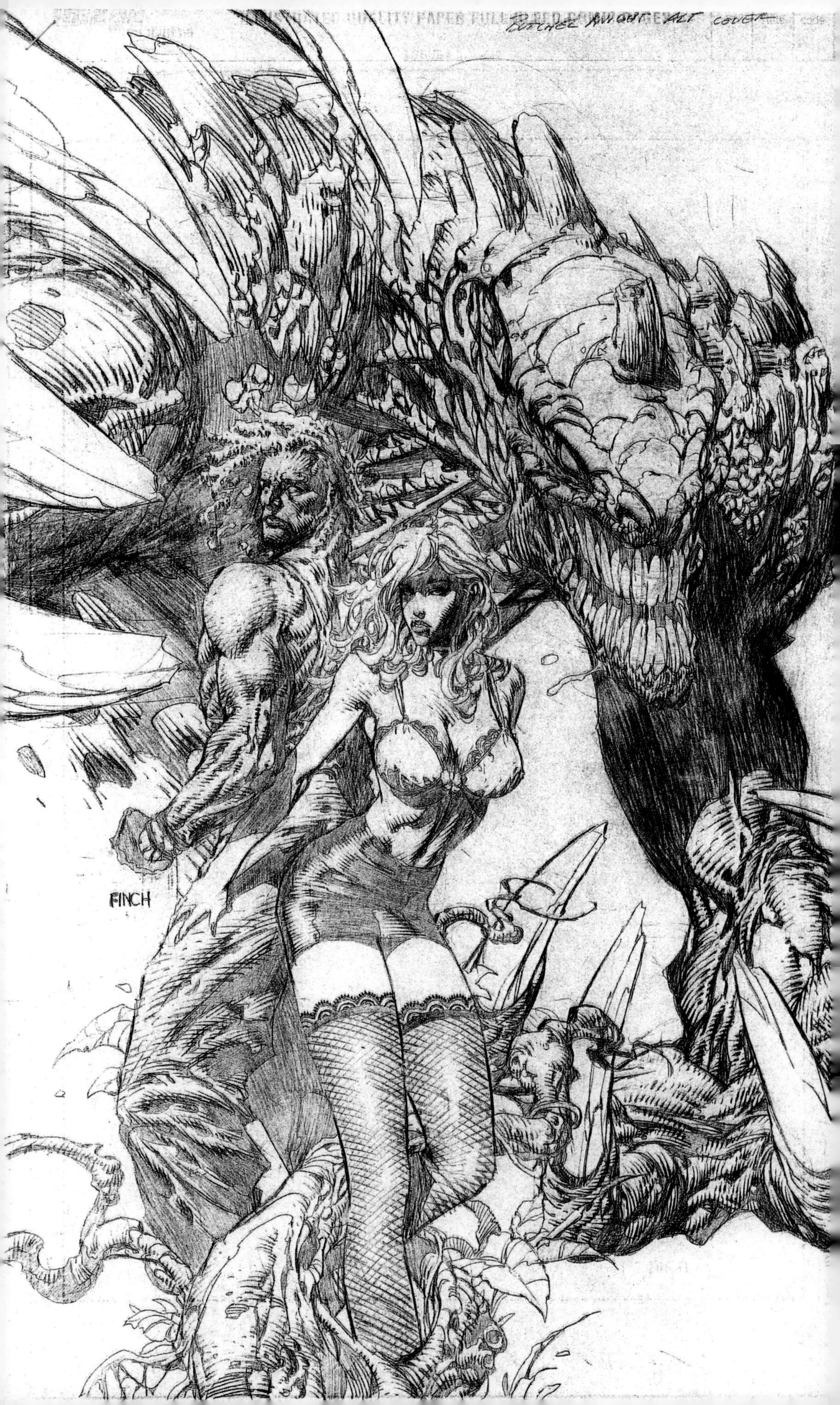
FINCH

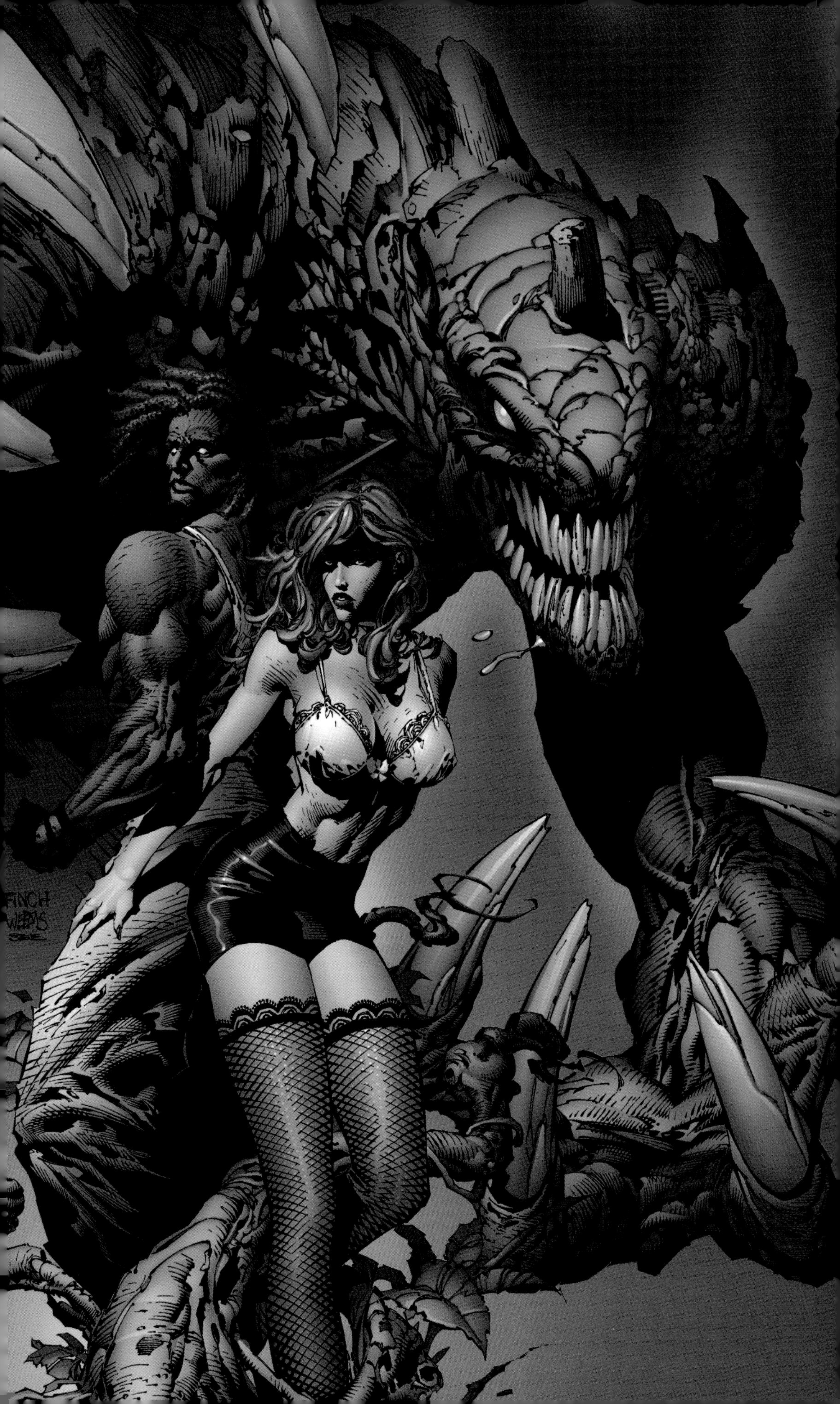
FINCH

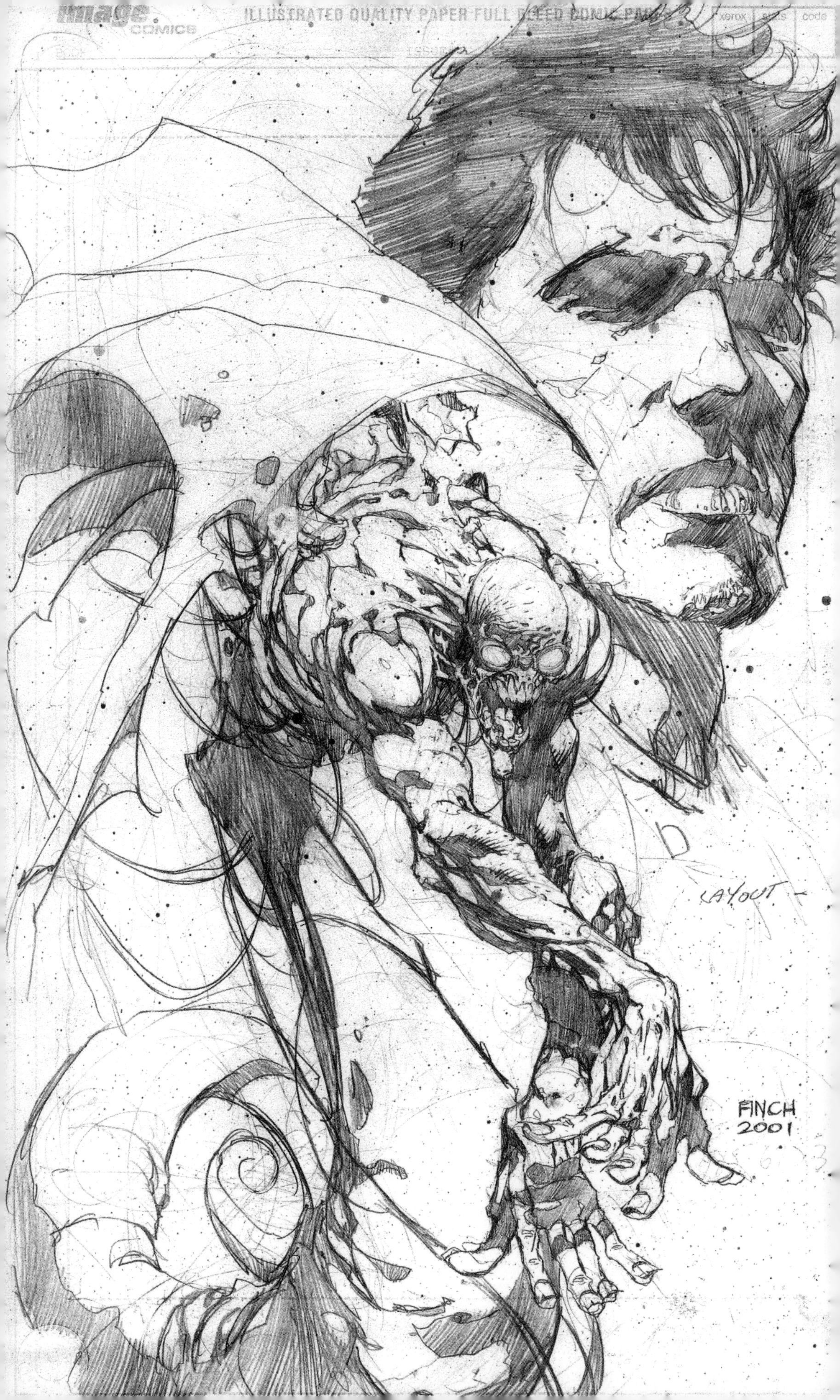

LAYOUT
FINCH
2001

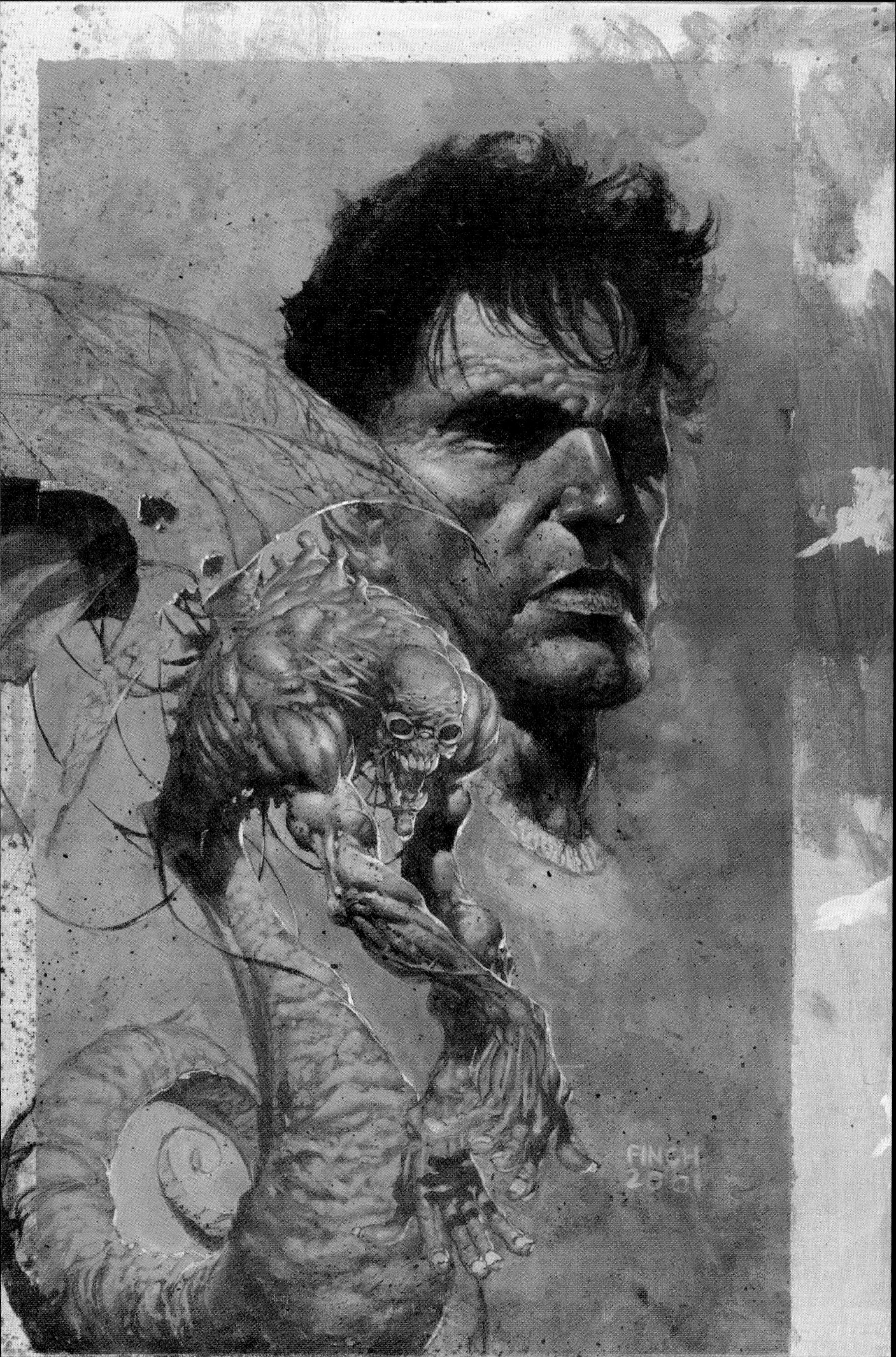
FINCH
2001

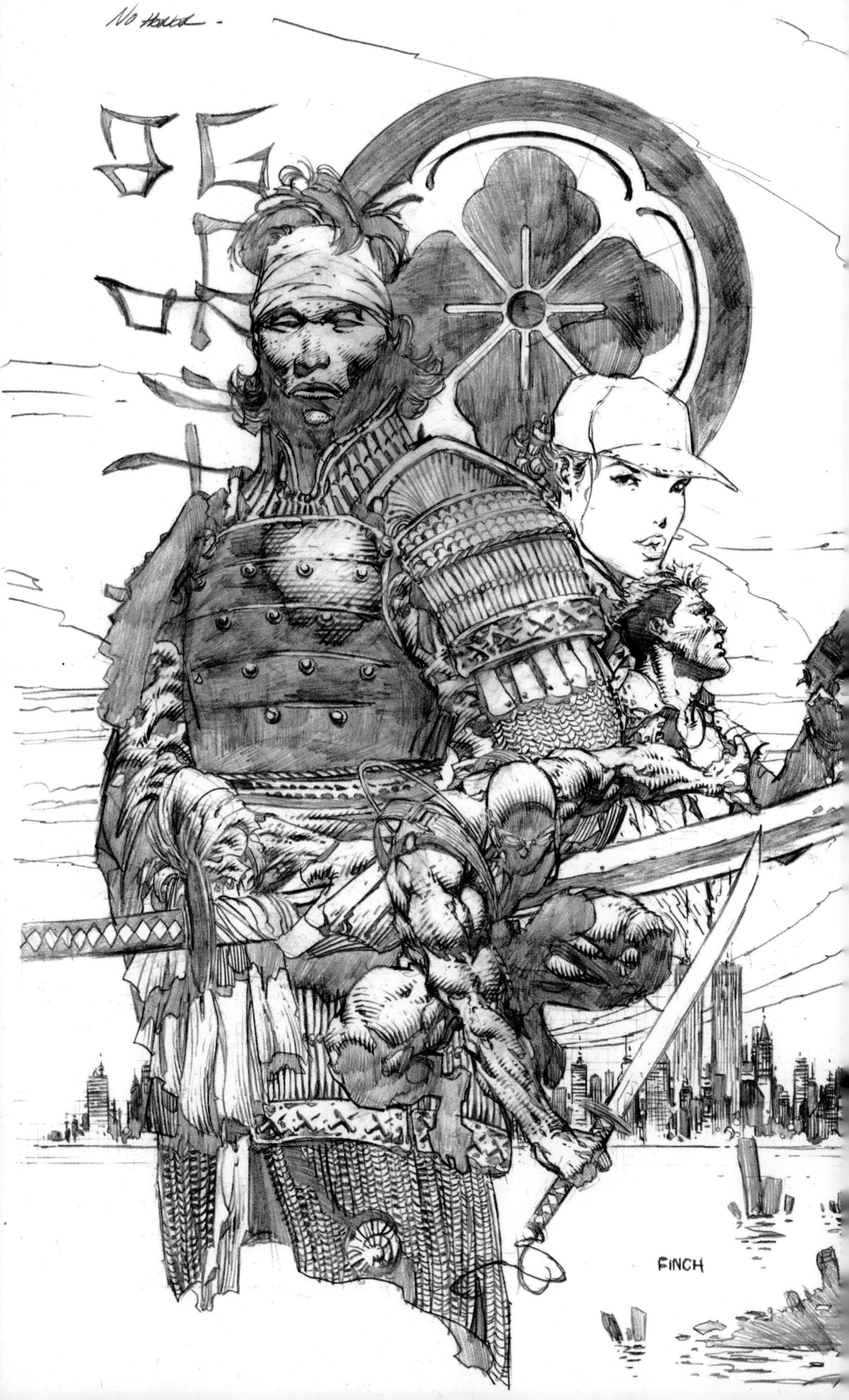
FINCH

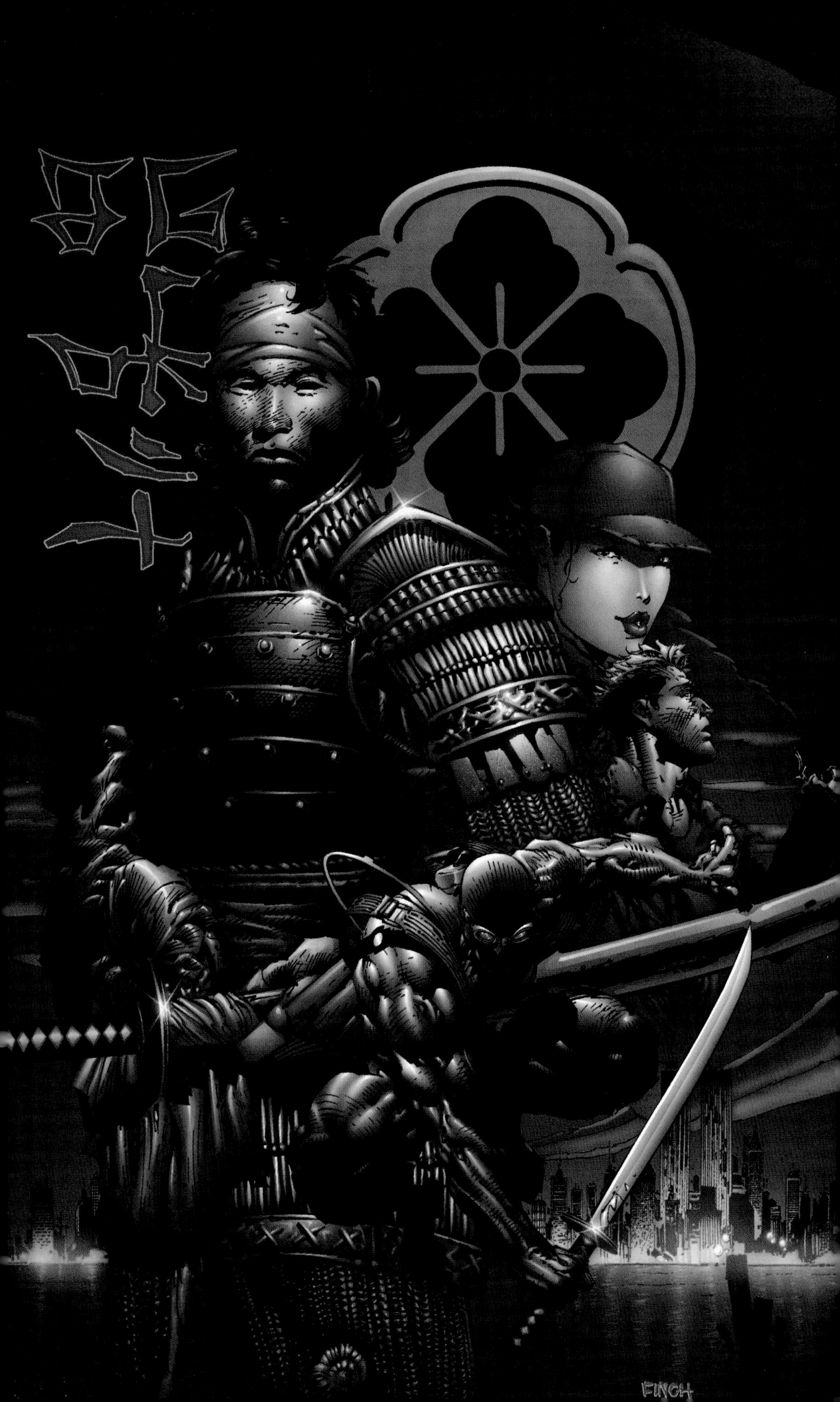
FINCH

TOP COW
image
APHRODITE IX
TIME OUT OF MIND

ASCENSION
Collected Editions

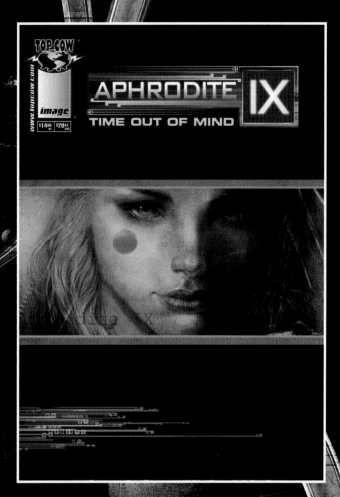

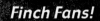

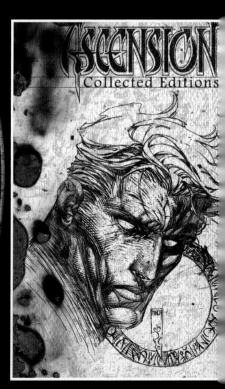

lso available from Top Cow Productions & Image Comics:

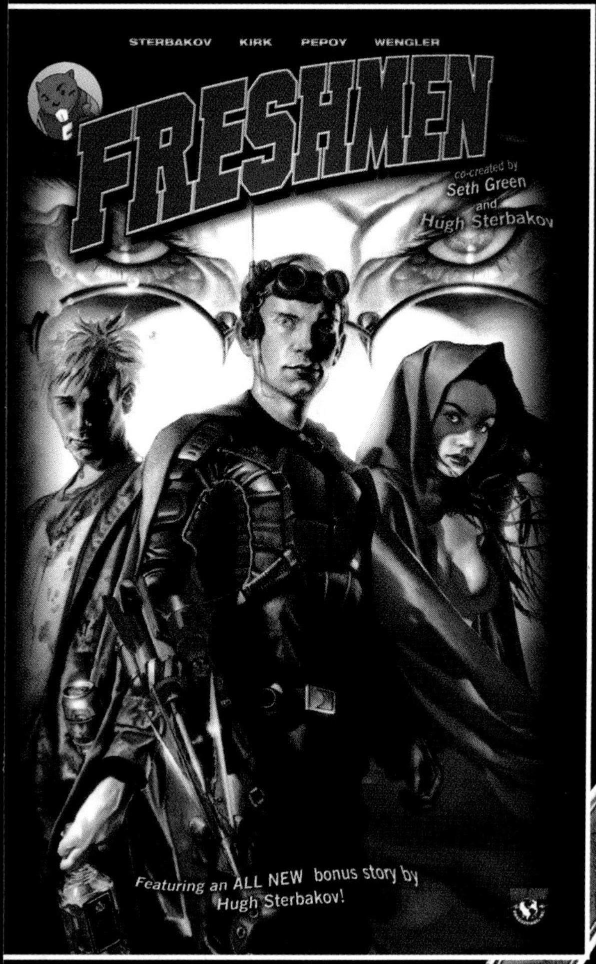
STERBAKOV KIRK PEPOY WENGLER
FRESHMEN
co-created by
Seth Green
and
Hugh Sterbakov
Featuring an ALL NEW bonus story by
Hugh Sterbakov!

Freshmen!

collects *Freshmen* vol. 1 issues #1 - #6,
plus the *Freshmen Yearbook* and more!
co created by Seth Green and Hugh Sterbakov!
This edition features an all new bonus story by
writer Hugh Sterbakov!
(ISBN # 1-58240-593-X) US $16.99

"Super powered teens, angst, action and comedy...I don't get it."

—*Joss Whedon*

Top Cow's Best of: Michael Turner

›p Cow's Best of: Michael Turner showcases this artistic erstar's early works, which established some of Top Cow's ship characters and his own stellar career. This collector's ıme reprints 9 full issues, including Witchblade and Tomb ler, plus rare promotional works including trading card ges, posters, pinups and variant cover images. For Turner :ionados this collection brings together 10 years of classic ıer in one package.

(ISBN: 1-58240-544-1) $24.99

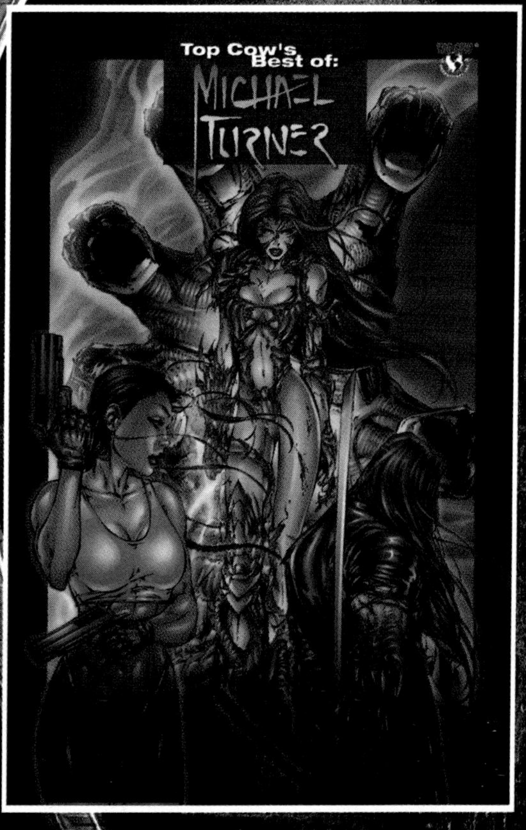
Top Cow's
Best of:
MICHAEL
TURNER